Public Sociology series

Series Editors: **John Brewer**, Queen's University, Northern Ireland and **Neil McLaughlin**, McMaster University, Canada

---

Public Sociology series addresses not only what sociologists do, but what sociology is for, and focuses on the commitment to materially improving people's lives through understanding of the social condition. It showcases the wide diversity of sociological research that addresses the many global challenges that threaten the future of humankind.

Forthcoming in the series:

The Public Sociology of Waste
Myra J. Hird

Out now in the series:

The Public and Their Platforms
Public Sociology in an Era of Social Media
Mark Carrigan and **Fatsis Lambros**

Public Sociology As Educational Practice
Challenges, Dialogues and Counter-Publics
Edited by **Eurig Scandrett**

Find out more at
bristoluniversitypress.co.uk/public-sociology

Public Sociology series

Series Editors: **John Brewer**, Queen's University, Northern Ireland and **Neil McLaughlin**, McMaster University, Canada

---

International editorial advisory board:

Michael Burawoy, University of California, Berkeley, US
John Brown Childs, University of California Santa Cruz, US
Craig Calhoun, London School of Economics, UK
Frances Fox Pivan, City University of New York, US
John H. Hall, McGill University, Canada
Katie Hughes, Victoria University, Australia
Linda McKie, Durham University, UK
Ann Nilsen, University of Bergen, Norway
Elisa P. Reis, International Panel on Social Progress, Brazil
John Scott, Exeter University, UK
Ari Sitas, University of Cape Town, South Africa
Linda Woodhead, Lancaster University, UK

Find out more at
bristoluniversitypress.co.uk/public-sociology

ERICH FROMM AND GLOBAL PUBLIC SOCIOLOGY

Neil McLaughlin

First published in Great Britain in 2023 by

Bristol University Press
University of Bristol
1-9 Old Park Hill
Bristol
BS2 8BB
UK
t: +44 (0)117 374 6645
e: bup-info@bristol.ac.uk

Details of international sales and distribution partners are available at bristoluniversitypress.co.uk

© Bristol University Press 2023

British Library Cataloguing in Publication Data
A catalogue record for this book is available from the British Library

ISBN 978-1-5292-1458-1 hardcover
ISBN 978-1-5292-1459-8 paperback
ISBN 978-1-5292-1460-4 ePub
ISBN 978-1-5292-1461-1 ePdf

The right of Neil McLaughlin to be identified as author of this work has been asserted by him in accordance with the Copyright, Designs and Patents Act 1988.

All rights reserved: no part of this publication may be reproduced, stored in a retrieval system, or transmitted in any form or by any means, electronic, mechanical, photocopying, recording, or otherwise without the prior permission of Bristol University Press.

Every reasonable eff ort has been made to obtain permission to reproduce copyrighted material. If, however, anyone knows of an oversight, please contact the publisher.

The statements and opinions contained within this publication are solely those of the author and not of the University of Bristol or Bristol University Press. The University of Bristol and Bristol University Press disclaim responsibility for any injury to persons or property resulting from any material published in this publication.

Bristol University Press works to counter discrimination on grounds of gender, race, disability, age and sexuality.

Cover design: Andrew Corbett
Front cover image: Müller-May / Rainer Funk (CC BY-SA 3.0 DE)

Contents

Acknowledgements		vi
Series Editors' Preface		x
Introduction: Erich Fromm's Global Public Sociology		1
1	Sociology in a World at War: *Escape from Freedom*	19
2	How Optimal Marginality Created a Public Sociologist	51
3	The Cold War, Conformity, and the 1960s	81
4	How Fromm Became a Forgotten Public Sociologist	111
5	Fromm's Political Activism in the 1960s	143
6	Studying Social Character and Theorizing Violence	183
Conclusion: The Revival of a Global Public Sociologist		221
Notes		241
References		251
Index		285

Acknowledgements

This book has a long history. It started with Lake of Two Mountains High School in Montreal, Canada, got going at First College, Cleveland State University, reached new heights at the Graduate Center of the City University of New York (CUNY) and in the Democratic Socialists of America (DSA), and was written at McMaster University in Hamilton, Ontario. High school friend Rick Hughes introduced me to *Escape from Freedom* after being assigned it by an American war resistor at Vanier College. Rick also told me about a job at McMaster.

I can't say enough about Donald Ramos and Elizabeth and Steve Cagan at Cleveland State University who showed me what it means to be professors who cared about teaching, intellectuals excited by ideas, and political people committed to changing the world. Don and Beth read the first draft at First College, a terrific cluster college whose history should be written about and built upon. First College confirmed to me that Fromm's critique of higher education held real insights, and my conversations with David Riesman while writing my dissertation convinced me that Fromm was too pessimistic. A better education is possible and great teachers and intellectuals are out there in state colleges and universities in the US. The Cleveland State soccer gang, Cleveland State students, faculty and staff, and the local DSA chapter opened up my eyes to the world, showing me that Fromm was too sweeping in his critiques. Joe Ventura, Karen Barber, and Randy Cunningham can't go unmentioned.

And then there is New York City. Bogdan Denitch reinforced my belief that I wanted to be an intellectual – not an academic – and let me into the CUNY graduate centre. Robert Alford, Stephen Steinberg, Cynthia Fuchs Esptein, Charles Kadushin, Alan Wolfe, and Catherine Silvers saved me from my own deep ambivalence, shall we say, about the academy. Their intellectual engagement and scholarly training allowed me to become a sociologist while still doing what I wanted to do. CUNY is special that way, and long may it live as a great public institution. Much of my analysis of American politics has come from my time listening to the high-level discussions at the famous Queens College Monday lunch, with Dean Savage, Charlie Smith, and Harry Levine while I was teaching there.

Then, there is democratic socialism. Michael Harrington, Frances Fox Piven, Barbara Ehrenreich, Irving Howe, the DSA youth section, New York and national DSA, Brian Morton and *Dissent*, and Cornel West and Jerry Watts inspired me to find my way to the left wing of the possible while expanding what visionary gradualism could mean.

Pamela Donovan, Lisa Baum, Bonnie Oglensky, and Catherine Spaeth were all so very important in my journey to becoming an intellectual and a New Yorker, at least for a time. I am not Sherri Levine's mother but she and John both know how much she means to me. Tom Canel and the DSA youth section, and Mark Levinson, Frank Llewellyn, Joseph Schwartz, Jo-Ann Mort, and Paul Meyer, taught me so much about politics. Frank even let me live in the castle. My critique of Fromm's political activism offered in this book is rooted in what I learned at the castle.

My colleagues and students in the sociology department at McMaster University mostly got in the way of me writing this book, but conversations with Scott Davies, Tony Puddephatt, John McLevey, Anna Vu, Dean Ray, Michelle Goldenberg, Kyle Siler, and Iga Mergler have been priceless. Johanne Jean-Pierre knows how important she was in pushing me to create this book. Both Sarita Srivastava and Vanina Leschziner inspired by example and friendship. Jeff Denis and Vanessa Watts helped me frame some things differently in politically important ways as they build a whole new Canada and sociology department. Gregory Hooks is a model of integrity and I am thrilled that he and Jane came to join McMaster sociology here in Canada. Rhoda Howard-Hassmann, Cyril Levitt, Charlene Miall, Victor Satzewich, and Dorothy Pawluck taught me much along the way, as did Louis Greenspan who was a joyful public intellectual in the ways Fromm was, at his best. Jackie, Danielle, and now Madeline have my appreciation for all they did to keep the department together, and Olga and Corinne know how much they did to allow me to do my job. I love laughing with Corinne, and we all miss Olga but know she is well.

Hilde Jacobson helped me see some feminist issues in new ways, and some of her insights and a pinch of her spunk and courage are reflected in some of my re-readings of Fromm in this book. Peter Baehr taught me much about theory and real political debate, and his courage in standing against totalitarianism is a model and a challenge for left-wing intellectuals. His reading of Arendt offered a critique of Fromm through his concept of 'unmasking', and I have tried here to find my own synthesis. Skaidra Triupaityte is following in the tradition of the democrats who are building a post-Soviet home in Lithuania and she helped me understand Fromm's work in Eastern and Central Europe in new ways.

The Fromm scholar community is growing. Rainer Funk has helped and inspired, as have Michael Maccoby, Daniel Burston, Maurico Cortina, Barbara Lenkerd, and Salvador and Sonia Gojman de Millan. Kieran Durkin and Matheus Romanetto, both brilliant new voices, make me confident about the future of radical humanism. Lawrence Friedman and I started writing a Fromm biography together after a Bard Conference panel we were taking part in with Paul Roazen. While this joint book was not to be since he published *The Lives of Erich Fromm: Love's Prophet* (2013) on his own, our work together and his research on his own was essential to making my own book better. We all owe Lawrence Friedman thanks for his relentless work in archives as a master intellectual historian. Friedman's book on Fromm borrowed from my own work, and I have borrowed some things back: it has all worked out for moving knowledge and ideas forward. Paul Roazen helped start the Fromm revival in the 1970s at York University and I will always remember talking to him in his office and at Bard in the early and mid 1990s. He helps explain the particular strength of Fromm scholarship in Canada. Catherine Silver and Lynn Chancer have been essential intellectual influences, connecting my Fromm project to a larger psychosocial vision that is essential today.

The book would never been written in the form you can read here without the intellectual salon that I have been running in my apartment in Toronto for over a decade, and which is now co-run on Zoom with Kathryn Exon Smith, a Toronto native living in San Jose. Andreas Hess from University College Dublin (UCD) started us off, and we have a scores of speakers from left, right and centre, academics and non-academics engaging with ideas not concerned with political organizing or academic status, but inspired, in my mind anyway, by proposals in Fromm's *The Sane Society* (1955). Academics need to get out a little. While *Erich Fromm and Global Public Sociology* (2021) is an academic book, it tries to have a real dialogue with my audience as we all have been doing in my salon. Najwa and my informal dinner salon friends in Lisbon also helped me think more globally, especially with regards to the Arab Spring and the Portuguese world and empire. As did Tanya in Taiwan while Ryan kept me in the game here in Toronto. Out of the salon, I am inspired by the book writing of historians Mark Solovey and Marga Vicedo after meeting them over yoga and then in a room full of historians. I thank Marga for not calling the police on me while I was talking to Lawrence Friedman, a funny story I will tell anyone in person who asks once COVID-19 is over. Thank you to everyone who gave talks at my salon, and to all who engaged ideas and different views together in good faith in our little public sphere.

Plum Publishing Coaching Services were essential in helping me pull together my ideas to produce this finished project. Cynthia Levine-Rasky is a terrific editor as well as my dear friend. Alison Gray and Alma Gardiner, Pamela Donovan Neil Gray and Sharang Sharma did what they could to make all this readable. The University of Bristol Press have been excellent, efficient, and high quality.

Luisa Montesinos and I have been talking about Fromm for a long time, and she knows how important that has been. Lisa Kowalchuk has always been there, and Steve has taught me so much. I wish I could have talked about the issues with Andrea, who is dearly missed. My mother Grace and father Neil McLaughlin would have loved to have seen this, as would my sister Kathleen and Vincent's father, my dear uncle and the intellectual in the family. Carole's love has sustained me, as has the caring of my brother Shaun. My dear Duntocher Aunt Bridget, Ian and Rita in Ireland, Vincent and Alison in Scotland, Michael and Sylvia in Montreal, and all my family as well as the larger chosen family I have mentioned above, have all made me feel at home, even after having travelled so very far. I am not escaping from any freedom but rooting again in new ways in a world that needs both transformation and social change as well as more love, laughter, and caring.

Neil McLaughlin, Toronto, 2021

Series Editors' Preface

Sociology is a highly reflexive subject. All scholarly disciplines examine themselves reflexively in terms of theory and practice as they apply what the sociologist of science Robert Merton once called 'organised scepticism'. Sociology adds to this constant internal academic debate a forceful, almost obsessive, concern about its very purpose and rationale. This attentiveness to founding principles shows itself in significant intellectual interest in the 'canon' of great thinkers and its history as a discipline, in vigorous debate about the boundaries of the discipline, and in considerable inventiveness in developing new areas and subfields of sociology. This fascination with the purpose and social organization of the discipline also reflects in the debate about sociology's civic engagements and commitments, its level of activism, and its moral and political purposes.

This echoes the contemporary discussion about the idea of public sociology. Public sociology is a new phrase for a long-standing debate about the purpose of sociology that began with the discipline's origins. It is therefore no coincidence that students in the twenty-first century, when being introduced to sociology for the first time, wrestle with ideas formulated centuries before, for while social change has rendered some of these ideas redundant, particularly the Social Darwinism of the nineteenth century and functionalism in the 1950s, familiarity with these earlier debates and frameworks is the lens into understanding the purpose, value and prospect of sociology as key thinkers conceived it in the past. The ideas may have changed but the moral purpose has not.

A contentious discipline is destined to argue continually about its past. Some see the roots of sociology grounded in medieval scholasticism, in eighteenth-century Scotland, with the Scottish Enlightenment's engagement with the social changes wrought by commercialism, in conservative reactions to the Enlightenment, or in nineteenth-century encounters with the negative effects of industrialization and modernization. Contentious disciplines however, are condemned to always live in their past if they do not also develop a vision for their future; a sense purpose and a rationale that takes the discipline forward. Sociology has always been forward looking, offering an analysis and diagnosis of what C. Wright Mills liked to call the human condition. Interest in the social condition and in its improvement and betterment for the majority of ordinary men and women, has always been sociology's ultimate objective.

At the end of the second millennium, when public sociology was named by Michael Burawoy, there was a strong feeling in the discipline that the professionalization of the subject during the twentieth century had come at the cost of its public engagement, its commitment to social justice, and its reputation for activism. The vitality and creativity of the public sociology debate was largely fuelled by what Aldon Morris called 'liberation capitalism', created in social movements of political engagement outside of the universities in the years after the social turmoil and changes of the 1960s.

The discipline has mostly reacted positively to Burawoy's call for public sociology, although there has been spirited dissent from those concerned with sociology's scientific status. Public sociology represents a practical realignment of the discipline by encouraging a focus on substantive and theoretical topics that are important to the many publics with whom the discipline engages. Public sociology, however, is also a normative realignment of the discipline through its commitment to enhance understanding of the social condition so that the lives of people are materially improved. Public sociology not only changes what sociologists do, it redefines what sociology is for.

Sociology's concern with its founding principles is both a strength and a weakness of the discipline. Nothing seems settled in sociology; the discipline does not obliterate past ideas by their absorption into new ones, as Robert Merton once put it, as the natural sciences insist on doing. The past remains a learning tool in sociology and the history of sociology is contemporaneous as we stand on the shoulders of giants to learn from earlier generations of sociologists. We therefore revisit debates about the boundaries between sociology and its cognate disciplines, or debates concerning the relationship between individuals and society, or about the analytical categories of individuals, groups, communities, and societies, or of the primacy of material conditions over symbolic ones, or of the place of politics, identity, culture, economics, and the everyday in structuring and determining social life. The boundaries of sociology are porous and, as many sociologists have asserted, the discipline is a hybrid, drawing ideas eclectically from those subjects closely aligned to it.

This hybridity is also sociology's great strength. Its openness facilitates interdisciplinarity, it encourages innovation in the fields to which the sociological imagination is applied, and opens up new topics about which sociological questions can be asked. Sociology thus exposes the hidden and the neglected to scrutiny. There is very little that cannot have sociological questions asked of it. The boundaries of sociology are thus ever expanding and widening; it is limitless in applying the sociological imagination. The tension between continuity and change – something evident in society generally – reflects thus also in the discipline itself. This gives sociology a frisson that is both fertile and fruitful as new ideas rub up against old ones and as the conceptual apparatus of sociology is simultaneously revisited and renewed. This tends to work against faddism in sociology, since nothing is entirely new and the latest fashions have their pasts.

Public sociology is thus not itself new and it has its own history. Burawoy rightly emphasized the role of C. Wright Mills and broader frameworks allow us to highlight the contribution of the radical W. E. B. DuBois, the early feminist and peace campaigner Jane Addams, and scores of feminist, socialist, and anti-racist scholars from the Global South, such as Fernando Henrique Cardosa in Brazil and Fatima Meer in South Africa. Going back further into the history of public sociology, the Scots in the eighteenth century were public sociologists in their way, allowing us to see that Burawoy's refocusing of sociology's research agenda and its normative realignment is the latest expression of a long-standing concern. The signal achievement of Burawoy's injunction was to mobilize the profession to reflect again on its founding principles and to take the discipline forward to engage with the relevance of sociology to the social and human condition in the twenty-first century.

Despite the popularity of the idea of public sociology, and the widespread use of such discourse, no book series is singularly dedicated to it. The purpose of this series is to draw together some of the best sociological research that carries the imprimatur of 'public sociology', done inside the academy by senior figures and early-career researchers, as well as outside it by practitioners, policy analysts, and independent researchers seeking to apply sociological research in real-world settings.

The reflexivity of professional sociologists as they ponder the usefulness of sociology under neo-liberalism and late modern cosmopolitanism, will be addressed in this series, as the it publishes works that engage from a sociological perspective with the fundamental global challenges that threaten the very future of humankind. The relevance of sociology will be highlighted in works that address these challenges as they feature in global social changes but also as they are mediated in local and regional communities and settings. The series will thus feature titles that work at a global level of abstraction as well as studies that are microethnographic depictions of global processes as they affect local communities. The focus of the series is thus on what Michael Ignatieff refers to as 'the ordinary virtues' of everyday life, social justice, equality of opportunity, fairness, tolerance, respect, and trust, and how the organization and structure of society – at a general level or in local neighbourhoods – inhibits or promotes these virtues and practices. The series will expose, through detailed sociological analysis, both the dynamics of social suffering and celebrate the hopes of social emancipation.

The discourse of public sociology has permeated outside the discipline of sociology, as other subjects take up its challenge and reorientate themselves, such as public anthropology, public political science, and public international relations. In pioneering the engagement with its different publics, sociology has therefore once again led the way, and this series is designed to take the debate about public sociology and its practices in new directions. In being the first of its kind, this series will showcase how the discipline of sociology has utilized the language and ideas of public sociology to change what it does and what it is for. This series will address not only what sociologists do, but also sociology's focus on the commitment to enhance understanding of the social condition so that the lives of ordinary people are materially improved. It will present the wide diversity of sociological research that addresses the many global challenges that threaten the future of humankind in the twenty-first century.

This latest addition to the series makes some significant contributions among those mentioned above. It resurrects the sociology of Erich Fromm to highlight his early contribution to public sociology, thus giving public sociology a history. Fromm is not normally accorded this recognition by public sociologists; not because his work is marginal to public sociology, more because Fromm has been forgotten. The word 'resurrect' is not too strong, for Fromm has been largely overlooked in sociology's interest in its history, in much the same way as other figures in the distant history of public sociology, such as Robert Morrison MacIver, whose thoughts on sociology in times of crisis, written on the cusp of the Second World War, bear modern consideration.

Neil McLaughlin is a noted Fromm scholar who has done much to keep Fromm's sociology contemporary. He wisely asks why we should reclaim Fromm now, and in answering this challenge he shows Fromm's relevance to understanding the modern condition. The spectre of fascism, the rise of Nazism, and the growth of authoritarianism that so dominated the critical thinking of the Frankfurt School, may seem to date Fromm's public sociology to times past, but the return of right-wing populism, so-called authoritarian populism, and neo-fascism has made Fromm relevant once more. Fromm's scholarly analysis of the sociological and psychological structures that undergird and root such emotions and behaviours is a public sociology for our era too.

One of the strengths of this book is that it seeks to rescue Fromm from the Frankfurt School by locating him in the tradition of public sociology, by which we mean that approach that is critically engaged with moral questions about the good society, is engaged publically with the social problems that hinder it, and which employs public sociology alongside cognate disciplines in an interdisciplinary approach to human betterment. This makes the latest addition to our series not only one of the most important books on Fromm for many years, it contributes further to our understanding of the distinctiveness of public sociology as a moral discipline.

John D. Brewer and Neil McLaughlin
Belfast, Northern Ireland, and Hamilton, Ontario
November 2020

Introduction: Erich Fromm's Global Public Sociology

As a practice and a vision, public sociology has swept through the discipline in the years since Michael Burawoy's 2005 call for action in his speech, 'For Public Sociology'. The German critical theorist Erich Fromm was among the most creative, visible, and influential practitioners of public sociology in the middle of the twentieth century until his death in 1980. The great American theorist Robert Merton taught Fromm's classic book *Escape from Freedom* in sociology courses at Columbia University and Fromm was widely cited in the top sociology journals in the Cold War era. Fromm was the author of a number of best-selling works of social science, selling millions of books in the age of the paperback well before the internet and social media. Yet his work is largely unmentioned among the canonical figures of the craft of public sociology such as W. E. B. Du Bois, Jane Addams, C. Wright Mills, and David Riesman.

Born in 1900 and brought up in Germany, he lived in the United States and Mexico for decades while enjoying a massive global influence, particularly in Latin America and Central and Eastern Europe. Fromm is an important part of the history of global public sociology. As the global neo-liberal consensus collapses in the fallout from the COVID-19 pandemic, Fromm's public sociology should be celebrated and renewed both within our discipline and in the broader public imagination.

Fromm earned a PhD at Heidelberg University in the department of national economy with a specialization in sociology under the supervision of Alfred Weber, Max Weber's younger brother. Centrally involved in the Frankfurt School of critical theory (Bronner, 1994; McLaughlin, 1999, 2008; Wheatland, 2009), Fromm worked closely in the 1930s with Robert Lynd in the Columbia sociology department, one of earliest proponents of public sociology who argued passionately that we need to ask 'knowledge for what?' (Lynd, 1939). Fromm's *Escape from Freedom* revolutionized how scholars understood the social psychology of fascism, putting an analysis of what Anthony Giddens later called 'ontological insecurity' at the centre of the historical social psychology of extremism (Giddens, 1990; Thorpe, 2020). Written in wartime while Hitler ruled Germany, the book made Fromm famous and established an important tradition of thought about the authoritarian character and sociology of emotions in politics that is all too relevant today.

Fromm's ideas and his role model were central to public sociology in both the Cold War and the 1960s era. He was the mentor to the Harvard sociologist David Riesman, the first in the discipline to be on the cover of *Time*. Fromm's ideas were central to the framework of Riesman's best-selling book *The Lonely Crowd* (1950) and they both helped create the substantial literature on mass society and the sociology of conformity (Kornhauser, 1959; McLaughlin, 2001b). Fromm's *The Sane Society* and *Marx's Concept of Man* helped create a research tradition on alienation in the sociology of work that would lead to analysis of the commercialization of feelings in the sociology of emotions (Hochschild, 1982).

Fromm's global best-selling book *The Art of Loving* made him a celebrity intellectual whose work offered a sociological as well as psychoanalytic perspectives on love in a market-based society. The book made Fromm an early prophet for what Anthony Giddens would call the 'pure relationship' (Giddens, 1992).

Playing the dual role of insider policy sociologist and expert on German politics with access to elite policy makers and politicians, Fromm was also an anti-war and anti-nuclear weapons activist. With his writing on American foreign policy *May Man Prevail?* and vocal opposition to American militarism, the dispossession of the Palestinian people and the Vietnam War (Jacobs, 2014), Fromm was the Noam Chomsky of the 1950s.

In the late 1960s, however, Fromm's reputation as a scholar declined dramatically; he was excluded from the public sociology debate that Burawoy inspired (Burawoy, 2005). *Erich Fromm and Global Public Sociology* tells the forgotten story of Fromm's global public sociology in order to contribute to a revisiting of his sociological legacy in light of current world events.

Fromm was the great sociological theorist of narcissism and the presidential election of Donald Trump in 2016 highlighted issues of psychosocial dynamics in politics in ways that have swept away our conventional hesitation about the psychoanalytic perspective. Fromm wrote extensively about the politics of authoritarianism in the 1930s and was the most prominent social psychological theorist of alienation and of what Arlie Hochschild would later describe as the commercialization of feelings. These political issues are at the forefront of our intellectual agenda once again as we confront far-right authoritarian regimes in Hungary, Poland, and Brazil, Communist China's status as a world power, the pervasiveness of social media, and the increasing dominance of the market in a world in political and social crisis. In the post-Trump era, moreover, Fromm's theories can help us understand what happened in 2016 and how we can understand Trumpism.

As a result of changes in the world and broader shifts in intellectual paradigms among scholars, we are seeing a revival of interest in Fromm's ideas.[1] The purpose of this book is to narrate the story of the rise, fall, and now revival of Fromm's sociology in relation to the broader scholarly literature on public sociology. The Australian theorist Raewyn Connell (2007) and the American sociologist Aldon Morris (2015), in particular, along with the towering influence of Pierre Bourdieu (1988, 1990b), have pushed sociologists to reflexively consider the empirical study of public sociology itself. *Erich Fromm and Global Public Sociology* sits squarely within these traditions of the sociology of sociology and ideas.

Fromm is an obvious missing figure in public sociology from the mid-twentieth century. Rediscovering his work and theorizing why he was forgotten is a valuable step that historians and sociologists can take towards making public sociology more global and relevant to the current political and cultural moment.[2] As we tell the story of Fromm's life through a sociologically influenced biographical lens, we will both evaluate his ideas in light of current scholarship and address a number of broader questions. What is a public sociologist, and did Fromm qualify as one? What role do best-selling books play in social movements and contemporary life? What is the difference between a public sociologist and a celebrity intellectual? How did the role of the public sociologist and activist shape the content of Fromm's ideas and his intellectual reputation? Can critical sociologists also be policy sociologists and what are some of the tensions involved in these roles? How could these issues be studied more systematically through a sociology of sociology? We start with the definition of public sociology and why it matters in the contemporary moment.

What is public sociology and why does it matter?

The debate about public sociology emerged in 2004 in San Francisco when radical ethnographer Michael Burawoy gave a powerful American

Sociological Association Presidential address, 'For Public Sociology'. The speech was published in the *American Sociological Review* in 2005, an intervention that triggered a global debate about sociology and its publics. Burawoy's tenure as President of the International Sociological Association and the world tour he undertook in that position gave rise to a global discussion of sociology's role in early twenty-first-century politics. The American-led 'war on terror' after 9/11, the 2008 economic meltdown, the rise of authoritarian populism around the world stimulated by Trumpism after 2016, the collapse of the neo-liberal global consensus in the wake of the COVID-19 pandemic, the revival of feminism after #MeToo, the democracy protests in Hong Kong, Peru, Belarus, and Poland, and the mass racial justice movement of 2020 all contributed to making public sociology newly relevant.

Burawoy claimed that the time was right for sociology to create a vibrant public engagement with mass audiences outside the university. To do so it was vital to build on the professional research in peer-reviewed journals, policy research created in collaboration with outside sponsors, and the critical debate regarding the normative dimensions of the field. Burawoy did not invent public sociology; there have been long-standing debates about applied versus theoretical scholarship and the politics of professors. Burawoy, however, created an analytic framework that allowed for fresh discussions about the value-free nature of the field, normative values, and reflexivity. The debate has been lively and contentious, drawing cohorts of young sociologists into a discipline that is directly engaging these issues with a moral and analytic agenda.

The major contemporary debate about public sociology, especially in the United States where it began, concerned the question of the scientific and value-free nature of sociology. For a significant number of sociologists, Burawoy's public sociology was a serious threat to the scientific status of the discipline. Overly concerned with politics and left-wing social engineering, public sociology was bound to fail. Its preachy arrogance would undermine the scholarly reputation of the discipline in research universities (Brady, 2004; Nielson, 2004; Tittle, 2004). There was even a contentious debate led by one American sociologist who called for sociology to be 'saved' from the threat posed by public sociology (McLaughlin, Kowalchuk, and Turcotte, 2005).

Burawoy is a well-known Marxist sociologist teaching at the University of California-Berkeley, a centre of critical sociology and left-wing student activism. For many mainstream scholars, especially in the quantitatively oriented professional wing of the discipline, public sociology was a cover for Marxist or activist sociology. Burawoy spent hard-won political capital in the core of the discipline trying to get mainstream American sociology to accept a compromise: critical and left-wing sociology would be allocated space in the discipline if it did less denouncing of mainstream sociology. For some in the radical and critical wing of the discipline, Burawoy's compromise gave away too much, leaving anti-racism, feminist, and anti-colonial sociologies as subordinate in a field that had to be radically transformed (Ghamari-Tabrizi, 2005).

Burawoy contributed to a global debate on public sociology by highlighting a critique of the hierarchal and elite American discipline housed in well-financed universities. These institutions present a provincial form of academic practice as a universal standard. In this context, the call for a global sociology implies the end of the dominance of American sociology, at least in its current form; a point debated widely in the literature.[3] The public sociology debate could have only started in the United States, something Burawoy recognized; the resources in higher education existed to carve out a space for elite research somewhat above and outside society. The long history of elite intellectual life pre-dates sociology. Philosophers and thinkers isolated themselves from popular discourse and everyday politics by using elite resources to first establish ideas and then, after the early 1880s, research universities and disciplines (Collins, 1998). But for most sociologists outside the United States, however, sociology always has been public, policy oriented, and often critical.

Public sociology has now been institutionalized in important ways and, in our polarized intellectual climate, has been targeted by extremists on the right. In the broader institutionalization of public sociology, the American Sociological Association created criteria for accessing and rewarding public sociology. It does so alongside a rich new scholarly literature where the concepts of 'professional', 'policy', 'critical', and 'public' sociology have become integrated into sociology's common sense (Vaughan, 2006). Sociology departments sprung up, branding themselves as specializing in public sociology. The American Sociological Association now gives an award for the 'public understanding of sociology'.

Things are not all going well for public sociology, however. There has been a broader cultural and global backlash that, in my homeland (Canada), for example, saw former Prime Minister Stephen Harper publicly advise that now was not the time to 'commit sociology'. More recently, sociology has been a central target in the attacks on democracy and intellect life led by, to just give two prominent examples, Brazilian far-right wing President Bolsonaro and Hungarian President Viktor Orbán, a proponent of illiberal democracy in that country (Plenta,

2020). Canadian social psychology and internet sensation Jordan Peterson publicly opines against what he views is a 'post-modern Neo-Marxist' takeover of modern universities led, he often suggests, by 'corrupted' disciplines like sociology. Public sociology needs to defend itself but it also needs to examine its internal practices self-reflexively (Bourdieu and Wacquant, 1992). This may be done by looking at its history and its heroes – including forgotten ones such as Erich Fromm.

Public sociology is defined and defended partly through the ways its history is told and who is chosen to represent its past. Burawoy focused our attention on important earlier practitioners of public and critical sociology, particularly C. Wright Mills, David Riesman, Dorothy Smith, Pierre Bourdieu, and W. E. B. Du Bois (Burawoy, 2005). Later American Sociological Association presidents, notably Frances Fox Piven (2006) and Eduardo Bonilla-Silva (2019) have broadened the debate. Raewyn Connell's book *Southern Theory* (2007) and Aldon Morris' vital scholarship on the erasure of W. E. B. Du Bois' pioneering and global public sociology in *The Scholar Denied* (Morris, 2015) have expanded the range of heroes with whom sociologists can identify.

The remarkable contemporary revival of the sociological reputation of W. E. B. Du Bois is worth particular attention. The Du Bois revival was created both by activist-scholars in the United States and Aldon Morris who wrote a painstakingly empirical case study. Although Fromm faced vicious and deadly anti-Semitism in his lifetime, including the murder of relatives by Nazis, he did not face the same level of systematic racist exclusion from American universities as did Du Bois. Fromm's exclusion and reputational revival, however, provides further empirical data for the development of general theories about public sociology, allowing us to envision a broader set of empirical research questions that could be addressed. From a sociology of reputation perspective, the number of scholars inspired by Du Bois willing to fight to restore his reputation is far greater than is the case with Fromm, most of whose dedicated followers do not tend to be academics or social scientists.

Both the cases of Du Bois and Fromm suggest that the standard debates about the normative value of public sociology versus traditionally professional sociology are becoming increasingly stale. The case of Erich Fromm is interesting on its own terms while also raising questions for broader research. These questions include: What are the sociological origins of individuals who make public sociology a career pathway and intellectual vocation? Why do some intellectuals choose to engage the public as social critics while others pursue narrower professional careers? How can we better theorize and understand the role of best-selling books in creating social change and political movements? How might the study of friendships and collaborations improve understandings of the intimate relations, network dynamics, and social supports that make public sociology possible (Farrell, 2001)? What does public sociology look like when you ask questions about its global reach and how it travels across national borders? What are the trade-offs involved in doing professional scholarly work, or public social criticism and therapeutically oriented social analysis, offering policy advice behind the scenes, or engaging in activism in radical and reformist political organizations? What are the special challenges for public sociologists engaging ideas in an interdisciplinary way? None of these questions can be conclusively answered with a case study on one individual scholar. Nonetheless, the example of Fromm as a public sociologist is rich and illuminating. One issue, however, needs to be directly addressed in thinking about Erich Fromm's public sociology before we proceed: was he a bona fide sociologist?

Was Fromm really a sociologist?

In the discipline's collective memory, if he is remembered at all, Fromm would be seen as a well-known psychologist, a therapist and Freudian, a spiritual thinker and self-help book writer and, more recently perhaps, a public intellectual. But was he a sociologist? Jennifer Platt, an authority in the history of sociology, has outlined the best guide to thinking about this question; it is not necessarily self-evident (Platt, 2007). To qualify, does one need a PhD in sociology or to teach in a sociology department? Does publishing in sociology journals, using sociological concepts and methods in research, being active in sociology's professional associations, or self-identifying as a sociologist count? Would showing little interest in one's sociological identity be a disqualification, or would it suffice to have one's work used by others? We may note the example of Karl Marx, a figure claimed as one of our own but who himself surely would have described much of what sociologists do as bourgeois claptrap. Are you a sociologist if other sociologists cite your work in sociology journals and review your books in core outlets in the discipline? Would claiming a primary professional identity as a scholar in a related discipline disqualify someone as a sociologist? Or do the disciplines' gatekeepers offer double or triple citizenship to psychologists, anthropologists, political scientists, or scholars of cultural studies or Black or Indigenous studies? These issues are important broader questions that we need to consider as we discuss Fromm as a public sociologist.

Fromm did not explicitly identify as a public sociologist since the concept did not exist at the time of his death in 1980, yet he certainly was a sociologist if we approach the issues in the ways that Platt encouraged. Fromm did his PhD in Heidelberg on a sociological topic, the law in four orthodox Jewish communities. His supervisor was Alfred Weber, Max Weber's younger brother and a prominent sociologist in his own right. Fromm admired the younger Weber but was less impressed with Max Weber because of his support for Germany in the First World War, an issue about which the young anti-nationalist and Marxist-influenced Fromm felt much passion. Fromm tells of how the irrationality of the First World War drew him towards Marxism as a teenager (Fromm, 1962). He was deeply influenced by sociologist Georg Simmel's social psychology, particularly his account of gender and insistence on taking a micro perspective on social life (Fromm, 1997).

Fromm was also involved in serious sociological research through his connection to the network of thinkers known as the Frankfurt School. In the late 1920s, Max Horkheimer, a German philosopher responsible for a significant endowment left by a wealthy patron to create the Frankfurt School, an essentially neo-Marxist think tank, hired Fromm to direct a sociological study of the emotional and ideological commitments of the working class in Weimar Germany (Jay, 1973; McLaughlin, 1999). Fromm was connected to these early critical theorists through his friendship with Leo Löwenthal, a scholar who later went on to become a professor of sociology at the University of California, Berkeley (Jay, 1973; Jacobs, 2014).

The empirical work Fromm did in that period would alone qualify him as a sociologist; this would be the case even if it had not been so influential on twentieth-century social science. Today, we think of the Frankfurt School as consisting of Jürgen Habermas and his theories of the public sphere, Theodor Adorno and Max Horkheimer's critique of the dialectics of Enlightenment and their analysis of the distorting lens of the cultural industries, and Herbert Marcuse's analysis in *One-Dimensional Man* (1964 [2013]) and his activism during the New Left era in the United States (McLaughlin, 1999, 2008). There are many other works of important scholarship in the Frankfurt School tradition including Löwenthal's work on the sociology of literature (Jay, 1973). Other lesser-known economists, philosophers, and historians who were associated with the Frankfurt School included Friedrich Pollock,

Otto Kirchheimer, Franz Neumann, and Henryk Grossman (Jay, 1973; Wiggershaus, 1995; Wheatland, 2009).

Fromm was central to early critical theory because of his study of workers in Weimar Germany. The core project of the Frankfurt School circle was to revise Marxism to explain how the economic crisis of the 1920s resulted not in a socialist revolution as Marxists had predicted, but in a significant shift to the nationalist right in Spain, Japan, Italy, and especially Germany. Fromm's training in both psychoanalysis and sociology made him attractive to Horkheimer in his efforts to address this troubling phenomenon. The Weimar study was conducted when 'there was almost no empirical research in the academic field' (Bonss, 1984 p 15). Indeed, Israeli sociologist José Brunner's article on the working class in Weimar study is subtitled 'How Erich Fromm Turned Critical Theory into Empirical Sociology' (Brunner, 1994).

There were two major competing streams of scholarship on the working class in Germany at the time. One was Robert and Helen Lynd's *Middletown* (1929) authored by Americans influenced by the Vienna School. This work led to Marie Jahoda's, Paul F. Lazarsfeld's and Hanz Zeisel's German-language research that eventually resulted in *The Unemployed of Marienthal* (1933) in English. The second stream was a new German critical theory tradition steered by Fromm under Horkheimer's sponsorship and funding. This critical social psychology was more theoretically oriented and committed to qualitative methods and, under Fromm's influence, concerned with theorizing emotions, the unconscious, and the dynamics of what Fromm would call the authoritarian character. We will discuss the limitations of the Fromm study and explain why it was not published until 1984 after German sociologist Wolfgang Bonss found the manuscript and prepared it for Harvard University Press. Although the study was little known until recently, it played a pivotal role in Fromm's career, establishing his sociological credentials as surely as did his PhD.

The study was also helped the Horkheimer circle finding shelter from Hitler in New York City at Columbia University. After the mostly Jewish Marxists of the Frankfurt School fled Nazi-ruled Germany to Switzerland, there were sustained negotiations between top officials at Columbia University, among whom was Robert Lynd from the sociology department. Lynd knew of Fromm's work through his own involvement in the research area. Arrangements were made for the Frankfurt School circle to spend most of the 1930s and the war years in Morningside Heights in the north-west part of Manhattan (Wheatland, 2009). The years that Horkheimer and the Frankfurt School researchers spent at Columbia University were pivotal for creating a beachhead for critical theory in America (Jay, 1973; Bronner, 1994). We tend to remember Adorno's involvement in critical theory although he was not formally involved until later in the 1930s (McLaughlin, 1999). It was Fromm's empirical work on the Weimar study that held the most interest for the university (Wheatland, 2009), despite the fact that Fromm was later written out of the origin myths critical theorists told about their history (McLaughlin, 1999).

Critical theory came to Columbia because of Fromm's sociological work on the working class in Weimar that was absorbed into a broader set of studies on authority and the German family (Jay, 1973; Wiggershaus, 1995). This work, in turn, led to *The Authoritarian Personality*, published after Fromm broke with Horkheimer and was replaced by Adorno, who then decamped to the University of California at Berekley to work with academic social psychologists on the issues Fromm pioneered (Adorno et al, 1950). Adorno and his social psychological collaborators developed the famous F-scale, which become one of the most influential works in empirical social science in the mid-twentieth century. What is often not recognized is that the measure was directly shaped by Fromm's original formulation of the authoritarian character in the 1930s (Burston, 1991; Brunner, 1994). One of the ironies of this history is that Paul Lazarsfeld, who would later become one of the most influential sociologists of the twentieth century working closely with Robert Merton at Columbia University's Bureau for Applied Social Research, worked as Fromm's research assistant in the early 1930s as Fromm unsuccessfully attempted to publish the Weimar study.

One of the consequences of Fromm's failure to publish the Weimar study is that it buried his early contributions to a sociology concerned with patriarchy and gender inequality. Fromm had been influenced by sociologist Simmel's writings on gender (Fromm, 1997) as well as by German Jewish revolutionary Marxist Rosa Luxemburg, an intellectual he thought was not taken seriously enough by the Social Democratic Party because she was a woman (Anderson, 2015 p 217). The Weimar study was centrally concerned with how the authoritarian character of some socialists and communists could be revealed through the interpretation of their conventional views on gender equality and the rights of children. Authoritarian character structures can contradict explicit egalitarian ideology (Fromm, 1984; Afary and Friedland, 2018).

Fromm broke with the Frankfurt School in the latter part of the 1930s. While he became famous as a public intellectual and best-selling author with *Escape from Freedom*, however, the sociological perspective he derived from Alfred Weber and practised in the Weimar study remained central to his work. *Escape from Freedom* was not a peer-reviewed work of scholarship. Instead, it was a powerfully written work of scholarly social criticism that offered a theoretical account of Nazism drawing on Freud, existentialist philosophy and, more crucially, a sociological framework. Drawing on both Marx and Weber, the book was framed by a critique of both Durkheim- and behaviourist-influenced social science.

After the book gained scholarly and popular attention, Fromm published an article in the *American Sociological Review* (1944) and the value of his work was debated in the *American Journal of Sociology* (Green, 1946). Fromm was clearly a sociologist although he was also a psychoanalyst and social critic who had little desire to be a professor. When given the opportunity, Fromm did not even respond to the critique of his work in the *American Journal of Sociology*, mostly because he simply did not care enough about what sociologists said about his work (Green, 1946).

Fromm was even more distant from sociology by the late 1940s and until his death in 1980, but his legacy demands that we view him through the public sociological lens, especially at key moments. *The Sane Society* was Fromm's most sociological book of the 1950s, an extended social psychological critique of modernity that was reviewed in the *American Journal of Sociology*, the *American Sociological Review*, and *Social Problems*. Fromm's analysis in *Marx's Concept of Man*, and his powerful critique of American foreign policy in *May Man Prevail?* were generally not reviewed in core sociology journals. By then, Fromm was defined more as a public intellectual and social critic than as an empirical social scientist. These books did, however, utilize sociological frameworks, were read by sociologists, and warrant a close revisiting.

By the last decade of Fromm's life, he viewed himself as external to what he would have regarded as the narrow disciplinary identity of a sociologist. Fromm continued to do work influenced by sociological theories, and he was read by sociologists. His books, *Social Character in a Mexican Village* (written with Michael Maccoby) and *The Anatomy of Human Destructiveness* were both reviewed by *Contemporary Sociology*, the American Sociological Association's official book review journal. *Anatomy* was also reviewed by the *American Journal of Sociology*. The reviews Fromm received from sociologists in the 1970s were far less positive than in the 1940s and 1950s. Nonetheless, Fromm was clearly a sociologist by the criteria Jennifer Platt recommends we use, even if his relationship to the field was complicated and ambivalent. It was Fromm's popular books, however, that made him a public sociologist.

The sociological importance of books for social movements: Fromm's paperback public sociology

Fromm was a public sociologist who took his sociology to mass audiences by writing best-selling books six decades before the concept of public sociologist existed. What is most distinctive about him was his ability to write best-selling book after book for nearly forty years. Starting with *Escape from Freedom* which had sold over 5 million copies by 2011 and has been translated into twenty-nine languages, through to *The Sane Society* which sold over 3 million copies also with twenty-nine translations, and ending with *To Have or To Be* which sold 8 million and was translated thirty-three times, Fromm was a writer of what sociologists have called 'big books'. None were bigger than *The Art of Loving* which sold over 25 million copies in thirty-three translations. No public sociologist has achieved this number of readers in so many different languages around the world. No one else comes close as a global public sociologist.

Important social movement scholarship has evoked a 'big book' myth that over-estimates the political influence of 1960s-era best-selling paperbacks (Meyer and Rohlinger, 2012). Meyer and Rohlinger (2012) assess the political influence of 'big books', such as Michael Harrington's *The Other America* (1962), Betty Friedan's *The Feminist Mystique* (1963), Rachel Carson's *The Silent Spring* (1962), and Ralph Nader's *Unsafe at any Speed* (1965) in relation to the anti-poverty, feminist, environmental, and consumer rights movements of the 1960s respectively (Meyer and Rohlinger, 2012). Meyer and Rohlinger's social movement perspective rejected the assumption that big books caused social movements, what Verta Taylor calls an 'immaculate conception' view of social movements that ignores the covert work that goes into movement building (Taylor, 1989).

It would be a mistake, however, to ignore the political influence of high-profile books, especially after the invention of the paperback and before social media. Throughout Fromm's career, he was centrally, although not exclusively, a political thinker directing his insights into the writing of books. Fromm thus had significant political influence on intellectual debate and social movements during the Second World War, the Cold War period, the social turmoil of the 1960s, and finally, in the late 1970s as the environmental and green movements spread across the world.

Fromm's *Escape from Freedom* was not his best-selling book at over 5 million copies,[4] though it was his ultimate 'big book' in relation to his intellectual agenda and career. Written as a hybrid of sociology, history, and an empirical sociology text, *Escape from Freedom* was also an impassioned anti-fascist manifesto and political intervention and represented the final severing of his association with the Frankfurt School. The Frankfurt School scholars are barely mentioned, and *Escape* was not read as part of the tradition. Fromm and the Horkheimer circle were happy to forget about their collective work and move on. Published by the major New York commercial press Henry Holt, the book influenced public and scholarly debate about Nazism and set in motion the sociological logic that guided the rest of his career. After *Escape from Freedom*, Fromm would never again be dependent on his academic or clinical career alone. His new fame and status ensured his financial security.

Fromm also wrote three big books in the Cold War era, each of them playing an important role in public sociology of the 1950s. An open secret in the history of American sociology is the central role that Fromm's book, *Man for Himself: An Inquiry into the Psychology of Ethics*, played in shaping David Riesman's *The Lonely Crowd* (1950), the best-selling sociology book of all time and a major inspiration for Cold War-era social science critiques of conformity. Fromm's *The Sane Society* continued this sociological social criticism, helping create a Marxist sociology of alienation. *The Sane Society* had such influence on the social movements of the New Left that Jamison and Eyerman read it as one of the 'seeds of the sixties' (Jamison and Eyerman, 1994).

Fromm's biggest-selling book, *The Art of Loving*, made him a global celebrity. It influenced Martin Luther King and inspired bell hooks' major black feminist analysis of love (hooks, 2002). *The Art of Loving* sold over 25 million copies and helped inspire a genre of books between self-help and social science on love and intimacy that is now a valuable part of public sociology.

Fromm would publish two major works of public sociology in the 1960s – *Man's Concept of Man* (1961a) and *May Man Prevail?: An Inquiry into the Facts and Fictions of Foreign Policy* (1961b). These two books contributed to Fromm's reputation as the most important Marxist sociologist before the rise of the New Left and academic Marxism of the later 1960s. Fromm's fame and writing abilities allowed him to appeal to mass audiences of millions of readers as he did in the 1940s and 1950s. *Marx's Concept of Man* was a mass-market book that sold over a million copies. It dealt with Karl Marx's philosophical and sociological thought – a remarkable achievement in retrospect. Michael Burawoy and many other radical sociologists of the 1960s benefited from the space for Marxist sociology that Fromm helped create, even though Fromm's own writings on Marx in this period were not of professional calibre. Not written for experts, Fromm did not make original contributions to political economy that others would in the 1960s and 1970s (Attewell, 1984; Wright, 2010). *May Man Prevail?* reached a smaller audience of scholars, activists, and general readers of 500,000 who were concerned about the dangers of war in a nuclear-armed world just before the Cuban Missile Crisis and the escalation of the colonial conflict in Indochina. Before Noam Chomsky's emergence in the late 1960s and 1970s, Fromm was the most prominent radical critic of American foreign policy who wrote to the public (Barsky, 2007; Lannigan and McLaughlin, 2017).

Public sociology and celebrity intellectuals

Fromm is unique. Most famous public sociologists are only famous among other scholars or, at the most, among elite intellectuals, while Fromm achieved the level of what Lewis Coser calls a 'celebrity intellectual' (Coser, 1965). Coser did not view celebrity intellectuals positively, regarding fame and the capitalist marketing of books to mass publics as leading to a reduction in intellectual standards. Any discussion of Fromm's public sociology needs to clarify the difference between the average sociologist's career and the sociological mechanism at play for scholars who reach the pinnacle of fame.

Fromm's notorious public sociological status shaped his activities, the content and quality of his ideas, the effectiveness of his political interventions, and the reception of his scholarship in significant ways. Trade-offs in both the quality of his political work and his intellectual contribution flowed from his fame and his multiple professional roles as a therapist, scholar, and activist. Margaret Mead in anthropology, Noam Chomsky in linguistics, and more recently Marxist Slavoj Žižek and conservative psychologist Jordan Peterson, are among the few scholars who have achieved prominence comparable to Fromm's.

David Riesman is often cited as one of the most renowned public sociologists of the twentieth century, but his eminence was acknowledged only by other scholars and intellectual elites and he was not particularly global. Riesman remains generally unknown outside the United States. C. Wright Mills is acclaimed outside of the United States, although still within sociology. Only W. E. B. Du Bois approaches Fromm's global influence on Pan-Africanism and on anti-colonial intellectuals around the world. Sociology has witnessed a recent revitalization of Du Bois' reputation (Morris, 2015) but we need more scholarly work on the general issue of global public sociologies.

Erich Fromm's Global Public Sociology will contribute to the sociological literature on the effect of fame on both the scholarship and the activism of public sociologists. The esteem Fromm received from publishing *Escape from Freedom* allowed him to stay out of professional sociological networks for decades. This gave him a unique and original angle on American and global society. The book also cleared a path for him to develop a powerful radical critique of capitalist modernity in *Man for Himself* and *The Sane Society*.

Fromm's work restructured scholarly debates within sociology in the post-war period from what I call the an 'optimally marginal' position in the field (McLaughlin, 2001a). Fromm was close enough to the intellectual energy and cultural capital of Weber, Durkheim, Simmel, and especially Marx and Freud to be able to bring powerful new insights into sociology. But Fromm was far enough away from the status hierarchies of mainstream sociology to resist the sociological orthodoxies that inhibited intellectual progress. Fromm's fame and his relationship to David Riesman, a consummate insider within American politics, gave him access to powerful politicians, influential intellectuals, and activists. Even a Pope would magnify the global reach of his work around questions of nuclear weapons and American foreign policy.

Fromm's prominence was a double-edged sword. It hurt his scholarly reputation and reinforced some of the insularity of his thinking. He was distant from sociological elites and this had advantages but also damaged his scholarly work. The more fame an intellectual has, the greater the incentive to avoid the hard work of research since one need only to trade one's name brand to sell books, a point Richard Posner has made (Posner, 2001). For Posner, some academics who are tempted by fame abandon serious and time-consuming academic scholarship, preferring income from the sales of books and speaking engagements. More public sociologists and public intellectuals can become celebrity intellectuals through social media. *Erich Fromm and Global Public Sociology* thus hopes to encourage the research and the publication of more case studies on fame and celebrity in public sociology, an increasingly important topic for the disciplines and for scholars of communication and the sociology of culture.

Chapter 1 tells the story of how Fromm burst onto the scene as a major intellectual figure with *Escape from Freedom* and evaluates the usefulness of his analysis in understanding the current moment of far-right populism and political polarization. Chapter 2 turns to Fromm's youth and early career as a case study of what I call optimal marginality in order to theorize how scholars become public sociologists. This chapter will describe Fromm's involvement with the critical theory of the Frankfurt School in the 1930s alongside his early involvement with German radicals, radical Jewish intellectuals, early feminist psychoanalysts, Weberian sociology, and his later connection to Margaret Mead and the cultural school of anthropology. Fromm had a remarkable ability to join the intellectual energy in each of these networks while staying on their optimal margins (McLaughlin, 2001a). This disposition cultivated his public sociology. While Fromm is an unusual case, I argue that similar dynamics operate for many of the most creative public sociologists today, despite new institutional and cultural context.

Chapter 3 discusses at length Fromm's close collaborative relationship with David Riesman and his influence as a role model for both Cold War liberal public sociology and the radical public sociology of the 1960s. I also discuss and evaluate Fromm's influence on the sociology of conformity in Cold War America represented by Riesman's *The Lonely Crowd* and Fromm's own neo-Marxist classic, *The Sane Society*.

This will lead to an analysis in Chapter 4 of how Fromm's public sociology was forgotten, involving a famous debate between Fromm and Herbert Marcuse in *Dissent* magazine and the reception of *The Art of Loving*. These two publishing events, along with his distance from feminism in the 1960s and sociologist Lewis Coser's influential negative opinion of Fromm, help explain Fromm's disappearance from public sociology's collective memory.

Chapter 5 will outline Fromm's political writing and activism in the 1960s with *Marx's Concept of Man*, *May Man Prevail?*, and *The Revolution of Hope* and his anti-nuclear weapons activism, policy work on the Berlin Crisis, socialist activism, involvement in electoral politics, and protest against the Vietnam War. Chapter 6 deals with Fromm's attempt to return to scholarly activity in his last decade, partly to leave an intellectual legacy. His books, *Social Character in a Mexican Village* and *The Anatomy of Human Destructiveness* are discussed, showing how Fromm's marginality to mainstream social science created insights but also undermined the quality of his research.

With this case material as a foundation, the concluding chapter discusses the beginning of what we are seeing now as a major revival of interest in his public sociology. I then evaluate how Fromm's specific theories and professional sociological work interacts with public sociological engagement and activism. This broader discussion contributes to current debates about how scholars can best engage the public, imbue American professional sociology with a global perspective, and suggest new directions for an empirical sociology of public sociology. We will start, however, with America on the eve of Pearl Harbor and its entry into the Second World War when, with the publication of *Escape from Freedom*, a global public sociologist was born.

1

Sociology in a World at War: *Escape from Freedom*

The world was in flames and chaos in 1940 when Erich Fromm was finishing writing his book *Escape from Freedom* (1941) and living in exile in New York City. Hitler dominated Europe with Nazi firepower and war making, and fascists were in power in Italy, Japan, and Spain. Stalin ruled Russia with brutality and an iron hand while fighting Hitler on his western front before the United States joined the war. The Battle of Britain raged in the air over the United Kingdom with Prime Minister Churchill promising a fight to the death while President Roosevelt in the United States was still debating America's role in this increasingly global conflict on the eve of the Japanese attack on Pearl Harbor. It was in this context that Erich Fromm published *Escape from Freedom* with Farrar and Rinehart, a major New York commercial book press. With this soon-to-be best-selling book, Fromm entered the stage as a public sociologist with a theoretical and political intervention that would help define the debate about fascism for a generation of intellectuals. The book outlined the research agenda he would follow for the rest of his life and it would make him famous.

Fromm was a left-wing Jewish exile from Nazism, living in New York City. He was making a living from his therapeutic practice with a safety net provided by a significant settlement he had received when he gave up his tenured status with the Frankfurt School led by Max Horkheimer. Before *Escape from Freedom*, Fromm's writings had been mostly theoretical and empirical papers (predominantly in German although increasingly in English) all written for academic and clinical audiences of his peers. Fromm had been writing the manuscript for a number of years around themes of authoritarianism, but it was in the course of a letter exchange with Robert Lynd, a well-known Columbia

University sociologist (Friedman, 2013), that he turned towards the meaning and implications of freedom in modernity. Fromm faced first hand the danger the Nazi regime posed to Europe and the world. He played a central role in persuading the critical theorists to leave Germany (Wheatland, 2009) and was engaged throughout the 1930s in trying to get Jewish relatives out of the country before it was too late. The book was a warning as well as a theoretical analysis.

Fromm was simultaneously conducting political work, contributing to intellectual debate on major philosophical questions regarding freedom, and outlining an agenda for a social psychological research agenda he would develop throughout his life. Fromm was a radical humanist and socialist (Durkin, 2014) but he was not a pacifist; a major goal of the publication of the book with a commercial press was to spread his analysis of the danger of Nazism as widely as possible partly to help make the case for American entry into the war against Hitler.

Escape from Freedom was not simply an extended political polemic, however, as it also outlined the theoretical agenda Fromm would develop up to his death in 1980. *Escape from Freedom*'s original theoretical synthesis of Marxist, Freudian, Weberian, and existentialist ideas had an enormous influence on sociology and general public intellectual debates on freedom and democracy in the middle of the twentieth century. The book prefigured his research agenda on the social psychology of authoritarianism, destructiveness, alienation, and conformity. This chapter will outline the core argument of *Escape from Freedom*, stressing its theoretical importance, discuss its reception and influence, and offer an analysis of its strengths, limitations, and current relevance as public sociology. The fame Fromm achieved with its publication shaped the logic of his career but we will begin with his argument in this first major book.

The social psychology of fascism

In Fromm's analysis, the modern world had created both new freedoms and increased anxieties, and the stage had been set for Nazism by both the breakdown of the security provided by feudalism and the political crisis of the 1930s. In Germany, defeat in war and economic depression had destroyed the legitimacy of democratic institutions. Hitler's 'evangelism of self-annihilation' had shown millions of Germans the way out of cultural and economic collapse (Fromm, [1941] 1969 p 259). The Nazi Party's racism, nationalism, militarism, and 'spirit of blind obedience to a leader' represented an 'escape from freedom' (Fromm, [1941] 1969 p 235).

Fromm argued that the dominant social science approaches to the problem of fascism were falsely polarized between psychological and structural levels of analysis. He explicitly criticized various Marxist theories of fascism that reduced Nazism to the expansionist tendencies of German imperialism. Fromm understood the role played by German militarism, the Junkers who dominated agricultural production, and opportunist right-wing industrialists in the rise of Hitler. Yet Nazism cannot be understood simply as the result of a minority's trickery and coercion of the majority of the population, the victory of madman Hitler, or a capitalist plot. Fromm insisted that the mass base of Nazism be accounted for with an analysis that avoids both what we now call an 'over-socialized' explanation of Nazism and psychological reductionism (Wrong, 1961).

Escape from Freedom follows the insights of historical materialism in tracing the origins of Nazism to the economic changes that over several hundred years transformed medieval Europe into a modern market society. Fromm was hardly an orthodox Marxist, arguing that Marx's nineteenth-century enlightenment tradition was unprepared theoretically to deal with humanity's powerful propensities for violence, lust for power, and yearning for submission. Nazism cannot be understood in purely rationalistic terms; Freud's theory of the unconscious helps fill the gaps in Marxist theory and provides tools to understand the human irrationality of the First World War and the rise of Hitler, events that shattered the confidence of all non-dogmatic Marxists. Fromm insisted that Freud and most of his disciples 'had only a very naive notion of what goes on in society, and most of his applications of psychology to social problems were misleading constructions' (Fromm, [1941] 1969 p 23). Yet he argued that Freud's ideas were essential for a social theory that could come to grips with the human potential for destructiveness inherent in the Nazi Party.

Theoretical core: an existentialist revision of psychoanalysis

To adapt psychoanalytic insights for sociology, Fromm argued, we must reject Freud's overly speculative, ahistorical, and biologically oriented social theory in favour of a revised version of psychoanalysis. As Jay Greenberg and Stephen Mitchell would later summarize from Fromm's contributions (1983 p 25), Freud's formulations reflect the 'influence of now outmoded neurological conceptions' as well as 'the influence of hydraulic metaphors'. The mainstream psychoanalytic view has shifted from the original Freudian model of humans as 'drive-regulating animals' to an object relations perspective that views us as 'meaning generating animals' (Mitchell, 1993 p 23). It is precisely this focus on emotions and meaning that recommends the psychoanalytic perspective to contemporary sociologists concerned with understanding the power of irrationality in contemporary extremist movements. Fromm had been moving away from Freudian orthodoxy for years and he would further develop his critique of psychoanalytic libido theory throughout the 1950s until his last book *The Greatness and Limitations of Freud's Thought* (1980). It was in *Escape from Freedom*, however, that he took his original thinking on the sociology of emotions to the public.

Drawing on Kierkegaard, Nietzsche, and Dostoevsky, Fromm says that the very conditions of human existence bring about 'the need to be related to the world outside oneself, the need to avoid aloneness' ([1941] 1969 p 34). Kierkegaard, according to Fromm, 'describes the helpless individual torn and tormented by doubts, overwhelmed by the feeling of aloneness and insignificance' ([1941] 1969 p 154). Nietzsche had foreseen the 'approaching nihilism which was to become manifest in Nazism', and his 'superman', for Fromm, was intended to negate the insignificance of the individual in the modem world ([1941] 1969 p 154). Dostoevsky's *The Brothers Karamazov* suggests that man has 'no more pressing need than the one to find someone to whom he can surrender, as quickly as possible, that gift of freedom which, he, the unfortunate creature was born with' ([1941] 1969 p 173). For Dostoevsky, eliminating the self also eliminates the burden of freedom – the basic thesis of *Escape from Freedom*. 'Moral aloneness' and 'lack of relatedness to values, symbols, patterns' is as 'intolerable as psychical aloneness' (Fromm, [1941] 1969 p 33). The need to relate to the world is an even more powerful driving force than instinctual dynamics. Humans will turn to religion or nationalism for refuge from 'what man most dreads: isolation' ([1941] 1969 p 34). Human self-consciousness, the awareness of one's self as distinct from nature and also from other humans is what makes man's fear of isolation so powerful.

Contrary to critics who argued that Fromm's Marxism was marred by idealism, Fromm understood the need to ground social analysis in concrete sociology and history. He later clarified this point, saying that unlike Kierkegaard and many others in the existentialist tradition, Marx saw 'man in his full concreteness as a member of a given society and of a given class, aided in his development by society, and at the time its captive' (1961a p vi). Existentialists wrote in broad abstractions about the human condition, dread, and death, whereas Fromm used existentialist insights and a Marxist philosophical anthropology to develop a psychological foundation for a historically informed and empirical social science.

Existential dread and moral aloneness provide a crucial motivational drive lacking in the rational choice, symbolic interactionist, and instinctual theories that dominated the social science thinking of the period. People certainly attempt to maximize utility and interact through symbolic meanings, and they are motivated by instinctual dynamics and biological hardwiring, but what explains the human passion to kill, take revenge, and destroy? How does one explain self-destructive behaviour and suicide? Rational choice theorists generally downplay the theoretical significance of irrational destructiveness, and most micro-level paradigms within contemporary sociology still derive from an overly cognitive view of human motivation. Dennis Wrong, in *The Problem of Order: What Unites and Divides Society* (1994), for example, argues that symbolic interactionism and ethnomethodology display a 'cognitivist' bias. And sociobiology, evolutionary psychology, as well as Freudian-influenced theories of 'death instincts' ignore the social and historical variability of human violence as well as the concrete reasons why nations go to war. The existentialist tradition provides a foundation for a fuller account of human irrationality and destructiveness even though existentialists themselves seldom developed these insights fully. Unlike most existentialist philosophers, Fromm understood modernity in its historical specificity, not simply as an abstract human condition. He drew from existentialist philosophy but returned to historical and sociological analysis.

For Erich Fromm, as for De Tocqueville and Durkheim, individualism was the central theme of modernity (Bellah et al, 1985). Drawing on the work of Carl Jung, Fromm called the process by which an individual emerges from original ties 'individuation' – something that 'seemed to reach its peak in modern history in the centuries between the Reformation and the present' ([1941] 1969 p 40). Fromm attempts to deal with these issues at the micro level, where the individual self develops, and in macro-historical terms.[1] The history of the human species is, for Fromm, a progressive move away from a behaviour determined by instincts (Cortina, 2015). Man is 'the most helpless of all animals at birth. His adaption to nature is based essentially on the process of learning, not on instinctual determination' (Fromm, [1941] 1969 p 41). Fromm argues that 'human existence and freedom are from the beginning inseparable'.[2] For Fromm, separation and individuation produce 'an unbearable feeling of isolation and powerlessness' that leads to psychic mechanisms ([1941] 1969 p 47).

These mechanisms cannot be understood purely in structural terms. Fromm was explicitly critical of Durkheim and his school for trying to 'eliminate psychological problems from sociology' and for neglecting the 'role of the human factor as one of the dynamic elements in the social process' ([1941] 1969 p 29).³ Modern freedom can be frightening; Fromm argued that psychological 'mechanisms of escape' allow people to overcome the anxiety inherent in modernity. While much of *Escape from Freedom* consists of a polemic against Freudian instinct theory, Fromm argued also against sociological thinking 'tinged with behaviorism' and what we now call rational choice theory. Although his Marxism highlighted the fundamental importance of economic relations in shaping human behaviour, Fromm insisted that utilitarian models are inadequate for understanding the complex sources of human action.

The clinical evidence we have on masochistic and sadomasochistic behaviour raises serious questions about contemporary social and political theory (later theoretically developed in Benjamin, 1988; Chancer, 1992). 'From Hobbes to Hitler', said Fromm, 'the lust for power has been explained as a part of human nature which does not warrant any explanation beyond the obvious', blurring, for Fromm, an understanding of the 'personality structure which is the human basis of fascism' ([1941] 1969 pp 169, 186). The characteristics of the 'authoritarian character' are familiar to contemporary readers because of Adorno's development of Fromm's ideas a decade later in *The Authoritarian Personality* (Adorno, et al, 1950).⁴ The most important aspect of an authoritarian character is his or her attitude towards power: Such a person tends to disdain and have contempt for the weak and powerless while also submitting to those more powerful.

Fromm had examined this question more than a decade before *Escape from Freedom* when he had conducted an empirical study on the social character of the German working class in the late 1920s and early 1930s as part of his work with the Institute for Social Research – what we know as the Frankfurt School. In 1941 this work was widely available only in German, as Fromm had published a summary of this research as part of Horkheimer's edited collection *Studien über Autorität und Familie* (1936). By the late 1930s, however, Fromm had broken with the other members of the Frankfurt School. For various reasons we will discuss in Chapter 2, the full text of the original authoritarian character study was not published until after Fromm's death, when German sociologist Wolfgang Bonss pulled the uncompleted manuscript together as *The Working Class in Weimar Germany: A Psychological and Sociological Study* (1984). Adorno developed Fromm's ideas with better empirical methods (helped by a group of social psychologists at Berkeley) in *The Authoritarian Personality* (Adorno et al, 1950) although arguably with less theoretical power and political insight and significant remaining methodological problems (Jay, 1973). In the text of *Escape from Freedom*, this history and context were very much in the background, but Fromm's theory of the role played by the sadomasochistic character in creating political authoritarianism was front and centre, with the empirical evidence an afterthought. The history of European and German authoritarianism, however, was foremost in Fromm's mind and, before he focused his analysis on Nazism, he highlighted the links between the crisis of the 1930s and the period of the Reformation in an extended engagement with Weberian sociology.

The Protestant Ethic and the Spirit of Authoritarianism

Drawing on Max Weber's *The Protestant Ethic and the Spirit of Capitalism* (1905), Fromm argues that scholars in Protestant countries have stressed only the positive aspects of Luther's legacy. The doctrines of Luther, Calvin, and Puritanism have often been linked to the development of modern political and spiritual freedom. Fromm accepts this historical account but argues that the Weberian theoretical tradition ignores Luther and Calvin's 'emphasis on the fundamental evilness and powerlessness of man'. Luther's stress on the worthlessness and insignificance of human action 'paved the way for a development in which man not only was to obey secular authorities but had to subordinate life to the ends of economic achievements' (Fromm, [1941] 1969 p 103). For modern fascists, 'the aim of life is to be sacrificed for "higher" powers, for the leader or the racial community' ([1941] 1969 p 103). Calvinism served the same sociological function for Anglo-Saxon countries. Fromm's revision of Weberian orthodoxy provides balance for the sociological literature from Weber to Merton that stresses the positive aspects of Protestant culture. It was Fromm's belief that Protestantism was intimately linked to political freedoms and economic progress as well as to Nazism.[5]

For Fromm, moreover, this was all linked to capitalism as Lutheranism and Calvinism emerged along with modern market societies. Fromm wrote that the 'mechanism of the new market seemed to resemble the Calvinistic doctrine of predestination', where the 'market day became the day of judgment for the products of human effort' ([1941] 1969 p 79). The roots of Fromm's analysis of Nazism lie in his analysis of Lutheranism's appeal for the middle class of the Reformation. This analysis of the cultural consequences of the Reformation led to his discussion of capitalist modernity. For Fromm, capitalism freed man from traditional bonds and created a 'critical and responsible self'. Yet, freedom has a cost, for it 'made the individual more and more alone and isolated', imbued 'with a feeling of insignificance and powerlessness' ([1941] 1969 p 123).

After laying this theoretical foundation, Fromm returns to a discussion of the political and psychological basis of Nazism. The political events he stresses are well known to contemporary students of history. Unemployment and inflation accelerated the loss of legitimacy caused by the collapse of the monarchy after the First World War. The older generation was bewildered by the rapid cultural changes, while young people rebelled against the authority of their discredited elders. Hitler rallied people to his ideology as the representative of a humiliated but now resurgent Germany. Although he stresses psychological dynamics, Fromm never denies the importance of specific political events, such as the debate over the Versailles Treaty. He argues, however, that Hitler's indignation at the injustice of the treaty was a rationalization for his real motives of hatred, lust for power, and conquest.

Fromm's analysis is a social psychology, however, since Hitler's hatred would have been relatively harmless had it not found a mass base. Fromm, following Wilhelm Reich, was interested primarily not in individual pathology but in the 'mass psychology of fascism'.[6] Whereas Reich stressed the passing on of authoritarian values through sexual repression in the German family, Fromm insisted that a full explanation of Nazism must account for larger sociological and political realities. The authoritarian character that Fromm claimed was dominant in the lower middle class and among Protestants, created a potential mass base that was exploited by the 'radical opportunism' of the Nazi Party (Fromm, [1941] 1969 p 245). Inflation played both an economic and a psychological role in the move towards fascism. Fromm points out that inflation was 'a deadly blow against the principle of thrift as well as against the authority of the state' ([1941] 1969 p 239). Just as Luther expressed the social and psychological insecurities of his supporters during the Reformation, Hitler was a representative of the threatened and marginalized lower middle class and a humiliated nation.

The reception of *Escape from Freedom*

The intellectual reaction to Fromm's book was immediate and widespread, particularly in newspapers and journals of opinion.[7] *Escape from Freedom* was reviewed enthusiastically by such prominent public intellectual figures as Margaret Mead, Ashley Montagu, and Dwight

Macdonald. The reaction from academic and professional audiences was less dramatic, but largely positive. The *American Journal of Sociology* described *Escape from Freedom* as a 'noteworthy book'.[8] It was initially ignored in professional psychology journals, and it would be some time before Fromm's work would have a major influence on academic psychology. The interdisciplinary psychoanalytic journal *Psychiatry*, however, published a symposium of reviews on *Escape from Freedom*. Psychologist Lewis B. Hill argued that 'this book must be read by every clinical psychoanalyst who, like Freud, regards psychoanalysis as capable of further expansion and application rather than as a closed rigid system of thought' (Hill, 1942 p 117).

The acclaim was hardly universal – Fromm was always a controversial figure. Orthodox Freudians in particular were unimpressed. Psychiatrist Karl Menninger, reviewing in *The Nation*, argued that although Fromm writes as if 'he considered himself a psychoanalyst', his lack of medical and psychoanalytic credentials disqualified him from serious consideration. Fromm is a 'distinguished sociologist' who, Menninger conceded, is 'wholly within his rights in applying psychoanalytic theory to sociological problems'. Yet, as Menninger put it, Fromm's analysis only 'purports to be psychoanalytic in character'. *Escape from Freedom* is a 'subjective' book, written in a 'heavy, tedious style' that contains 'many flatly incorrect statements, especially of Freudian theories' (Menninger, 1942 p 317). The doctrinaire Freudian and political radical, Otto Fenichel, also attacked *Escape from Freedom*, accusing Fromm of abandoning psychoanalysis (Fenichel, 1944). The literary intellectual, anarchist, and ardent Reichian, Paul Goodman, also dissented from Fromm's critique of Freudian libido theory, suggesting that 'every part of this general indictment is either wrong or absurd' (Goodman, 1945 p 198).[9]

Orthodox Marxists also were offended (although less so) by Fromm's *Escape from Freedom*. Francis Bartlett's review in *Science and Society* suggested that the work had made 'significant contributions' but was 'blighted by ... many faulty interpretations' (1942 p 188). Bartlett was impressed by *Escape from Freedom*'s stress on how character was shaped by the economic development of society and argued that Fromm's revision of psychoanalysis provided a 'valuable contribution to the struggle against reactionary psychological theories' (1942 p 188). The major problem for Marxists, however, was that Fromm did not emphasize enough that psychological character plays only a subordinate role relative to the 'total economic and political development' (1942 p 189).[10] In addition, *Escape from Freedom* is marred by 'pessimism' and a 'defeatist mood', which suggest that the petty bourgeois is doomed 'to succumb to fascist propaganda', the working class 'act blindly', and the 'finance capitalists alone act rationally' (1942 p 189). Far from the Marxist stress on the revolutionary character of the proletariat, Fromm presents the working class as a 'weak second fiddle' to the bourgeoisie in decline.[11]

Fromm had also offended some important sociological orthodoxies, besides the Freudian and Marxist (Green, 1946). The University of Chicago sociologist Louis Wirth wrote a blistering attack on Fromm's 'cosmic' thesis, 'ambiguous terms', and 'predilection to play with riddles and anomalies' (Wirth, 1942 pp 129–130). Wirth made several valuable substantive points about the limitations of *Escape from Freedom*, but much of his review is unnecessarily nasty and uncharitable. According to Wirth, Fromm underestimated the rational reasons why people would support Hitler. Fromm's theory of self would have benefited from the work of Cooley, Dewey, Mead, Baldwin, and James, as well as empirical research conducted by child psychologists. And Fromm overgeneralized about the lower middle class and modernity without adequate evidence. Although most reviewers were impressed with Fromm's analysis of the dialectical quality of freedom, Wirth asks 'how freedom can be at one and the same time a passionately cherished goal and an oppressive burden?' (1942 p 129). The uncharitable nature of Wirth's critique can be seen here:

> Fromm seems to take it for granted that in the fascist countries, although here and there may have been some struggle to resist the dictator, on the whole people have willingly submitted to a leader and even lovingly embraced him. Mr. Fromm asserts that millions of Germans willingly surrendered their freedom. But, the armies of refugees and the countless thousands in concentration camps furnish at least some reason to suspect that not all Germans deliberately and willingly gave up their freedom. (1942 p 129)

One can reasonably argue that Fromm underplays both internal resistance to Nazism and the role of coercion in securing support for Nazism. But Fromm's point was that coercion had been stressed in the contemporary discussions of Nazism in the West to such an extent that the mass support for Hitler had been underestimated. This is all debatable, but Fromm's position can hardly be disposed of simply by pointing to refugees from Nazism, a phenomenon Fromm was quite familiar with as he was focused behind the scenes throughout the 1930s in getting Jewish relatives out of Germany alive (Friedman, 2013).

Wirth was a prominent sociologist at the University of Chicago in what was becoming the symbolic interactionist tradition, so Fromm was not well received in the most important qualitative research tradition in sociology. Over time, Wirth's dismissal and the general hostility to Fromm from within the symbolic interactionist tradition would play a significant role in the marginalization of his work within sociology.

Despite the reservations of *Escape from Freedom*'s critics, Fromm had arrived on the intellectual scene. As Dan Hausdorf has put it, 'In one stroke, the book established Fromm's reputation as one of the most provocative thinkers of his time' (1972 p 42). Over the next few years, *Escape from Freedom* was widely cited in major social science journals and books.[12] According to Alex Inkeles, 'Fromm has added something to social history and to our understanding of modern man' (1963 p 345). Even those who would become sceptical of Fromm's later work recognized the genuine accomplishment this book represented. John Schaar, one of Fromm's harshest critics, conceded that *Escape from Freedom* is one of the 'finest examples of modern social science of what C. Wright Mills calls the sociological imagination' (1961 p 94). Fromm had, as John Schaar once put it, 'the gift of putting profound ideas simply' (1961 p 6). Although the war effort led to much anthropological speculation into the cultural roots of totalitarianism, Fromm's analysis stood out because he opposed simplistic national character theories (Lenkerd, 1994). With a nod to John Dewey, Fromm argued that 'the crisis of democracy is not a peculiarly Italian or German problem, but one confronting every modern state' ([1941] 1969 p 19). Where theories of national character promoted simplistic generalizations, Fromm's analysis raised larger questions about human motivation and the condition of modernity. At the time, anthropologist Ashley Montagu predicted that *Escape from Freedom* would have a 'wider and deeper influence upon modern thought' than the larger theoretical work of which it was part, arguing that it will always be read as 'the essence of the author's considered conclusions' (Montagu, 1942 p 122). At one level, Montagu was right, for all of Fromm's later writings can be seen as attempts to provide evidence for and revise the basic thesis of this first and most famous book. Ultimately, Montagu's comment was facile, however, because Fromm's strength was as a theorist, not an empirical researcher; the contemporary relevance of *Escape from Freedom* comes from its theoretical insight, not its concrete analysis of Nazism.

The most widespread general influence Fromm's book had on twentieth-century intellectual life was to play a role as a foil for Isaiah Berlin's famous analysis of negative and positive freedom (Berlin, 1969). Fromm was opposed to the limits to freedom represented by dictatorships and state oppression, but central to the argument of *Escape from Freedom* was the importance of what he called 'freedom to' not simply 'freedom from'. For Fromm, if human beings are liberated from extreme poverty and state/religious control to live in societies that do not support the freedom to develop human creativity, love, and productive work, then the danger of people escaping from freedom to authoritarianism and destructiveness are almost inevitable. Berlin, as perhaps the great liberal political theorist of the twentieth century, rejected this very notion of 'freedom to' preferring to argue for limited government and freedom from while suggesting that socialist utopianism would lead to tyranny.

Escape from Freedom also had a positive and direct influence on the discipline of sociology at the time both in its professional core and its radical public sociology offshoot. Talcott Parsons, the dominant sociological theorist in mid-century America, read Fromm's *Escape from Freedom* and engaged it seriously, although he ultimately moved to develop his own very different theoretical framework, preferring the orthodox Freudian theory he picked up while training as a psychoanalyst in Boston. Parsons' student Robert Merton, the most important sociological theorist of the 1960s era in American sociology, was influenced by *Escape from Freedom*, and taught it in Columbia sociology graduate classes in the 1950s (for details on Fromm at Columbia, see Wheatland, 2009).

C. Wright Mills, probably the most important radical public sociologist of the twentieth century (Geary, 2009; Aronowitz, 2012), was impressed with and influenced by *Escape from Freedom* and he went on to follow a similar career path of writing books that appealed to popular audiences while addressing scholarly debates (Oakes and Vidich, 1999). C. Wright Mills had different political and theoretical commitments to Fromm, of course. Mills opposed American entry into the Second World War as a pacifist, while Fromm believed that Hitler had to be defeated militarily and his movement destroyed by force. Fromm was to a greater extent Marxist in his theoretical orientation and politics, while C. Wright Mills was ultimately a radical Weberian American utopian pragmatist (Aronowitz, 2012). Ironically, this led to Fromm being far more critical of communism, Stalinism, and Maoism than Mills was, although we will never know how Mills would have reacted to the excesses of the cultural revolution and the brutal Soviet invasion of Czechoslovakia because he died in 1962. In terms of social psychological theory, Mills was committed to the ideas of George Herbert Mead, not Freud (Gerth and Mills, 1953), and while there is much in common between Mills' theory of social character and Fromm's, the role of emotions is not central to Mills' sociological imagination. Mills deserves his place in our collective memory as a more important public sociologist than Fromm as he focused more of his energy into doing sociological research and making the case for the discipline. At the same time, however, something is lost by forgetting the historical role Fromm played in creating the template that Mills followed in writing his public sociology classics such as *The Power Elite* (1956).

Even more importantly, both Merton and Mills moved away from psychoanalytic insights and thus left us with a public sociology that has done less than it could to follow the insights about emotions and passions than Fromm pioneered in *Escape from Freedom*. Fromm's move from sociology to becoming a famous public intellectual and psychoanalyst operating largely isolated from professional sociology had consequences both for his career but more importantly for the power of his influence on the discipline and the power of analysis. Merton was central to the discipline of sociology in the middle of the twentieth century onwards, Mills remains a significant radical critic of mainstream sociology, while Fromm moved to the margins of both our professional practice and our collective memory. Yet, Fromm's insights in *Escape from Freedom* are powerful and relevant today even if they must be reformulated and revised for contemporary sociologists and current social reality.

Escapes reformulated: professional historical sociology

Escape from Freedom has much to offer both contemporary public sociology and professional research in the discipline. But as we evaluate Fromm's legacy for today, his status as a public sociologist and interdisciplinary thinker as well as nature of the book and its goals must be kept in mind. Peter Baehr's important work in the history and sociology of sociology entitled *Founders, Canons and Classics* (2016) provides an essential framework for thinking about the value of *Escape from Freedom*.

Fromm was certainly not a 'founder' of the discipline as was Durkheim in France in the late nineteenth century or Talcott Parsons or Herbert Blumer were in the United States because, unlike these far more committed sociologists, he was not interested in establishing, building, or even participating in the creation and sustaining of sociological professional associations, journals, and departments. *Escape from Freedom* is not part of the canon of key theoretical texts or exemplary empirical works of research that is taught in sociology PhD graduate seminars, cited regularly in core peer-reviewed journal articles in the field, or integrated into the professional identity of practising sociologists as is the work of Durkheim, Weber, Marx, Merton, or Goffman. *Escape from Freedom* is, however, a greatly neglected 'classic' in Baehr's sense, meaning that it is worth revisiting and rethinking as sociologists attempt to grapple with both the theoretical traditions of the discipline and, I would add, the current crisis of democracy around the world in the age of Trump, Brexit, rising populist revolts, and growing political authoritarianism.

We must remember, however, that for any evaluation of *Escape from Freedom*, Fromm was not primarily a professional sociologist even in the late 1930s; the book must be thought of as a work of public sociology. Fromm did empirical research in the 1930s, 1950s, and 1960s (Brunner, 1994), but he did not train PhD graduate students, nor was he employed full time in major research universities rooted in an academic culture premised upon peer-reviewed scholarship. Therefore, the empirical grounding of *Escape from Freedom* was not its core strength. *Escape from Freedom* was not written in a style designed for academic journals or university presses, and his audience was the general educated reader, not academic specialists. It is true that in this period of his career, Fromm was engaging in dialogue with some of the top social scientists of the era; the book is sophisticated and cutting-edge for its time. But *Escape from Freedom* is not a work of professional history or sociology, and needs to be revised given the massive scholarly literature done on this issue since the 1940s.

Professional sociologists today do not think we can understand contemporary suicide simply by reading Durkheim's *Suicide* (1897), or explain the current work ethic among young people in our market society by reading Weber's *The Protestant Ethic and the Spirit of Capitalism* (1905), or think critically about mental health either in the 1960s or today by simply accepting the framework in Goffman's *Asylums* (1961). *Escape from Freedom* is a book worth re-reading because of the questions it helps us ask and the critique it offers of our existing theoretical paradigms. In this sense, Fromm is a critical sociologist in the ways that Burawoy later theorized (Burawoy, 2005).

Escape from Freedom is not a book comparable to canonized works of sociological theory represented by Durkheim, Weber, or Marx, partly because Fromm was not concerned with establishing a distinctive sociological approach. In theoretical terms, Fromm's *Escape from Freedom* is a useful book to teach theory to undergraduates because it puts Marx, Weber, Durkheim, and Freud up against each other and raises important critical questions about rational choice and behaviourist models for thinking about human motivation. While Fromm is not an original thinker in the way Marx or Freud was, *Escape from Freedom* is indispensable for thinking about how to use Marx and Freud productively within the discipline; he was rooted in these two intellectual traditions while not being wedded to some of their core dogmas. Fromm pulls out some of the most important insights in the Marxist and psychoanalytic traditions while rejecting key flaws in these frameworks and putting them into dialogue with each other and also drawing on Weber and Durkheim.

The core insight of Fromm's analysis useful for sociology and public intellectual debate today, however, is the existentialist–psychoanalytic theory of the emotional dynamics of the search for meaning in the modern world connected to revised Weberian and Marxist frameworks. It is within the context of broader public intellectual debates about the rise of populism, nationalism, and extremism that public sociologists contribute to where Fromm's insights are most useful.

Empirical and historical limitations

The key dilemma faced by sociologists who think about Nazism is how to give an adequate account of historical and situational processes and structural forces while avoiding simplistic psychohistory and excessively abstract attempts to explain political events by the personalities of politicians or dictators. Just as it was easy to see Nazism as being a function of a 'mad man' Hitler, contemporary debates are not moved forward by excessive focus on Trump's pathologies. At the same time, however, there is a powerful mass politics of emotions that social scientists are widely acknowledging today in ways they did not do so in the past. In addition, individual character does matter in political leadership. How does one balance the rational and irrational in politics, and who defines what is rational? How do we think about the role of the individual without simplifying social life beyond recognition? Fromm never argued for a psychoanalytic sociology, narrowly defined, as his work always insisted on the necessity of sophisticated depth psychological insights without reducing politics to psychology. His analysis fits well within what we would call today psychosocial analysis (McLaughlin, 2019).

We must acknowledge, however, that his specific analysis of Nazism is inadequate given the state of current scholarship. Discussing the empirical problems is essential because as professional empirical sociology, *Escape from Freedom* does not hold up. Fromm's central assertion that the base of mass support for fascism lies primarily with the urban lower middle class of shopkeepers, artisans, and white-collar workers is almost certainly wrong. Writing today with the benefit of fifty years of modern research, Richard Hamilton convincingly argues that there is little empirical evidence for a lower-middle-class affinity for Nazism, particularly in urban areas.[13] He describes a linear positive relationship between the social class and the Nazi vote in major German cities. Those of the upper middle class, not the lower middle class, were more likely to vote for the Nazi Party, relative to their numbers in Germany at the time. The evidence is not as clear when one considers party membership instead of voting (Kater, 1983).

The scholarship in Michael Mann's brilliant theoretical account of both ethnic cleansing and fascism (2005, 2004), however, further challenges a simplistic lower-middle-class theory of fascism. Mann defines fascism as 'the pursuit of a transcendent and cleansing nation-statism through paramilitarism' (Mann, 2004 p 13), and through a comparative analysis in Austria, Germany, Hungary, Italy, Romania, and Spain, he shows the Marxist-influenced lower middle-class theory to be inaccurate and deeply misleading. Stressing the origins of fascist activism in war making, not economic crisis, Mann shows the inadequacy of overplaying class explanations since Romanian fascism drew from working-class mobilization, Italian fascism was mostly bourgeois, and in Germany, the Nazi movement drew equally from all classes (Mann, 2004). Mann points out that the Nazis did extremely well among students, often drawing their greatest numbers of converts from the highly educated, not the lower-middle-class outsiders and small businesspeople (Mann, 2004). Fromm, following the widespread conventional wisdom common in the 1950s and 1960s it should be said, was wrong on the urban lower-middle-class roots of Nazism. This obviously holds implications for research on the social basis for Trumpism and the alt-right today on social media and in the streets.

One important aspect of *Escape from Freedom* that was right, however, is the link between the sixteenth and seventeenth centuries and the 1930s. Protestantism is the single best predictor for Nazism, a point blurred by a Marxist-influenced orthodoxy that focuses on the lower middle class. And while Fromm stressed how the uprooting of community led to Nazism, Hamilton's data suggests that rural, not urban, Protestants were the single most likely social stratum to vote for the Nazi Party. It is likely, as Barrington Moore stressed in *The Social Origins of Dictatorship and Democracy* (1966), that fascism emerged partly out of the militaristic values of rural Germany, not from an escape from freedom created by the conditions of mass society. But Fromm's framework, neither fully Weberian nor orthodox Marxist, was correctly attuned to the role of Protestant culture in shaping the Nazi movement. Fromm's critique of the Protestant bias of much historical sociology is useful, furthermore, as a corrective to the literature in political sociology that simplistically links Protestantism with democracy and political liberalism.

Contemporary sociologists read Max Weber as a critic of capitalism, signified by his famous quote about the iron cage of modernity, but this account of Weberianism underplays how the tradition was used in American social science to promote an excessively rosy view of Protestant culture. Parsons, for example, wrote in 1940 that there is 'an authoritarian element in the basic structure of the Catholic Church itself which may weaken individual self-reliance and valuation of freedom' (quoted in Gerhardt, 1993 p 106). This tradition of emphasizing the democratic nature of Protestant culture, furthermore, was a major element in the modernization theory that was so important in the Cold War social science that dominated the American academy after the Second World War. The reception of the Weber thesis in American and British sociology in the 1950s and 1960s often subtly and sometimes polemically linked Protestant culture in the Anglo-American world to democracy and development, unlike Catholic Latin America, fascist Spain and Portugal, and Irish Catholic backwardness. Fromm was not simplistically arguing that Catholicism was inherently democratic, an absurd position given the history of the Catholic anti-Semitism, the Inquisition, the Catholic fascism of Franco, and Salazar's dictatorship in Portugal that he was well aware of. And Mann has documented over-representation of Catholics as staff in German concentration camps (Mann, 2004).

Fromm was arguing against the intellectual conventional wisdom of the time, rooted as it was in a broader Protestant cultural framework. Randall Collins' (1992) contemporary work offers a compelling critique of this traditional sociological view of Protestant liberalism and Catholic authoritarianism consistent with Fromm's writing in the 1940s. And Mann's comparative work reminds us that the Protestant nature of the Nazi movement was more linked to the fact that the Protestant Church in Germany saw itself as linked to the 'soul of the nation', something untrue of German Catholicism irrespective of various compromises and complicity that historians have emphasized in more recent debates about the Pope and Hitler (Mann, 2004).

Indeed, Collins' stress on the organizational structure of the respective churches as the key to their political stances is more compelling than Fromm's Weber-influenced account that privileges ideas. *Escape from Freedom*'s identification of the early roots of Nazism within elements of the Reformation is one-sided in stressing only the authoritarian aspects of Luther and Calvinist doctrines (Erikson, 1958).[14] Fromm's account can hardly explain Italian, Spanish, and Japanese fascism, nor the widespread Nazi support in Austria and Catholic Bavaria as Mann's work addresses with sophisticated historical analysis (Mann, 2004). Nor does it help us understand political authoritarianism in a wider framework as we confront Islamist movements and the deadly dialectic between terrorists and the war on terror. Fromm's emphasis on Protestant culture can best be seen as a complement rather than an alternative to more detailed macro-historical explanations of the paths to dictatorships (Moore, 1966; Skocpol, 1979; Greenfeld, 1992). Yet his unorthodox and intentionally exaggerated challenge to the conventional wisdom on the democratic nature of Protestantism is a contribution that still has not been fully utilized, both in sociological research, but even more so, as we shall see later in this chapter, when engaging with popular right-wing public intellectuals and politicians in the current period.

Although Fromm was often criticized for being a Freudian and Marxist revisionist, the irony is that *Escape from Freedom* is marred by its orthodox theoretical commitments. While his revised version of psychoanalytic theory is compelling, his analysis of Nazism remains overly psychological. Fromm, like many Freudians, assumed that psychological insight gained through clinical practice could translate relatively easily into understanding of broader social dynamics – a questionable proposition. And, although Fromm's Marxism gives historical materialism a needed cultural and psychological analysis, *Escape from Freedom*'s account of Nazism ultimately relies on an outdated class model. Contemporary research suggests that Hitler's movement can be understood not primarily as a lower-middle-class revolt, but as a nationalist *Volks* movement.

Like many Marxists, Fromm puts far too little emphasis on the role of ideas in the emergence of Nazism, particularly German anti-Semitism. Finally, while Fromm's engagement with Weber's historical sociology allowed him to highlight the importance of Protestant support for Hitler, *Escape from Freedom*'s stress on the ideological roots of Lutheran authoritarianism is not compelling, nor does it help us understand fascism from a comparative perspective. Fromm's analysis relies far too heavily on Weber's account of the Protestant ethic and spirit of capitalism, where an organizational analysis of the role of religions in political life would be more illuminating alongside a focus on military cadres and the mobilization of nationalism in political life. And while a simplistic Marxist lower-middle-class theory of populist reaction should be rejected, there *is* working- and lower-middle-class support for right-wing populism in, for example, Hungary, Poland, Canada, and among Trump supporters in America. We need a new theoretical framework to understand and study the social processes at play.

Reframing Fromm's sociology of emotions and nationalism

By the same token, however, Fromm's existentialist-influenced sociology of emotions provides a useful foundation that can be combined with organizational models to provide an intellectually powerful way to understand the rise of Nazism, something we can apply to other cases today. Hamilton explains Nazism with an organizational model that views Hitler's movement as members of a right-wing ex-military cadre who gained access to potential followers in places with the least organizational resistance (Hamilton, 1996). Thus Hamilton, along with Randall Collins, argues that the central sociological difference between the Catholic and Protestant Churches was organizational, not doctrinal, as Fromm posited. The German Catholic Church provided a thick institution of culture and commitment that helped isolate Catholics from outside political influence. The Nazi Party's early anti-Catholic rhetoric had cut the party off from the leadership of the church. Consequently, Catholic priests were not allowed to join the Nazi Party, a policy that could be enforced only by a centralized church. In contrast, the decentralized Protestants responded to Nazi appeals based on more local considerations and personal beliefs. Some Protestant ministers led resistance to Hitler, while others joined and recruited for the party. The relative individualism of Protestant communities also left people less tied to church culture and institutions, providing an opening for mobilization from the far right (Hamilton, 1996).

Analysing the rise of the Nazi Party within the context of Hamilton's organizational model is illuminating. Unions and left parties in the cities and the Catholic Church in the countryside complicated the Nazi mobilization, while rural Protestants and the anti-socialist and anti-communist upper middle class were the obvious source of potential recruits. The upper middle class supported the Nazi Party partly to protect their privilege from the left, a political force Hitler promised to destroy. Hamilton found that humiliation in war and the demobilization after the Treaty of Versailles laid the foundation for Nazism, not the economic and social squeeze of the lower middle class between the workers and the industrialists. Mann's analysis highlights some of the complexities of all this, because defeat in war helps explain Austrian and Hungarian fascism but not Romanian or Spanish.

Neither Hamilton nor Mann, however, offer us an adequate account of the motivations of the Nazi cadre. Certainly, demobilized officers and soldiers were socialized into a militaristic culture, were angry at their defeat in war, and needed jobs. But what explains the level of anger, hatred, and far-right commitment and sacrifice these cadres exhibited over the many years it took for the Nazi Party to gain power? What explains the level of irrationality and fanaticism exhibited by Hitler and the Nazi Party once they controlled the state, and the emotional hatred that made the Holocaust possible? Historians can attempt to answer the specific questions and Mann has offered the best sociological framework we have for theorizing ethnic cleansing (Mann, 2005), but there is a psychological flatness to most sociological models that Fromm's existential-psychoanalysis can fill in, and a revised theoretical model could be applied to help us understand contemporary events.

Contemporary historical accounts of the rise of the Nazi Party and other extremist movements often rely on an undertheorized analysis of the emotional appeals of extremism.[15] Richard Hamilton's great strength is to insist on solid evidence for class for grand theoretical claims that stress class, religious, status, or 'power-knowledge' aspects of social dynamics that are ultimately rooted in concrete people in specific times and places, trying to build and make sense of their lives. It is valuable to move beyond counting and testing specific theories as Hamilton tends to do, in order to posit more ambitious general theories seeking to explain the rise of the neo-fascist movements and governments, the recruitment and mobilization of violent non-state actors, the creation of conspiracy theories in the space of opinion and in networks of 'truthers', and in the maintenance of symbolic violence in colonial fields. In addition, Randall Collins has convincingly shown the analytic pay-off for looking at the roots of violence in the situational space between macro-historical structures and the micro dynamics of individual psychology (Collins, 2009).

Fromm's *Escape from Freedom* operates best at both the historical-comparative macro level and the internal emotional level while leaving undertheorized the situational and organizational levels of analysis as contemporary sociologists will highlight. A fuller analysis of far-right movements will require a better understanding of the ways in which situational dynamics and interaction chains can bring people together into organizations and movements promoting irrational ideologies and actions as Randall Collins has rightly emphasized (Collins, 2009). There is a situational space between psyche and social structure, and an excessive focus on internal psychological dynamics hides the extent to which similar people can behave in different ways, depending on the group dynamics that can create racist mobs, anti-Muslim riots, and the scapegoating of stigmatized Roma, for example. Mann's work provides the essential framework for a comparative analysis of political extremism (Mann, 2004, 2005). Sociological theory influenced by Fromm's insights, however, can add to our understanding of far-right extremism, militant ultra-nationalism, and non-state actor violence by highlighting the micro-level roots of social action with an existentialist-psychoanalytic theoretical foundation, a theoretical issue to which we now turn.

A micro-foundation for political sociology

The psychological roots of Hitler's mass appeal can be traced to the fact that 'this combination of insecure social bonds and humiliated fury was endemic among the German masses' (Scheff, 1994 p 117). According to Thomas Scheff, a sociologist who wrote decades after *Escape from Freedom* and who was also influenced by psychoanalytic insights, many Germans had harsh fathers and 'loving' mothers who yielded to the cruelty inflicted on children. Thus, Hitler's charisma can be explained by the 'emotional, not the cognitive, content' of his message. Scheff suggests that the 'leader who is able to decrease the shame level of a group, interrupting the contagion of overt shame, no matter how briefly or at what cost, will be perceived as charismatic' (1994 p 118). Although there are many important questions about the empirical basis of Scheff's analysis of Nazism, *Bloody Revenge* (1994) is significant because it sharply raises the theoretical importance of a sociology of emotions for a political sociology of nationalism.[16] Nonetheless, Scheff fails to theorize fully the psychological roots of shame.

Fromm's existential-influenced analysis of the human awareness of both our individual existence and inevitable death provides a theoretical micro-foundation for Scheff's sociology. For Fromm, human beings fear isolation as much as death itself, because only through connections to other people and society can humans find meaning in a universe that otherwise appears arbitrary, capricious, and absurd. This is the human root of the sociological dynamics of shame and humiliation central to Scheff's argument. Shame operates differently in distinct historical periods, societies, and institutional settings, of course, but its enormous power to enforce social norms is ultimately rooted in the human condition and the dynamics of individual psychology. For Fromm, individuals are drawn to the dangers of symbiosis because it provides the relations with others that humans require if they are not to go insane. The human need for recognition creates deeper and more powerful human passions than the simple avoidance of shame (Benjamin, 1988).

For Fromm, the psychological dynamic of symbiosis is 'the union of one individual self with another (or another power outside of the own self) in such a way as to make each lose the integrity of its own self' ([1941] 1969 p 157). *Escape from Freedom* stresses how modernity undercut the traditional religions that provided consensual meaning for solidly integrated societies with little individualism. Consequently, modernity creates people drawn to symbiotic relationships with new systems of meanings – like nationalism and fascism. This is a commonplace insight today but was far less so in 1941 when *Escape from Freedom* was published. And the logic of symbiosis is perhaps more powerful and certainly it is more widespread in the age of social media, suggesting powerful contemporary applications for Fromm's theoretical framework.

Fromm argues that 'the emergence of man can be defined at the point in the process of evolution where instinctive adaption reached its minimum' (1947 p 39). As a result, humans are different from animals because of man's 'awareness of himself as a separate entity' and his ability to understand the world through symbols, imagination, and reason (1947 p 39). Fromm writes,

> Reason, man's blessing, is also his curse; it forces him to cope everlastingly with the task of solving an insoluble dichotomy. Human existence is different in this respect from all other organisms; it is in a state of constant and unavoidable disequilibrium. Man's life cannot 'be lived' by repeating the pattern of his species; he must live. Man is the only animal that can be bored, that can be discontented, that can feel evicted from paradise. Man is the only animal for whom his own existence is a problem which he has to solve and from which he cannot escape. He cannot go back to the pre-human state of harmony with nature; he must proceed to develop his reason until he becomes the master of nature, and of himself. (1947 p 40)

Fromm argued that this 'split in man's nature' leads to 'existential dichotomies' that cannot be overcome because they are rooted in the human condition. The central explanation for human motivation is, for Fromm, the human need to react to the fear of death and the fact that the 'short span' of individual human life does not permit the 'full realization' of human potential under 'even the most favorable circumstance' (1947 p 42).

Human beings respond to this contradiction in various ways, relative to their character and their culture, but this existential dichotomy shapes humanity's universal search for meaning and transcendence.[17]

Rural Protestants were the single most important voting bloc for the National Socialists, but Fromm only gets this half right. Standard histories of the *Kulturkampf*, as well as an analysis of the political collapse of German liberalism in Weimar Germany explain most of this phenomenon. Hamilton offers an additional sociological emphasis on the organizational dynamics that made rural Protestants more vulnerable to the appeals of Nazi cadre. And, as Talcott Parsons once pointed out, the Nazi appeal, while 'not primarily religious', had a 'good many resemblances to that of fundamentalism' (quoted in Gerhardt, 1993 p 111). In the Weimar period, communists and social democrats in the cities and the Catholic Church in the countryside all provided competing worldviews that were disseminated through comprehensive ideologies and maintained through communal-like institutions. Rural Protestants were the least tied into an ideological system that provided meaning and an 'imagined community'. Protestants were thus the most vulnerable to a Nazi worldview that answered all doubts, showed a way out of confusion and social breakdown, and promised symbolic immortality through a thousand-year Reich. In this sense, Fromm was right that Nazism was an 'escape from freedom'.

There is thus much worth building on and debating, then, in Fromm's analysis (for a valuable alternative theory of nationalism, see Greenfeld (1992, 2009, 2013). Fromm's existentialist-influenced revision of psychoanalysis is useful for thinking about the role of expressive and emotional appeals in ethnic nationalism and fascist movement. Political and nationalist movements involve far more than purely instrumental forms of mobilization. Social theory requires a theoretically informed sociology of emotions that Fromm provides in a form that can be utilized for thinking about both extremist movements and mass culture and politics in advanced industrial democracies. Other scholars have engaged these issues, of course, and there is little doubt that Fromm's analysis of the 'authoritarianism' and 'destructiveness' of Nazism could have benefited from more stress on youth culture, gender, family, and sexuality (Mitscherlich, 1969; Loewenberg, 1971; Koonz, 1987; Theweleit, 1989; Afary and Friedland, 2018). Fromm's analysis puts very little theoretical and historical stress on the role of anti-Semitism in the Nazi movement although he certainly was aware of the violence and hatred directed at Jews in Germany, including his relatives. Moreover, contemporary scholars must avoid Fromm's tendency for overgeneralization and romanticism, particularly with regards to medieval Catholicism and feudalism,[18] and his excessively pessimistic account of advanced industrial 'mass societies' embedded in his concept of 'automatic conformity'. Fromm never developed a sociological approach as empirically sophisticated as Michael Mann, for example, that would allow us to understand the social basis of right-wing reaction and left-wing authoritarianism in ways that ask historical-comparative questions about when working and lower middle classes are central as opposed to contexts where corporate elites and the upper middle class, as in Brazil today, are central to fascism. Nonetheless, Fromm's *Escape from Freedom* remains a neglected social science classic; his insights into the often-irrational roots of human motivation demand our renewed attention.

The current crisis and public sociology

Fromm's *Escape from Freedom* should not be read solely as a theoretical contribution to professional sociology as it also serves as a classic example of a 'big book' that can stimulate insights, inspiration, and a corrective to contemporary forms of public sociological interventions (Meyer and Rohlinger, 2012). While Fromm's intellectual reputation went into decline in sociology and more broadly among elite intellectuals in the 1970s, there is new interest in his theories created both by events in the world and trends within the academia. The rise of Trumpism, the chaos of Brexit, the emergence of far-right populism all over Europe and Latin America, the continuing expansion of authoritarian Chinese and Russian state-dominated capitalism, and the spread of extremism (both Islamist and right-wing Zionism) and civil wars throughout the Middle East has created new interest in Fromm's insights about the social psychology of freedom.

In an age of academic specialization, academic scholars tend not to lead with the big-picture generalizations central to *Escape from Freedom* (Brint, 1994), but the historical analogies between the crisis of the 1930s and today warrant serious reflection. The fall of communism in the former Soviet Union in 1991 was one of the great victories for freedom in the modern world, but similar sociological mechanisms are operating as Fromm analysed in *Escape from Freedom*. Freedom from communism did not lead to human liberation but to the emergence of crony and authoritarian capitalism and the social pathologies created by globalization and social media that we now can see in Putin's tyranny and in the illiberal democracies in Hungary and Poland.

The exiled Russian journalist Masha Gessen is one of the most knowledgeable and courageous critics of Putinism and they draw insightfully from *Escape from Freedom* in their important book *The Future is History: How Totalitarianism Reclaimed Russia* (2017). Building on a marginalized tradition of Soviet sociology pioneered by Marina Arutyunyan and her student Lev Gudkov, Gessen emphasizes that the concept of *Homo Sovieticus* helps explain the continuity between Russian autocracy, Stalinism, totalitarianism, and contemporary Putinism in ways that were suggested by the analysis in *Escape from Freedom*. Quoting at length from Fromm's account of the Middle Ages, the Protestant Reformation, and his theory of the 'magic helper' that offers an 'escape from freedom' for individuals caught up in rapid and confusing social change, Gessen argues compellingly that Fromm's broader theory of the 'authoritarian character' helps illuminate the current Russian situation.

Gessen further suggests that Fromm's description of Germany in the immediate post-First World War period in *Escape from Freedom* fits perfectly the post-Soviet Russian dilemma in the 1990s. Drawing also from Arendt's description of 'homelessness' under totalitarianism and quoting Fromm, Gessen compellingly makes the case that both Nazism and Putinism represent an unprincipled radical opportunism that plays on people's sense of personal insignificance and both masochistic and sadistic emotional yearnings in ways that compensate for the fact that their lives 'have been impoverished, economically and culturally' (Fromm, 1941 p 219, cited in Gessen, 2017 p 303). Gessen is a journalist, not an academic sociologist, but their analysis is powerful and has much to offer public sociologists who wish to return to the kind of work Fromm pioneered in *Escape from Freedom*.

There are also clear elements of an 'escape from freedom' in the contemporary resurgence of Islamism, as the fall of autocrats and the spread of modern freedoms create the political space for historically specific and varied Muslim and Arab forms of the evangelism of annihilation. Using the model of *Escape from Freedom* for thinking about the Middle East today holds potential both for insight but also for traps laid by Orientalist thinking and political polemics. Fromm did not write extensively about Islam although he was interested in Muslim mystics and intellectual traditions and was a principled critic of Israeli dispossession of Palestinians and an opponent of anti-Arab bigotry. He would have been critical of ways in which his analysis would later be used by some conservative thinkers to blame Palestinians, Arabs, and

Muslims for freely choosing the tyranny of Islamofascism, a concept popularized by the far-right American polemicist David Horowitz (Horowitz, 2019).

Escape from Freedom was a popular book in Egypt and the Middle East during the Arab Spring (Friedman, 2013), reminding us of the powerful call to freedom central to the book. Fromm would have insisted on contextualizing discussion of authoritarian political regimes and movements in insurgency in the Middle East within the history of European colonialism in the region and with attention to the human carnage wrought by British, French, and now American and Israeli militarization. He would never have justified or explained away the suicide bombings, death cults, and extremist terror networks that have emerged out of a combination of traditional warrior cultures, unjust occupation, and modern freedoms. Fromm's attention to both the independent power of religious ideas and the need to conduct serious historical and sociological analysis of how particular ideas and religions become influential is a helpful counterbalance today to the simplistic popular books being written that suggest that there is something inherently authoritarian or violent about Islam understood in static ahistorical ways.

Fromm's *Escape from Freedom*, alongside the argument in Benedict Anderson's *Imagined Communities* (1983) is useful for highlighting the centrality of the ever-present search for meaning alongside the economic and political forces that are driving these contemporary events. The powerful social psychological quest for certainty that Fromm wrote about at length in his analysis of Weimar Germany has combined with the social dynamics set in motion by the internet to create an unprecedented global spread of conspiracy theories and radicalization (McLaughlin and Trilupaityte, 2013), something that was far slower and nationally bound in the era of the fascist axis of Germany, Japan, and Italy. The eclectic sociological theoretical orientation that runs through Fromm's work is useful for thinking about recent right-wing movements in psychoanalytical terms even as we must reject excessive focus on psychoanalysing Trump and his followers in ways that blur the boundaries between the psychological and the political (Maccoby and Fuchsman, 2020).

It is precisely Fromm's sophisticated position on the balance between individual personality factors and large-scale historical-sociological forces in creating authoritarianism that makes *Escape from Freedom* such a classic text worth returning to today. Fromm made important contributions to the political sociology of character, allowing us to insert a social psychological analysis of leaders into structurally oriented field and political sociological theory. He was right to argue that the debacle of twentieth-century communism and the horrors of Nazism could not be understood without analysis of the pathologies of Stalin and Hitler, just as these political tragedies cannot be reduced to personalities. Character matters in the political and social sphere, although one must study and debate these issues without descending into simplistic psychohistory. While a simplistic focus on individual leaders in these far right-wing movements cannot substitute for political analysis, the emotional power and psychological motivations of such charismatic leaders as Geert Wilders in the Netherlands and Viktor Orbán in Hungary must be part of our sociological account. Even more importantly, we must understand the emotional appeal of movements that call for a return to simpler days.

Focusing on Donald Trump's obvious psychological problems and almost limitless narcissism is not a viable electoral campaign strategy for opponents of his authoritarianism. But the rise of Trumpism has created new interest in the politics of narcissism and Frankfurt School-inspired analysis of authoritarianism (Langman and Lunskow, 2016) that are often simplistic. Yet Fromm was certainly right that one cannot understand or predict political dynamics without an adequate theory of personality and emotions. *Escape from Freedom* does not reduce politics to psychology as many popular accounts of the current crisis are prone to do, and the importance of the book increases as our popular culture becomes dominated by individualistic and therapeutic accounts of political issues.

The lower-middle-class thesis on fascism and Lipset's theory of working-class authoritarism (Lipset, 1959) are both being revived (Hetherington and Weiler, 2009) partly because there clearly is significant blue-collar and non-college-educated white support for Trumpist authoritarian populism, although it appears less so with Trump's defeat in 2020. We should certainly track movements of economic capital, booms and busts of economic insecurity, and ask the questions about classes and class dynamics that the Marxist tradition asks. Yet Fromm's refusal to fully embrace Marxism while also insisting on engaging the tradition's insights represents an important intellectual resource for today's public intellectual debates about the current political and cultural crisis.

Most radical intellectuals after the 1970s became critical of Fromm because he was not Marxist enough, not because he was too Marxist. The core flaw in *Escape from Freedom* was, however, that he was too uncritical of the assumption in the *Communist Manifesto* (Marx and Engels, 1967) that the lower middle class or petty bourgeois would be the source of the type of reactionary movements that would lead to fascism in the twentieth century. This was true in Romania and Hungary in the 1930s and there are elements of this dynamic going on today in among Trumpist Americans. But assuming, not documenting, that reactionary movements flow from the lower middle class as Fromm did, downplays corporate and upper-middle-class reaction. Fromm exhibited a class bias in this argument in *Escape from Freedom*.

In Fromm's defence, his tendency to view the lower middle class as the source of reactionary movements was common among historians throughout the mid- to late twentieth century, and this error lives on today in the common reframe that Trump's base is the white working and lower middle classes in the United States. This is a narrative with major elements of truth, and populists such as Steve Bannon are trying to unite far-right populism with capitalism as the wave of the future (Beiner, 2018; Teitelbaum, 2020). But this account downplays the central role played by the upper middle class and conservative business elite in forming the core voting bloc for Republicans in the electoral victory of 2016. Too many pundits and sociologists today share the class biases that Fromm himself had brought to his analysis of the class basis of reactionary movements leading intellectuals to explain reactionary voting patterns by focusing on markers of crassness, lack of elite higher education, and politically correct language and terminology.

This new version of the lower-middle-class thesis common among the chattering classes and sociologists in the United States, Britain, and throughout Continental Europe serves to hide the extent to which authoritarianism is not exclusively or even primarily a working-class phenomena, as sociologist Seymour Martin Lipset once argued (1959). It is a human tendency that has just as deep roots among lawyers, doctors, technological professions and, most importantly, the global financial elites who are creating the economic and cultural crisis that populists such as Trump, Bannon, and Orbán are exploiting. Working-class Trump voters are an important element in the Trump base and they are highly visible in his rallies and among the Proud Boys, but we cannot forget the obvious truth that the core voting bloc for Republicans today remains well-off middle-class and elite Americans in suburbs, rural areas, and urban centres, particularly white voters. It is impossible, further, to understand Trumpism without a serious analysis of gender, sexuality, and racism, linking these issues to a broader authoritarianism.

Looking at *Escape from Freedom* as a sociological classic, not a Marxist bible, helps us to identify political and intellectual errors and biases that are being reproduced among the contemporary academic and public intellectual left. Public intellectual and public sociological accounts of far-right and anti-immigrant movements in places as diverse as France, the Netherlands, Hungary, or Russia require us to look beyond Marxist orthodoxies while taking social class and capitalist power seriously. We must examine religious, status, class, economic, gender and sexuality, or historical-cultural variables to predict participation in extremist movements alongside social class, as the empirical cases and evidence demand. Fromm said little about anti-Semitism in *Escape from Freedom*, writing before the Holocaust and influenced by a combination of Marxism and psychoanalysis that led him to emphasize economics and emotions, not discourse and ideas. Modern versions of public historical-comparative work would certainly have to be more attentive to the politics of sexuality and more concerned with the specifics of different forms of bigotry, such as anti-Muslim hatred, anti-gay and anti-trans hatred, and conspiracy theories rooted in ancient anti-Semitic tropes.

When you look beyond the academic literature to examine public intellectual far-right thinkers, you will find that the pro-Protestant bias that Fromm believed was often linked to extremism is, in fact, openly promoted on the far-right today. In the United States, one can find this in David Horowitz in his *The Dark Agenda: The War to Destroy Christian America* (2019) as a secular right-wing Zionist and far-right extremist finds common cause with the fundamentalist Protestant right. *New York Times* columnist Michelle Goldberg (2017) has drawn on Fromm's *Escape from Freedom* explicitly to help us understand the relationship between Trump and his Protestant evangelical followers in the Republican Party as less a marriage of convenience, and more a sadomasochistic relationship and submission to blind authority. One can also see the sociological and political importance of evangelical religion all over Latin America today, as traditional far-right Catholics unite with Protestant extremists in opposition to the left as we see in Bolsonaro's neo-fascist elected regime in Brazil. *Escape from Freedom* inspires us to think about far-right extremism in both Marxist and Weberian terms, while highlighting emotions.

To do this kind of work, the methodological approach of Fromm's *Escape from Freedom* is inadequate, while ethnographic works such as Arlie Hochshild's *Strangers in Their Own Land: Anger and Mourning on the American Right* (2016) are essential. Fromm lacked ethnographic training and he was far more willing to directly rely on his general historical knowledge, theoretical insights, and the understanding of human psychology he gained from his clinical practice than any responsible public sociologist would do today.

Fromm's theoretical orientation and his personality itself led him to just the kind of judgemental critiques of followers of far-right movements that ethnographers are trained to avoid. Fromm's judgement of the Nazi movement is perfectly understandable, of course, given the context of Hitler's pathological violence and hatred. But Trumpism is not Nazism, and Fromm's ability to draw these kinds of distinctions was one of the things that set him apart from the other Frankfurt scholars, particularly Adorno and Marcuse. Yet there is a fundamental tension between Fromm's theoretical deductive analysis and the kind of introspective interpretive work that allowed ethnographers to talk to Tea Party activists, Trump supporters, Brexit proponents, and followers of populist movements more generally, while putting the researcher's own assumptions and biases on the table.

Hochschild's beautifully written *Strangers in Their Own Land* (2016) improves on the model of public sociology that Fromm's *Escape from Freedom* helped create by theorizing beyond what she calls an 'empathy wall' between left and right to try to understand what she calls the 'deep story' of Trump supporters in a profoundly divided America. Hochschild can be critiqued for getting too empathic with her research subjects, and for downplaying deep psychological insights into racial, gender, and religious hatreds (Smith and Hanley, 2018; Smith, 2009). In addition, Hochschild does not make the mistake of substituting clinical analysis of personal pathologies for political analysis and arguments. Simply labelling Trump supporters as deplorables, as Hillary Clinton did, or dismissing them as authoritarian characters as some recent critical sociologists and philosophers have done (Kellner, 2016) is not likely to help defeat Trumpism politically.

Today, a dialogic public sociology must be supplemented by an analysis of the emotional dynamics created by social media. Indeed, the rise of social media makes the social psychological dynamics of rationalization and projection that were set in motion in the 1930s even more important to understand. In the 1930s, Germans attempted to make sense of the decline of their nation due to forces that seemed beyond their control and understanding. Today, economic insecurity, rapid changes in cultural norms, and new religious and ethnic diversity are shaking the worldviews and meaning systems of millions of people in Western, Central, and Eastern Europe, as well as in Latin American societies. The political dynamics are different when it is the scapegoating of Jews and Roma in post-communist Hungary or Poland, Muslims in Britain or France, Latin American immigrants or African-Americans in the United States through the mobilization of anti-black racism, or gays, women and trans people throughout the world, or cultural Marxists and Indigenous people in Brazil and the United States and Canada today. The psychological dynamics of various similar escapes from freedom and emotional logics, however, are similar enough that we can benefit from theorizing them together. And when these debates take place on Twitter and Facebook, not on mainstream TV and in newspapers, Fromm's analysis of psychological projections, emotional displacements and irrational rationalizations is even more important.

Fromm's *Escape from Freedom* remains an important part of the history of public sociology. Public sociology today is of course different, as individual books tend not to have the same influence as blockbluster social science best-sellers did in the classical age of the public intellectual. Academic scholarship is far more extensive today, and thus it is far more difficult to write a general book of broader social critique and analysis. Public sociology today tends to be focused on specific issues (Brint, 1994). There are sociologists who have attempted to engage with the rise of the extremism and political crisis in the old genre of public sociological books such as Alan Wolfe in *The Politics of Petulance: America in an Age of Immaturity* (2018), but this kind of work is rare and tends not to theorize emotions in the depth Fromm did. Public intellectual life today is dominated by YouTube videos and podcasts as much as big books and powerful social theories. The example of *Escape from Freedom* thus remains an important part of the legacy and the promise of public sociology worth re-examining and revisiting.

Escape from Freedom certainly transformed Fromm's career, leading him to become one of the most famous and influential social scientists and social critics of the twentieth century. I will pick up this story in the late 1940s and the 1950s, during which time Fromm helped create the template both for liberal traditional public sociology through his influence on Harvard sociologist David Riesman and the radical public sociological Marxists and critical theorists of the 1960s. Before doing so, we will first take a step to the early years of the twentieth century, and the 1920s and 1930s, in order to explore Fromm's youth and the making of *Escape from Freedom* as a case study to help theorize the broader sociological origins of big books and public sociologists.

2

How Optimal Marginality Created a Public Sociologist

Public sociology runs against the grain of the professionalizing logic of modern academic disciplines (Burawoy, 2005). We do not have adequate theories about how this kind of intellectual activity is produced and sustained in the era of the research university.[1] Scholarship on particular public sociologists is often tinged with either hero worship or giant killing. 'Great thinker' or 'excluded genius' tropes get in the way of systematic explanations of how sociologists actually come to write and speak to the public.

Sociology today is a profession embedded in modern research universities, having left behind its origins in conservative religious defenders of the medieval traditionalism and hierarchy (Nisbet, 1952), the positivist sects of Saint-Simon and Comte (Coser, 1965), social work reform (Deegan, 1988), and the grand theories of its founders Durkheim, Weber, and Spencer. With the creation and expansion of tenure within research universities, most young scholars see becoming a professor as a career path, not a vocation aimed at changing the world. This is true, even though many young scholars are recruited into the discipline through political engagement. Public sociologists who see their primary goal as engaging the public with ideas will always be a minority in the discipline because of the reward structures that encourage 'professional' and 'policy' over 'public' and 'critical' sociology (Burawoy, 2005). Traditional public sociologists who speak and write to the public based on their specialized knowledge emerge as scholars establish their credentials and careers close to the centre of the field.

The kind of general interdisciplinary, normative, and best-selling books like that of Fromm's *Escape from Freedom* are rare. Although Fromm did have a PhD like Margaret Mead in anthropology, he operated closer to the model of more general public intellectuals like Betty Friedan, Michael Harrington, and Rachel Carson (Meyer and Rohlinger, 2012). What we are theorizing is the kind of public sociologist who gains a major audience outside of the academic field, like W. E. B. Du Bois and C. Wright Mills in the middle of the twentieth century (Aronowitz, 2012; Morris, 2015), and Arlie Hochschild and William Julius Wilson today (Gans, 1997). Earlier in the twentieth century, these kinds of thinkers would often make their name by writing best-selling books as Daniel Bell and David Riesman did *before* attaining academic stature although by the 1960s and 1970s this pathway became far less possible as the research university professionalized.

To explain the rise of this kind of public sociologist on the border between the professional sociologist and celebrity intellectual, we need to highlight two major ways that intellectuals who might aspire to gain mass audiences can fail. The most common trap is that they become swallowed by the logic of professionalism and specialization. Sociologists often come into the field with a concern for class inequality, crime, racism, violence, or similar social issues. By the time they are finishing graduate school, these action agendas (Alford, 1998) are translated into researchable questions. Theory, methods, and publications then become the core focus. This is true, especially in the United States with its highly professional and competitive disciplinary culture after the 1960s. The sociologists who succeed in getting tenure at major research universities and elite liberal arts college tend to be highly professionalized and involved in grant-seeking policy sociology and/or peer-reviewed specialized research. There is sociological variation in all this, and book-writing sociologists more open to public engagement sometimes do succeed, often on the East and West Coasts (Merton and Wolfe, 1995).

Professional and policy sociology tends to be the dominant form of sociological practice at elite research institutions (Burawoy, 2005). The more activist-oriented scholars at institutions with fewer resources focus on teaching and may well speak to local audiences. Often these scholars and teachers, however, will not even have the time to write outside of heavy teaching and administrative loads. There is a pull as well as a push factor involved as talented and ambitious intellectuals are excluded from mainstream professional sociology; others actively choose to leave academia to be journalists, political activists, or politicians. The heroes that are memorialized in the public sociology debates as role models, like W. E. B. Du Bois and C. Wright Mills, are just the kind of public sociologists who stay in the discipline long enough to be claimed for its collective memory, but who also break away from the norms of professional and policy sociology so that they gain mass audiences for their work. What kind of sociological dynamics explain such examples?

To theorize public sociologists, we need to avoid the polarization that exists within the creativity literature – paradigms stress either the need for resources, status, and cultural capital that comes from cultural, geographic, institutional, and demographic centrality or they draw on newer literatures that suggest public sociologists must inevitability come from the margins, the excluded and liminal spaces (McLaughlin, 2001a). Rooted in larger, also often polarized, debates about canons and cultural elites, the discussions about what factors give rise to public sociologists often stress how either elite educational institutions, privileged demographic groups, and dominant political and cultural views lead to the creation of public sociologists from the center of the academic field or, conversely, that the public sociologist is created by what Aldon Morris calls the liberation capital that flows from the experience of being excluded, marginalized, or oppressed (Morris, 2015). There is evidence for both perspectives. The lighter teaching load of a Harvard professor and the tendency of elite journalists to search out the opinions of established professors at prestigious institutions makes it easier to be a public sociologist while simultaneously publishing professional scholarship and doing policy work (Burawoy, 2005). The examples of Jane Addams, W. E. B. Du Bois, and C. Wright Mills on the other hand, suggest that gender, regional, political, and racial marginality can push a scholar outside of mainstream reward structures and publishing outlets, creating a public sociologist on the margins.

Addams faced sexist exclusion (Deegan, 1988), racism prevented Du Bois from teaching at elite American universities (Morris, 2015), and C. Wright Mills' less-than-urbane presentation of self and roots in Texas certainly helps explain why they each never entered into the very core of professional sociology (Aronowitz, 2012; Geary, 2009). Addams' upper-class background, Du Bois' connections to Harvard and his time in Germany around Weber's circles, and C. Wright Mills' connections to Columbia's Merton and Lazarsfeld (Sterne, 2005), as well as his ability to leverage networks at elite New York-based book presses, played important roles in creating the uniqueness of their ideas and the influence of their work. In each of these cases, however, their marginalization as well as their relative advantages helps explain why they took a path of writing to the public as a method of avoiding elite peer review orthodoxy.

Marginalization on its own cannot explain their success since there were many more women, African-Americans and regional outsiders who never succeeded at all in twentieth-century American sociology. Those who did were more likely to take a safe path of professional or policy sociology closer to the mainstream. Public sociology is produced by particular combinations of marginality and centrality. To think about this analytically it is necessary to break down the issues into questions of personality and psychology, race, class, gender, and religion, as well as training, institutional location, and networks. As intersectionalist theorists (Crenshaw, 1989) have taught us, marginality and centrality are not unidimensional factors, but instead can be broken down into various variables (sex, class, religion, gender, nationality, geography, personality, and family background, for example) that must be understood as interacting. The most influential and innovative of public sociologists are usually created by combinations of marginality and centrality.

We need not choose between seeing public sociology as being created by either elites or liminal outsiders. I will look at the development of Fromm's intellectual development before the publication of *Escape from Freedom* with an eye to theorizing how both his marginalization and marginality helped spur his creativity. But that was not enough on its own. Fromm's links to sources of cultural capital, elite networks, and what Jerry Watts has called 'marginality facilitators' (Watts, 1994) combined to set him on a path to producing a major work of public sociology. When one looks at Fromm's early life, education in both sociology and psychoanalysis, and his period with the Frankfurt School through the lens of optimal marginality, questions arise about how his social location and network/organizational involvement shaped his career. One can see how his centrality in some networks interacted with forms of marginalization that helped create an innovative synthesis of ideas. From this analytic approach, a broad picture of how a public sociologist was created becomes clear.

I will narrate the story of Fromm's development as the author of *Escape from Freedom* in three distinct stages. The first two periods are formative (youth and education in the early 1920s, and early career in late 1920s to early 1930s), while the third period sees Fromm's active leveraging of the independence he had created for himself in the middle of the 1930s by having a dual career as a psychoanalyst and social science researcher. In Fromm's youth, he had combined the prophetic Judaism he acquired from his upbringing with an interest in the insights of Marx and Freud. In Fromm's university years and in his twenties, he received a PhD in sociology, while maintaining links with

Jewish religious radicalism, deepening his knowledge of Marxism, and training in psychoanalysis. In the pivotal decade of the 1930s, Fromm gained research experience by working closely with the Frankfurt School on a study of German support for Nazism, while also acquiring psychoanalytic training in circles of dissident Freudians in Berlin.

The combination of these two sources of both economic support and intellectual inspiration meant that he neither became a sociology professor nor exclusively a professional therapist. Fromm had also become close to both Karen Horney (Westkott, 1986; Quinn, 1987; Sayers, 1991; Paris, 1995; McLaughlin, 1998b) and Margaret Mead (Lutkehaus, 2008), two intellectuals who had been marginalized in psychoanalysis and anthropology respectively. Horney and Mead thrived by writing popular books to the general public in ways that modelled a future for Fromm. In the period of Fromm's development just before *Escape from Freedom*, he had moved beyond exclusive connections to psychoanalysis or critical theory and was sustained by the 'culture and personality' school of anthropology, an informal network of scholars. All of this together produced *Escape from Freedom*, a work that was not as scholarly or technical as most professional sociology or anthropology but was also not orthodox psychoanalysis or Marxism. Writing to the public was his path to avoiding professional or intellectual orthodoxies of any kind, and this allowed him to turn his status as a Jewish exile from Nazi Germany to his advantage. It all produced a classic of public sociology.

Youth on the margins of German capitalism

Major public sociology interventions like *Escape from Freedom* (1941) require emotional and intellectual energy (Collins, 1998). Passion for public sociology often has deep roots in early life. Raised in Frankfurt am Main, near Germany's major industrial city, Fromm came from a family of orthodox Jewish Rabbis on both sides (Funk, 2019). Fromm's youth, from his birth in 1900 to before his university years, set in motion his prophetic vision for both his theorizing and political work. Fromm experienced marginalization as a Jewish young man in a Christian dominant nation, but he was also sustained by the ethical vision of the orthodox Judaism of his family. His father was a wine merchant, who seemed slightly embarrassed by his profession in comparison to the distinguished stature of the Talmud scholars in his family. This dual experience of living close to a major industrial city and being raised by a small businessperson while being deeply rooted in Jewish orthodoxy left him both with an understanding of the social changes capitalism was bringing to Germany and the human costs of modernity (Burston, 1991; Funk, 2019).

Fromm's intellectual autobiography emphasizes an incident where one of his relatives, working at a family-owned business, asked a customer to shop somewhere else because he was busy reading the Torah. This story illustrates the attitude Fromm had about market society and profits (Fromm, 1962); reading Torah was more important than making money. Fromm's own account of his upbringing in a traditional and non-assimilated culture stressed how almost medieval it was, with a focus on traditional learning and suspicion of market values. Fromm remembers himself as a youth who did not quite feel at home, neither 'in the world I lived in, nor in the old world of traditions' (Friedman, 2013 p 4). *Escape from Freedom* was a defence of the pre-capitalist community values of his upbringing combined with an analysis that highlighted the Marxist critique of market logics. But Fromm also defended the benefits of modernity, as Marx himself certainly did.

Fromm's sense of alienation was not all about books and ideas. Fromm's feelings of psychological marginality within his own family, the tragic suicide of a young next-door neighbour, and the brutality of the First World War which broke out when he was fourteen, shaped his teens and led him on a path to Freud, Marx, and sociology. From all accounts of his youth, Fromm was a neurotic young boy (Funk, 1982, 2019; Burston, 1991; Friedman, 2013), the only child of a unhappily married middle-class Jewish couple, Rosa and Naphtali. Fromm was born just about nine months after his parents were married, and his later psychoanalytic way of thinking led him to believe that perhaps his birth had kept together a couple who were not happy or well suited to each other. More scholarly than athletic, pampered and feeling smothered by his mother, Fromm felt closer to his father, but was unimpressed by his authority and example. Out of this, Fromm developed a dependant nature in his youth alongside a sense of insecurity, since his father did not appear to have much confidence in Fromm's abilities. Fromm's parents loved him, but it was not a warm, nurturing, or happy childhood. His own unease in his family clearly played a central role in his interest in Freud. Fromm felt 'out of place', as the great Palestinian literary critic and public intellectual Edward Said would later put it in his own memoir of his youth and family life (Said, 1999b). Fromm's desire to understand and heal the world was partly rooted in an emotional marginality he felt within his own family, psyche, and body that cannot simply be reduced to anti-Semitism in

Fromm's case, or to the dispossession and anti-Arab bigotry that Said experienced (Said, 2012b).

The appeal of the Freudian theory of neurosis and the unconscious had a powerful pull on the young Erich Fromm that reached its nadir after the suicide of a twenty-five-year-old female neighbour he romantically admired as a thirteen-year-old. A beautiful and talented artist, from the perspective of Fromm's memory and imagination, the woman's widowed father had died and instead of going on to live her own life after mourning, she killed herself. How could it be, the young teenage Fromm asked, that someone with so much to live for would end everything in an act of irrationality and self-destructiveness? Was the bond she felt to her father so deep and all-consuming that she could not imagine living without him? This deeply personal mystery led Fromm on a lifetime path of Freudian discovery and clinical practice, but it also left him sceptical of all Marxist and sociological perspectives that did not leave a place for irrationality and passionate emotions. Fromm would never be an orthodox Marxist and sociologist precisely because of the Freudian account of emotions that was central to his intellectual development.

If an individual death pointed Fromm towards Freud and sociological theories of suicide, it was the mass killings and brutal destructiveness of the First World War that made him a Marxist, albeit an unorthodox one. Fromm's intellectual autobiography tells the story of how he saw one of his secondary school teachers promote unrealistic nationalistic propaganda as they argued that Germany was in the right, and victory was inevitable, morally just, and right over the horizon (Fromm, 1962). As the war dragged on and on, and hundreds of thousands and then millions of young military men and defenceless women, children, and the elderly were slaughtered in trenches, bombed from the air, and machine gunned, raped, and bayonetted on all sides of the conflict, Fromm learned to appreciate Marx's critique of ideology, propaganda, and the distorting and hate-promoting lens of nationalism. Fromm had been introduced to Marx by a boarder who had lived in his home while working for his father, a young man who likely died in the First World War. Fromm also had a sober and thoughtful teacher at school, who saw through German war propaganda, showing his students the value of reason in the face of mass emotion (Friedman, 2013). The Marxist analytic perspective that shaped *Escape from Freedom*'s analysis of the business elite and landowning classes' role in promoting nationalist propaganda was rooted in Fromm's teenage years where he saw the consequences of war. It was a Marxism, however, tempered by a prophetic Judaism, that became central to Fromm's intellectual project (Braune, 2014; Funk, 2019).

As much as Fromm felt ill at ease in his parental home, he was always connected to their Judaism (Jacobs, 2014; Funk, 2019), a central influence on his ideas and career as a public sociologist. As a young boy, Fromm was influenced by his uncle Ludwig Krause, a prominent Talmudic scholar who gave Fromm an appreciation for the intellectual contributions of his great-grandfather, Bamberger, and exposed him to the 'prophetic writing of Isaiah, Amos, and Hosea and their visions of peace and harmony among nations' (Friedman, 2013 p 7). During the First World War, Fromm came under the influence of Rabbi Nehemiah Nobel, the leader of Frankfurt's orthodox Jewish community (Friedman, 2013 p 10). Nobel had been influenced by a well-known neo-Kantian and socialist Jewish thinker, Hermann Cohen (Friedman, 2013 p 10), and Cohen's 'universal code of ethics' that can be 'discovered through reason, ethical ways applied to all humanity, irrespective of time and place' (Friedman, 2013 p 10). Fromm became close to Nobel, listening to his sermons, taking walks with him outside of Frankfurt, and visiting him in his apartment, absorbing his 'strong Hasidic bent' and deepening his understanding of the 'messianic ideas of the prophets' (Friedman, 2013 p 10).

Fromm solidified his knowledge of Jewish mysticism and radicalism in the Nobel circle, a network that would later evolve into the Free Jewish Teaching Institute in Frankfurt. Fromm would be involved in this network along with the major Jewish philosophers Martin Buber and Gershom Scholem. Fromm introduced his close friend Leo Löwenthal to the Nobel circle, and they both would end up being central members of the Frankfurt School circle around Horkheimer, where Jewish mysticism and Enlightenment thinking would meet neo-Marxism and sociology. Fromm entered graduate school with a prophetic vision for social change rooted in the Judaism of his youth and the Marxism he read as a young man (Maccoby, 1995; Braune, 2014).

A prophetic empirical social psychology, Jewish psychoanalysis and utopian socialism

Fromm's twenties were spent training as a PhD in sociology and a psychoanalytic clinician while engaging with the German Marxism that had emerged out of the First World War and the failed German revolution. During this process, Fromm was mentored by three very different intellectual figures: the sociologist Alfred Weber, the psychoanalyst Frieda Reichmann, and the Jewish Russian philosopher and rabbi Salman Rabinkow (Funk, 2019). It was the combination of the critical but non-Marxist sociology of Weber, the innovative community-based psychoanalysis of Reichmann, and the Jewish socialism of Rabinkow that laid the foundation for Fromm's own synthetic public sociology. In each of his engagements with sociology, psychoanalysis, socialism, and Judaism, Fromm engaged with core elements of the traditions while never becoming the orthodox practitioner of any profession, political view, theoretical camp or – after he broke with orthodox Judaism – religion.

It was the combination that led to the core ideas in *Escape from Freedom*. Fromm's PhD education in sociology with Alfred Weber allowed him to engage with the great sociological tradition of Weber, Simmel, and Durkheim without becoming a professional sociologist. Fromm's political involvement with German Marxists in the 1920s connected him to the theory of historical materialism and the humanism of the early Marx (Anderson, 2015; Durkin, 2014), but he was always outside the orbit of the German Communist Party. Fromm's training with psychoanalysts linked him to Freud and exposed him to the psychoanalytic Marxists in Berlin in the 1920s. Fromm's collaborative work with Frieda Reichmann enriched his social theory with psychoanalytic insights outside the core of Freudian orthodoxy, particularly around questions of patriarchy and gender. Fromm's deep connection to the Jewish socialist Salman Rabinkow grounded his thought in the prophetic tradition (Funk, 2019), an ethical core that would be central to his efforts at developing his sociology and activism outside of both the academy and traditional parties of the left.

In this crucial period of his intellectual and political development, Fromm needed what the political scientist Jerry Watts called marginality facilitators (Watts, 1994). Drawing from the experiences of African-American intellectuals who are attempting to address their precarious social status as creative thinkers without control of their own cultural institutions and resources, Watts defines marginality facilitators as 'strategies that are employed by black intellectuals in order to navigate black artistic social marginality' (Watts, 1994 p 16). Some of the strategies that African-American intellectuals, writers, and social scientists employed in the 1920s included joining communist or socialist parties, going into exile to Paris or other magnet places for creativity (Farrell, 2001), moving to bohemia, or establishing and getting involved in black-run magazines, organizations, and colleges.

Watts' theory, modified for the case of German Jews in the same period, is illuminating. For Fromm, in this period of the 1920s, anti-Semitism had not yet driven Jews out of German cultural institutions as it would during the Nazi period. There was not yet a need for exile or the fear of violence that African-American intellectuals had to constantly face although there were storm clouds on the horizon. Fromm did not want to become a sociology professor in German universities where anti-Semitism remained significant and Marxist and prophetic ideas were rejected. Fromm also had no desire or temperament to become a political activist in German trade unions or socialist or Marxist parties.

Fromm entered his PhD programme as an orthodox Jew and did a dissertation on Jewish law and culture. But Fromm was having what Erik Erikson would later call an 'identity crisis', and he spent these years experimenting with Marxism and various countercultural ideas while also being deeply shaped by the Jewish socialism of Rabinkow. Fromm found his initial marginality facilitator in his involvement with the Jewish psychoanalytic institute he worked at, along with Freida Reichmann, a brilliant psychoanalytic clinician. These were his pathways out of the academy, orthodox Marxism, and doctrinaire psychoanalysis.

The story must start, however, with the sociologist Alfred Weber. Fromm had considered becoming a lawyer as he entered adulthood as the First World War was ending, but was more interested in the close study of the Hebrew Bible and had wanted to go to Lithuania, an innovative centre of Talmudic scholarship (Friedman, 2013 p 12). His parents wanted him to stay closer, so he entered Heidelberg University in 1919, experimented for a year and finally settled into the department of national economy. He specialized in sociology under the supervision of Alfred Weber, whose seminars and lectures he attended. An accomplished economic, historical, and cultural sociologist in his own right, Alfred Weber's mentorship worked for Fromm partly because the younger Weber did not share the same liberal nationalist viewpoints of his brother, Max Weber. Here is how Lawrence Friedman puts it, 'Fromm was impressed by the courage and integrity with which the professor expressed his thoughts and commitment to universal humanism over the rigid nationalism that Fromm ascribed to his brother' (Friedman, 2013 p 12). Alfred Weber introduced Fromm to the great German sociological tradition of Wilhelm Dilthey and Georg Simmel, providing him with a path to writing about Jewish law, culture, and history with a sociological lens.

Fromm's career as a professional sociologist began with his dissertation 'Jewish Law: A Contribution to the Study of Diaspora Judaism', on social cohesion and culture in three communities, the Karaites, the

Reform Jews, and the Hasidim. Lawrence Friedman summarizes Fromm's conclusions nicely:

> Without a state, a common secular language, or even the opportunity to build a place of worship, Fromm argued, a Jewish social body is bound by a belief system and a unique culture. By 'law,' Fromm meant the applied religious and moral code of a people. Indeed, there was a 'soul' within Jewish law, which established the moral-ethical unity of the people. The collective content within the law was sufficiently flexible to allow individuals to interpret and implement its requirements; freedom of interpretation was embedded in the ethos of the community. (Friedman, 2013 p 13)

This work, which is not yet translated into English, is very much part of the pre-history of Fromm's psychoanalytic sociology since it was not until after he finished his PhD that he met Frieda Reichmann and was introduced to psychanalytic theory (Funk, 2019 p 47). But even then, Fromm was not a mainstream sociological thinker because unlike more functionalist sociologists, he 'was not primarily interested in the function that institutions had for social cohesion' but was more concerned with 'what allowed people to think, feel, and act similarly when they had no such exterior institutions' (Funk, 2019 p 47). For Fromm, at that period of his thinking, the key to ethical behavior and social cohesion lay in 'the lived form of ethics or the ethos, internalized through religious practise' (Funk, 2019 p 47), something he would later theorize as social character with insights from both Marx and Freud. At that time, however, Fromm was a young orthodox Jewish man with left-wing sympathies and some training in sociology.

After his successful PhD defence, Fromm had a choice that many left-wing sociologists face. Should he become a professor or stay more organically connected to the intellectual, political, and spiritual visions that brought him into sociology in the first place? Fromm had the talent and basic temperament to become a sociology professor, as he enjoyed close readings of texts, had an analytic mind and, while he loved philosophy and theology, he also had an empirical and scientific side to him. This empirical sensibility led him to study prophetic Judaism through case studies of specific communities. Alfred Weber thought highly of Fromm and encouraged him to pursue an academic career, something Fromm felt was constraining (Friedman, 2013 p 15).

There were pull as well as push factors involved in Fromm's choice not to prioritize academic sociology. Throughout his PhD years and into his late twenties, Fromm also under the tutelage and influence of Salman Rabinkow. Rabinkow was a Jewish socialist originally from Russia who introduced Fromm both to revolutionary Marxist ideas and the Lithuanian Talmudic tradition of focusing on the 'psychological and spiritual truths' (Friedman, 2013 p 15) of a text. As Friedman puts it, Rabinkow 'had a knack for synthesizing Marxism and socialist protest politics with traditional Jewish pietism' (Friedman, 2013 p 16).

As a role model and substitute father, Rabinkow was pivotal to the development of Fromm as a public sociologist. They met in Rabinkow's sparse apartment for tutorials regularly over many years. Fromm came to distrust academic credentials and the worshipping of power, money, and status partly from observing Rabinkow. Fromm also picked up Rabinkow's disciplined approach to study, along with the notion of radical humanism that Fromm turned into his theoretical analysis of what he would later call the 'productive character'. Rabinkow had started out an ardent Zionist, but was moving away from this position when, in 1923, Fromm rejected his early Zionism to become a lifelong critic of all nationalism. Without Rabinkow's influence, Fromm may well have become a traditional German professor, but instead spent his twenties preparing for the role he would later play in the discipline as a public sociologist.

As important as Rabinkow's influence was on Fromm, he was different from his mentor in significant ways. Rabinkow rejected worldly success and professional striving and was not an adventurous person, staying put in his home in Frankfurt. Despite his intellectual prowess, he suffered from writer's block (Friedman, 2013) only publishing one article during his career. In contrast, Fromm was ambitious, was willing to travel around Germany for new experiences and to gain intellectual capital, and soon learned that he could write well and with relative ease. Not ready yet to leave orthodox Judaism but willing to seek professional training and employment outside the university, the next major stage of Fromm's career after defending his dissertation was intense participation in an experimental Jewish psychoanalytic commune led by Frieda Reichmann. She, an established psychoanalytic clinician eleven years his senior, would be his first wife.

Frieda Reichmann also came from an orthodox Jewish family and had earned a medical degree at a young age with a dissertation on schizophrenia. She later received specialized training working with brain-injured soldiers returning from the war (Friedman, 2013).

While Fromm was working on his sociology dissertation in Frankfurt where they had briefly met, Reichmann was in Dresden as an assistant physician-psychiatrist determined to be a psychotherapist (Friedman, 2013 p 19). Reichmann had received a training analysis in Berlin with Hans Sachs, an orthodox psychoanalyst close to Freud himself. Fromm went into analysis with Reichmann and came out of it with intimate knowledge of Freudian theory as well as a new romantic partner. Both knew this was inappropriate, of course, but they were rebels in a time of cultural upheaval and experimentation before our modern ethical standards on such matters were fully formed and enforced.

Reichmann and Fromm established a therapeutic facility for Jewish patients in Heidelberg that was essentially a large communal house where people lived by orthodox cultural practices and read and talked about social justice and socialism. They engaged in group therapy and psychoanalysis led by Reichmann and Fromm. The relationship with Reichmann facilitated Fromm's entry into an intense period of psychoanalytic training, intellectual networking, and scholarly exploration that would be central to his later development as a public sociologist and psychological theorist.

In these years, Fromm learned psychoanalysis in Munich, the resort town Baden-Baden, and Frankfurt, setting the stage for his lifelong involvement in the world of Freudian theory and clinical practice. Fromm moved to Munich in 1925 to complete an analysis with Wilhelm Wittenberg and to learn neurosciences with Reichmann's former teacher Emil Kraepelin. Fromm and Reichmann married in 1926, and by 1927 they announced their exit from Jewish orthodoxy in separate articles written for the psychoanalytic journal *Imago*. Just as the communal therapeutic enterprise had failed, the marriage between Fromm and Reichmann also fell apart, as she was having numerous extra-marital affairs and Fromm had developed a connection with Karen Horney, another psychoanalyst a decade older than him. Fromm also developed an interest in the work of clinician Georg Groddeck, a psychoanalyst based near the spas of Baden-Baden who had the support of Freud himself. Groddeck was concerned with the body, massages, psychosomatic issues, and had a therapeutic approach that stressed openness, warmth, and directness not theory, that inspired Fromm's own practice.

It was in the Groddeck circle where Fromm began to break with Freudian orthodoxy, a revisionist move that would define his career and social theory. Groddeck was not as intellectually and theoretically oriented as Fromm but his clinical skills and charisma inspired Fromm's involvement in the Southwest German Psychoanalytic Study Group in

Frankfurt. Fromm joined the study group along with Reichmann in 1927 (Friedman, 2013 p 25) as the therapeutic social circle began to unravel. This would soon lead him to Horkheimer and the Frankfurt School later in the 1920s.

Before that would happen, however, Reichmann and Fromm moved to Berlin for more opportunities within the psychoanalytic world. Freida Fromm-Reichmann opened a clinical practice that provided support for Fromm's further psychoanalytic training. Fromm worked with Hans Sachs, a member of Freud's inner circle, and Theodor Reik, an important and creative orthodox Freudian interested in religion. Fromm was thus not totally marginal to the cultural capital and intellectual energy that was circulating within the psychoanalytic movement. In the end, however, Fromm was not impressed by the orthodox Freudian institutions and their ideas partly because he remained connected to his Jewish identity as well as to his radical political and cultural sensibilities.

Fromm would soon break with orthodox Freudianism, but it was in Berlin where he gained intense exposure to the core of the tradition and got involved with Marxist Freudians such as Otto Fenichel and Wilhelm Reich. Fromm knew Wilhelm Reich in those years, although he was not impressed with Reich's orthodox Freudian and Marxist synthesis and almost exclusive focus on sexual freedom as key to what he would later call 'the mass psychology of fascism' (Burston, 1991).

It was in Berlin where Fromm also reconnected with Karen Horney, whom he had met at Baden-Baden. This was pivotal to his development as a public sociologist. Horney was now a founder of the Berlin Institute and was developing her own original critique of the Freudian orthodoxy on women. Fromm's relationship with Horney would play a part in leading him out of his failing marriage with Reichmann and she would show him the way beyond psychoanalytic libido theory. It was the combination of Horney's proto-feminist critique of Freud's patriarchal assumptions about women and the 'Mother Right' work of nineteenth-century aristocratic romantic thinker Johann Jakob Bachofen that led Fromm to reject core elements of Freudian theory such as the Oedipus Complex and instinct/drive theory.

Horney was herself on a path to developing a career as a public psychoanalytic writer a decade before *Escape from Freedom*, a key intellectual role model for Fromm as well as an important personal relationship that would develop in the 1930s in America (Paris, 1995). The neo-Freudians' network served as a marginality facilitator (Watts, 1994) for both Fromm and Horney during the early years of their exile in New York after Hitler came to power.

Fromm could just as easily have created a career as a clinician and perhaps public psychologist. Instead, Fromm returned to his social science interests, presenting the paper 'Psychoanalysis and Sociology' to the Frankfurt psychoanalytic community in 1928. By this time, the Southwest German Psychoanalytic Study Group was now the Frankfurt Psychoanalytic Institute and they shared an office building with the Institute for Social Research, a neo-Marxist circle led by a philosopher named Max Horkheimer. Horkheimer had trouble with public speaking and had a short psychoanalysis with Karl Landauer to address the issue (Friedman, 2013). When Horkheimer was looking for a psychoanalyst with training in the social sciences to assist with bringing Freudian and social psychological perspectives into the emerging 'critical theory' research agenda, Landauer suggested Fromm. In 1929, Fromm was brought into the Frankfurt School, first as a part-time investigator and later as a central member of this interdisciplinary circle of unorthodox Marxists. Fromm thus began a return to sociology that would lead to *Escape from Freedom* and eventually a career as a public intellectual alongside the clinical work he loved.

Three key circles: Frankfurt scholar, neo-Freudianism, and the national character tradition

Fromm's youth and early professional training prepared him well for the role of public sociology, but it was not until his thirties that it came together. In the 1930s, Fromm was able to develop the theoretical framework and non-academic voice that produced *Escape from Freedom*. The framework emerged neither from within mainstream professional sociology nor the clinical world of psychoanalysis, but from a combination of three intellectual movements/collaborative circles: the critical theory of the Frankfurt School, the neo-Freudian psychoanalysts, and the culture and personality anthropologists concerned with questions of national character.

Fromm did the empirical research that went into *Escape from Freedom* on the psychological roots of Nazi authoritarianism in the late 1920s and early 1930s in Germany as part of a major funded research project directed by Max Horkheimer. Fromm broke with the critical theory circle in 1936 over a variety of political, intellectual, financial, and personal issues. The innovative revision of psychoanalysis that sits at the core of the insights of *Escape from Freedom* was shaped not from Fromm's involvement in the centre of the powerful Freudian institutes so important in American psychiatry and psychology in the 1930s or in elite networks of mainstream professional anthropology/

sociology. Fromm's ideas were forged on the optimal margins of both psychoanalysis and social science (McLaughlin, 2001a).

Each of these intellectual movements and collaborative circles were marginality facilitators for Fromm (Watts, 1994). Fromm was a Jewish Marxist in Weimar Germany and then a radical exiled in America. *Escape from Freedom* was produced by the interaction of the emotional energy and cultural capital (Collins, 1998) produced by the marginality facilitators and movements he was involved with combined with the economic bargaining power Fromm gained from being doing all this at the same time. Fromm was able to avoid becoming a full-time psychoanalyst outside the world of social science research because his involvement in the Frankfurt School in Germany and then at Columbia University kept him linked to sociology.

Fromm gained the courage to break from both Freudian orthodoxy and the conventional wisdom of Horkheimer's critical theory because of the independence that flowed from the success of his clinical practice and the creativity forged in the close and often intimate connections to revisionist critics of psychoanalysis such as Karen Horney and Harry Stack Sullivan. Fromm was able to bring sociological and anthropological insights into the psychoanalytic tradition because of his collaborative work with Margaret Mead and anthropologists involved in the 'culture and personality' school in America just before the United States entered the Second World War. To tell this story, we will need to consider each separate network of intellectuals in turn, then do an analysis of how this came together to create *Escape from Freedom*.

Critical theory, neo-Freudianism, and theorizing among the anthropologists

Fromm took longer than many young creative intellectuals to find his own path, partly because of the ambition of his vision but also because of the danger and trauma of the Nazism and world war. As a result of the delays in his career, partly chosen and partly imposed on him, there were three central methods of marginality facilitation that Fromm engaged in as a young man in the decade before writing *Escape from Freedom* (1941). Each of these strategies involved networks that we theorize here as intellectual movements or collaborative circles: the critical theory of the Frankfurt School in Germany and in exile at Columbia, the neo-Freudian movement of clinicians, and the cultural and personality movement – the latter two based largely in New York City.

I will offer an analysis of how: (1) the critical theorists helped Fromm avoid becoming an academic while sharpening his empirical research skills; (2) the neo-Freudians allowed him to stay out of the stifling influence of orthodox Freudians while developing his revision of Freudian libido theory; and (3) the culture and personality circle created the debate about nationalism and national character/culture that *Escape from Freedom* was part of and allowed him to stay connected to social science while critiquing its core assumptions. The power of Fromm's public sociology was created by the social processes by which these three intellectual movements channelled, refined, and combined Fromm's cultural capital (Bourdieu, 1986), liberation capital (Morris, 2015), and emotional energy (Collins, 2014).

The critical theorists

Escape from Freedom was made possible by the critical theory network of the Frankfurt School which Fromm was involved in from the late 1920s to 1939. In the late 1920s, Fromm was on a path to carving out a career as a clinician and perhaps then as a psychoanalytic writer as the more ambitious psychoanalysts tend to do. Fate would put him in contact, however, with Frankfurt School critical theory.

The Frankfurt School was a network of independent radical philosophers, economists, and sociologists associated with the German Institute for Social Research – essentially a Marxist think tank bankrolled by the radical son of a German millionaire grain merchant who had made his fortune in Argentina (Jay, 1973; Wiggershaus, 1995; McLaughlin, 1999). The Institute was founded in the early 1920s with the goal of developing radical intellectual ideas not controlled by traditional Marxist and social democratic parties or academic disciplines (Jay, 1973). In the mid-nineteenth century, Marx had predicted that the economic booms and busts of capitalism combined with the growing wealth of the bourgeois and increasing poverty of the working class would lead to the victory of the revolutionary left. The revolution, in fact, only succeeded in Russia, a largely rural society, in the context of the First World War led by Lenin's Bolsheviks in 1917.

Germany and the world were in economic and cultural crisis in the 1920s with the Great Depression but by the late 1920s and early 1930s, the rise of fascism in Spain, Italy, Japan, and Germany exposed a major problem with Marxist theory. What if capitalist crises were to lead nations to the right not the left, with authoritarian populist leaders such as Hitler gaining enough support from traditional elites, the capitalist class, workers, and the new middle class? That is precisely what was happening, destroying the credibility of orthodox Marxism among any thoughtful observer. The Frankfurt School was concerned with reformulating Marxism to explain why Marx's predictions did not come true and providing the theoretical basis for a new radical project.

The Frankfurt School was interdisciplinary, involving philosophers, economists, and political scientists. They needed both a sociologist and a psychologist, and Fromm fit the bill. Max Horkheimer was its director during its most productive period (Jay, 1973). Members and collaborators of the early Frankfurt School were Carl Grünberg (whom Horkheimer replaced as director in 1930), Leo Löwenthal, Friedrich Pollock, Otto Kirchheimer, Franz Neumann, Theodor Adorno, Herbert Marcuse, Karl Wittfogel, and Henryk Grossman. Fromm's childhood friend Leo Löwenthal was involved, and this connection was renewed in Frankfurt in the late 1920s when Löwenthal helped facilitate Fromm's employment with the Horkheimer circle. Fromm then brought psychoanalysis into the Institute, helping create the distinctive mixture of Marx and Freud that Herbert Marcuse later developed in his distinctive way, bringing the Frankfurt School notoriety as part of the New Left.

Frankfurt School scholarship has, until very recently, underestimated Fromm's importance to the early development of critical theory (but see Rickert, 1986, Kellner, 1989; Wolin, 1992; Bronner, 1994; Wiggershaus, 1995; Durkin, 2014). Even Martin Jay's enormously influential and otherwise excellent book, *The Dialectical Imagination* (1973), repeats some of the origin myths about critical theory promoted by Horkheimer and Adorno. Adorno, Horkheimer, and Marcuse, as well as Walter Benjamin, became the central figures within a revised history, and Adorno's student Jürgen Habermas became the heir to the tradition. The story of how this remarkable rewriting of the history of a school of thought came about has been told elsewhere (McLaughlin, 1999, 2008). What is important here is how critical theory helped Fromm return to sociological research, now with a PhD and the financial support provided by the Frankfurt School.

Unlike in psychoanalytic institutes and sociology departments, the resources and journal of critical theory were controlled singlehandedly, after 1930, by Max Horkheimer, as he managed and shaped the Frankfurt School.[2] The major figures in the Frankfurt School thus were far more dependent on the economic resources of one institution than is the case for either psychoanalysts or sociologists. Horkheimer used his control over the Frankfurt School resources to ensure that he and a limited number of scholars could avoid the pressures of attaining a mainstream academic job. Horkheimer guarded this money carefully, always attempting to support a small core of thinkers loyal to him. He used the money as a 'seed' to try to keep a peripheral group associated with the Institute but supported by outside teaching, foundation grants, or government employment. Horkheimer had initially been interested in merging Marxist politics with the psychological insights of the Freudian tradition. Yet Horkheimer's knowledge of psychoanalysis was minimal, having only been analysed briefly for his public-speaking inhibition. Fromm was made the tenured director of the Institute for Social Research's Social Psychology Section in 1930 precisely because of his psychoanalytic expertise (Wiggershaus, 1995 pp 57–58).

Fromm's major project with the Institute had begun a year earlier with a study on the social psychology of German workers, research that played a major role in Fromm's bitter break with his colleagues (Bonss, 1984). In 1929, Fromm began research on *German Workers 1929 – A Survey, Its Methods and Results*. The theory of the F-scale that Theodor Adorno would make famous with *The Authoritarian Personality* (Adorno et al, 1950) came directly out of this empirical research (Adorno et al, 1950). The early Frankfurt School was interested in understanding the sources of the mass appeal of the Nazi Party, as well as why the German working class did not resist Hitler. This project proceeded slowly partly because of the forced migration of the Institute from Germany in 1933 as Hitler came to power. Historian Thomas Wheatland has shown that Fromm played a central role in pushing the critical theorists to get their money out of Germany into Switzerland and then negotiating a temporary home for their work in exile at Columbia University with the help of sociologist Robert Lynd (Wheatland, 2009).

Fromm's *German Workers* study is an unappreciated classic in the social sciences despite some real methodological limitations. A first report of the study appeared in German in the context of Horkheimer's edited collection, *Studien über Autorität und Familie* (1936), where it was suggested that the larger work would soon be published (Bonss, 1984). While many of Fromm's later works were best-sellers and were greeted with critical acclaim, he had to fight hostility and indifference to this project from the beginning. Fromm left the Institute in 1939 and the revised plan for a publication of the *German Workers* project was dropped. The study disappeared, as Wolfgang Bonss puts it, 'into Fromm's desk drawer' and 'was later also partly deleted from the annals of the Institute' only to be published after Fromm's death in the 1980s (Bonss, 1984 p 2).

There is dispute among scholars as to why this study was so unpopular among the inner circle of the Frankfurt School. Fromm himself stressed Horkheimer's concern that the controversial Marxism of the study would hurt the Institute in anti-communist America (Bonss, 1984). Martin Jay repeated the Institute's official justification that the research design was flawed and that many questionnaires had been lost (Jay, 1973). Herbert Marcuse was concerned that the study might be used to show that German workers were really fascists at heart (Jay, 1973; Bonss, 1984).[3] Horkheimer's refusal to publish the Fromm study under the auspices of the Institute was a major factor in the rift between Fromm and the Frankfurt School. In addition to these ideological and intellectual conflicts, the strong personal animosities between Fromm and Theodor Adorno, theoretical differences, as well as questions of money and resources, played a major role.

Adorno replaces Fromm

The fundamental reason for Fromm's departure from the Frankfurt School for Social Research was conflict between Adorno and Fromm over both resources and Freudian theory. Adorno was not central to the Institute until the late 1930s. While in Germany and abroad in England during the early Nazi rule, Adorno had been supported by his well-off parents. Horkheimer had initially wanted to tie Adorno to the Institute without committing to him financially (Wiggershaus, 1995). The Institute had substantial, but finite, resources and Horkheimer's priority was maintaining his own material security as well as control over the content of the work produced. Horkheimer saw Fromm as an intellectual equal and collaborator in the early 1930s, but gradually Adorno replaced him as a core member of the Frankfurt School and Horkheimer's trusted ally.[4] This competition and struggle played itself out most dramatically over the use of psychoanalysis within critical theory.

Adorno argued that Fromm's emerging break with Freud was a serious threat to the political and intellectual 'line' of the Frankfurt School. Adorno had been suspicious of the collaboration between Horkheimer and Fromm while the Institute was based in Frankfurt. The beginning of open conflict, however, can be dated to Fromm's essay 'The Social Determination of Psychoanalytic Therapy', an early version of his later criticisms of orthodox Freudian theory and therapy published in the critical theory's journal in 1935 (Wiggershaus, 1995).[5] In March 1936, Adorno wrote to Horkheimer defending Freud against Fromm's revisionism. For Adorno, Fromm's revision of Freudian theory inevitably led away from a truly radical critique of modern society – substituting soft-hearted therapy for rigorous analysis. By the late 1930s, Horkheimer had accepted Adorno's critique of Fromm's psychoanalytic theory. Both Adorno and Horkheimer insisted that 'biological materialism' was 'the theoretical core of psychoanalysis which was to be maintained against the revisionists' (Wiggershaus, 1995 p 271). This issue had little to do with therapy since no one in the Frankfurt School other than Fromm was an expert in the clinical and empirical basis of Freudian theory.[6]

This intellectual conflict happened at the same time as a major conflict over resources, something almost uniformly ignored in the secondary literature. In the spring of 1939, Fromm was essentially dismissed from his tenured position at the Institute by Friedrich Pollock because of financial problems flowing from bad investments made in American real estate. Fromm was asked to go without his salary since he had an income from therapy, an arrangement he declined (Jay, 1973; Bonss, 1984). Horkheimer and Fromm engaged in discussions at the end of 1939, but as Wiggershaus puts it, 'the breach had already taken place, and only the arrangements for the separation remained to be dealt with' (Wiggershaus, 1995 p 271). Fromm received $20,000 for giving up his tenure (a significant sum during Depression-era America) and he turned his energies to therapy and to writing what would become *Escape from Freedom*. Adorno entered the core of the Institute and Horkheimer and especially Adorno became bitter enemies of Fromm and attempted to exclude him as best they could from the history of the Institute. Adorno and Horkheimer would go on to publish major works on their own, coming to dominate what we think of as Frankfurt School critical theory especially by the 1970s when the 1960s student movements created a following for Western Marxism (Horkheimer and Adorno, 1972; Horkheimer, 1974; Adorno, 2002, 2005).

The neo-Freudian intellectual movement

Fromm was financially sustained by the Horkheimer circle during the early 1930s and did empirical research under their auspices but was also deeply committed to clinical work and psychoanalytic theory. Throughout the 1930s, Fromm was both involved in the critical theory network and an alternative Freudian intellectual movement led by German psychoanalyst Karen Horney and the American psychiatrist, Harry Stack Sullivan (McLaughlin, 1998b). Horney, Sullivan, and Fromm were widely known as the leading proponents of the 'cultural' or neo-Freudian school of psychoanalysis. Their collectively created theoretical perspective was a key ingredient in the intellectual mix that would lead to *Escape from Freedom*.

The label neo-Freudian is misleading despite the fact they shared criticisms of Freudian orthodoxy. All three were sceptical of the usefulness of orthodox instinct theory. Horney insisted that cultural values and norms had a powerful influence on standards of mental health and definitions of neurosis. Sullivan captured this point clearly with his stress on 'interpersonal relations'. Fromm, Horney, and Sullivan all downplayed the importance of instincts, arguing that the individual search for identity, self-esteem, and secure relations with others in work, family, and the broader society should be the central focus of psychoanalytic theory (McLaughlin, 1998b). The consequence of this perspective was a stress on sociological, not biological, factors, a major break with both classical Freudian theory and the increasingly medically oriented American psychoanalytic establishment. There were important differences of emphasis between Horney, Sullivan, and Fromm but their critique of orthodox Freudian libido theory was pivotal in the success of *Escape from Freedom*.

Horney, Sullivan, and Fromm were sceptical of Freud's cultural values. Horney, in particular, was a pioneer in developing an early feminist critique of the patriarchal bias embedded in Freud's theories of the Oedipus Complex and penis envy (Westkott, 1986; Paris, 1995). Sullivan, while not a political radical, looked for the social roots of schizophrenia and was an early critic of the labelling that constructs deviance and delinquency. Neither Horney nor Sullivan would accept Fromm's Marxist critique of modern society, but they all insisted on opening the Freudian tradition to a broader set of theoretical influences. Horney's psychoanalysis drew on cultural anthropology and the sociology of her German acquaintance, Georg Simmel (Westkott, 1986). Sullivan's very American psychology was partly based on the theories of the self that were developed by the University of Chicago philosopher George Herbert Mead (Perry, 1982; Huebner, 2014). Fromm contributed his Marxist and Weberian training and empirical experience in the Frankfurt School network to this exciting mix of ideas (Burston, 1991; McLaughlin, 1999).

The version of Freudian theory that Fromm outlined in *Escape from Freedom* came out of this collaboration. Sullivan helped promote the book through his journal *Psychiatry*. The social circle of the neo-Freudians was a key marginality facilitator for Fromm as he negotiated hostility he faced from both the Horkheimer circle and orthodox Freudians. While Fromm was close to both and Sullivan was important in connecting him to the William Alanson White Institute within the psychoanalytic world – it was Horney who helped make Fromm a public sociologist, not just a clinician and theorist.

Fromm and Horney's collaboration

The three major neo-Freudians had come together not as separate individuals. Horney and Fromm collaborated first and then together they developed a working relationship with Sullivan. Horney and Fromm had met initially at the Berlin Institute for Psychoanalysis while Fromm was being trained in Freudian theory and clinical work. In the 1920s and the early 1930s, the Berlin Institute was the most intellectually exciting centre of psychoanalysis in Europe (Jacoby, 1975; Harris and Brock, 1991), and Horney was a founding member and important figure in its intellectual life and training.

Although the Berlin Institute was an orthodox institute that treated Freud's writings as quasi-scriptural, it was remarkably vibrant and open. The first generation of German Freudian enthusiasts trained a dedicated cadre of psychoanalysts schooled with a unique blend of clinical and humanistic education (Harris and Brock, 1991). Associated with the cultural radicalism of the Weimar period, the Berlin Institute fostered a movement, not a professional culture (Jacoby, 1986). The Berlin Institute provided inexpensive treatment to German workers and the middle classes and functioned to educate social workers, teachers, political activists, and nurses in psychotherapy (Harris and Brock, 1991; Hale, 1995). It was in this milieu that Fromm learned to think about psychoanalysis as a movement not a narrow professional occupation.

Younger than Horney, Fromm was trained at the Berlin Institute where he was influenced by the renegade Freudian-Marxist Wilhelm Reich. For a time, Fromm was part of a circle of radical psychoanalysts led by Otto Fenichel. Although Fromm would soon fall out with both Reich and the psychoanalytically orthodox but politically radical Fenichel, Fromm's work was shaped by these early attempts to combine Freudian depth psychology with Marxist historical materialism and Horney's feminism. Fromm remained a relatively orthodox Freudian-Marxist until the late 1930s, several years after he had emigrated to the United States and just before publishing *Escape from Freedom* (Harris and Brock, 1991). Fromm initially came to the United States at the invitation of Horney who attempted to secure a position for him at Franz Alexander's Chicago Institute for Psychoanalysis after she had moved there in the early 1930s to serve as its associate director. Her scheme fell through because Alexander objected to Fromm's status as an analyst without a medical degree (Funk, 1982; Burston, 1991; Hale, 1995).

Lay analysis was widely accepted among the first two generations of European psychoanalysts, and some of the most important of Freud's followers in Europe did not have medical degrees. The master himself had written an essay defending the practice of 'lay analysis'. Freud had, after all, been rejected by the European medical establishment even though he held a medical degree.

Freud's vision of psychoanalysis was much broader and more ambitious than a subfield within medical psychiatry. Several important followers (including his daughter, Anna) were not physicians. Most American psychoanalysts, however, wanted to increase the professional status of psychoanalysis by establishing it as a speciality in psychiatric medicine. European psychoanalysts who emigrated to the United States without medical degrees often suffered rejection at the hands of American psychoanalysts because of this emerging professionalization strategy among American Freudians. Unlike many other European psychoanalysts who came as refugees, however, Fromm had other options and moved to New York City to his position as a tenured member of the Frankfurt School for Social Research now based at Columbia University, at the same time establishing a private practice in the city. Horney herself found the Chicago Institute stifling and she soon also relocated to New York, joining the New York Psychoanalytic Institute (Funk, 1982; McLaughlin, 1998b, 1999).

Fromm and Horney were collaborators as well as lovers, and together they established contacts with a number of anthropologists, sociologists, psychoanalysts, and psychiatrists who were interested in merging revised Freudian insights with the social sciences as part of an emerging concern with 'culture and personality'.[7] Both Horney and Fromm participated in Sullivan's eclectic Zodiac Club, an informal network of like-minded psychoanalysts and social scientists. Through this network, Horney and Fromm got to know anthropologists Margaret Mead, Ruth Benedict, and Ralph Linton. Neo-Freudianism emerged out of this exciting mix of ideas and energizing network of support and marginality facilitation.[8]

While Fromm's work with Horney and Sullivan helped develop a critique of Freudian orthodoxy, Fromm failed to establish a solid alternative institutional home for his brand of unorthodox Freudian analysis. While the reputation of all three thinkers suffered from the hostility directed at them by dogmatic Freudians, Horney and Sullivan, especially, were able to develop far more secure institutional support in psychoanalysis in America. Horney later established her own institute, and Sullivan was a central figure and had many loyal followers in both the Washington School of Psychiatry and the William Alanson White Institute.

Conflicts among Horney, Sullivan, and Fromm are central to this story. Horney and Fromm had become romantically involved in the early 1930s, and the break-up of their relationship caused bitterness, particularly on Horney's part. The deterioration of the relationship is a complex story that Quinn and Paris have told in detail, but one contributing factor was that Karen Horney had asked Fromm to take her daughter into analysis. Fromm agreed and proceeded to help Marianne Horney to see her conflicts with her mother in a new light. Marianne Horney gained the confidence to stand up to her mother, and Fromm and Karen Horney's relationship went into decline. For all his psychoanalytic insights, he shared with other early psychoanalysts a remarkable blindness to the obvious psychological and sociological conflict of interest involved in analysing one's lover's daughter. There were deeper causes to their problems (Quinn, 1987; Paris, 1995).[9] Sullivan's and Fromm's relationship has also become strained, even if Sullivan's early death prevented an open break. Contrary to the focus in much of literature, however, the major difference between Fromm and Sullivan was not personal or related to Freudian theory but was instead rooted in politics.

The most important differences between Horney, Sullivan, and Fromm were not primarily personal but were rooted in professional and political differences that had important sociological implications. Fromm was too Marxist for Horney, and certainly for Sullivan. While Fromm was a committed professional therapist, he was far more concerned with reforming the world through radical political activity and social criticism than he was establishing a school of psychoanalysis, either neo-Freudian or Frommian.[10]

Both Horney and Sullivan were more focused than Fromm on the internal politics of psychoanalysis and the mental health professions. Horney wrote for a general not radical audience, while Sullivan had political influence on elite policy makers and was critical of political radicals. Fromm's emergence as a public sociologist owes much to what he learned from both Horney and Sullivan. Indeed, *Escape from Freedom* was written in ways that combined Horney's strategy of publishing psychoanalytic ideas aimed at the general educated public but published by elite commercial presses (particularly in *The Neurotic Personality of Our Time* [1937]) with Sullivan's insider policy orientation aimed at policy makers and elite professionals. Both Horney and Sullivan, however, were clinicians who were ultimately neither deeply political nor social scientists. The neo-Freudians shared too little to become a school of thought but they were central to his early career and intellectual development (McLaughlin, 1998b). There was one final influence, however, that allowed Fromm to become a public sociologist concerned with issues of fascism, war, and American foreign policy.

Margaret Mead and the culture and personality school

Fromm's *Escape from Freedom* would not have been possible without the marginality facilitation provided by the culture and personality movement of anthropologists Margaret Mead, Edward Sapir, John Dollard, and Ruth Benedict. It was among a network of anthropologists on the optimal margins of their own field that Fromm was exposed to a vision of a public social science that could address the issues of culture, war, nationalism, and destructiveness central to *Escape from Freedom*.

The informal Monday night Zodiac Club meetings led by Sullivan in the mid-1930s discussed psychoanalytic theory, family dynamics, and clinical issues. By the later 1930s, a wider gathering was convened in Horney's apartment, concerned now with the broader societal influences on the psyche rather than strictly clinical topics. It was in Horney's network where Fromm met Margaret Mead and the other anthropologists whom historians of the social sciences now call the culture and personality movement. An example of what Gross and Frickel call a 'scientific intellectual movement' (2005), the 'culture and personality' school was concerned with taking psychoanalytic insights into the mainstream of anthropological theory while also engaging with policy makers and the public on major political and cultural questions. Mead's influence on *Escape from Freedom* and his developing career as a public sociologist was pivotal.

Fromm had long been an excellent networker, and he had come to know a range of faculty members at Columbia University and had fine-tuned his English language skills early on. Fromm was thus able to take full advantage of the opportunities that connection to the culture and personality movement made possible. Sociologist and social psychologist John Dollard and anthropologist Edward Sapir invited Fromm and the neo-Freudians into their homes and had them participate in their Rockefeller-funded 'Culture and Personality' seminar at Yale University (Friedman, 2013 p 77). Fromm would later teach a seminar at Yale in 1949 with the anthropologist Ralph Linton. Psychoanalyst and culture and personality theorist Abram Kardiner's early work cited Fromm extensively. By the 1950s, however, Fromm would largely be rejected by this network of thinkers just as they themselves started to lose prestige and influence in the discipline. Kardiner, in particular, disliked Fromm intensely, had a personal loyalty to Freud, and dismissed Fromm's revisionism in his later writings (Kardiner, 1961). A negative view of Fromm's work would later be diffused among young social scientists through the extremely influential Linton/Kardiner culture and personality seminar at Columbia University. For Fromm, however, the key contact that emerged out of this network of thinkers would be Margaret Mead.

Margaret Mead played a particularly important role in connecting the neo-Freudians to her expansive professional and intellectual networks. Fromm benefited enormously from his interactions with a woman who would soon become the most famous public anthropologist of the twentieth century. Trained at Columbia under the mentorship of Franz Boas, the dominant liberal anthropologist of the period, Margaret Mead became famous with *Coming of Age in Samoa* (1928) and was on the way to an iconic status in American society (Lutkehaus, 2008) even by the middle of the 1930s, when Fromm and Mead met. Fromm and Mead became personal friends and by 1939 they were sharing each other's ideas and work, a relationship that Michael Farrell has called 'instrumental intimacy' (Farrell, 2001; Friedman, 2013 p 91).

Fromm's concept of social character drew on Mead's attempts to understand how self, culture, and emotions interacted in different national contexts (Friedman, 2013 p 91). Fromm had been influenced by Mead's *Sex and Temperament in Three Primitive Societies* (1935), along with the example of Karen Horney's popular selling *The Neurotic Personality of Our Time* (1937). By the time Fromm and Mead became friends, she had written three major books in that crossover space of academic and commercial presses that his own work would soon occupy (Mead, 1928, 1935). Margaret Mead faced a sexism that Fromm did not but he saw how Mead's marginality in mainstream professional anthropology, her job at the American Museum of Natural History, and ability to sell books on the mass market combined to allow her to avoid academic orthodoxies.

The culture and personality movement was far more directly politically active than either the neo-Freudians or the critical theorists. Mead was skilled at framing her analysis of American society in ways that both tapped into and critiqued American nationalism. Fromm and Mead were very different while sharing much in common. Fromm retained the socialism and Marxism he embraced in his twenties for the rest of his life, while Mead was always a democratic left-liberal, not a political radical. Following from this, Fromm would never be comfortable as an insider to policy circles unlike many of the culture and personality scholars in America, especially during the Second World

War and the Cold War that followed. Both Fromm and Mead were intellectually ambitious while being critical of the mainstream versions of their academic disciplines, sociology and anthropology respectively. Fromm and Mead shared an ability to write often, well, and clearly on topical issues of the day while connecting to both empirical and theoretical scholarly concerns.

Fromm and Mead also shared some of the same intellectual limitations. The public academic work of both in the 1930s, 1940s, and 1950s is vulnerable to a critique of its Eurocentric and uncritical modernist assumptions. Fromm and Mead both uncritically wrote about 'primitive' societies, and while they both were critical of mainstream developmental research in what would later be called modernization theory, they were rooted in some of the same assumptions about modernity that post-colonial scholars would later critique after the 1960s. The quality of the scholarship of both Fromm and Mead suffered from the inevitable simplifications and short-cuts that came from writing social science for mass audiences, a problem that got worse over time as they both became academic celebrities isolated from peer review.

Fromm's connections to the culture and personality network and his close relationship with Margaret Mead was the final piece of the puzzle that explains how Fromm became a world-famous public sociologist. *Escape from Freedom* was concerned with the origins of Nazism in Germany just as Mead and her collaborators among the culture and personality school were. Fromm was not, however, committed to a national character theoretical frame. Indeed, it was precisely Fromm's critical engagement with national character theories that made *Escape from Freedom* so influential.

While Fromm insisted in *Escape from Freedom* that the specifics of German history and class structures be taken into account when analysing the rise of Hitler's movement, he argued that the mechanism of escape in authoritarianism and destructiveness that led to Nazism was not a uniquely German phenomenon. Fascism could happen in Western democracies and the escape from freedom represented by what he called automation conformity was a threat to freedom created by capitalist modernity itself. While the national character work on German and Japanese fascism created by the 'culture and personality' school opened up space for Fromm's social character theory in America, his rejection of the concept of national character itself helped his book stand out and gain both a mass audience and scholarly recognition. The appendix to the book laid out a theoretical framework for social character work that he would develop over the rest of his working life.

A general theory of the public sociologist

The case of Fromm holds several important lessons for theorizing the emergence of public sociologists. Academic PhDs in sociology who are ambitious and well trained with prospects for success as professional sociologists do not just leave the world of peer-reviewed scholarship and potential academic tenure without support and role models that come from outside the profession.

W. E. B. Du Bois became a public sociologist, not just a scholar of slavery and racism in America, partly because racism pushed him out of the profession, but also because of his involvement in the Niagara movement for black civil rights in the period before the First World War and then the communist and Pan-African movements in his later years (Morris, 2015). Du Bois learned to speak and write to the public not from his sociology teachers but from activism with the National Association for the Advancement of Colored People (NAACP) and during his years as editor of the monthly magazine *The Crisis* (Morris, 2015).

This is a general process. Jane Addams was sustained by networks of activist social workers and middle-class political reformers that made her more than a philanthropist but not fully a professional academic (Deegan, 1988). C. Wright Mills published in the elite journals of the American sociological profession in his years as a graduate student, but it was his involvement with New York-based intellectuals associated with commercial book presses and politically engaged opinion magazines that made him a public sociologist even though he taught at Columbia and was more connected to the discipline than Fromm (Aronowitz, 2012).

In each of these cases, informal networks of intellectuals around journals and political organizations (*The Crisis* and Communist Party with Du Bois, the settlement houses with Addams, and the magazine *Politics* with Mills) and connections with powerful elites and institutions (Harvard and Max Weber with Du Bois, the University of Chicago with Addams, and Merton and Lazersfeld at Columbia Sterne (2005)) were essential for each thinker in overcoming their marginality due to race, gender, and religion/ethnicity respectively. Not all thinkers associated with small journals and various political movements will become famous public sociologists like Du Bois, Addams, Mills, and Fromm. In each of these cases, there is a story of intellectual talent, hard work, fortunate circumstances and fateful decisions that would lead outside of the relative safety of professional sociology and social work towards careers writing for the public.

The writing and publishing of a major public sociological book like *The Souls of Black Folk* (1903), *The Power Elite* (1956), and *Escape from Freedom* (1941), flowed from both individual inspiration and genius that cannot be fully explained by existing sociological theories of creativity. There is much comparative research to be done on the origins of great books of public sociology now operating in a social media environment and a far more crowded book market. I have offered and theorized the details of one case while suggesting a framework for further research for understanding the making of public sociologists.

In Fromm's case, this was only the beginning. The critical acclaim, fame, and financial security that Fromm gained from *Escape from Freedom* made it possible for him to spend the next forty years of his life developing the theoretical and political agenda he outlined in the book while also writing public sociology and social criticism. Fame and influence brought attacks directed at him, and a complicated and difficult reputation (Fine, 2001) as is often the case for public intellectuals.

It is to the sociological and intellectual consequences of Fromm's emergence as a global public sociologist that we now turn as he becomes the most influential public sociologist in the world by critiquing American conformity and capitalism first during the Cold War period and then the 1960s.

3

The Cold War, Conformity, and the 1960s

At the end of the Second World War, Fromm was a well-known social scientist, psychoanalyst and social critic living in New York City poised to become the most influential public sociologist of his time. Financially secure and no longer constrained by his connection to the Frankfurt School network or to orthodox Freudian sponsorship and institutions, Fromm was well positioned to take his social theory and sociology directly to the public. Fromm was connected to top commercial press editors in New York, their respect earned from the success of *Escape from Freedom*. Able to write clearly and quickly in English, Fromm entered the period of the height of his fame and influence throughout his forties, fifties, and early sixties.

There was a brief moment in the wake of *Escape from Freedom*'s critical success where Fromm had an opportunity to gain influence inside professional sociology in the United States.[1] Fromm rejected a sustained engagement with the discipline,[2] preferring to write books to mass audiences. Best-selling books *Man for Himself: An Inquiry into the Psychology of Ethics* (1947), *Psychoanalysis and Religion* (1950), *The Sane Society* (1955a), and *The Art of Loving* (1956a) made Fromm the most visible and important popularizer of the ideas of both Freud and Marx in America in the Cold War era. Fromm had moved from the role of empirical researcher to social critic and public sociologist. Fromm interpreted, popularized, and revised Marx, Freud and the broader European intellectual tradition for Americans in an age of the paperback, mass conformity, and anti-communism. No simplistic popularizer, Fromm outlined a powerful public sociological critique of American capitalism, culture, and militaristic foreign policy. Fromm would shape the politics of the 1960s era in profound ways (Jamison and Eyerman, 1994).

Fromm was doing a kind of sociology but one that was in accordance with his 'intellectual self-concept' (Gross, 2013). Fromm's ideas were important, but he also provided the single most influential role model – indeed a template – for the public sociologist of the 1950s and 1960s, both for the broader public but also for the sociology profession itself. Fromm was a role model and intellectual influence on both David Riesman's brand of liberal 'traditional' public sociology and C. Wright Mills' radical public sociology of the 1950s and early 1960s. These two templates of 'traditional' and 'critical' public sociology, respectively, would indirectly inspire Burawoy's formulations of the public sociology debate in the early years of the twenty-first century. By then, Fromm's role in all of this had been generally forgotten despite his pivotal contributions in creating both types of public sociology.

Fromm was the mentor to David Riesman, the iconic representative of public sociology from the 1950s era who retains an important place in current debates within the discipline. Riesman himself went on to create the prototype of public sociology we would see in the work of Robert Bellah and his collaborators in *Habits of the Heart* (1985) and Alan Wolfe's sociological social criticism on American politics and culture (Wolfe, 1989, 1993, 2011, 2018). These well-respected social scientists were not generally operating at the center of mainstream peer-reviewed professional sociology. Practitioners of the public sociological imagination, they would write sophisticated sociological social criticisms in ways that were framed as liberal sociological dialogues on political and cultural issues of broad interest, most often published by commercial presses. Bellah and especially Wolfe were generally uninterested in Fromm's ideas, but their work built on the earlier example of David Riesman.

Fromm's public sociological ideas helped shape contemporary sociology. Fromm's theorizing of the politics of emotions, analysis of American culture's social character of excessive individualism (what Bellah later called habits of the heart), insistence on the need to understand both far-right populism and left-wing authoritarianism travelled into sociology partly mediated by Riesman. Fromm also was a significant direct influence on C. Wright Mills in the 1940s and early 1950s and on many Marxist and critical sociologists from the mid-1950s through to the late 1960s. Fromm helped popularize the Marxist concept of alienation and offered a critique of the pathological cultural and political consequences of market fundamentalism. He also offered an analysis of the inconsistencies and paranoia of American foreign policy and he defended the humanist anti-Stalinist Marxist tradition that helped create the New Left on campuses in the 1960s. These were major contributions that have disappeared from sociology's collective memory.

Mills read Fromm and was influenced by him even though he eventually went his own way with his Meadian and Weberian analysis of *Social Character and Social Structure* (Gerth and Mills, 1953). Mills would replace Fromm as the most famous radical public sociologist in the 1960s. After Mills died in the early 1960s, there was a massive explosion of sociological research on alienation, on Marxist theorizing, and on radical public sociology. Arlie Hochschild's pioneering writings on the commercialization of feelings and on the negative consequences of the capitalist logic on character, personality, and emotions in the American culture is one example. Fromm was pivotal to this explosion of psychosocial influenced ideas that first rippled through both the profession and the culture in the 1950s and continues today. To understand all this we start with Fromm's relationship to a then young David Riesman in the 1940s and 1950s.

Riesman meets Fromm: from therapist to mentor

In the early 1940s, in the wake of the fame *Escape from Freedom* had brought him, Fromm had been the therapist for a young American named David Riesman. Riesman was a lawyer who would go on to make major contributions as a sociologist and public intellectual. Riesman was raised in an agnostic and elite Jewish Philadelphia family; his father was a learned clinical medical professor and his mother a cultivated Bryn Mawr graduate. Educated at Harvard and Harvard Law School, Riesman went to teach law at the private University of Buffalo at the age of twenty-seven, after a clerkship with Supreme Court Justice Brandeis. He also had a brief stint at a law firm in Boston and a short spell as a district attorney in New York.

Riesman agreed to undergo psychoanalysis with Fromm to please his mother who was in analysis with Karen Horney. The matriarch of the Riesman family was concerned that young David was underachieving. After Horney recommended Erich Fromm to Eleanor Riesman, David would fly or take the train on alternative weekends for two-hour sessions with Fromm in Manhattan. The formal analysis was unconventional often resembling a teacher–student rather than a psychoanalyst–patient relationship. The analysis continued for some years, however, and was the beginning of a long-standing intellectual relationship and friendship. Fromm furthered Riesman's training in the European intellectual tradition that Riesman had first been introduced to by Carl Joachim Friedrich of the Harvard Government Department.[3] Fromm, according to Riesman, 'greatly assisted me in gaining confidence as well as enlarging the scope of my interests in the social sciences' (Riesman, 1990a p 46).[4]

Fromm and Riesman did politics together, and had a productive intellectual and personal relationship, what sociologist Michael Farrell calls 'instrumental intimacy' (Farrell, 2001). They maintained a close personal friendship and an extensive correspondence until Fromm's death in 1980 (Burston, 1991).[5] The creative tension between their different politics was an important part of the mix that went into the making of *The Lonely Crowd* (1950). When Riesman first met Fromm, he noticed a large shelf of Marxist texts in his apartment and worried that his analyst 'would seek to propagandize me' (Riesman, 1990a p 45). Riesman never shared Fromm's radicalism or his Marxist theoretical bent and felt that Fromm's 'view of the United States and especially its middle classes was too monolithically and stereotypically negative' (Riesman, 1990b p 46). Riesman did, however, integrate Fromm's interest in revising psychoanalytic ideas into his own emerging intellectual agenda, a key theoretical component of Riesman's sociology. Riesman and Fromm, moreover, shared a passionate concern with American foreign policy, particularly the nuclear arms race. In the 1940s and 1950s, Fromm was widely known as one of Riesman's mentors (Glazer, 1990; Wrong, 1990). The Fromm–Riesman relationship was central to the development of liberal traditional public sociology.

Man for Himself (1947) and the critique of conformity

While mainstream sociology today has moved far from the kind of public sociological work Riesman did in the 1950s, the conservative political philosopher Allan Bloom could never be accused of failing to take David Riesman's sociology seriously. One of the seldom remarked upon aspects of the controversial best-selling *The Closing of the American Mind: How Higher Education Has Failed Democracy and Impoverished the Souls of Today's Students* (1987) is the special place given to Riesman. Bloom argued that *The Lonely Crowd* (1950) facilitated the decline of intellectual and cultural standards in contemporary America that he saw coming out of the social movements of the 1960s.

For Bloom, Riesman's sociology turned America upside down. Bloom's *The Closing of the American Mind* (1987), it should be remembered, claimed that American intellectual life had been corrupted by a nihilism and relativism that had become widespread with the social turmoil of the 1960s and omnipresent in the popular culture of the 1980s. The roots of this cultural decay, for Bloom, were not political or economic, and cannot be blamed on the social conflicts associated with the civil rights movement or the Vietnam War. Instead, the violence that Bloom observed first hand at Cornell University, the cultural decay epitomized by Woodstock (the Nuremberg rally of the 1960s, according to Bloom!), and the study of popular culture in contemporary universities that Bloom saw as a lowering of intellectual standards, were the natural consequence of Nietzsche's influence on the American Left. Just as National Socialism flowed from German philosophical traditions, the importation of German ideas into American life in the twentieth century laid the foundation for the degradation of North American cultural and intellectual life since the 1960s (Bloom, 1987).

According to Bloom, Riesman played a central role in this process by absorbing German ideas from 'his analyst', Erich Fromm, and then spreading these destructive theories widely through his academic bestseller *The Lonely Crowd* (1950). There is certainly an element of paranoia in Bloom's attribution of such widespread cultural influence to the work of two once influential but now largely forgotten intellectuals (McLaughlin, 1998a). It is difficult to accept Bloom's one-sidedly negative account of the cultural consequences of the 1960s. Bloom is simply inaccurate about much of the intellectual content of both Riesman's and Fromm's work. His claim that Riesman and Fromm were simplistic popularisers of nihilism is an absurd notion to anyone familiar with their work (Burston, 1991; Bronner, 1994).[6]

Bloom is right, however, that Riesman's *The Lonely Crowd* is an important example of how German intellectual traditions and European theories of mass society were transported across the Atlantic, adapted to American intellectual traditions, and then spread into the culture. Riesman was a sociologist who also functioned as a social critic as well as having a major influence on American cultural life more broadly. A re-examination of Riesman's work and its relationship to Fromm's critical theory will tell us much about the hidden history of contemporary public sociology, particularly with regard to Riesman's *The Lonely Crowd* (1950), the best-selling sociology book of all time (Gans, 1997).

Riesman wrote far more than *The Lonely Crowd* (1950). He wrote extensively and insightfully for decades about American popular and intellectual culture, social and cultural theory, higher education in the United States, foreign policy, nuclear weapons, and the consequences of modern consumer culture. Writing in that strange boundary space between intellectual social criticism and academic social science, Riesman provides us with an important role model for the sociologist as public intellectual or a traditional public sociologist, in Burawoy's terms. And unlike the many European critical theorists that Allan Bloom attacks, and post-modern sociologists applaud, Riesman is a very American theorist whose work was shaped by pragmatist traditions. It is free of pretence, anti-empirical abstraction, and tortured prose. Riesman's unique and creative positioning at the crossroads of American social criticism and European theory, however, has seldom been analysed sociologically.

Riesman was more than a popular writer and the first social scientist to appear on the cover of *Time*. Riesman's work combined American pragmatist thinking with European critical theory and suggested original and provocative themes that later sociologists and social critics would develop. As historian Rupert Wilkinson suggests,

> [*The Lonely Crowd*] heralded later findings to a degree that is seldom appreciated. Narcissism and 'diffuse anxiety'; the shifting of authority from 'dos and don'ts' to manipulation and enticement; the flooding of attitudes by media messages; the channelling of achievement drives into competition for the approval of others; and the splintering of society into myriad interest groups—all these tendencies of modern American life that so worried commentators in the 1970s and 1980s were spotted by Riesman et al. (and well before television had become an everyday staple). (Wilkinson, 1988 p 16)

Riesman's *The Lonely Crowd* provided the model for public scholarship that addressed these issues such as Robert Bellah et al's *Habits of the Heart* (1985) as well as historian Christopher Lasch's *The Culture of Narcissism: American Life in an Age of Diminishing Expectations* (1979).

Capitalism and the Reformation

The framework for *The Lonely Crowd* came from Fromm. *Escape from Freedom*'s theoretical account of the social psychology of capitalism (Riesman 1990b). Fromm's account of modern society emphasized the cultural importance of the urban middle class, the group that Max Weber argued was the 'backbone of modern capitalist development in the Western world' and also central to Riesman's account of 'the lonely crowd'. Fromm focuses on the economic changes that brought about modern capitalism and the resultant cultural upheaval, arguing that,

> Significant changes in the psychological atmosphere accompanied the economic development of capitalism. A spirit of restlessness began to pervade life toward the end of the Middle Ages. The concept of time in the modern sense began to develop. Minutes became valuable; a symptom of this new sense of time is the fact that in Nuremberg the clocks have been striking hours since the 16th century. Too many holidays began to appear as a misfortune. Time was so valuable that one felt one should never spend it for any purpose which was not useful. Work became increasingly a supreme value. A new attitude toward work developed and was so strong that the middle class grew indignant against the economic unproductivity of the institutions of the Church. (Fromm, 1941 p 76)

This capitalist marketplace had become the master instead of the servant of human affairs. The ambiguity of freedom emerged during the Renaissance but became even more extreme during the Reformation. Fromm writes of the influence these changes would have on the individual,

> Not having the wealth or power which the Renaissance capitalist had, and also having lost the unity of men and the universe, he is overwhelmed with a sense of his individual nothingness and helplessness. Paradise is lost for good, the individual stands alone and faces the world – a stranger thrown into a limitless and threatening world. The new freedom is bound to create a deep feeling of insecurity, powerlessness, doubt, aloneness, and anxiety. These feelings must be alleviated if the individual is to function successfully. (Fromm, 1941 p 80)

It was in Fromm's next book, *Man for Himself*, however, where he first fully develops his social criticism of American 'mass society' that influenced Riesman's writings on conformity among the 'lonely crowd' in the United States.[7] *The Lonely Crowd*'s famous concept of the 'other-directed' personality was, as Riesman himself puts it, 'stimulated by, and developed from, Erich Fromm's discussion of the 'marketing orientation' in *Man for Himself* (Riesman, [1950] 1961 pp 67–82).

American capitalism and the marketing character

Man for Himself: Towards a Psychology of Ethics is a continuation of *Escape from Freedom*'s theoretical project of developing a social psychology of modernity. While *Escape from Freedom* dealt with the pathology and destructiveness of Nazism, *Man for Himself* was an attempt to theorize the 'problem of ethics, of norms and values leading to the realization of man's self and his potentialities' (Fromm, 1947 p vii) in modern democratic societies. Modern capitalism, for Fromm, is fundamentally different psychologically from earlier societies and economic systems. Building on Marx, Simmel, and Lukács, Fromm's *Man for Himself* suggests that,

> The modern market is no longer a meeting place but a mechanism characterized by abstract and impersonal demand. One produces for this market, not for a known circle of customers; its verdict is based on laws of supply and demand; and it determines whether the commodity can be sold and at what price. No matter what the use value of a pair of shoes may be, for instance, if the supply is greater than the demand, some shoes will be sentenced to economic death; they might as well not have been produced at all. The market day is the 'day of judgement' as far as the exchange value of the commodities is concerned. (Fromm, 1947 p 68)

This economic situation leads, for Fromm, to a new conception of value regarding people and the self. As a consequence, the 'marketing character' emerges, a character orientation that is rooted in the 'experience of oneself as a commodity and of one's value as exchange value' (Fromm, 1947 p 68). Although the explicit ideology of modern society is built around the search for individual life and happiness, Fromm argues that with the development of a 'personality market', people have become more concerned with 'becoming salable'. This marketing personality has been growing rapidly only in the last few decades and finds its dominant social base among upper middle-class professionals, business executives, clerks, and those associated with sales and the mass media. While the earlier social characters were largely transmitted by the family, this new 'marketing orientation' is increasingly being formed by motion pictures, popular magazines, newspapers, and mass advertising and today, most of all, by social media. Instead of identifying with great poets and writers, or saints, modern people are connected to 'great people' by movie stars, sports heroes, or, more recently, TV celebrities and rock musicians.

Fromm insists that the marketing orientation has its positive aspects, particularly a flexibility and openness to change relative to the rigidity of the 'hoarding character' typical of those socialized with a nineteenth-century industrial work ethic or the conservative orientation of pre-modern peasants. Yet, ultimately, Fromm is a harsh critic of the modern personality. Since in modern society worth is determined by market forces that are beyond the individual's control, Fromm argues that,

> one's self esteem is bound to be shaky and in constant need of confirmation by others. Hence one is driven to strive relentlessly for success, and any setback is a severe threat to one's self-esteem; helplessness, insecurity, and inferiority feelings are the result. If the vicissitudes of the market are the judges of one's values, the sense of dignity and pride is destroyed. (Fromm, 1947 p 72)

Modern identity is as shaky as modern self-esteem for 'it is constituted by the sum total of roles one can play'. Since human beings cannot live doubting their identity, they must, Fromm argues, 'find the conviction of identity not in reference to himself and his powers but in the opinion of others about him'. For individuals shaped by the marketing orientation,

> prestige, status, success, the fact that he is known to others as being a certain person are a substitute for the genuine feeling of identity. This situation makes him utterly dependent on the way that others look at him and forces him to keep up the role in which he once had become successful. If I and my powers are separated from each other then, indeed, is my self constituted by the price I fetch. (Fromm, 1947 p 73)

These ideas had an enormous influence on American intellectual life, as Fromm's best-selling works of social criticism became one of the 'seeds of the 1960s' (Jamison and Eyerman, 1994). But these ideas also entered both American culture and sociology mediated by Fromm's intellectual relationship to Riesman. Fromm's concepts were central to the theoretical structure of *The Lonely Crowd: A Study of the Changing American Character* (1950), one of the founding classics of contemporary public sociology.

The Lonely Crowd revisited

Rooted in Fromm's theory of social character as well as the 'culture and personality' anthropology of the 1930s and the larger sociological tradition of historical comparative analysis from De Tocqueville to Weber, *The Lonely Crowd* is a book 'about the differences in social character between men of different regions, eras, and groups' (Riesman, [1950] 1961 p 3). The most enduring and interesting aspect of *The Lonely Crowd* is, of course, Riesman's famous distinction between 'tradition', 'other', and 'inner'-directed social characters which ensure conformity in different historical periods and types of societies. Riesman uses this provocative albeit overstated theory to examine the cultural and political consequences of the dramatic change from the 'inner-directed' character of nineteenth-century America to the 'other-directed' nature of contemporary life.

Modern American society, for Riesman, is dominated by a concern for 'niceness', not achievement, leisure, or competition; and 'consumerism', not production. Modern parents and teachers are anxiety ridden as their authority over children and students has been undermined by the media, youth culture, and a rapid social change that creates a situation where the 'other-directed child is often more knowing than his parents' (Riesman, [1950] 1961 p 50). Political life is also transformed by the rise of the 'other-directed' characters, as cynical 'insider-dopesters' replace the moralizing style of nineteenth-century American politics. Riesman outlined a provocative sociological analysis of conformity in contemporary American society that created a surprise academic best-seller and helped jump-start a rich tradition of mid-century social criticism.

The originality of *The Lonely Crowd* was its combination of the long-standing sociological interest in the transition from traditional '*Gemeinshaft*' to '*Gessellshaft*', Fromm's 'neo-Freudian' sociology of emotions, and Riesman's own insights and remarkable skills of observation of American culture. Fromm added a sophisticated psychological foundation to the sociological analysis of the decline of community and tradition and Weber's account of the culture of the modern Protestant ethic (essentially the 'inner-directed' character). Fromm himself, however, was tone deaf to the nuances and dynamics of the American middle-class and overgeneralized, as was typical of the German critical theorists.

Riesman's concept of 'tradition-directed' societies and character provides a social psychological analysis of *Gemeinshaft*. Human beings with 'tradition-directed' characters live in societies with a low level of individualism and strong ties to primary groups. Society is held together by belief systems based on religion, magic, and tradition. The conformity of an individual to a social role 'tends to reflect his membership in a particular age-group, clan, or caste' (Riesman, [1950] 1961 p 11) and he 'learns to understand and appreciate patterns which have endured for centuries' (Riesman, [1950] 1961 p 11). The tradition-directed character has, for Riesman, all but disappeared in modern American society except in pockets of black, French-Canadian, Southern, rural, and immigrant cultures.

'Tradition-directed' is clearly the least well-developed aspect of *The Lonely Crowd*, for the concept is a catch-all term modelled on earlier sociological accounts of the European Middle Ages and traditional societies throughout world history. Covering far too much history and anthropological data to be analytically compelling, and sharing a simplistic modern versus pre-modern view of societies outside European and American capitalism,[8] Riesman's focus on tradition as an organizing model for conformity simply provides a useful foil for his provocative analysis of modern American culture since the nineteenth century and the general 'inner'- 'other'-directed characters that came into being in modernity. It is Riesman's sociological analysis of the social psychology of the transition from early capitalism and modernity to contemporary society that remains most useful to social theorists.

For Riesman, as for Fromm, modern capitalism produces a new psychology. As the control of the primary group in a tradition directed society loosened because of industrialization, urbanization, and modern technology, 'a new psychological mechanism appropriate to the more open society is "invented"'. Social conformity is ensured for 'inner-directed' social characters by 'a tendency to acquire early in life an internalized set of goals' (Riesman, [1950] 1961 p 8) and a 'psychological gyroscope'. As Riesman describes this process, 'the source of direction for the individual is "inner" in the sense that is it implanted early in life by the elders and directed towards generalized but nonetheless inescapably destined goals' (Riesman, [1950] 1961 p 15). Set in early life, the gyroscope keeps the person 'on course' and 'capable of maintaining a delicate balance between demands upon him of his life goals and the buffetings of his external environment' (Riesman, [1950] 1961 p 16).

Modern society, particularly twentieth-century American society, is in the process of replacing both 'tradition'- and 'inner-directed' characters with 'other-directed' characters. 'Other-directed' individuals are not tied to either tradition or an internalized gyroscope. Conformity instead is ensured by people's 'tendency to be sensitized to the expectations and preferences of others' (Riesman, [1950] 1961 p 8) and a 'radar' that clues the individual in to the signals of contemporaries 'known to him or those with whom he is indirectly acquainted, through friends and through the mass media' (Riesman, [1950] 1961 p 21).

Three different forms of sanction for deviant behaviour correspond to Riesman's three types of societies and characters: shame for the tradition-directed, guilt for the inner-directed, and anxiety for the other-directed. Coercion and communal pressures of shame ensure conformity in traditional societies. Internalized guilt keeps the inner direction character in line with social expectations. The need to be 'liked' and a diffuse anxiety is the 'prime psychological lever' operating on the 'other-directed person' living in a society dominated by media messages and the constant pressures for conformity enforced by the inescapable pressure of 'a jury of his peers' (for a contemporary analysis of these dynamics that would have benefited from Riesman's work, see Lukiannoff and Haidt, 2018).

As a result of these social changes, schools in other-directed society will teach getting along more than getting smart and educated. Manipulation comes to dominate parent–child relations as well as the work environment, and consumerism is enforced by peer pressure-dominated culture, leisure activities, and popular narratives. The media and eventually higher education and politics will suffer from what Riesman called 'false personalization' where the boundaries between the personal and political become blurred and inauthentic emotions dominate public life. Much of Riesman's analysis is overplayed and his evidence thin. But his insights hit a deep chord in the 1950s and remain relevant. The damage done by the widespread desire for 'likes' on Facebook and the decline of the public sphere we see on Twitter, Instagram, and modern social media were prefigured in Riesman's analysis long before the digital revolution (Gardner and David, 2013).

The Lonely Crowd is an idiosyncratic book from sociology's past. The most glaring problem with the book is Riesman's attempt to link his theory of character with demographic trends, an aspect of the book that was widely criticized and from which Riesman dissociated himself. Talcott Parsons argued that Riesman's analysis of American society emphasized psychological character issues at the expense of larger and more important cultural norms and values best illuminated by functionalist sociological theory (White and Parsons, 1961). Seymour Martin Lipset suggested that Riesman's stress on the recent alleged historical transformation from 'inner'- to 'other'-directed character obscures the Tocquevillian insight that Americans have always been other directed relative to Europeans (Lipset and Löwenthal 1961). Radical sociologists like C. Wright Mills were critical of Riesman's argument that American politics is run by pluralistic veto groups rather than a power elite or a capitalist class. Sociologists like Dennis Wrong, Herbert Gans, and Alan Wolfe argue that Riesman's account of conformity is unfair to the culture, political good sense, and personal experience of what Gans (1988) has called 'middle American individualists'. Riesman's work can be understood as part of the long tradition of sociological analysis of the 'state of the masses' that Richard Hamilton and James Wright have shown often lacks empirical evidence and balance (Hamilton and Wright, 1986). Riesman was relatively inattentive to the pre-civil rights movement black liberation struggle that would soon shake the nation to its core, and he never was a leader in promoting feminist ideas and consciousness.

The flaws in his social science and limitations of his political sensibility are serious. Modern American society does not live with the leisure and abundance that Riesman and many other social critics from the 1950s assumed. For those who have jobs, the pace of life has increased, and work–family balance is far more of a concern than figuring out what to do with all our leisure time, as Riesman thought. Nor has American competitiveness been totally undermined by a culture of niceness and concern for feelings. If anything, sport and business competitiveness has spread to young women as well as men as Americans live in an era of mean and lean corporations and winning the 2019 FIFA Women's World Cup.

There are important elements of Riesman's analysis that could be given a social structural explanation as opposed to a social-psychological and cultural account. Steven Brint's comparative analysis of schooling around the world, for example, suggests that the focus on sociability in American high schools can be understood as a social structural characteristic of a school system weakly linked to job training and career advancement relative to the German or Japanese systems (Brint, 1998). Riesman's work would not pass the methodological demands of modern social science (Turner and Turner, 1990; Abbott, 1999). As a final point, *The Lonely Crowd* does not deal with gender, race, or the perspectives of North America's Indigenous peoples in ways that are adequate for contemporary sensibility and commitments.

Yet, there is much of Riesman's analysis that rings true today. Riesman makes a compelling argument that traditional forms of socialization in family, neighbourhood, and schools have been undermined by a culture that produces young 'consumers in training' not educated citizens and community participants. Riesman was surely onto something when he pointed to the undermining of traditional sources of socialization by youth peer culture, mass media, and now social media. The continued rise of celebrity-dominated culture and the enormous influence that new YouTube sensations hold over young people from Jordan Peterson to Joe Rogan along with the broader power of celebrity culture suggests that Riesman's analysis of 'false personalization' was on to something important. New age culture, armies of business consultants dealing with teamwork and getting along, and schools that seem to focus excessively on niceness and psychological adjustment do exist alongside the highly competitive, achievement oriented, and cut-throat culture of modern America (Brint, 1998).

While one would want to resist simplistic psychohistories or political psychology, there is a sense in which a growing number of politicians today exhibit 'other-directed' characteristics with few convictions of their own. Politicians suggest that they feel everyone's pain and have become masters of emotional manipulation to please others and thus get elected. And as sociologist Meštrović has pointed out, Riesman's analysis of how modern other-directed individuals would subject themselves to a 'jury of their peers' appears brilliant now in a world of TV and radio talk shows where 'ordinary people as well as celebrities literally bare all, disclose details of their lives that are so intimate that previous generations could not have imagined such confessions' (Meštrović, 1997 p 44). In a world where a reality TV star became president, shaking the nation to its core, Riesman's insights remain relevant.

Sociology, however, will only produce quality public sociologists if the discipline remembers that good social criticism must balance society's need for what Jeffrey Goldfarb has called both 'civility and subversion' (Goldfarb, 1998). When one thinks about how critical theory met America in the 1930s, 1940s, and 1950s, Fromm and the Frankfurt School represent the need for subversive intellectuals who challenge the core assumptions and legitimating myths of modern society and culture. Riesman's moderate temperament, grounded analysis, and respect for expertise and evidence, in contrast, provides a needed counterweight to a radical post-modern sociology that can become shrill, unreasonable, and excessively romanticized if it loses connections to mainstream culture and sociology (Brint, 1994). The post-colonial, queer, feminist, and critical theorists whom Lemert and Seidman value can bring much into sociology as a discipline (Seidman, 1994; Lemert, 1995), no doubt, but such contemporary thinkers who follow in the Riesman tradition such as Robert Bellah and Alan Wolfe are a valuable corrective to what Burawoy called the potential dogmatism of critical sociology (Burawoy, 2005). Wolfe, in particular, best represents the Riesman tradition of public sociology with his *The*

Politics of Petulance: America in an Age of Immaturity (2018), a book that sings the praises of Riesman along with other similar public sociologists such as Daniel Bell and Seymour Martin Lipset from the golden age of the public intellectual.

The genius of *The Lonely Crowd* was to raise larger critical questions about modern culture while allowing the analysis to be moderated by what Wolfe calls 'sociological realism' (Wolfe, 1993). The collaboration between Fromm and Riesman was so powerful precisely because Fromm provided subversive insights while moderating Riesman's civility. Yet Riesman was not simply a proponent of 'sociological realism' marginalized in the middle, as Wolfe suggests; he was a utopian thinker who seriously engaged the speculations and theoretical insights of great European thinkers such as Freud and Weber. Wolfe is right to insist that we must always ask whether our theoretical ideas have some relation to social reality, but we must also guard against theoretical complacency and loss of imagination (Wolfe, 1993). It was Wolfe, after all, who would write *One Nation, After All: What Americans Really Think about God, Country, Family, Racism, Welfare, Immigration, Homosexuality, Work, the Right, the Left and Each Other* (1998), a popular survey-based public sociological book. Wolfe argued that America really was not all that divided politically and culturally, a remarkable example of public sociological complacency that does not hold up well after Donald Trump.

Fromm is simply more predictive than Riesman and Wolfe about the forces that are tearing America apart, a good argument for keeping the radical and liberal versions of public sociology in dialogue with each other. Wolfe wants sociologists to lead in promoting maturity (Wolfe, 2018), but for many young people today watching their life prospects disappear in the wake of the recession caused by COVID-19 and the broader crisis of declining economic prospects under globalized capitalism, this can look more like complacency than insight.

There is a sociological dynamic to all this. More than Fromm, Riesman was able to place himself in a unique sociological position that holds lessons for those of us today who would like to see a renewal of public sociology. While Fromm largely reached his audiences through books and increasingly withdrew from the academic peer-review process, Riesman ended his career teaching at Harvard, and collaborated with younger sociologists and historians engaged in cutting-edge academic research as well as writing his own books and essays on social criticism.

Part of this story is about students as the first public for public sociology. Appointed to sociology at both the University of Chicago and Harvard, Riesman mostly taught undergraduates and was not central to the training of professional sociologists among graduate students. While not generally cited in major sociology journals today because he did not create a research programme for professional sociology, Riesman mostly published books, taught undergraduates, and consulted with elites on questions of higher education. Riesman came to be honoured as sociology's 'last public intellectual' (Patterson, 2002) and his example gave rise to a new genre of public sociology that combined more methodological care than either Riesman or Fromm possessed.

This is seen in the work of Robert Bellah and his collaborators *Habits of the Heart* (1985) and *The Good Society* (1991), whose research on individualism and community in America is explicitly inspired by *The Lonely Crowd* (1950). Bellah knew of Fromm's influence on Riesman, of course. The concept of 'expressive individualistic type' that the *Habits of the Heart* research team developed was similar to Riesman's 'autonomous character' (Bellah et al, 1985 p 49) and Fromm's own 'productive character'.

Fromm and Riesman had different politics, to be sure, and distinct network ties to mainstream sociology and the global intellectual elite. Fromm maintained his closest relationships with other similar social critics who wrote about society from the margins such as thinkers like Paulo Freire, Ivan Illich, and Lewis Mumford. Fromm was a global figure with strong connections to intellectuals in Latin America and Continental Europe. In contrast, Riesman was a very American thinker with limited global reach to his networks and influence. In effect, Riesman's thought maintained an engagement with research findings while still addressing larger social issues with a remarkable balance as an American moderate. Fromm's work, in contrast, sometimes veered off into an excessively prophetic mode with the one-sided tone we see again in many works of contemporary critical theory such as Allan Bloom's conservative rant against modern society (Maccoby, 1995). But Fromm also had a far more global appeal in his work, arguably becoming, like W. E. B. Du Bois a generation before him, one of sociology's first global public sociologists and intellectuals.

Finding the right balance between civility-realism versus utopian subversion remains a dilemma for public sociology. It was Riesman, more than Fromm, Bloom, or various contemporary social theorists like Zygmunt Bauman, who best combined the role of public sociologist while maintaining the proper respect for evidence and the craft of empirical sociological research. When Riesman met Fromm,

American social criticism and pragmatism met the grand tradition of European critical theory and American social science was made better for it.

There remains much historical work to be done, however, to gain a better picture of Riesman's relationship to twentieth-century American sociology especially concerning the strengths and the weaknesses of his public sociology. Andrew Abbott's discussion of Riesman in *Department and Discipline: Chicago Sociology at One Hundred* (1999) raises questions that deserve examination. While Abbott shares the professional vision that underlies the Turner and Turner (1990) critique of Riesman as a popular, not sociological, thinker, Abbott's critique is more substantial. He presents evidence that Riesman was far more involved in department politics, hiring battles, and the like, than the view of Riesman as public intellectual ambassador for sociology outside the professional trenches would suggest. The Abbott book is a cautionary reminder not to construct a 'Saint Riesman' for intellectuals as with 'Saint George Orwell' earlier in the century (Rodden, 1989).

Contemporary public sociologists still have much to learn from Riesman's work and career. It would be a mistake to dismiss Riesman's insights, principled concern with undergraduate teaching, and his broad interdisciplinary orientation either because of his liberal politics and relative marginality in a professional sociology that has become increasingly narrow and specialized. Fromm's radical public sociological vision is an essential resource for getting the best out of the Riesman tradition and moving beyond it because he was also central to the emergence of the New Left era radical public sociology. Fromm's influence can be seen both inside the discipline, through public intellectual debate among general readers, and in the streets of America during the protest movements of the 1960s. Let us turn now from Fromm's influence on liberal traditional public sociology to his even greater influence in shaping post-1960s radical and critical public sociology from Mills, to Hochschild and Sennett.

The Sane Society (1955) and the seeds of the 1960s

As close as Fromm and Riesman were personally, they had very different politics. Fromm was a socialist and critical of American capitalism in ways that Riesman never was. By the middle of the 1950s from his new home in Mexico after writings on ethics and religion in the 1940s and early 1950s (Fromm, 1947, 1950), Fromm was becoming as concerned about political issues as he had been in the 1930s. Beginning to write *The Sane Society* in 1953, the year of

Stalin's death, Fromm was entering the most intensely political years of his life. While Fromm's critique of German fascism had made him famous in *Escape from Freedom*, his political writing in *The Sane Society* was undertaken this time in the context of the Cold War, the nuclear arms race between the United States and the Soviet Union, and the growing power of American capitalism and culture in the post-Second World War period. Fromm feared both a global nuclear war and the degradation of modern societies created by market fundamentalism and the commercialization of everything.

The Sane Society was a best-selling critique of capitalist modernity with over 3 million copies sold worldwide. It would eventually play a major role in creating the political movements and academic Marxism of the 1960s, a major forgotten contribution to contemporary public sociology. *The Sane Society* represents a continuation of *Escape from Freedom* focused less on the authoritarianism and destructiveness of fascism and more on the mechanism of escape he had called 'automation conformity'. With fascism defeated and Stalin dead, Fromm turned his attention to how the capitalist marketing character produced mass conformity, epidemics of suicide, alcoholism, and an undermining of real democracy in a media-saturated individualistic corporate-dominated world. With the publication of the book, Fromm was at the height of his fame and influence. Sociologists Robert Merton and C. Wright Mills were both influenced by *The Sane Society*. A popular campus speaker, Fromm was invited to give the Distinguished George W. Gay Lecture at Harvard and was asked to give hundreds of talks at various venues (Friedman, 2013 p 185). *The Sane Society* is an important work of public sociology, both because of its influence and its content.

After reintroducing and refining the theory of the human condition he had developed in *Man for Himself*, Fromm offered a normative theory of human needs in *The Sane Society* that shapes the rest of his academic and popular writings. Human nature was not a blank slate, Fromm would argue, a position that Steven Pinker (2011) took later from a different theoretical and political position. Pinker's best-selling book was written from a more strictly evolutionary psychological perspective offering a set of answers to limited, but universal and unavoidable, questions posed by the human condition. Fromm, in contrast, saw the human condition as not purely hard-wired but flowing from the fact that humans were what Fromm called a 'freak of nature' who had developed individual consciousness and awareness of the inevitability of death. While the behaviour of other animals was largely determined by instincts, humans lived in culture based on and developed across generations by language, religions, and myths and thus had to choose how to live and cope with the anxiety that flowed from this freedom.[9]

Fromm's theory of social character was posited as the core mechanism that socializes human beings into a mode of existence. It functions as an unconscious emotional matrix whereby people come to want to live as they must live in order to survive in the society in the historical period they were thrown into without their pre-knowledge or choice.

Fromm leverages the new revision of Freud's ideas that he developed in *Man for Himself* and posits a theory of human needs that he argues is essential in order to evaluate whether societies are sane and healthy. Fromm rejected both the liberal relativism of the anthropology of the period as well as sociological functionalism dominant in sociology that suggested modern American society is near the pinnacle of emotional health. Fromm argues that a comprehensive theory of human needs can allow scholars to evaluate societies based on how well they serve human needs, a core issue for the socialist that Fromm was. Human beings, from this perspective, have a need for relatedness, transcendence, rootedness, identity, and a frame of orientation and devotion. Humans enjoy health and meaning if these needs are well served by the institutions and culture of a sane society. A pathological society, on the other hand, creates rampant narcissism as opposed to relatedness, destructiveness instead of creative transcendence, blood and soil fascism instead of healthy rootedness, herd conformity instead of true individuality, and the worship of irrationality over reason.

At the height of American intellectual's celebration of what democratic socialist Irving Howe called this 'age of conformity' (Howe, 1954), Fromm was having none of it. Fromm offered a powerful public sociological critique of modern capitalist society that would soon help define both a broader mass society literature (Kornhauser, 1959) and the radical politics of the New Left era. American society was affluent in ways that no nation had ever been before, Fromm was quick to concede, but in human terms it was producing suicide, alcoholism, and what Fromm called a pathology of normalcy and collective insanity. Fromm was not an expert in the empirical sociology of mental illness, alcoholism, and suicide, even by the standards of the time, but he believed in a science of society. Unlike much of the almost purely philosophical critiques of modernity produced by his former Frankfurt School collaborators in the *Dialectic of Enlightenment* (Horkheimer and Adorno, 1944) and *Eros and Civilization* (Marcuse, 1956a), however, Fromm marshalled data to make the case that modern society was producing emotional pathology in the form of increased levels of suicide, alcohol, drug addiction, and anxiety/depression.

Pushing against the boundaries that had emerged in post-war sociology between the psychological and the social as French sociologist Durkheim had earlier argued for, Fromm made a powerful case based on empirical data and historical-comparative analysis that there was a mental health crisis in advanced democratic societies. The affluence and peace that emerged after the Second World War were creating new and deep social problems.

Contemporary scholars would criticize Fromm's specific analysis based on decades of methodological improvements and empirical findings, but in retrospect, his general insights remain relevant. This is especially so given the current widespread mental health issues we see in contemporary societies and on relatively privileged college campuses (Lukiannoff and Haidt, 2018) as well as the broader contemporary opioid crisis in North America (Hedges, 2018). By the 1980s and 1990s, post-structuralist and post-modern critiques of humanism would lead many academics to be sceptical of attempts to judge societies by a universal standard. Fromm's analysis is certainly flawed by his tendency to erase and even pathologize the cultural values of pre-modern societies that he was still calling 'primitive'. But even with these caveats and critiques on the table, it is hard to argue against Fromm that modern societies were as healthy as their functionalist apologists were arguing at the time.

Fromm's critical perspectives retain relevance even today as we see new generations of scholars downplaying the problems that modern individuals face by comparing them to past sufferings and poverty (Pinker, 2018). Both Parsons then and Pinker now have held up modern advanced industrial societies as models for human health and development, a form of modernist propaganda for Fromm. Fromm argued that relative material wealth and economic security alone would not produce a sane society given the passionate need for meaning and relatedness inherent in the human condition that could not be satisfied under market fundamentalism.

Ever the neo-Marxist, Fromm insisted that we understand the modern dilemma in a historical materialist context. *The Sane Society* outlines an analysis, in turn, of pre-modern medieval Europe, early seventeenth- and eighteenth-century emerging capitalism, nineteenth-century laissez-faire capitalism, and mid-twentieth-century welfare state corporate-dominated capitalism. In each of these various stages of the emergence of the modern society, Fromm lays out an analysis of the means of production, the political and cultural conditions that flowed from the economic conditions, and the psychological glue, or form of social character as he would call it, that would make each type of society possible and functioning.

For the nineteenth century, for example, the social character was 'essentially competitive, hoarding, exploitative [and] aggressive' (Fromm, 1955a p 99) although in Europe some of the positive elements of feudal societies mitigated the brutality with non-market values promoted by religions and elites. These institutions retained a sense of honour, dignity and responsibility that would disappear in the twentieth and twenty-first centuries. As a student of Leon Trotsky and Rosa Luxemburg and as a deeply universalistic and prophetic thinker, Fromm was not blind to both the class and global implications of his analysis. He argued that the exploitative and hoarding character of nineteenth-century capitalism in Europe caused 'Europe to exploit Africa and Asia and her own working classes ruthlessly and without regard for human values' (Fromm, 1955a p 100).

The bulk of *The Sane Society* focuses on economic sociology, culture, and psychology of the mid-twentieth-century American version of capitalism. Fromm offers a devastating critique of Cold War America's domination by technology and centralized capital where both self-employed entrepreneurs and farmers were on the decline. Drawing on the work of Berle and Means, Fromm stressed how management had increasingly become separate from ownership. The social character was increasingly one of people who 'co-operate smoothly in large groups', who are oriented to mass consumption and whose 'tastes are standardized and can be easily influenced and manipulated' (Fromm, 1955a p 110). This type of capitalism required the 'Organization Man' (William H. Whyte's book of that name was published the same year) who 'feels free and independent, not subject to any authority or principle, or conscience' but are 'willing to be commanded, to do what is expected, to fit into the social machine without friction' (Fromm, 1955a p 110).

While Fromm's sociological analysis of this form of corporate capitalism was standard for the period (in the work of Riesman, Whyte, and C. Wright Mills), he offered a distinctively Marxist psychoanalytically inflected critique of American society that gained him a mass audience among students, activists and scholars well into the mid-1960s. Capitalism was not just an economic system that created structural unemployment and the exploitation of workers, it was a cultural system that permeated the very character structure and personalities of the population. Modern capitalism was no longer just about low wages and dangerous work, it was a system that was making quantification and abstractions central to people's way of life, replacing craft work, local community and human interaction with alienated work, culture, and personalities.

Four decades before political theorist Marshal Berman would pen the classic book *All that Is Sold Melts into Air* (1982) and half a century before sociologist Zygmunt Bauman would lament the rise of *Liquid Modernity* (1999), Fromm powerfully described a world where 'science, business, politics, have lost all foundations and proportions' (Fromm, 1955a p 120). Drawing directly from Marx's early economic and philosophic manuscripts of 1844, Fromm (1955a p 22) claimed that man has become 'estranged from himself'. Over half a century before the creation of the internet and social media and over a decade before Donald Trump was old enough to evade the Vietnam War draft, Fromm put it in ways that seen all too relevant today despite the obviously gendered humanist language he used:

> We live in figures and abstraction; since nothing is concrete, nothing is real. Everything is possible, factually and morally. Science fiction is not different from science fact, nightmares and dreams from the events of next year. Man has been drawn thrown out from any definite place where he can overlook and manage his life and the life of society. He is driven faster and faster by the forces which originally were created by him. In this wild whirl he thinks, figures, busy with abstractions, more and more remote from concrete life. (Fromm, 1955a p 120)

A critic of modern bureaucratization as much as capitalist exploitation, Fromm believed, as Herbert Marcuse would argue almost a decade later in *One-Dimensional Man* (1964 [2013]), that 'alienation as we find it in modern society is almost total' (Fromm, 1955a p 124). This was true not just on the worker assembly line or in the mines as Marxists would argue. Along with C. Wright Mills in *White Collar* (1951), Fromm believed that managers were alienated themselves even while they see the people they must administer as things to be manipulated (Fromm, 1955a p 126). Unlike Riesman who was a liberal, and William Whyte who was explicitly pro-capitalist, both Fromm and Mills were radicals and shared a critique of the bureaucratic mentality that they felt had entered into contemporary socialist and labour parties, organized unions, and indeed, the statist communism in the Soviet Union that had consolidated itself after Stalin's terror.

Fromm was far more explicitly Marxist than Mills, however, and more deeply schooled in the writings of Marx, Engels, Trotsky, and Rosa Luxemburg. Fromm's Marxism is evident in the middle section of *The Sane Society* when he embarks on a remarkable and detailed discussion of the concept of alienation and how it permeates human work, everyday experience, even religion and especially consumption, culture, play, and mental health in modern society. While capitalism was undermining the traditional authority of monarchies, elites, and their culture, it was replacing authoritarian rule not with what Fromm called 'rational authority' but with the anonymous authority of mass conformity, rumours, peer pressure, and the manipulation and propaganda of films, television, advertisements, and newspapers. Parents are now their children's friends, 'every desire must be satisfied immediately', and no wish 'must be frustrated' (Fromm, 1955a p 164). Love has now become 'a short lived sexual desire, which must be satisfied immediately' (Fromm, 1955a p 165) and people talk about and share their most intimate secrets and trivial details of their lives, in a context where there is 'no inhibition, no sense of shame, no holding back' (Fromm, 1955a p 168). Fun and consumption have replaced insight and psychological depth as the goal for therapists, and psychologists have become 'specialists of manipulation' (Fromm, 1955a p 169). Even religion has been commercialized where God can become your 'partner in business, to "sell" religion with the methods and appeals used to sell soap' (Fromm, 1955a p 177).

In our social media-dominated world, anxiety is now widespread and the public–private divisions in modern societies have broken down – both central predictions in *The Sane Society*. Fromm was never as pessimistic as his Frankfurt School collaborators, however, so he outlines a history of various critiques of modernity and a set of proposal for 'answers' and 'roads to sanity'. Fromm's great strength was never as a political strategist, but his ideas for change still have much to offer contemporary public sociology.

More than most contemporary public sociologists, Fromm engaged with ideas across a broad range of political and disciplinary perspectives. For Fromm, the decay and barbarism that we saw in the twentieth century was illuminated by nineteenth-century ideas coming from 'varied philosophical and political views' ranging from 'the Swiss conservative, Burckhardt; the Russian religious radical, Tolstoy; the French anarchist, Proudhon as well as his compatriot, Baudelaire; the American anarchist, Thoreau, and later his more politically minded compatriot, Jack London; and the German revolutionary, Karl Marx' (Fromm, 1956a p 210). From twentieth-century thinkers, Fromm drew insights and inspiration from a range of thinkers including British socialist R. W. Tawney and his classic *The Acquisitive Society*

(1921), Australian-born Harvard organizational theorist and industrial psychologist Elton Mayo, sociologist Émile Durkheim, novelist Aldous Huxley, and scientist and socialist Albert Einstein.

Influenced as he was as a young man by the Polish-German Marxist Rosa Luxemburg, Fromm argued for a socialist alternative to modern capitalism while being aware that the barbarism of authoritarian fascism, anti-democratic communism or elitist super-capitalism were possible futures. Fromm's own preferred vision drew from Marxism, to be sure, but it was ultimately a version of democratic utopian socialism that was less concerned with purely economic issues than orthodox Marxism and more focused on community engagement, democratic participation, and ethical humanist principles. *The Sane Society* played a pivotal role in popularizing the Marxist theory of alienation and the broad humanistic socialist critique of capitalism in America during the late 1950s and early 1960s.

Yet Fromm was no doctrinaire Marxist. The emergence of the innovative New Left era student movement as represented by the Students for a Democratic Society (SDS) and their Port Huron Statement (an important political manifesto for young radicals in the 1960s) was shaped by Fromm's nuanced defence and critique of Marxist ideas. Tom Hayden and the young American radicals were most influenced by C. Wright Mills' radical utopian pragmatism (Aronowitz, 2012), but they also read and drew on *The Sane Society*. Fromm's ideas were far more visionary than the social democratic perspectives they were exposed to through the young Michael Harrington and the Socialist Party of America (Isserman, 2000).

Fromm was critical of the bureaucratic and anti-democratic nature of Soviet Communism that he saw as unequal, unjust, and a distortion of the original Marxist humanist vision. Fromm was also critical of European social democracy, a politics appealing to young radicals in the late 1950s and 1960s. Communitarian socialism required ethical and moral leadership, a concern with freedom and emotions, decentralization, and a focus on human scale for community life, work, and democratic participation. Believing that capitalism deepens the cultural pathologies he had outlined in the early sections of the book, Fromm argued for a modification of Marxist socialism that puts more emphasis on the role of 'cultural factors' that 'influence the economic basis of society' (Fromm, 1955a p 263). Rejecting Marx's 'romantic idealization of the working class' (Fromm, 1955a p 263), Fromm dissents from Marx's mistaken view that the 'socialization of the means of production was not only the necessary, but also the sufficient condition for the transformation of the capitalist into a socialist co-operative society' (Fromm, 1955a p 265). Fromm argued that Marx, despite his own theoretical insight into historical materialism, did not fully understand that 'the only things that matter are the actual and realistic conditions of work, the relation of the worker to his work, his fellow workers, and to those directing the enterprise' (Fromm, 1955a p 166).

Fromm offered a powerful theoretical critique of the foundations of the Marxist tradition that he claimed did not fully grasp the 'complexity of human passions' (Fromm, 1955a p 262). Marx thus grossly overestimated the prospects for socialist revolution in the late nineteenth century and underestimated the prospects for barbarism that we would see in Nazism and Stalinism in the twentieth century. For Fromm, there was lack of realism in Marx that other socialist as well as conservative thinkers avoided. This 'oversimplified, overoptimistic rationalistic picture' of human nature was 'responsible for many of the theoretical and political errors in Marx's and Engels' thinking and it was the basis for the destruction of Socialism which began with Lenin' (Fromm, 1955a p 265). Fully aware of the economic, political, and moral brutality of Stalin and Soviet communism and how different this was from Marx's humanist vision, Fromm believed that some of the roots of this political monstrosity were due to Marx's 'dangerous errors' particularly his 'neglect of the moral factor in man' (Fromm, 1955a p 264). Fromm argued that Marx assumed that 'the goodness of man would assert itself automatically when the economic changes had been achieved'. Marx did not understand that a 'new moral orientation' was required, without which 'all political and economic changes' would be 'futile' (Fromm, 1955a p 264). Most fundamentally,

> The famous statement at the end of the Communist Manifesto that the workers 'have nothing to lose but their chains,' contains a profound psychological error. With their chains they have also to lose all those irrational needs and satisfactions which were originated while they were wearing the chains. In this respect, Marx and Engels never transcended the naïve optimism of the eighteenth century. (Fromm, 1955a p 164)

Fromm drew heavily from the earlier non-Marxist radical traditions such as the utopian socialism of Charles Fourier and Robert Owen and anarchism of Proudhon and Bakunin. Fromm also drew from examples of local communities of work in Belgium, Switzerland, and the Netherlands, with a particular focus on the French watch-case factory in Boimondau (Fromm, 1955a p 306). He engaged research on industrial social psychology to explore concrete plans to democratize and humanize the actual conditions of work in ways that traditional social democratic parties had not succeed in doing.

Fromm also offered a set of proposals for political and cultural transformation, a form of a policy sociology. One of his most important proposals in *The Sane Society* was his argument for the establishment of a national guaranteed income, what Fromm called a 'universal subsistence guarantee'. For Fromm, people were not naturally lazy; they desired meaningful work that would allow connection to society although there ought to be limits to benefits in order to 'avoid the fostering of a neurotic attitude which refuse any kind of social obligation' (Fromm, 1955a p 336). In the 1960s and 1970s, the idea of a national guaranteed income was promoted by conservatives such as free-market economist Milton Friedman and American President Richard Nixon. In the early months of 2020, the idea was given prominence again among liberals and was adopted as the signature idea of the American Democratic Party presidential primary candidate Andrew Yang. Fromm developed the idea of a national guaranteed income in more detail in 'The Psychological Aspects of the Guaranteed Income', a chapter in a book entitled *The Guaranteed Income* (Theobald, 1966a) published at the height of Fromm's political involvement in the 1960s.

With automation putting more and more people out of work, the powerful forces of globalization creating structural unemployment, and the COVID-19 crisis exposing the vulnerability of the population to economic disruption, Fromm's proposal from the 1950s appears to be an idea whose time has come. Others will have more detailed things to say about the economics of this, as Fromm was never a first-rate policy sociologist. Fromm generally thought the economic problems of modern capitalism were on the way to being solved, something that was clearly not true. Yet Fromm's ideas on the social psychology of the issue are worth reconsideration and empirical study in light of new circumstances.

The crisis of democracy created by social media-inspired fake news, conspiracy theories, and the increasingly outrageous propaganda promoted by cable TV in the United States vindicates Fromm's pessimism about the possibilities for democratic deliberation. Fromm was right about the destructive influence of mass media-mediated emotional manipulation in political matters, something he saw first in Nazi Germany but recognized again in the culture industries of the mid-twentieth-century United States. Fromm argued that it was important to reintroduce town hall meetings into modern industrial democracies so that small groups could regularly meet face to face to discuss political issues free from media propaganda. Basic information for these discussions would be provided by what Fromm called a 'non-political cultural agency' composed of 'personalities from the fields of art, science, religion, business and politics, whose outstanding achievements and moral integrity are beyond doubt'.

Fromm was not a practical political organizer and talented organization builder, so these ideas never became reality in anything that Fromm himself created. Nonetheless, the 'participatory democracy' championed by the New Left generation in the SDS came out of a dialogue stimulated by *The Sane Society* and C. Wright Mills' grittier American utopianism (Miller and Miller, 1994) The rise of Trumpism and global right-wing authoritarianism, as well as various populist revolts and revulsion against the technocratic liberal elite, has created new interest in attempts to build face-to-face democracy around the world. Practically speaking, it is a tall order to address this crisis of democracy, but it vindicates Fromm's basic insights.

Fromm's ideas about education outlined in *The Sane Society* and elsewhere are also relevant today, particularly as we face a growing dissatisfaction with the state of higher education. Fromm argued for reforms of educational systems for children and young and older adults so that they combine both practical and theoretical knowledge, an unhelpful division critiqued by his close friend Ivan Illich's concept of 'deschooling society' (1971). Fromm was not as active and talented an undergraduate teacher as David Riesman and he had no interest in the administration and practical reform of higher educational institutions. Riesman wrote extensively and insightfully about higher education and university leadership issues (Riesman, 1956; Jencks and Riesman, 1968; Grant and Riesman, 1978; McLaughlin and Riesman, 1990).

Yet Fromm was deeply committed to alternative forms of education, having written the foreword to A. S. Neill's influential *Summerhill: A Radical Approach to Child Rearing* (1960). Fromm knew Paulo Freire and the Brazilian radical's classic, *The Pedagogy of the Oppressed* (1970) drew explicitly from Fromm's analysis of irrational versus rational authority. Building on *Escape from Freedom* and *Man for Himself*, *The Sane Society* had an influence on Freire's 'banking model' critique of traditional education which in turn led to the creation of what we call critical pedagogy today.

The core of Fromm's critique in *The Sane Society* of today's 'neo-liberal' higher education remains valid. Fromm would be appalled by professors who are obsessed by their citation counts or their scholarly brand on Twitter. Fromm would also be rightly contemptuous of the ways that scholars have been turned into celebrities selling their services, charisma, and personalities on the academic marketplace in universities managed by administrators Veblen once called the 'captains of erudition'. These pathologies are ultimately created by the very structures and logic of our societies analysed in *The Sane Society*.

The final vision for the future offered *in The Sane Society* takes Fromm out of the policy realm and closer to what Michael Maccoby would call his 'prophetic voice' (Maccoby, 1995). Fromm believed that modern societies would not be sane and healthy without a revival of collective art and rituals and eventually new humanistic religions. Fromm rejected the idea that the choice between religion and atheism was the most important division in societies as new atheists such as Richard Dawkins and the late Christopher Hitchens would argue. *The Sane Society* contended that the core choice faced by humanity was between authoritarian or humanistic belief systems. Existing religions were themselves divided by both authoritarian and humanistic elements, an argument Fromm had developed in *Psychoanalysis and Religion* (1950), a book that came out of lectures he had given at Yale.

Fromm argued for a humanistic spirituality partly because he saw the deeply authoritarian potential of Stalinism as an atheistic alternative religion. More broadly, he offered a political vision that recognized the greater freedom and wealth in Western democracies relative to Soviet communism while also insisting that war, and what he called 'robotism', were fundamental threats to humanistic values everywhere. Fromm argued for a spiritual as well as a political revival of humanistic values, an argument connecting *The Sane Society* to Fromm's earliest professional sociology contributions in his essay 'The Dogma of Christ' first appearing in German in 1930. Fromm's analysis of the social origins of Jesus Christ's ideas as expressing the revolutionary stirrings of oppressed social classes and groups remains an important early contribution to the sociology of religion but it also represents Fromm's prophetic voice and visionary politics, something that does not fit well within the logic of professional sociology.

Part professional sociology and part prophetic politics, *The Sane Society* was pivotal to Fromm's vision and practice of public sociology. The world and Fromm's priorities were changing and his status as a public sociologist would never again reach the same heights. Perhaps this will change as his sociological vision gets rediscovered as seems to be happening today but for a Fromm revival to succeed it is necessary to move beyond some of his limitations as a thinker.

Conclusion: Fromm's influence on professional Cold War/1960s-era sociology

Fromm's reputation as a scholar and public intellectual was at its height in the middle of the Cold War before the rise of the 1960s movements. *The Sane Society* sold over 3 million copies and was reviewed positively in *The New York Times* and in various sociology and other academic journals (McLaughlin, 1998a). Versions and revisions of Fromm's ideas would enter the core of American professional sociology in the decades after 1955 but they tended not to be associated with Fromm himself for a variety of sociological reasons.

The stress on personality, culture, and class that Fromm helped pioneer would enter mainstream professional sociology through the enormous productivity and creativity of Melvin Kohn's social structure and personality school (Kohn, 1989). Kohn was influenced by Fromm early on but possessed professional research skills and an academic appointment that allowed him to develop a professional sociology version of social character theory that went far beyond that which Fromm accomplished (Kohn, 1989).

Nancy Chodorow and a generation of psychoanalytic feminists found inspiration in the revised versions of Freud and the critiques of the patriarchal biases of the Freudian movement that both Horney and Fromm developed (Chodorow, 1978, 1989, 1999). Chodorow and other feminist psychoanalytic sociologists often did not draw on Fromm even though they were clearly building on foundations he had created. Psychoanalytic sociologists were generally more concerned with engaging professional forms of sociological knowledge than Fromm was. Chodorow created a broader theory of object relations that influenced psychosocial theories and sociological research but with very little engagement with Fromm's work.

Arlie Hochschild also built on Fromm's analysis of the marketing character and the commercialization of feeling. To it, she added a more rigorous attention to methods, more precision in focusing in on specific industries, professions and jobs, a feminist lens and, Goffman's insights into impression management and surface and deep acting (Hochschild, 1979, 1982). Alongside the development of the sociology of emotions that Hochschild pioneered, 1960s- and 1970s-era sociology would see the explosion of Marxist influenced theories of alienation, many of them influenced by Fromm's popularization of Marx's ideas in America especially after the publication of *Marx's Concept of Man*.

Fromm was a major international public sociologist in the middle of the twentieth century but there were storm clouds on the horizon for his reputation. The analytical and methodological demands of professional sociology increased dramatically in post-war America in the 1950s and 1960s as increasing credentialism, disciplinary consolidation, and higher publication demands made the old-fashioned public intellectual in the style of Fromm and Riesman less influential in the modern research university.

There was a pull as well as a push involved as Fromm moved away from a focus on scholarly work to political activism. Throughout the 1950s and 1960s, his political engagement in the United States from his base in Mexico became more explicit. Fromm's public standing declined after the publication of *The Sane Society* and *The Art of Loving* and what become known as the Fromm–Marcuse debate in *Dissent* magazine in 1955–1956. It is because of the broader decline of Fromm's intellectual reputation in the 1960s and 1970s in the United States that we do not remember his role as a global public sociologist. Revisiting this history is essential work in rediscovering sociology's great global public sociologist of the Cold War era. It is to the intellectual history of the mid-1950s in America that we now turn in order to understand how Fromm became a 'forgotten public sociologist' (McLaughlin, 1998a).

4

How Fromm Became a Forgotten Public Sociologist

Fromm was at the height of his fame and scholarly status in 1955 after the publication of *The Sane Society* but in 1955–1956, two publishing events occurred that led to his rapid decline in prestige. This broader reputational decline led to the eventual forgetting of his role as one of the disciplines' great public sociologists. The Fromm–Marcuse debate in *Dissent* magazine in 1955–1956 and the publication of *The Art of Loving* in 1956 seriously damaged Fromm's intellectual reputation. The decline in his scholarly stature took decades but Fromm was no longer cited in professional sociology by the 1980s and early 1990s. This in turn made him unavailable as a resource and inspiration for the revival of 'public sociology' in the early years of the twenty-first century. This history is worth revisiting.

In 1955, Frankfurt School-associated German philosopher Herbert Marcuse was in exile in the United States and was just about to publish *Eros and Civilization: A Philosophical Inquiry into Freud* (1956a). Marcuse adapted the appendix of his book on what he viewed as the radical Freud and published it as an essay attacking Fromm and the neo-Freudians in the left-wing magazine, *Dissent*. *Dissent* was a journal with low circulation but high intellectual status and was central to the world of what intellectual historians call 'The New York Intellectuals' (Wald, 2017). The rebuttal and counter-rebuttal exchange between Fromm and Marcuse eventually became known as the Fromm–Marcuse debate among critical theorists and intellectual historians. Their dialogue played a major role in both creating Marcuse's reputation as an important radical intellectual during the 1960s era and in damaging Fromm's scholarly and intellectual standing, especially in the United States.

The fact that Fromm published the best-selling book *The Art of Loving* just after the Fromm–Marcuse debate was a fateful coincidence. *The Art of Loving* was an analysis of the contradictions of love in market societies. It sold over 25 million copies worldwide and was translated into more than twenty-two languages. Fromm's enemies jumped on the book, using a distorted reading of it to unfairly define him as the Norman Vincent Peale of the left. Peale was a popular Protestant minister famous in the United States for his notion of the 'power of positive thinking'. Associating Fromm with Peale was defining him as a lightweight popular writer who was neither a first-rate scholar nor a radical thinker. This all reinforced a negative framing of Fromm for many radical intellectuals, especially later as the culture wars of the 1960s took off.

This war of reputations damaged Fromm's standing among American sociologists because it occurred in the context of the discipline's continued attempts to professionalize and secure a stable position as a scientific discipline in research universities during the Cold War. *The Sane Society* had been well received in the discipline and *Escape from Freedom* and *Man for Himself* were cited in major sociology journals. After 1955–1956, however, professional sociologists would increasingly define him as a popular writer rather than a scholar.

This chapter will offer an analysis of how the Fromm–Marcuse debate and the publication of *The Art of Loving* led to Fromm's dismissal as an important public sociologist. I will draw partly on Bourdieu's field theory framework for help in understanding the tensions between public sociology and the relatively autonomous field of academic status hierarchies (Bourdieu, 1988; Burawoy, 2005). Understanding the depreciation of Fromm as a public sociologist, however, requires emphasis on the influence of the small journals, non-academic intellectuals and commercial presses (Coser, 1965; Kadushin, 1974).

Fromm became a forgotten public sociologist because of important sociological mechanisms that remain relevant today as we ponder the fate of public sociology in the age of social media. Firstly, Fromm's appeal to millions of readers in *The Art of Loving* was a major challenge to the professional boundaries that sociologists were attempting to secure in the post-war period. Sociologists have long realized that writing to the public could have important benefits for individuals' careers and for the discipline as a whole. Even Robert Merton, the major representative of professional sociology in the United States in the 1960s, published his books with commercial presses while aspiring to make sociology a science (Wolfe, 2018). The professional reaction to Fromm's success in reaching mass publics, however, makes visible the symbolic boundaries operating in the field (Lamont and Fournier, 1992) that distinguish public intellectual/public sociological work in elite outlets from popularization/common sense. The status hierarchies upheld by elite newspapers, magazines, commercial book publishers, and book reviewers remained important for an insecure discipline.

The forgetting of Erich Fromm's public sociology has to do with the policing of the boundaries between professional and popular sociology. Burawoy (2005) asserted that professional and policy sociologists are responsible for situating public and critical sociology outside the borders of the core of the discipline. There is much truth to this perspective. The most quantitative, technical, and specialized scholars in sociology have indeed been central to keeping out public sociologists, activists, undergraduate teachers, and scholars who write like journalists from the core peer-reviewed journals that define the elite of the discipline.

The implicit debate about whether Fromm was a serious public sociologist is connected to this larger division in the discipline. Are we analysing society from above looking for general laws, patterns, and explanations (Collins, 1981), or are sociologists just professional moralists giving students and the public advice about right and wrong (Wolfe, 1989)? Fromm's *The Art of Loving* draws from sociology, psychoanalytic insights, philosophy, and historical analysis to theorize how love operates in modern market societies while giving people direction to what he viewed as the 'art of living'. Most scholars would insist that public sociology is not 'self-help' or advice for living, but there is a major contradiction in public sociology that the reaction to Fromm's work highlights. The response to Fromm's left-wing *The Art of Loving* in the 1950s illuminates an implicit set of assumptions. While left-liberal sociologists often have a vision for how life should be lived, we generally reject explicit attempts to write about this openly. Work that does is defined as self-help, social work, therapy, or common sense.

There is a current debate about the politics of professors whereby sociology is seen as an excessively radical discipline that promotes Marxism and political correctness rather than analysis (Gross and Fosse, 2012). This debate cannot be understood without a deeper analysis of the academic field in the environment of research universities and liberal arts colleges. The logic of this field is structured by constructed divisions between facts and values, and analysis, moral judgement, and advice (Townsley, 2006). We will illustrate this division by showing how *The Art of Loving* was placed outside the realms of sociology even while it helped create a genre of public sociological advice on love, relationships, intimacy, *and* a research tradition on the commercialization of feelings and sex. But first we must start with the Fromm–Marcuse debate.

The Fromm–Marcuse debate

The bitter conflict between Fromm and the Frankfurt School led him to under-emphasize his connections to the critical theorists. Nor did the Horkheimer circle go out of their way to write about Fromm's pivotal role in the early years of their work. Fromm was hardly mentioned in *The Authoritarian Personality* (1950), even though Fromm had been pivotal to the development of the F-scale, the central theoretical innovation of that highly influential work of social psychology. Adorno had made the case against Fromm and his Freudian revisionism in the late 1930s and, in various essays and articles in the 1940s, 1950s, and early 1960s (Adorno, 1967, 1968), where he criticized Fromm's views on Freud and American culture. Generally, however, both parties to the conflict moved on to their own careers and intellectual agendas; Fromm as a social critic and psychoanalytic therapist and clinician. The Frankfurt School operated as philosophers and academic researchers in the United States and then in Germany for Horkheimer and Adorno when they returned home.

Marcuse was relatively obscure in 1955 and not a central figure in the Horkheimer circle. He had been a student of the great German philosopher Martin Heidegger who turned out to be militantly pro-Nazi. Marcuse did not share Heidegger's politics but, like Hannah Arendt, he learned a great deal from his philosophical teaching. Along with the other Frankfurt School scholars, Marcuse went into exile during Nazi rule, but he was never in the inner core of the Horkheimer circle. In fact, Horkheimer wanted Marcuse to get a job as a professor so that he would not have to support him with the significant but finite funds he had at his disposal (Wiggershaus, 1995). Getting an academic job was not generally easy for German war refugees (Coser, 1984); this was true for Marcuse despite the fact that he had published an important book on Hegel (Marcuse [1941], 1956). Like many émigré intellectuals, Marcuse fell between the cracks in wartime and post-war America (Coser, 1984). He ended up working for the United States Government's Office of Strategic Services (OSS) and then the State Department, providing analyses about Marxism, Russia, and Germany in the Cold War.

The publication of *Eros and Civilization* created a higher intellectual profile for him, beginning his rise in academic status and fame. By the late 1960s and early 1970s, he would be widely seen as the major

Frankfurt School philosopher and, for his critics, the guru of New Left radicals in America. In 1955, however, it was Fromm who was famous, and Marcuse was relatively unknown and attempting to make his mark with a critique of Fromm in *Dissent* magazine.

Dissent and the anti-Stalinist left

Dissent magazine was founded by Irving Howe and Lewis Coser in 1953 as a home for the anti-Stalinist left in America in the context of the Cold War and McCarthyism. *Dissent* recruited Fromm for its original editorial board in 1953 as they positioned themselves to raise money and add intellectual prestige. Coser and Howe were relatively unknown at the time and *Dissent* politics was on the margins of American intellectual life. Fromm was among the most famous American socialists of the time and he gave significant amounts of money to left-wing causes (Friedman, 2013). It made sense that Coser and Howe would recruit Fromm to *Dissent*'s board, but they did not like each other personally, it turns out, and they had different political sensibilities despite shared democratic socialist identities.

Howe and Coser both played a key role in constructing Fromm's reputation among the American left. Howe had been a Trotskyist in the 1930s as part of the network at young radicals' Alcove 1 at the City College of New York (CCNY), a social circle that included such later intellectual luminaries as Daniel Bell, Irving Kristol, Nathan Glazer, and Seymour Martin Lipset. By the early 1950s, Howe had moved from Trotskyism to a democratic socialist position; *Dissent* was his attempt to keep radical ideas alive when revolutionary politics were not on the table. Two decades later, Howe wrote his best-selling history of Jewish immigration to New York City, *World of our Fathers* (1976). A masterful literary critic, Howe played an important role in reviving Yiddish literature in America. Today, he is an iconic example of what we would call a public intellectual, known more for his essays than his academic work as an English professor at the City University of New York until his death in 1993. In the 1950s, Howe was deeply anti-Stalinist and active in American socialist politics, a key left intellectual figure outside the American Communist Party. Howe disliked Fromm intensely because he saw him as too utopian and sentimental and he would not have been impressed with his views on Israel.[1]

More important for Fromm's reputation among sociologists, however, was Coser. Lewis Coser had fled Nazi-controlled Germany and, following Rose Coser's example, studied sociology with Robert Merton at Columbia. A social democrat and left-wing intellectual,

Coser was in the process of building a career in the 1950s as a future American Sociological Association president. Coser would later make his mark in sociology by writing about the theoretical work of German sociologist Georg Simmel and contributing to the development of a synthesis of Parsonian functionalism and 'conflict theory'. Coser and Howe shared democratic socialist politics and collaborated on writing a history of the American Communist Party (Coser and Howe, 1957).

Fromm was never close to either Howe or Coser but was willing to give money and lend his prestige as a major socialist intellectual, anti-Stalinist, and popular author to this fledgling magazine of the democratic left. Fromm later came down on different sides in battles within the left in the late 1950s and early 1960s, but their relationship had been undermined before that because of Howe and Coser's decision to publish Marcuse's polemical critique of neo-Freudians and Fromm in *Dissent* in 1955–1956.

Marcuse's critique of Fromm: conformist revisionist?

'The Social Implication of Freudian Revisionism', published in the summer 1955 issue of *Dissent*, was a brilliant piece of polemical writing. Marcuse argued that orthodox psychoanalytic instinct theory was truly radical, suggesting that Fromm and other 'revisionists' Karen Horney and Harry Stack Sullivan had transformed powerful and radical Freudian ideas into conformist banalities. Echoing arguments that Theodor Adorno had been making in various publications since the late 1930s, and the internal polemics within Horkheimer's critical theory circles (Funk, 1982; Burston, 1991; McLaughlin, 1999), Marcuse claimed that even though Freud and most psychoanalysts were committed to bourgeois society, 'psychoanalysis was a radically critical theory' (Marcuse, 1955b p 221).

Borrowing the language of revisionism from the Marxist tradition, Marcuse argued that Fromm's move from orthodox Freudian theory had conservative political implications. The neo-Freudian purging of Freud's theory of the death instinct and the hypothesis of the primal horde along with the metapsychology based on libido theory had meant, for Marcuse, that the 'explosive connotations of Freud's theory of the unconscious and sexuality were all but eliminated'. The central theme of the revisionists, according to Marcuse, was that the present environment caused more conflict than allowed for in the orthodox Freudian biological model that focuses on sexual instincts and the first five or six years of life. As Marcuse puts it, revisionists, move from past to present, from biology to culture and constitution to environment, discarding libido theory and substituting 'relatedness'. The result is an eclectic and banal theory and the laboring of the obvious, of routine wisdom.

Marcuse prefers orthodox Freud to the revisionist critics, claiming that Freud's writings are full of irony, insight, and a willingness to squarely face the inevitable conflict between instinctual necessity and society. In contrast, the neo-Freudian 'mutilation' of instinct theory simply accentuates the positive, preaches about 'inner strength and integrity', and turns social issues into spiritual concerns. As a consequence, 'neurosis becomes a moral problem and people are blamed for not being able to be self-realizers'. The writings of the neo-Freudians, 'come frequently close to that of the sermon, or of the social worker ', suggesting Norman Vincent Peale's 'power of positive thinking' instead of radical politics. In the defence of his argument, Marcuse undertakes a brief discussion of such early Freudian revisionists as Adler, Jung, and Reich. Marcuse quotes a passage from Sullivan that links neurosis with political radicalism, and contrasts Fromm's analysis of love (that would soon find its way into the book *The Art of Loving*) with Freud's discussion of what he sees as the inherent conflict between male sexual desire and respect for women. Marcuse then quotes and dissents from Karen Horney's critique of the Freudian theory of the death instinct.

Arguing against what he claims is the revisionist goal of 'optimal development of a person's potentialities and the realization of his individuality', Neo-Freudians, despite their internal differences, help adjust people to present society as opposed to encouraging 'transgressions beyond the established form of civilization and to radically new "modes" of "personality" and "individuality", incompatible with the prevailing ones'. While Marcuse's essay is framed explicitly around the issue of Freudian theory, there was obviously a Marxist and Nietzschean subtext to the polemic. Ever since Marx's attacks on the utopian socialists, Marxists have looked poorly on moral discourse preferring hard-headed 'materialism' to ethical appeals. Marcuse is rooted in this tradition, as well as a Nietzschean philosophy when he claims that:

> Fromm revives all time-honored values of idealist ethics as if nobody had ever demonstrated their conformist and repressive features. He talks of the productive realization of the personality, of care, responsibility, and respect for one's fellow men, of productive love and happiness as if man could actually practice all of this and remain sane and full

of 'well-being' in a society which Fromm himself describes as one of total alienation, dominated by the commodity relations of the 'market'. (Marcuse, 1955b p 231)

Thus Fromm, for Marcuse, is not a real Freudian, a genuine Marxist, or a serious philosopher. The 'style betrays the attitude' since the revisionists are moralistic not political, conformist not critical. Marcuse rejects both therapy and traditional radical politics as solutions to the modern dilemma, instead arguing for a 'fundamental change in the institutional as well as cultural structure' (Marcuse, 1955a p 238). An important step towards this radical project must be, as anyone familiar with Marxist sectarianism would know, an internal intellectual and theoretical battle within the left and, for Marcuse, a defence of orthodox Freudian ideas against revisionism.

Fromm's response, entitled 'The Human Implications of Institutional Radicalism', appeared in the autumn issue of *Dissent* in 1955, with rebuttals published in the winter issue of 1956. Fromm's first response took Marcuse to task for indiscriminately lumping Horney, Sullivan, and Fromm together. Fromm argued that this 'lumping together has the unfortunate result that Marcuse substantiates his brief against me by quoting Horney or Sullivan whenever there is no passage from my writings which would serve the purpose'. Fromm certainly did not agree, he pointed out, with Sullivan's attempt to psychologize political radicals as neurotics (McLaughlin, 1998b). Fromm also argued that Marcuse had made an elementary misreading of both Sullivan and Freud on important theoretical issues. Responding to Marcuse's critique of the alleged neo-Freudian neglect of early childhood, Fromm points out that 'Sullivan's work is almost entirely concerned with the development of childhood', and Fromm himself had long argued that the 'character of a person is mainly determined by his [sic] childhood situation' (Fromm, 1955b p 347). Fromm further rejects Marcuse's account of the politically radical implications of Freud's thought pointing out that while Freud was a 'critic of society', this 'criticism was not that of contemporary capitalist society, but of civilization as such' (Fromm, 1955b p 342). Fromm argued that Freud's arguments for a loosening up of sexual norms in modern civilization were largely a reformist project, hardly revolutionary given the hedonistic culture encouraged by capitalist consumerism.

More fundamentally, for Fromm, Marcuse's argument was an unsubstantiated assertion that the rejection of drive theory somehow leads to naïve pre-Freudian social theory and conservative conformist politics. Drawing on years of psychoanalytic therapy and engagement with Freudian theory, Fromm dissents from Marcuse's largely philosophical Freud, instead emphasizing the roots of psychoanalytic insight in the detailed observation of human beings that emerge from the therapeutic context. Fromm furthermore argued that Marcuse's analysis of capitalism is compelling but dissents from what he saw as Marcuse's almost total rejection of the society. Marcuse seemed to leave people with the options of being a martyr or going insane, a politics of nihilism according to Fromm.

Marcuse's rebuttal largely sidestepped a detailed engagement with Freudian theory. Marcuse argued that Fromm misinterprets Freud's views on sexuality, instinct, and modern civilization and suggests that Sullivan's treatment of childhood development is 'not essentially different from its most ancient presentations at the surface level of "interpersonal relations"'. The core of Marcuse's response, however, shifted the terms of the debate from Freudian theory to Fromm's political programme. Marcuse quotes from Fromm's just-published *The Sane Society* in an attempt to illustrate that Fromm's work is conformist and promotes alienation. Focusing on Fromm's practical suggestions for change, Marcuse accused Fromm of being a 'promoter of industrial psychology and scientific management'. Marcuse concludes with a response to Fromm's challenge to provide alternatives to capitalist culture with what would later become a famous argument for what he calls the Great Refusal. 'Nihilism', Marcuse argues, as the indictment of inhuman conditions, may be a truly humanist attitude – part of the Great Refusal to play the game, to compromise with the bad 'positive'. Fromm penned a short counter-rebuttal largely concerned with the details of Freud's view of civilization and its discontents, arguing that Marcuse is guilty of a narrow and erroneous reading of the founder of psychoanalysis.

Fromm's fall from intellectual grace

This contentious and deeply personal exchange in the pages of a relatively low-circulation, left-wing, non-academic periodical turned out to be a pivotal moment in the reception of Fromm's public sociology in America. The immediate consequences were relatively minor and personal largely involving friendships and network dynamics within the German émigré community and small intellectual world of the New York left. Marcuse and Fromm had known each other for many years as part of the Frankfurt School in Germany and in exile (Wheatland, 2009), and they shared many political and intellectual ideas. The nastiness of the *Dissent* exchange drove a wedge between them.

Marcuse won the debate if one measures that by support from other intellectuals and scholars (Rickert, 1986), although over time Fromm's intellectual position gained scholarly support (Burston, 1991; Durkin, 2014). Hardly any psychoanalysts today, moreover, would defend the libido theory for which Marcuse made the case with such passion (Greenberg and Mitchell, 1983). The intellectual issues were not, however, central to what was going on; seeing the Fromm–Marcuse debate through a sociological lens is more illuminating (McLaughlin, 1998a, 2017a, 2018).

Marcuse published *Eros and Civilization* (1955a) in the same year, and with the publication of *One-Dimensional Man* (1964 [2013]) he started to become well known in the United States. Given his association with student radicalism in his California years, the various political controversies of the New Left era in the later part of the decade made Marcuse a celebrity leftist just as Fromm had been in the 1940s and 1950s. Over the years, Marcuse backed off from many of the arguments he made in the *Dissent* exchange about Freud. Marcuse rarely mentioned Fromm's ideas or person in writings or in public after this exchange, moving on as he did to develop his own intellectual and political identity as someone who was often referred to as a 'guru' for (by his critics) or major inspiration for (by his students and followers) the New Left. Marcuse became famous for his critique of repressive tolerance in modern liberal democracies and his vision of the marginalized coming together in a politics of liberation; both arguments gained him a major audience among young radicals. Marcuse also mentored radical African-American intellectual Angela Davis and was famously attacked by then California Governor Ronald Reagan during the 1960s. Marcuse's views on Freud became a footnote in intellectual history for a relatively small number of scholars interested in the history of the Frankfurt School and combining Marxist and Freudian ideas. Marcuse generally let the Fromm–Marcuse debate go having served its purpose by helping jump-start his stalled career in the mid-1950s.

Fromm, on the other hand, was obviously angered by the exchange, and very likely understood that he had 'lost' the debate in the court of general intellectual opinion, even if not in any clear-cut scholarly terms (Friedman, 2013). In the many books Fromm wrote throughout the 1960s and 1970s, he often mentions Marcuse and the ideas he outlined in the Fromm–Marcuse debate (Fromm, 1964, 1970, 1973) even writing a long critique of Marcuse (Fromm, 1992 [1963]). The Fromm–Marcuse debate essentially solidified the divide between Fromm and his former critical theory collaborators. The

Fromm-as-a-conformist thinker myth would be institutionalized in the literature on the Frankfurt School throughout the 1970s and beyond as the critical theory perspective became part of radical academic social science, philosophy, and cultural studies (Burston, 1991; Braune, 2014; Durkin, 2014; McLaughlin, 1999).

The Fromm–Marcuse debate also aggravated an emerging division between Fromm and the social democratic and democratic socialist network around *Dissent* magazine, and this turned out to be pivotal to his reception among sociologists. Their alliance of convenience based on a general political affinity was seriously damaged when *Dissent* printed this attack. Fromm's feelings of alienation from this key network of the New York intellectuals turned out to have important implications for his political activities.

Fromm was at a disadvantage in this debate because many orthodox Freudian psychoanalysts and intellectuals influenced by classical libido theory picked up on Marcuse's critique of Fromm and popularized it in various books, articles, and essays (Rickert 1986). Fromm indeed was a major critic of both orthodox Freudian theory but also later the professional practice of the traditional psychoanalytic institutes (Fromm, 1958, 1959, 1992 [1963]; Burston, 1991; McLaughlin, 2001a). Highlighting and amplifying a radical German philosopher in a magazine of the intellectual left gave Freudians an opportunity to marginalize Fromm, one of the major internal critics of Freudian orthodoxy (Roazen, 1996). After the Fromm–Marcuse debate, Fromm had become more public in his critiques of Freudian orthodoxy particularly when he published 'Psychoanalysis: Scientism or Fanaticism' in the mass-market magazine *Saturday Review* (1958). *Sigmund Freud's Mission: An Analysis of His Personality and Influence* (1959) further angered orthodox Freudians who saw Fromm as what they would call a Freud-basher.

On the theoretical issues at stake, Fromm was largely correct. Psychoanalysts and social theorists have generally rejected Marcuse's defence of orthodox libido theory, something few clinicians will defend today (Chodorow, 1985; Rickert, 1986). But in terms of intellectual history, Marcuse's view dominated left-wing intellectual mythology for decades.

What must be emphasized here, as we theorize the reputational logics that shape public sociology careers, is that it was not the Fromm–Marcuse debate itself that destroyed Fromm's reputation in sociology. The debate was reframed well after the fact in the 1970s and 1980s through the lens of scholars schooled in the 'critical theory' tradition. In the 1970s, American historians Christopher Lasch and

Russell Jacoby both amplified the orthodox Freudian critique of Fromm (McLaughlin, 2018). It was only after Adorno, Marcuse, and Adorno's student Habermas in particular, became icons for what Burawoy calls 'critical sociology' in the 1970s that what, in the end, was a very narrow and sectarian debate between two exiled Frankfurt School-style scholars became conventional wisdom on the academic left. That would not have happened if it were not for the influence of American historian Russell Jacoby and his book *Social Amnesia: Conformist Psychology from Adler to Laing* (1975). Fromm's own publishing decisions also created reputational dynamics within sociology, a discipline undergoing major professional consolidation and expansion in the 1960s and 1970s.

A public sociologist of love and intimacy

If not for the publication of Fromm's *The Art of Loving* almost at the same time as the Fromm–Marcuse debate, then all of this would have remained a minor footnote. Instead, Fromm's reputation among intellectuals and sociologists began a decades-long decline, especially in the United States and the English-speaking world, where he increasingly became known as a simplistic popularizer, a self-help guru, and a conformist and conservative thinker – not a major radical public sociologist. We will outline the core arguments and influences of *The Art of Loving*, showing that the book, despite obvious flaws and limitations, remains a major intellectual contribution to a new genre of public sociology. After doing so, we will return to sociology and narrate how the book was received within the sociology profession.

Fromm offered a public intervention designed to help people think deeply and critically about love and society. Fromm took Marxist, psychoanalytic, philosophical ideas and applied them creatively to offer insights into love particularly within a modern capitalist society where market values were turning everything, even the most intimate relations, into commodities. Specifically arguing against the modern ideology of romantic love deeply institutionalized into American life with Hollywood movies and TV, Fromm offered instructions for living as well as social critique.

In the years after the invention of the paperback and decades before the creation of the internet and social media, Fromm created a mass audience for his books. Already well known, Fromm entered the realm of the celebrity intellectual when he published *The Art of Loving*. At under 140 pages long, written in a conversational and inspirational style that also offered historical, sociological, and philosophical analysis alongside deep psychoanalytic insights, *The Art of Loving* was published by major New York commercial publisher Harper & Row.

While Fromm was often attacked by intellectual elites and scholars for penning a self-help book, *The Art of Loving* was explicitly framed as a new genre of writing that was emerging in the United States. Its largely, but not exclusively, college-educated audience found inspiration in the 'easy instruction in the art of loving' (Fromm, 1956a p vii). *The Art of Loving* is fundamentally rooted in a sophisticated theory of love. Fromm sees love not as something you 'fall into' in some magical way as American romantic comedies suggest, nor is it a chemical reaction rooted in sexual instincts. While Fromm was certainly aware of the historical and anthropology literature that highlights societal variability in the social structural and cultural logics of mating and marriage, he viewed love as a broader and existentially rooted 'answer to the problem of human existence' (Fromm, 1956a p 7).

The more public Fromm became, the more he necessarily repeated his core philosophical and theoretical assumptions ensuring new readers became familiar with his terms. *The Art of Loving* thus begins by asserting that human beings are 'gifted with reason' and we are 'life aware of itself'. Our awareness of our separateness and eventual death brings about extreme anxiety that is expressed in various forms in different world religions. In the Biblical story of Adam and Eve, Fromm argued that our new awareness of the need to choose between good and evil led to intense feelings of shame, guilt, and anxiety. But he stressed, like Jung before him, the universal nature of the dilemma religious traditions seek to resolve is the question of how to live. For Fromm, love was the ultimate answer to the question posed to man by the 'prison of his aloneness' (Fromm, 1956a pp 8–9).

Fromm's account of the human existential dilemma is flawed by his tendency to refer to the 'needs of man' in ways that are antagonistic to our modern feminist sensibility and theoretical and political insight. On this question, feminist sociologist Lynn Chancer is right to stress both the value and the problems in Fromm's work for advancing an egalitarian understanding of sex and gender within a dated formulation (Chancer, 2017), something that was reinforced by how gender was expressed in his first language of German (Funk, 2019). Fromm also assumed that 'primitive' cultures (Fromm, 1956a p 8) are an example of human society 'in its infancy' (Fromm, 1956a p 10), a dated view that is deeply problematic. Fromm shared with the Freudians of his day a theoretical framework and a set of broad attitudes rooted in the orthodoxy of his class and gender that pathologizes gay and lesbian sexualities, although he did move beyond this in his later writings. He certainly never addressed questions of intersex, trans and queer rights that contemporary scholars must surely do as well as the complex set of debates that have emerged into mass politics among feminists since the early 2010s.

These serious limitations aside, from the perspective of 1950s sociology and public debate in the United States, Fromm's analysis was both remarkably anti-patriarchal and cosmopolitan. The core of the book assumes that patriarchal domination of man over woman is wrong and must be challenged by a universal theory of love. Fromm's is a global vision, drawing examples from international history and philosophy and various world religions including Buddhism. Fromm used a long quote from Rumi, the Muslim poet and mystic (Fromm, 1956a p 9) about the power of love. The theoretical analysis posits a theory of universal needs for love before it describes the degradation of love in capitalist society. At its core, his theory is concerned with the existential realities of death.

Death is universal for human beings, but Fromm suggested the anxiety this reality produces always haunts human consciousness, while responses differ in time and place. Fromm began by talking about what he calls orgiastic union with nature and others through intense and sometimes violent rituals, alcoholism and drug addiction, and intense sexual encounters. He then discussed the mass conformity to tribe, nation, religion, or political ideology that allows humans to feel part of something larger and greater than themselves. This sometimes occurs through healthy social and democratic practices, but in other times and places, it is associated with the authoritarianism escape he outlined in *Escape from Freedom* and the mass conformity both he and Riesman critiqued in *The Sane Society* and *The Lonely Crowd* respectively. A third answer to the dilemma of aloneness is creative activity, the subject of extended discussion of alienated labour and the possibilities for craft work in *The Sane Society*. *The Art of Loving*, however, focused in detail on the role of love which is neither 'transitory' like 'orgiastic fusion' nor 'pseudo-unity' like mass conformity. It was love in relation to creative work that was central to Fromm's Marxist and Freudian vision for sane societies.

Fromm argued that the desire for love is the most powerful drive in human existence and cannot be explained by simplistic theories of instinct and sexual drives. It is rooted in deeper existential needs since the 'desire for interpersonal fusion is the most powerful striving in man' (Fromm, 1956a p 18). While rooted initially in the biological pattern in the relationship of symbolic union between pregnant mother and foetus, Fromm stresses that interpersonal fusion comes in many forms, some deeply destructive and others central to productive human life and societies. There is a passive form of symbolic union that is clinically called masochism (Fromm, 1956a p 19) alongside active forms of sadism and domination that are common in all human relationships and central to many forms of love. These are distinct, however, from what Fromm sought to identify as 'mature love' which he defined as 'union under the condition of preserving one's integrity, one's individuality' (Fromm, 1956a p 20). *The Art of Loving* is essentially a theoretical account of and practical guide for active and mature love under the modern capitalism conditions that make it difficult to achieve.

Fromm argued that love must be understood as an active choice, an art that must be learned and practised, one that is even more important to give than to receive. Drawing on his own existentialist-influenced stress on anxiety and death, as well as his revised version of Freud, Fromm synthesized these insights with Marx's early philosophical manuscripts, which he drew upon in *The Sane Society*. Quoting Marx directly and at length, Fromm suggested that if we assume that:

> Man, as man and his relation to the world as a human one, and you can exchange love only for love, confidence for confidence, etc. If you wish to enjoy art, you must be an artistically trained person; if you wish to have influence on other people, you must be a person who has a really stimulating and furthering influence on other people. Every one of your relationships to man and to nature must be a definite expression of your relationship to man and to nature must be a definite expression of your *real, individual life* corresponding to the object of your will. If you love without calling forth love, that is, if your love as such does not produce love, if by means of an *expression of life* as a loving you do not make of yourself a *loved person*, then your love is impotent, a misfortune. (Fromm, 1956a p 25)

Writing decades before Freud and without the language to express this insight, Marx's philosophical position leads, Fromm argued, to the central role of character and character development. For Fromm, a productive approach to love and loving requires the productive character he had theorized in *Man for Himself*.

This active character of love requires four main interactive elements common to all forms of love: care, responsibility, respect, and knowledge. Care flows from the fact that love is 'active concern for the life and growth of that which we love'. Taking responsibility is key to love, not just as an external obligation or responsibility but as an inner choice and capacity to respond to needs of the loved one. This can turn into domination or possessiveness, and often did so historically and still does today under patriarchal and capitalist conditions. In this context, respect means the 'ability to see a person as they are, to be aware of their unique individuality' and to be genuinely concerned with the person's growth and development without exploiting them for one's own purposes. Love is not possible without deep enough knowledge of the other that enables connection to the core of someone's being in ways not shaped only by one's own self-interests.

The interdependence of these elements is required to produce mature love. Taking care and responsibility without respect and knowledge can easily lead to control and domination. Caring without responsibility is impotent and lacks maturity. Attempts to understand someone at their core can easily become sadism and control especially if one combines inaccurate knowledge and lack of respect of the other's autonomous growth with taking responsibility for them. Selfless caring for the other without concern for one's own growth and autonomy, something Fromm analysed extensively as self-love, is not love but masochism; it can be deeply destructive and harmful. Mature love, for Fromm, requires giving up 'narcissistic dreams of omniscience and omnipotence' to love with humility based on an 'inner strength' that can only come from 'productive' activity (Fromm, 1956a pp 32–33). Fromm took this model and applied it to various kinds of love depending on the object and the form of relationships: between parent and child, brotherly love, self-love, love of God, and most importantly for the influence of the book, erotic love.

Fromm was a part of a larger intellectual movement in psychoanalysis to move Freudian theory away from an excessive focus on the father towards pre-Oedipal relations with the mother (often called object relations theory and linked to attachment theories). As a result, his discussion of parental love highlights what he calls matriarchal principles of unconditional love versus patriarchal principles of work and competition. For Fromm, these were both Weberian 'ideal types' and Jungian archetypes (Fromm, 1956a p 41). Even though his thought was certainly flawed, Fromm did not argue for extreme versions of essentialism that would link each principle to women and men per se (Chancer, 2017). Fromm's discussion of brotherly love was linked to his broader discussion of socialism and love for all of humanity beyond the narrow nationalism discussed in *The Sane Society*. Fromm's analysis of self-love argued that it was not possible to productively love others without loving oneself, a critique of the Freudian libido theory on love as a substance that can be directed either inwards or outwards. Building on the analysis outlined in *Psychoanalysis and Religion*, Fromm makes the case for humanistic and non-authoritarian forms of spirituality, either theistic or non-theistic. His account of love within religious traditions was influenced by his own brand of Jewish mysticism but he aimed to develop a universal theory (Fromm, 1962, 1966a; Funk, 2019). Attempting to move beyond battles between Jewish, Christian, Islamic, Chinese, and Indian religious texts, Fromm focused attention on the right ways of living, not the right ways of thinking and believing.

The central focus of *The Art of Loving*, however, and the reason for its mass appeal, was his analysis of erotic and romantic love. While the book is not focused on sexuality per se, Fromm outlines a theoretical analysis of sexuality rooted in his own revised Freudian theoretical framework, dated as it certainly is. Fromm explicitly addressed a misconception about his 'neo-Freudian' revision of psychoanalysis that suggests he was critical of Freud for putting too much importance on sex. Fromm argued that his problem with Freud's view of sex was his emphasis on an excessively biological libido theory that underestimated how sexual desire can merge with other powerful passions to control, humiliate, dominate, and even destroy others as well as to care for, respect, and find intimacy/oneness with.

Fromm's understanding of sexuality was deeply flawed by his assumption that heterosexual attraction and an essentialist binary between man and woman was central to erotic love. There is little room in his analysis for complexities that contemporary sexuality scholars who would highlight, particularly playfulness, technique, societally based cultural scripts, and challenges to heteronormativity. *The Art of Loving* is not, in the end, a book about sex but instead is concerned with romantic intimacy and healthy interpersonal relationships in long-term partnerships. Fromm argued, years before Foucault, that Western societies were no longer repressed about sexuality; they were obsessed with it. For Fromm, sexuality is a form of narcissistic love of youth and beauty amplified by advertising and by a marketplace for emotionally barren forms of entertainment and status competition.

It is Fromm's analysis of the disintegration of love in advanced capitalist societies that explains the popularity and power of *The Art of Loving* as a classic work of a certain kind of public sociology. For Fromm, intimate love in modern society has been pervaded and perverted by the logic of the market. In the mid-1950s, Fromm was ahead of his time in saying that two people often feel what they perceive and understand as love when they meet a partner who offers desirable and matching qualities of attractiveness, wealth, and status. Years before the rise of internet dating, Fromm had the insight to see that in a market society love will be the feeling that both parties experience when feel they are getting a good deal. Modern people are seduced by an ideology of romantic love and a consumer culture that suggests sexual happiness will be easily available for everyone as you 'fall' in love. Fromm argued that the practice and art of loving requires a rejection of market logics and a disciplined commitment to character development. This is difficult in modern society because 'our character is geared to exchange and to receive, to barter and to consume' (Fromm, 1956a p 87).

Fromm's account of love in modern advanced capitalist democracies drew from Aldous Huxley's *Brave New World* (1932). Huxley suggests that too many people in modern society are now guided by cultural slogans: 'never put off till tomorrow the fun you can have today'; 'when the individual feels, the community reels'; 'everybody is happy nowadays'. Modern marriage is saturated by this orientation to exchange the right 'personality package' for fair value while remaining strangers to each other at a deeper emotional level. Without claiming to be a professional historian or historical sociologist of family and sexual life, Fromm historicized his analysis. He focused on post-First World War years in North America when sexual satisfaction was supposed to be the core of a healthy and successful marriage, and on post-Second World War when teamwork and mutual tolerance emerged as core values.

The Art of Loving offered a vision and model for a mature love that promotes real intimacy, something Lawrence Friedman has documented that Fromm had found in his personal life in the years he was writing it (Friedman, 2013). The book was so influential because it combined a positive vision with a critique of the forms of pseudo-love that so many people experience. One form of pseudo-love flows from an excessively emotional dependency on one's partner often rooted in earlier attachments to either a mother or father figure in one's life. Idolatrous love begins with an intensity and power that overwhelms. Experienced as a 'one true love', it often explodes in disappointment and anger as reality sets in or settles into a 'folie a deux' whereby both partners unite against the world while not ever realistically seeing each other. Sentimental love is probably the most common pseudo-love experienced by modern people as love 'experienced only in phantasy and not in the here-and-now relationship to another person who is real' (Fromm, 1956a p 100). This form of pseudo-love is encouraged by 'screen pictures, magazine love stories and love songs' (Fromm, 1956a p 100).

Many relationships in modern societies are pervaded, Fromm argued, not by idolatrous idealization, but by the psychoanalytic mechanisms of projection. One form of projection in relationships is when people's own faults are externalized onto one's partners. This sometimes results in a mutual hell of accusations and counter-accusations of exaggerated flaws alongside a refusal to look at one's own contributions to the relationship's problems.

Another pathological form of projection is trying to make sense of one's life through the lives of one's children. This can operate in terms of the motivations for having children and getting married. It can also involve staying together in a miserable marriage for the children's sake, something Fromm generally thought does more harm than good by discouraging courageous decisions to end intolerable situations. Not a professional or policy sociologist concerned with divorce laws and researching their consequences, Fromm is clearly on the side of the liberalizing divorce laws in the 1950s.

The Art of Loving concluded by offering specific suggestions for improving the art of loving. Fromm clearly attempted to distance himself from what he viewed as simplistic self-help books that had emerged in the 1930s to the 1950s, paperback books such as Dale Carnegie's *How to Win Friends and Influence People* (1938) and Norman Vincent Peale's best-selling *The Power of Positive Thinking* (1952). Fromm's suggestions for practising the art of loving were not intended to be passively consumed as a 'do it yourself' set of easy instructions but were offered as guidance for a disciplined and difficult craft to master for successful living.

Today we face conservative reactions to the anti-authoritarianism of the 1960s spreading through the culture in the examples of Trumpism and the popular writing of Jordan Peterson. In this context, Fromm's positions are subtle and nuanced. In the battle against authoritarianism, which he supported and help lead, Fromm was cautioning against the abandonment of what he called 'rational authority'. Fromm never argued for the rejection of all authority, in fact he advised discipline for without it, 'life becomes shattered, chaotic, and lacks in concentration' (Fromm, 1956a p 108).

To practise the art of loving, Fromm outlines a series of requirements that involve individual initiative, choice, and focus. One requirement is the discipline to work on love and relationships. This also requires concentration and focus, often involving time away from the frenzy of modern life. One cannot practise the art of loving without patience and a rejection of quick fixes and immediate results. One must also commit to the supreme concern with the mastery of the art, not viewing it as a secondary issue like a dilettante might.

Drawing on insights from Zen Buddhism, Western science, and various forms of Christian and Jewish mysticism, Fromm ends the book with an appeal for the power of faith, reason, and humility to overcome the narcissism and despair permeating the consumerist and conformist culture of modern capitalist democracies. Contrary to the conventional wisdom about Fromm among intellectuals in the 1960s and 1970s, *The Art of Loving* was not a conformist and conservative argument for adaptation to modern society. In fact, it argues that the 'principles underlying capitalist society and the principles of love are incompatible' (Fromm, 1956a p 131). Fromm recognized that all societies in their concreteness and complexity offer space and opportunities for non-conformity and personal latitude, and some of this differs by occupations that allow for more honesty than others. Ultimately love is a 'marginal phenomenon in present day Western society' because the 'spirit of a production-centered, commodity-greedy society is such that only the non-conformist can defend himself successfully against it' (Fromm, 1956a p 132). Far from arguing that people should adapt to the society they are living in, Fromm wrote: 'society must be organized in such a way that man's social, loving nature is not separated from his social existence, but becomes one with it' (Fromm, 1956a p 133).

The influence of Fromm's *The Art of Loving* was substantial. Like *The Sane Society*, which shaped the political movements of the 1960s with its communitarian vision and reformist proposals, Fromm's *The Art of Loving* was a precursor to the 1960s' and 1970s' feminist insistence on the personal being political. Fromm had a major influence on Martin Luther King who, in arguing for his own politics of love in the late 1950s and early 1960s, referred to Fromm's distinction between radical love and sentimental love and, like Fromm, rejected both. Fromm's radical humanistic version of the politics of love also shaped the writing of bell hooks in the 1970s, an important African-American feminist public intellectual (hooks, 2002). hooks argued for the importance of black self-love in a world shaped by far too many degrading images of black culture. She made the case against the domination of black women by men, both white and black, and wrote in a similar popular intellectual style aimed at mass audiences. hooks drew inspiration from Fromm's *The Art of Loving* since it complemented the deeper vision she drew from the black liberation struggle (hooks, 2002).

Fromm was relatively marginal to the mainstream sociology of the period since he lived mostly in Mexico after 1950 and was not active in the sociology profession. Fromm had moved to Cuernavaca largely because of the health concerns of his second wife, Henny Gurland (Friedman, 2013). Further reasons for the move are that he had a personal preference for the pace of life there and he was able to shape the psychoanalytic profession from his appointment at the National Autonomous University of Mexico in ways that would not have been possible in New York City where he was opposed so strongly by orthodox Freudians and was disadvantaged by not having a medical degree (Friedman, 2013). The negative consequence of this for his reputation in sociology, however, was he was no longer networked as closely with elite American social scientists as he had been in the 1930s and 1940s.

Nonetheless, *The Art of Loving* helped inspire a new genre of public sociology. After the 1960s, we started to see young intellectuals entering professional sociology after having lived through the Cold War era and having been active or influenced by the civil rights, anti-war, and feminist movements. Feminists like Lillian Rubin, who had both a sociology and psychoanalytic background, wrote crossover books that were similar in style and politics to *The Art of Loving*, like her *Worlds of Pain* (1976), *Intimate Strangers* (1983), and *Just Friends* (1985). Closer to the professional mainstream and peer-reviewed core of the discipline, with Arlie Hochschild's emergence in the 1960s and 1970s, we saw the creation of the field of the 'sociology of emotions'. Scholarship in the sociology of work like *The Managed Heart* (1982) proffered an analysis of the pathological dynamics of what she called the commercialization of feelings (1982). Other sexuality scholars such as Adam Green drew from Bourdieu's field theory more than Fromm's social character approach in developing the 'sex fields' approach while arguing for an object relations and interpersonal psychoanalytic theory (Green, 2008a, 2008b), precisely the kind of perspective that *The Art of Loving* helped to create. Fromm's marginality to the field meant that he was often not credited for pioneering this kind of work.

The audiences Fromm was targeting was a key dynamic for sociologists. While Fromm had broken into the real mass markets selling millions of books outside elite intellectual circles, most of these sociological self-help or popular books that emerged in the 1970s and beyond were aimed at undergraduate or graduate book markets. Some sociologists in gender and sexuality, such as Pepper Schwartz (Schwartz, 1995, 2005, 2006), delved into writing sexual love self-help books in consultation with internet dating companies. More recently, Eric Klinenberg broke into mass markets with the *New York Times* number-one best-seller, *Modern Romance: An Investigation* (2015) written by popular comedian Aziz Ansari. All these books can be seen as being more concerned with feminist theory and feminist practice than Fromm's *The Art of Loving*.[2] Fromm's personal behaviour was not beyond reproach (Friedman, 2013), although the details are complex and require more careful research than Friedman's biography provides on this score. Fromm's contributions, however, were not as the model human being but as a pioneering creator of a new genre of public sociology. Despite the improved methodological sophistication of these new public sociology interventions into love, marriage, intimacy, and the sociology of emotions, however, they were all indebted, either directly or indirectly, to Fromm's *The Art of Loving*.

The fall from grace of Fromm's public sociology was also partly a function of flaws and limitations of his work. His use of 'man's nature' and similar gendered language would cost him support among later generations of feminists (Chancer, 2017). There can be no defence of his outdated views about homosexuality rooted both in Freudian theory and in his own upbringing. It did not help his reception among scholars that his retreat to Mexico and his general uncomfortableness with political organizations meant that in the 1960s he had little contact with North American feminist and later gay liberation activists who could have pushed him to change his language and address more directly the essentialism in his theoretical framework.

In addition, while the book gestures towards using social science research to evaluate, say, the advantages of divorce for the mental health of children over the disadvantages of living with unhappily married parents, Fromm was too distant from academic social science by that point in his career. The book is shaped more by his own philosophy than by empirical social psychological research; the popularity of *The Art of Loving* sprang from the power of his writing and use of a fresh and insightful theoretical framework. The book both tapped into and helped shaped the 'liberation capital' (Morris, 2015) of the emerging social movements of the 1960s. But it would have been a better book had he retained closer links to professional sociology.

Fromm's reputation in sociology never survived the mid-1950s despite the influence of *Escape from Freedom*, *Man for Himself*, and *The Sane Society* on individual sociologists like Robert Merton, David Riesman and C. Wright Mills, and on the young, radical intellectuals of the New Left. Sociology in the 1950s was becoming more professionally oriented, focusing its energy on what Columbia sociologist Robert Merton called 'middle range' theory, and thus increasingly rejecting the 'big picture' social science criticism practised by Fromm (for a discussion of the general issue in social science, see Wolfe, 1996, 2018, as well as Haney, 2008). From the 1950s onwards, sociologists were concerned with establishing academic credibility by doing mainstream and rigorous social science research in the research universities that came to dominate intellectual life in North America.

Just as Freudian institutes in the 1950s rejected Fromm because of his critique of Freudian orthodoxy, sociologists in the post-war period were moving in a different direction, away from the depth psychology that had such influence on their work in the 1920s, 1930s, and 1940s. Sociologists had drawn on psychoanalytic insights in the early and middle decades of the twentieth century. But as George Cavalletto and Catherine Silver (2014) have painstakingly documented, there was a dramatic decline in references to Freud and psychoanalytic ideas in sociology journals beginning in the late 1950s. They persuasively argue that Freudian ideas had a significant influence on sociological thinking in the early twentieth century, especially after the First World War. This peaked in the late 1940s and throughout the 1950s, so that Freud and depth psychology had become accepted elements of intellectual life in general and in sociological research and theoretical tradition (Cavalletto and Silver, 2014).

This changed dramatically at the end of the 1950s. Using a systematic method to calculate references to Freud and psychoanalytic ideas in core journals such as the *American Sociological Review* and the *American Journal of Sociology* from 1900 to 2005, Cavalletto and Silver (2014) document a dramatic 'closing' of a previous 'opening' of the sociological mind to psychoanalysis, created by what they describe as a ferocious backlash. Sociologists came to see the insights of the psychoanalytic tradition as too speculative, overly focused on psychological rather than sociological factors, and harmful to the development of a rigorous scientific sociology to compete with economics, psychology, political science, and the natural sciences in the research-oriented university (Cavalletto and Silver, 2014).

This move away from psychoanalysis was not a purely intellectual shift or strategic decision taken by rational sociological actors but, as Catherine Silver (2014) shows, associated with what she calls 'paranoid and institutional' dynamics. Based on a careful sociological analysis informed by psychoanalytic theory, Silver discusses what she calls 'paranoid anxieties and paranoid theory' and describes how the 'struggle to position sociology as a science inflicted narcissistic injuries on both organizational and individual levels' (Silver, 2014 p 54). Fromm's decline in sociology was clearly linked in important ways to the broader move away from psychosocial perspectives within post war social science and sociology in America in the late 1950s and early 1960s.

Fromm's decline in sociology was tied to the influence of Talcott Parsons, a sociologist trained as a psychoanalyst at an orthodox psychoanalytic institute in Boston. The dominant sociologist of the middle of the twentieth century, Parsons developed a theoretical system that shaped the intellectual agenda for the discipline for decades. Although Parsons was influenced by Fromm early in his career, in later decades he ignored his work clearly preferring both orthodox Freudian theory and professional sociology to Fromm's revisionist social criticism. Although psychoanalytic sociology retained some influence in the discipline due to Parsons' status – and to some important American Sociological Association presidents and the feminist psychoanalyst Nancy Chodorow – public psychoanalytic sociology was not on the rise in the discipline in the late 1950s.

Scholars influenced by Adorno and Marcuse in the discipline helped ensure this by promoting the anti-Fromm consensus established in the Fromm–Marcuse debate. While all of this certainly helped delegitimize his scholarly profile, Frankfurt critical theory was relatively marginal in the discipline so Fromm's decline as a public sociologist must have had other causes.

Fromm's decline consolidated

It was not until the middle of the 1970s that Fromm would be clearly and univocally marked as existing outside sociology and thus was not rediscovered as an early model of public sociology during the public sociology debate of the early 2000s. The Fromm–Marcuse debate and the reception of *The Art of Loving* had begun the process of forgetting that would be fully realized after the political events of the late 1960s. Once critical theorists associated with the Frankfurt School gained a foothold in research universities in North America bringing with them Adorno and Marcuse's dismissive view of Fromm, his negative reputation was fixed. When Jacoby's (1975) influential account of Fromm's allegedly 'conformist psychology' gained prominence among intellectuals, reinforced by Jacoby's teacher Christopher Lasch's orthodox Freudian and explicitly anti-Fromm perspective on the culture of narcissism (Lasch, 1979, 1985), Fromm would become seen as inconsequential among social theorists and sociologists, especially in the English-speaking world.

Within sociology, citations to Fromm dropped off dramatically in the 1970s, 1980s, and 1990s (McLaughlin, 1998a). One factor was sociology's distinction from social work, clinical psychology, prophetic religious preaching, self-help therapeutic practice, or radical political activism, forms of intellectual practices that Fromm was often engaged in. Citing Fromm as a predecessor was a reputational liability (Camic, 1992). Emerging in this period was a new generation of public sociologists inspired by David Riesman, C. Wright Mills, or by the anti-racist socialist and communist wing of American politics and sociology represented by W. E. B. Du Bois. By the early 2000s, feminist sociologists would soon take the lead in much public sociology building on Arlie Hochschild, Cynthia Epstein, and honorary sociologist Barbara Ehrenreich. By this time, Fromm's social theory seemed outdated; some of his language and elements of his analysis of gender certainly was (Chancer, 2017).

Geography, agency, and chance were involved in this story of how Fromm became a forgotten public sociologist. By the time of Marcuse's attack and the various critiques offered by American intellectuals from both the left and the right (McLaughlin, 1998a), Fromm had been living in Mexico for years. He was no longer at Columbia and part of key academic networks in the 1950s as he had been in the 1930s and 1940s. While he did return to the United States regularly to teach and lecture, the reputational battles there over his work in the late 1950s and 1960s took place without his ability to intervene.

Fromm's personal choices are integral to this narrative. He did not care as much as Mills or Merton did, for example, about reputations within the field of sociology. Fromm was more like Du Bois, who cared far more about social change that he did about scholarly reputations (Morris, 2015). The final blow to Fromm's reputation as a public sociologist came down to chance and bad luck. After the mid-1950s, Fromm entered into an intense period of radical political activity ending in 1966 when he had a heart attack after giving an anti-Vietnam War speech at Madison Square Garden. After that, Fromm was far less active in scholarly and political circles, just when Marcuse becoming more well known and influential. This confluence of events undoubtedly damaged Fromm's intellectual reputation and helps explain why we do not remember him as one of the discipline's great public sociologists. But Fromm's strengths and weaknesses as a political activist are an important part of the story. It is thus to the period of Fromm's activism in the late 1950s and 1960s that we now turn to in order to analyse the many forms of engagement that activist public sociologists undertake. The trade-offs between professional scholarship and public writing and activism that we see in the case of Erich Fromm require exploration and analysis.

The trouble with fame and the social construction of Marcuse as a left icon

Fromm's reputational decline as a public sociologist was due to two sociological dynamics. We need to consider both the role that fame plays in scholarly reputations and the interaction of the publication of *The Art of Loving* with the Fromm–Marcuse debate. We will conclude this sociological account of how Fromm became a forgotten public sociologist by highlighting how his writing to mass audiences damaged his scholarly reputation and the ways in which the Fromm–Marcuse debate was read after the publication of *The Art of Loving*.

Public sociology is risky business because of the reputational damage that can come with political engagement and controversies outside of peer-reviewed scholarship. Mainstream professional acceptance and status often comes from doing either professional sociology or policy sociology funded by establishment foundations and elected governments, while public sociology can lead scholars to be dismissed as activists or popularizers (Burawoy, 2005). In reputational terms, doing public sociology is easier for 'traditional' public sociologists writing for elite newspapers like *The New York Times*, *The Guardian*, or *Le Monde* alongside high-status opinion journals such as *The New Republic*, *Commentary*, or *Dissent* (Kadushin, 1974). Sociology of intellectualls scholars who have studied these questions in the United States, Britain, France, and elsewhere, almost always focus on precisely these kind of publishing outlets read by elite non-academic audiences and scholarly elites (Brint, 1994).

Fame at the celebrity level requires more mass appeal than possible from writing in elite intellectual journals and Fromm reached a level of renown. Fromm's success as a public sociologist in the 1940s and 1950s was created and sustained precisely by his crossover appeal in *Escape from Freedom*, *Man for Himself*, *Psychoanalysis and Religion*, and *The Sane Society*. While *Escape from Freedom* sold over 5 million copies, and *The Sane Society* sold over 3 million, their core audience was among highly educated readers and they were well received among intellectual elites. *The Art of Loving*, in contrast, sold well over 25 million copies, extending his ideas and name recognition into a whole new level of celebrity influence. After *Escape from Freedom* Fromm was a famous academic, but after *The Art of Loving* he become famous among the general public.

For the public sociologist, the reputational consequences of public fame can be negative as scholars begin to suspect that ideas have been watered down to appeal to mass audiences. Envy and elitism are not unknown among academics, two further possible explanations. Ideas do tend to get picked up and further diluted and diffused into the culture and this can result in distortion and damage to the rigour of academic debate (Merton and Wolfe, 1995). Scholarly status tends to decline as popularity increases among what intellectuals and academics regard as audiences of lower status – that is the general public outside of academic and elite networks and publishing outlets.

In the 1930s and 1940s Margaret Mead in anthropology suffered this fate as her fame began to eclipse her more professionally esteemed colleagues, something that was surely amplified by the pervasive sexism of the period (Lutkehaus, 2008). Works like *Coming of Age in Samoa* (1928) and *Sex and Temperament in Three Primitive Societies* (1935) made Mead a celebrity. As she was asked to do more public lectures as her fame increased and take professional leadership roles in promoting anthropology, time pressures pulled her away from disciplined field work. This, in turn, served as a magnet for her critics who built careers by attacking Mead often with political motives and sometimes driven dogmatic theoretical commitments (Lutkehaus, 2008). There are certainly legitimate political and intellectual problems with Mead's work from a contemporary perspective but there is little doubt her fame was a double-edged sword both helping her career and damaging her scholarly reputation. Envy and sexism are also part of the story.

Fromm's audience for *The Art of Loving* was even more popular than that for Mead's books on the lessons foreign cultures hold for the American middle class. Fromm was explicitly and directly giving practical advice for love, relationships, and marriage. It was predictable, even inevitable, that Fromm's reputation would decline among sociologists as he gained a mass audience that went well beyond elite academic and intellectual circles. The fact that the book was published right on the heels of the Fromm–Marcuse debate played a central role in how intellectual elites viewed Fromm because it made Marcuse's critique more plausible, at least on the surface.

The sociological reception of the Fromm–Marcuse debate in the late 1950s, 1960s, and 1970s

The argument that Marcuse made against Fromm in *Dissent* was relatively arcane even for a highbrow New York intellectual journal. But Marcuse's ultimately unfair and inaccurate case that Fromm was recommending that people adapt to an alienated society became more credible after the publication of *The Art of Loving*. Marcuse argued that Fromm was making the case for the 'power of positive thinking', a brilliant rhetorical move. Some of the hard-headed socialist and radical liberal, as well as the elite intellectual readers around the *Dissent* social circle were predisposed to Marcuse's critique of Fromm.

Some were adherents of orthodox Freudian theory while others were drawn to the even more biological sexual politics of Wilhelm Reich. Some *Dissent* readers were also unimpressed with Fromm because of his far more critical view of the founding of Israel in the late 1940s (Jacobs, 2014), something Marcuse and Irving Howe both supported with far more enthusiasm. Others may have preferred Marcuse's more abstract philosophical style in comparison to Fromm's concern with feelings, emotions, and caring over a decade before the rise of a mass feminist movement in the United States. Whatever the reasons, the fact that Fromm explicitly criticized Norman Vincent Peale's 'the power of positive thinking' in *The Art of Loving* made little difference. Marcuse's attack in an elite left-wing journal had landed some heavy blows on Fromm's intellectual reputation despite the weakness of some of his arguments and to many in *Dissent* he became known as the 'Norman Vincent Peale of the left' (Howe, 1984).

By the mid-1970s, Fromm's reputation as an elite intellectual and public sociologist had declined in the United States. It was further damaged by the reintroduction of the major themes of the Fromm–Marcuse debate into American intellectual life by Russell Jacoby, a radical historian and New Left era devotee of the work of Adorno and Marcuse. We now know Jacoby as the author of *The Last Intellectuals* (1987), a book that popularized the term 'public intellectual', but in the early 1970s he was a relatively marginal historian who mostly had written highly philosophical accounts of the work of Adorno and Frankfurt School scholars in *Telos*, a critical theory journal. In 1974, Jacoby published *Social Amnesia: Conformist Psychology from Adler to Laing* (Jacoby, 1975) a polemical defence of the allegedly radical implications of Freud's libido theory. At the centre of the book was an extended attack on Fromm's neo-Freudianism that essentially updated Adorno's critique of Fromm after Marcuse in the *Dissent* debate. Jacoby was successful in painting Fromm as a conservative, conformist, and simplistic thinker for a new generation of young radical intellectuals who had not necessarily read *Escape from Freedom* or *The Sane Society*.

Many radical scholars were more interested in Marcuse in the 1970s than was the case during the original debate in the 1950s because of the changing political and cultural context. After *One-Dimensional*

Man (1964 [2013]) and his influence on the New Left in the late 1960s, Marcuse had become more well known. Marcuse had taken the Frankfurt School critique of instrumental rationality to new heights arguing that mass society led not just to conformity but to a totally administrated and alienated society. Marcuse later wrote *An Essay on Liberation* (1969) and *Counterrevolution and Revolt* (1972) and mentored militant activist Angela Davis. Marcuse had given many talks at anti-Vietnam War rallies, and survived attempts to get him fired from his university position at the University of California at San Diego by then California governor Ronald Reagan. These ideas and controversies together had made Marcuse famous as defender of New Left radicalism in the later 1960s and 1970s. The more famous Marcuse became among the left, the less credibility Fromm would have among radical activists, elite intellectuals, and Marxist academics.

Russell Jacoby played a pivotal role in resurrecting Marcuse's attack from the 1950s and reframing it for the left culture of the 1970s (McLaughlin, 2018). Jacoby's success in damaging Fromm's reputation among critical theorists can also be explained by the fact that Fromm's counterattacks on Marcuse after the 1955–1956 debate were so angry, personal, and excessive, that he left himself vulnerable to Jacoby's acerbic rhetoric. Fromm perceived that he had lost the exchange in the court of intellectual opinion (Friedman, 2013). Fromm often took shots at Marcuse, responding with anger in his writings throughout the 1960s and 1970s (Fromm, 1964, 1970, 1973), Jacoby quotes Fromm's attack on Marcuse, psychoanalysing his former colleague as 'an alienated intellectual who presents his personal despair as a theory of radicalism' (Jacoby, 1975 p 14). These conflicts made Fromm look bad, an opening that Jacoby exploited.[3] Fromm's activism in the 1960s was marred by a certain detached elitism and thus Jacoby in 1975 was able to effectively attack Fromm's ideas from the 1950s by a bait-and-switch tactic.

The level of hostility Fromm had for Marcuse can be seen most clearly in an essay 'The Alleged Radicalism of Herbert Marcuse' written for an appendix to *The Crisis of Psychoanalysis* but did not appear in print in *The Revision of Psychoanalysis* until after his death (Fromm, 1992 [1963]). Aware of the potential political risks in attacking Marcuse too sharply while he was being attacked by the far right in Nixon's America, Fromm refrained from publishing his more sustained critiques during his lifetime.

The tone of Fromm's unpublished critiques of Marcuse suggest that Fromm viewed Marcuse as a radical who practices the 'Great Refusal' which involves 'a childish sybaritic and egotistical experience' representing 'cynicism masquerading as a super-radical theory' (Fromm,

1992 p 129). This shows us how deeply Marcuse had troubled Fromm. Fromm had legitimate and compelling answers to the specifics of Marcuse's argument about Freud and about politics. But when Fromm went beyond critiques of ideas to offer psychoanalytic interpretations of Marcuse's personality at the time when he had become famous as a militant representative of the New Left, he left himself vulnerable to Jacoby's allegations that Fromm had collapsed the political into the therapeutic. Fromm had indeed done so on occasion; Jacoby's criticism resonated. It made no difference that Marcuse had been deeply unfair in his original remarks and Jacoby repeated these misrepresentations.

Jacoby's historical imagination and the quality of his writing allowed him to contextualize Marcuse's critique of Fromm in the broader history of the Freudian movement, the topic of his next major book *The Repression of Psychoanalysis: Otto Fenichel and the Political Freudians* (1986). Otto Fenichel was a Viennese émigré Marxist psychoanalyst who, along with Wilhelm Reich, had pioneered the kind of Marxist-Freudian synthesis based on libido theory that Marcuse argued was so important for the radical project. Marcuse's critique of Freudian orthodoxy had originated with Adorno in the 1930s when Fromm was centrally involved with the Horkheimer circle (Jay, 1973). Since neither Marcuse nor Adorno had extensive clinical knowledge of Freudian practice, Fromm's response to Marcuse on this point had a power and resonance. Jacoby, however, succeeded in changing the subject.

Jacoby played a key role in diffusing the Marcuse critique of Fromm facilitating his status as a 'forgotten intellectual', at least in the English-speaking world (McLaughlin, 1998a). Jacoby engaged in some historical digging that identified other Marxist Freudians who opposed Fromm's revision of libido theory. This effort resulted in *The Repression of Psychoanalysis* (1986), Jacoby's most archival-based book on the life and work of the Austrian Otto Fenichel, who had known both Freud and Fromm and who had died young in exile in the United States. Intellectual movements love heroes who die young (Rodden, 1989). Jacoby succeeded in taking the Marcuse critique of Fromm out of a personal animosity-rivalry frame rooted in a narrow technical theoretical question and making the issue into a larger political question about the radical Freudian traditions. When Jacoby gave the 1960s and 1970s generation of critical theorists a compelling defence of two Marxist Freudian heroes, Reich and Fenichel, Fromm became the foil as an alleged cultural conservative. This devastated his reputation among 1960s radicals, especially in North America.

Looking at the intellectual and political limitations of Fenichel and Reich today, it is unlikely they would gain a mass following among contemporary young leftists. They both were, for example, far less progressive on gender issues than Fromm, and Reich's homophobia was extreme. But Jacoby's New Left work of historical reconstruction struck gold in in that period of American cultural history, papering over these contradictions to create a myth of the radical Freud that still resonates today (Zaretsky, 2015).

Allan Bloom's *The Closing of the American Mind* (1987) had argued that Fromm was responsible for the radical excesses of the 1960s while Jacoby (1975) had earlier argued the opposite. The conservative attacks on Fromm from the 1940s to Bloom have been consigned to oblivion in the collective memory of the North American left. Largely because of the Fromm–Marcuse debate, and with Jacoby's help and Christopher Lasch's seal of approval and his own polemics (1979, 1985; 1991), Fromm became widely known in America as a conformist, simplistic, and conservative thinker. He was written out of the 'origin myths' of the Frankfurt School (McLaughlin, 1999, 2008).

At the very centre of Jacoby's critique of Fromm in *Social Amnesia* was a deeply problematic assertion that one must choose between trying to change the world by addressing historical and structural sources of injustice *or* look inside for psychoanalytic insights into one's unconscious patterns of self-defeating behaviours and irrational emotions. The best answer to contemporary Canadian conservative Jordan Peterson's 'clean your room' rhetoric is Fromm's position that people should be aware of *both* the political, historical and structural barriers to productive and decent lives *and* the psychological mechanisms that can best be dealt with through therapy, self-help, and the efforts of friends, families, and professionals. It was precisely Fromm's insistence that Marcuse, Adorno, and the Marxists of his generation were not dealing seriously with the clinical basis and implications of Freud's thought that helps explain why Fromm then, like Peterson today, had readers and followers in the millions. Unlike Peterson, however, who really is conservative, Fromm was and always remained a political radical.

It was not until the later years of the 1970s that the critical theory of Adorno and Marcuse was integrated into scholarly debates in the United States as the more scholarly of the young radicals of the 1960s era made their way into academic careers. Critical theory was more influential in philosophy, literary studies, and eventually cultural studies than in sociology, but there was a Frankfurt School tradition within the discipline of sociology that eventually made it into the scholarly literature by the 1980s and 1990s. Burawoy was influenced by the critique of instrumental reasoning developed within the Frankfurt School when he coined the category of 'critical sociology' as an example, along with public sociology, of what he called reflexive sociology in contrast to the instrumental orientation professional and policy sociology (Burawoy, 2005). Fromm was indeed both a critical and reflexive public sociologist. By this time, however, Fromm's reputation as a major public sociologist was long forgotten. Scholars influenced by Adorno and Marcuse in the discipline helped ensure this by promoting the anti-Fromm consensus established in the Fromm–Marcuse debate.

5

Fromm's Political Activism in the 1960s

Just after *The Art of Loving* brought celebrity fame, Fromm entered into an intense decade of activism. Fromm was not directly involved in sustained political activism for most of his life. Beginning in the mid-1950s and lasting for more than a decade until he was sixty-eight years old, Fromm began a long personal campaign for nuclear disarmament, human rights, global peace, humanistic socialism, presidential electoral politics, and the protests to end the brutality of the American war in Vietnam. The increasing danger of nuclear war that careful observers of Soviet–Chinese and US tensions could not fail to notice in the Cold War period pushed Fromm into action. Fromm would sustain his activist work for a decade.

Fromm's active clinical practice and involvement in the institutional life of both the Frankfurt School and various psychoanalytic institutes, along with teaching and his active publishing regime, left him little time to be politically active. By the time he moved to Mexico City in 1950, Fromm was busy taking care of a gravely ill wife, involved in the practical and factional political work of the Mexican Psychoanalytic Institute he had established, and travelling for regular part-time university teaching at various universities in the United States (Friedman, 2013; Funk, 2019). Fromm had been attempting to cut back his formal responsibilities at the Mexican Psychoanalytic Society and Institute for a number of years (Friedman, 2013 p 292) and in 1965 retired from the National Autonomous University. This left him more time for politics as well as writing.

Fromm was never what Burawoy calls an organic public sociologist who worked to represent his class, racial, or ethnic group or political ideology with roots in local communities, political parties, or social movement organizations. His most important political activism started after he was already world famous as a political intellectual, a status that changes one's relationship to mass publics. Financially independent and wealthy enough by that time (Friedman tells us Fromm's income tripled after *The Art of Loving*), Fromm became a significant philanthropist for various human rights causes, electoral campaigns, and political organizations. He was at his most politically active in the United States and Eastern and Central Europe from around 1955 to 1966, driving himself to his first heart attack while undertaking frantic anti-war activism. After recovering by 1968, he again threw himself intensely into political activism until the election of Richard Nixon as President of the United States in November of that year.

This chapter discusses Fromm's major public sociological writings during this period while telling the story of the political work that served as the backdrop to his books, manifestos, and essays. We describe Fromm's anti-weapons nuclear campaigning, his socialist and human rights activism, and his involvement in the anti-war presidential campaign of Eugene McCarthy. I will then examine how Fromm's activities affected the quality of his public sociology.

Fromm would publish three major works of public sociology in the 1960s – *May Man Prevail?: An Inquiry into the Facts and Fictions of Foreign Policy*, *Marx's Concept of Man*, and *The Revolution of Hope*. These books would make Fromm the most important Marxist sociologist before the rise of the New Left and academic Marxism in the later 1960s. He also became the most prominent radical critic of American foreign policy writing to the general public before Noam Chomsky.

Marx's Concept of Man, a mass-market book that sold millions of copies, dealt with Karl Marx's philosophical and sociological thought. Fromm's writing on Marx stretched back to *The Sane Society* but was reflected most prominently in the widely read introduction to *Marx's Concept of Man*, a translation of Marx's early philosophical writings. These works played an important role in popularizing radical ideas during the New Left era and laid the foundation for empirical Marxist professional sociology in the late 1960s and 1970s.

May Man Prevail? reached a smaller audience of 500,000 readers consisting of scholars, activists, and the general public concerned about the dangers of war in a nuclear armed world just before the Cuban Missile Crisis and the escalation of the Vietnam War. This book flowed from his anti-nuclear activism undertaken with David Riesman. It was also linked to his behind-the-scenes policy advisement to American foreign policy elites on Cold War incidents such as the Berlin stand-off and the Cuban Missile Crisis.

The Revolution of Hope was linked to the mainstream American politics of the day, coming as it did out of Fromm's electoral work in the 1968 democratic primaries. It was both an anti-war statement and critique of the alienation created by modern technology. Fromm's critique of modernity was increasingly framed by radical humanist commitments by the mid-1960s (Durkin, 2014). Despite the fact that *The Revolution of Hope* was neither the most commercially successful nor intellectually impressive of Fromm's books, it influenced millions of readers around the world.

Key to the story of how Fromm got involved in politics in the late 1950s is his connection to liberal public sociologist David Riesman. Fromm's own prophetic utopian socialist commitments were in creative tension with Riesman's insider elite status and liberal politics. Fromm's friendship and collaboration with David Riesman, however, shaped Fromm's political activism especially in the late 1950s and early years of the 1960s.

Instrumental intimacy, David Riesman, and the fight against nuclear war

While Fromm taught David Riesman social theory and thus helped create the public sociological critique of conformity that Riesman pioneered in the 1950s, the influence flowed two ways. The beginning of their relationship was one of therapist–client and mentee–mentor, but this changed once Riesman gained fame with *The Lonely Crowd* (1950). Riesman was teaching at the University of Chicago and Harvard, mostly focusing on undergraduate students. Over time, Fromm and Riesman became equals and close personal friends sharing what Michael Farrell calls an 'instrumental intimacy' that facilitated their creativity on the optimal margins of their respective professions (Farrell, 2001). Riesman never entered the core of the sociological field publishing in the peer-reviewed journals and training graduate students in professional sociology despite being at Harvard. Instead he played a role as a critic of higher education, an informal policy advisor, and a public intellectual teaching sociology at elite universities near the core of the American establishment (Kadushin, 1974; Kerr, Harden, and Aldredge, 2015).

Fromm and Riesman shared a concern with the polarization of world politics during the Cold War and while both were consistently anti-Stalinist, they were not military hawks. Both were committed to putting an end to the nuclear arms race between the United States and the Soviet Union and lowering the threat of catastrophic global war. Riesman's practicality, connections to American elites and constitutional moderation, provided a valuable foil against which Fromm developed his activist agenda. With Riesman's guidance and support, Fromm became the most influential critic of American foreign policy in the Cold War and Vietnam War period. Fromm was essentially the Noam Chomsky of the 1950s before the MIT linguist emerged to replace Fromm as the most visible English language intellectual voice opposing the American empire in the late 1960s (Lannigan and McLaughlin, 2017).

There was a pre-history to Fromm's political work during the height of the Cold War and the 1960s. Fromm had been a Zionist in his youth but by the middle of the 1940s he was a vocal and principled critic of Israeli dispossession of Palestinian land. As Lawrence Friedman puts it, 'In 1947, Riesman prodded Fromm to join with other American Jews to provide a non-Zionist alternative in the Middle East—namely to lobby for the creation of a multinational Jewish-Arab state in Palestine' (Friedman, 2013 p 206). Weeks before the establishment of the State of Israel, Fromm was involved in publishing a letter in *The New York Times* that Jacobs (2014) describes as condemning 'Arab and Jewish extremists' and urging 'peaceful co-existence in Palestine'. Fromm was the most Jewish identified and the most critical of Israel of the Frankfurt School critical theorists, making public statements defending Palestinian rights and writing about the issue in his books and essays (Jacobs, 2014).

It was Fromm's relationship to David Riesman, however, that took him from the general political interventions in the 1940s and early 1950s 'up to the next level' (Friedman, 2013) in the early 1960s. Fromm's own political instincts led him to a role as a prophet for justice and principle outside the channels of mainstream politics (Maccoby, 1995) even from within established socialist and social democratic parties. Riesman, on the other hand, was a consummate insider who was well connected to governments, major university leadership, and the media and intellectual elite. When network sociologist Charles Kadushin asked government elites in the early 1970s which American intellectuals they most trusted, David Riesman's name came up most often (Kadushin, 1974).

The combination of Fromm's prophetic radical views and Riesman's moderate and reformist insider orientation led to a productive political collaboration, partly because Riesman appreciated outsiders. Riesman, for example, was willing to help student activists at Harvard and even SDS when Todd Gitlin was president (personal communication with Gitlin, June 2020). Fromm and Riesman's personal correspondence documents how Riesman and Fromm strategized together and supported each other emotionally and intellectually (Friedman, 2013). The Fromm–Riesman collaboration is a case study on two public sociologists helping each other intervening in politics, using their sociological and psychological knowledge, and Fromm's world fame to engage with policy makers, social movement organizations, political parties, and the general public. Fromm's activist work with Riesman would inform *May Man Prevail?* I will first discuss the content of the book then outline the activism that led to it.

Beyond militarism and ideology: *May Man Prevail?*

Concerned with the possibility of nuclear war and exaggerated fears of Marxist plans to take over the world, *May Man Prevail?* is a work of public sociology/policy sociology aimed at opening up Cold War America to a level-headed analysis of the Soviet Union, Chinese communism, and the Berlin issue. The book is not professional political science, international relations, or historical sociology; it is a crossover work published with a commercial press and aimed at a sophisticated general audience. Fromm uses his psychoanalytic insights, knowledge of Marxism, and observations and sociological analysis of world events to offer Americans an alternative view alongside proposals for preventing nuclear war. Fromm's evidence was secondary texts, newspapers and his analysis draws from access to elites and knowledge of Marx and Marxism.

May Man Prevail? was concerned with 'anticipatory' change to prevent the further catastrophic use of nuclear weapons after the destruction of Hiroshima and Nagasaki that ended the Second World War. Fromm began the book with a social psychological analysis of what he calls 'sane' versus 'pathological' thinking in foreign affairs. Building on the social psychological mechanism discussed in *Escape from Freedom*, Fromm theorized what he called 'paranoid', 'projective', and 'fanatical' forms of thought processes that had made it difficult for American elites to understand the real threats to democracies posed by the Soviet Union and Chinese communism. Fromm argued that Soviet Russia after Stalin's death, was essentially a 'conservative, state-controlled, industrial managerialism, not a revolutionary system' (Fromm, 1961b p 14). It was possible, Fromm conceded, that Khrushchev's Russia wanted to conquer the United States by force and/or destroy it with a nuclear strike. This was extremely unlikely, however, given then-recent Russian history and the war against Hitler which had nearly destroyed the Soviet Union.

Paranoid thinking focuses on possibilities not probabilities. Fromm argued that Americans needed to look more closely at both the Russian and Chinese regimes before escalating the Cold War to bloody conflicts and potential nuclear war. The mechanism of projection in foreign policy issues involves a process whereby the 'enemy appears as the embodiment of all evil because all evil that I feel in myself is projected on to him' (Fromm, 1961b p 22). A number of years before Noam Chomsky would make these kinds of arguments (Chomsky, 1972, 1995), albeit without psychoanalytic theory, Fromm suggested that the 'Stalinist terror system was inhuman, cruel and revolting, although no more so than the terror in a number of countries that we call free—no more so, for instance, than was the terror of Trujillo or Batista' (Fromm, 1961b p 22). Fromm was certainly aware that Stalin's violence was at a much larger scale. Americans, he was emphasizing, only feel indignant about the lack of democracy and human rights in countries they consider enemies and ignore or minimalize injustices perpetrated by their own state and its allies.

Fanatical thinking is characterized by a 'cold fire' of emotions (Fromm, 1961b p 24) and a blind unfeeling worship of idols such as 'God, salvation, the country, the race, honour, etc.' (Fromm, 1961b p 25). Fromm deals with fanatical thinking within the communist movements led by Stalin, Mao, and revolutionaries committed to radical social transformation without concern for the human consequences. Fromm insisted that Americans and Europeans convinced of their own superiority, innocence, and goodness were also guilty of fanatical thinking that could lead to world destruction.

Fromm's critical view of American arrogance was not a false equivalence that ignored the differences between the deeply flawed but democratic Western nations and Stalinist tyranny. Intensely and consistently anti-Stalinist, Fromm insisted that we look carefully at the nature of the Soviet system after Stalin's death and ask questions about the function of communist ideology as well as Khrushchev's political goals. Fromm presents a detailed and sophisticated account of the origins of Lenin's Bolshevik movement and the brutality of the Stalinist regime and Khrushchev's police state. Contrary to American experts who warned of the regime's ambitions to conquer the world, Fromm argued that the Marxism within the Soviet Union under Khrushchev functioned largely as a ritualistic justification for the privileges of the communist managerial elite. For Fromm, the ideas of Marx were transformed into an ideology in the Soviet Union. American foreign policy should be based on a careful analysis of Russian realities and should not take the ritualistic invocations of Marxism too seriously.

As fears spread of the Soviet and Chinese communist alliance, Fromm was remarkably insightful about the tensions between these two great powers. He believed that future historians might well decide that the 'most outstanding event in the twentieth century was the Chinese revolution' (Fromm, 1961b p 141) signifying, as it did, the 'end of Western colonialism and the beginning of industrialization throughout the rest of the world' (Fromm, 1961b p 142). While many young radicals in the United States and Europe later in the 1960s would become enamoured with Maoism, Fromm was always a sharp and principled critique of Chinese communism. Drawing on Robert Jay Lifton's important *Thought Reform and the Psychology of Totalism* (1961), Fromm viewed Chinese communism as a totalitarian form of a new quasi-religion that industrialized a largely peasant nation through collectivism, brain washing, brutality, and one-party rule. Fromm did not have a romantic and uncritical view of the Chinese warlords who ruled the nation before Mao; he also recognized the injustices imposed on China by colonialism. Yet he viewed Chinese communism as a social system that was in fundamental opposition to humanistic Marxism.

In foreign policy terms, Fromm insisted that while China and Russia shared a common antagonism to the West and a Marxist ideology (Fromm, 1961b), their interests were different. The growing schism between them that Fromm saw clearly, was not emphasized in the American debates. Russia was increasingly becoming part of the industrialized world while in 1961 China was still a have-not nation. These two leaders of world communism were, for Fromm, likely to compete and get into conflicts over leadership of the movement. The Russian position on revolutions and nuclear conflict was more moderate, cautious, and largely concerned with the Soviet national interest, while the Chinese communists were more militant, less afraid of nuclear war, and more of a threat to world peace. Fromm viewed the Soviet Union as anti-democratic and Maoism as totalitarian but insisted that America reject paranoid fears of a united communist movement allegedly set to control the world.

Fromm outlined a historical and social psychological analysis of the rise of Nazism in *Escape from Freedom* but also highlighted political economy and class analysis of the German question. The Russians remained fearful of Germany in 1961, only sixteen years after the defeat of Nazism, while Cold War ideology in the United States had shifted to the threat of Soviet communism. Fromm was deeply anti-Stalinist, a commitment that was deepened by the experience of his cousin who was an anti-Stalinist left-wing political prisoner in a German Democratic Republic (GDR) prison at the time (Friedman,

2013). Fromm understood full well that the Soviet-controlled regimes in Germany were not democratic or just. Fromm believed that essentially the same coalitions of industrialists and Prussian militarists who had backed the German Kaiser's war aims in the First World War and, more reluctantly, Hitler's rise to power in the 1930s, remained powerful in West Germany in the 1960s. Germany was not a military power in the two decades after the end of the Second World War, but Fromm's analysis of the deeper sociological roots of German nationalism suggested that Russia had more reason to fear Germany than most American policy analysts were willing to concede. While motivated by his socialist and anti-war values, Fromm was also pragmatic. The book made proposals to the Kennedy Administration that were designed to reduce tensions in the divided Berlin partly by recognizing Russian fears and concerns. The conclusion of *May Man Prevail?* offers Fromm's political interventions on questions of the nuclear arms race and development.

May Man Prevail? represents an example of policy sociology because it is based on a sociological analysis of the logic of competing capitalist and communist social systems, a social psychology of disarmament, and a sophisticated political perspective on Third World politics. Fromm played the dual role of public intellectual and policy sociologist when he powerfully and persuasively argued against Herman Kahn whose RAND think tank-sponsored book *On Thermonuclear War* (1960) argued that the United States should prepare to fight and win a nuclear war. Fromm passionately opposed the false sense of security that proponents of nuclear deterrence theory were promoting among policy leaders. He believed that an accidental nuclear war between the United States and Russia was possible and the proliferation of atomic weapons made this more likely. Fromm was particularly appalled by Kahn's view that if a nuclear war were to occur, 'objective studies indicate that even though the amount of human tragedy would be greatly increased in the postwar world, the increase would not preclude normal and happy lives for the majority of survivors and their descendants' (Fromm, 1961b p 190).

Fromm argued that Kahn's prediction that civil society would survive a major nuclear war was mistaken. From a social psychological perspective, Fromm made the case that it was far more likely that 'the sudden destruction, and the threat of slow death to a large part of the American population or the Russian population or large parts of the world will create such a panic, fury and despair, as could only be compared with the mass psychosis that resulted from the Black Death in the Middle Ages' (Fromm, 1961b p 194). Fromm's position was that Kahn's hawkish view must be rejected as impractical, unrealistic, and dangerous.

Fromm's alternative proposals would have represented a major change for American foreign policy in the 1960s but that was not to be. Fromm's ideas did diffuse into government policy during the Kennedy/Johnson era, and he had more influence on nuclear weapons policy and Berlin than on general foreign policy questions. His ideas about 'universal controlled disarmament' and his reluctant acceptance of Russian interests and East German control of East Berlin were a serious part of policy discussions during this period of American history, contributing to a focus on negotiating nuclear disarmament deals that would emerge during the 1960s. Part insider, part outsider, Fromm was a vocal supporter of peace activism even arguing the case for unilateral steps for nuclear disarmament in *Daedalus* (Fromm, 1960b) and actively supporting SANE, an anti-nuclear weapons organization named after *The Sane Society*.

In *May Man Prevail?*, Fromm's broader politics led him to argue that American and European nations should compete with communist Russia and China for the hearts and minds of the Third World. Fromm predicted the Sino-Soviet split before it happened. Fromm also argued against the continuation of colonial wars like the French in Algeria and the more indirect American support of reactionary far-right pro-Western governments in Latin America and increasingly in Vietnam. He advocated for the development of a neutral third way where democratic socialism could develop in Cuba and Latin America, in Egypt and the Middle East, and throughout Africa.

In the end, of course, polarization continued. In Cuba, Castro became closer to the Soviets. Russia, not the United States, would support anti-colonial movements in Africa and the anti-apartheid struggle. And the Vietnam War would lead to deforestation and brutal bombings, as well as millions of deaths in a violent counter-insurgency war out of which Cambodia's murderous Pol Pot regime would rise. In the United States, Noam Chomsky would replace Fromm as the most prominent public intellectual critic of American empire with a view that was sharper, harsher, and less compromising than Fromm's and often less balanced (Chomsky and Herman, 1979a, 1979b). Chomsky also got things right that Fromm did not. In any case, Fromm would not write a book like *May Man Prevail?* again. Fromm's anti-nuclear activities were the backdrop to *May Man Prevail?*, an important part of his global public sociological activism.

How Fromm become a peace activist

The Committee for a Sane Nuclear Policy (SANE) was, along with the Committee for Non-Violent Action (CNVA), one of the 'twin engines of an accelerating peace movement' in the late 1950s (DeBenedetti, 1990 p 31). Fromm was involved with SANE from its formation in 1957, two years after the publication of his book *The Sane Society* that gave the organization its name. Fromm's involvement in anti-war activism and defence policy work can be traced to his attendance at an important peace movement meeting at the Bear Mountain Lodge near the Hudson River in March 1960. Along with David Riesman, he was joined by a few dozen important writers and academics, and representatives of the American Friends Service Committee (AFSC), a key Quaker organization central to pacifist activism in the United States. Unlike C. Wright Mills who opposed American entry into the Second World War, Fromm was never a pacifist. Indeed, Fromm wrote *Escape from Freedom* partly to encourage the entry of the United States into the war. But he was more than willing to work on peace issues with A. J. Muste, the militant American pacifist.

It was out of the Bear Mountain meeting that the Committee of Correspondence newsletter developed. With David Riesman taking the lead and Fromm providing some funding, the board included Muste, liberal historian H. Stuart Hughes, and the sociologist Seymour Martin Lipset. Michael Maccoby, then a young scholar-activist at Harvard who was close to Riesman, was also involved. Maccoby would go on to become an important collaborator with Fromm. Riesman played a mediating role in the circle around the Committee of Correspondence, allowing the airing of various positions and perspectives. Eventually the newsletter was successful in creating space for criticisms of the arms race and the war in Vietnam.

Todd Gitlin, then a Harvard undergraduate student before he would become a major leader of the radical student movement SDS, was first exposed to anti-nuclear weapons activism in October 1960 during the Eisenhower Administration amid Test Ban Treaty debates. Gitlin attended a SANE rally at the Boston Arena on 1 October 1960 'starring Erich Fromm', a number of liberal politicians, and with music provided by Pete Seeger and Joan Baez (Gitlin, 1993 p 87). That evening, SANE handed out excerpts from Mills' *The Causes of World War III* in an arena jam-packed with 6,000 people (Gitlin, 1993 p 87). We remember Mills' influence on the student movement but at the time Fromm was more famous and his involvement in the movement more sustained.

As well as being a public face of the movement, Fromm also was operating as an elite insider. Fromm attended meetings in the United States where he confronted American strategists of nuclear war, criticizing what he viewed as their underestimation of the consequences of nuclear war. He also attended a World Council of Peace Meeting in Moscow in 1962 where in front of high-ranking Russian officials, he challenged Khrushchev's bellicosity while also chastising Western celebration of militarism (Friedman, 2013).

Later, after 1965 when the Vietnam War escalated and the protests spread, Fromm turned up the heat at rallies and protests moving beyond these early elite-led debates. SANE was at the centre of many controversies during the 1960s as they were largely a membership organization which aimed to mobilize mainstream liberals, moderate Republicans, students, religious leaders, and suburban voters. Fromm represented the left of the organization and was their most famous and visible writer and speaker. SANE was controversial on the left wing of the anti-war movement because it favoured the exclusion of communist involvement in the organization. This view was consistent with Fromm and Riesman's opposition to Stalinism, authoritarianism, and manipulation, but did not impress the more militant anti-war activists especially as the polarization of the later part of the 1960s led from peaceful protest to resistance and the 'the days of rage' (Gitlin, 1993).

Fromm's politics were a challenge to the nihilistic and destructive elements in the New Left. One of the most telling stories in Friedman's biography is about when Fromm was asked to offer expert testimony at the trial of a member of the German Baader-Meinhof group. Sometimes known as the Red Army Faction, this was a far-left anti-capitalist and anti-imperialist urban terrorist organization founded in 1970 that engaged in bombings, kidnappings, and assassinations in West Germany. The lawyer wanted to leverage Fromm's anti-capitalist politics and psychoanalytic expertise to provide testimony that would help him defend a Red Army Faction member. Fromm refused because he believed their actions were nihilistic violence and not a revolutionary politics that he could support or justify. Out of step with the radical Maoist sensibilities of some in the student movements of the time, Fromm's decision flowed from his own experiences.

Fromm's knowledge of the general human rights violations within the Soviet bloc and his opposition to ultra-leftism were sharpened by his direct involvement in getting his own anti-Stalinist radical cousin Heinz Brandt discharged from an East German prison where he languished as a result of his political beliefs. This led Fromm to increase his involvement in the politics of human rights, particularly

Amnesty International. Amnesty International was formed in 1961 in London, at the height of Cold War tensions. Its chief founder, Peter Benenson, wanted an organization that took a principled position against political persecution around the world, equally in Western democracies, the communist bloc, and the developing world (Neier, 2012 p 187). Benenson's commitment to oppose human rights violations committed by Western allies derived from concern for two Portuguese men who had been arrested in a Lisbon bar for criticizing their own right-wing government. Amnesty International is now a massive global organization that raises many millions of dollars a year but in the early 1960s, its focus was on gaining support for prisoners of conscience who did not engage in violence but were imprisoned for their political views. They also opposed torture (Neier, 2012 p 191).

Friedman provides an extensive discussion of how, with the help of British philosopher Bertrand Russell – an admirer of *Escape from Freedom* – Fromm skillfully negotiated for Brandt's eventual release. Friedman corrects the common view of Fromm as a politically naïve utopian. Brandt was the Prisoner of Conscience of 1963 for Amnesty, part of a global campaign to apply pressure on the East German regime. Fromm gave significant money to the organization in its early years, another example of his human rights activism and political philanthropy (Friedman, 2013). Fromm knew, as some academic Marxists do not, how authoritarian Stalinist Marxism could be. Fromm's human rights activism led him to develop and amplify his moral commitment to a humanistic alternative socialism in *Marx's Concept of Man*, his most important contribution to public sociology in the 1960s.

Socialist public intellectual: *Marx's Concept of Man*

Marx's Concept of Man consists of a short eighty-page introduction to the first widely available English translation of Karl Marx's early unpublished work, 'Economic and Philosophical Manuscripts of 1844'. Fromm's intention for the book was neither to present a scholarly treatise on Marx's philosophical works nor offer a comprehensive analysis of Marxist social theory. *Marx's Concept of Man* consists of dense philosophical writings from a young philosophical Karl Marx (translated by British sociologist T. B. Bottomore), as well as personal letters and a selected set of short excerpts from key Marxist texts.

Not an original contribution to Marxist academic scholarship, it is a targeted public intervention against widespread distortions of Marx's ideas. Fromm's purpose was twofold: to correct widely circulated mythologies about the ethical core of Marxism; and to introduce the notion of alienation and Marx's theory of human nature to the English-speaking world. *Marx's Concept of Man* was thus a sustained critique of the dismissal of Marxism promoted by American intellectual elites during the Cold War as well as theoretical protest against Russian and Chinese communist orthodoxy and the neo-Stalinist account of 'dialectical materialism'.

Fromm believed that Marx's ideas had been distorted by his political opponents in the major capitalist nations and by Soviet and Chinese communist leaders who used his texts to justify their own path to political power. American politicians and intellectual elites presented an ignorant version of Marx's ideas as the 'word on the Devil's tongue'. They read Marx's work as an anti-spiritual and 'materialist' scientific philosophy and cast him as the enemy of Enlightenment inspired freedoms. For millions of people in the developing world, Marxism represented opposition to class inequality and colonialism as embodied in the radical political movements led by Russian and Chinese communist parties. Fromm argued that both Marx's capitalist and Western democratic enemies and his communist intellectual supporters misrepresented the philosophical foundations of his work.

Marx's ideas are not represented by the Soviet and Chinese anti-democratic states focused primarily on ending mass starvation and poverty through dictatorial methods. Marx's thought was humanistic and democratic aiming as it did at the 'full realization of individualism, the very aim which has guided Western thinking from the Renaissance and Reformation far into the nineteenth century' (Fromm, 1961a p 3). Far from being a 'materialist' thinker unconcerned with humanist and spiritual values, Fromm argued that Marx's ideas 'represents a protest against man's alienation, his loss of himself and his transformation into a thing; it is a movement against the dehumanization and automatization inherent in the development of Western industrialism' (Fromm, 1961a p v).

Fromm offers political, textual, and cultural reasons for the distortions of Marxist ideas while acknowledging the history of socialist thought and movements detailed in *The Sane Society*. The communist movement in Russia in the early years of the twentieth century, led first by Lenin and then taken over by Stalin in the 1920s and 1930s and modified by Mao in the 1950s, took elements of Marxist ideas out of their philosophical mooring in the Hegelian humanist tradition. Marxists in the communist movement used these ideas first to inspire their revolutionary actions and then to legitimize the bureaucratic elites who rule the Soviet Union in a 'conservative state capitalist' regime that undermine the 'emancipation of the individual person which is the very aim of socialism' (Fromm, 1961a p vii). Western elites unwilling to give up colonial empires and the economic inequality that capitalism produces and reinforces have, for Fromm, made a terrible error in allowing the Soviets and Chinese communists to represent Marxism, an ideology that is popular among colonialized people for good reason.

Fromm was combining social science analysis with efforts to influence American politics. *Marx's Concept of Man* was both a theoretical account of Marxian theory and a polemical text designed to educate the American public and political elites. Fromm wanted to push American foreign policy towards less belligerence in the world. Fromm was also concerned with discrediting Soviet and Chinese Communist Party attempts to lay claim to the legacy of Karl Marx's ideas, something he believed was legitimizing anti-democratic regimes.

Fromm attributed ignorance of Marx's humanistic philosophy partly to the fact that the 'Economic and Philosophical Manuscripts' that laid out his core assumptions about human nature were not published until the 1920s and were not widely available in English. As a consequence, Marx had been misread as a 'materialist' and 'scientific' thinker who allowed little space for human agency and choice, preferring an economic deterministic theory that served the interests of labour and social democratic parties. This interpretation of Marx also served the world communist movement that stressed class equality and material well-being as the core goals of the socialist tradition.

The book had its strengths and weaknesses linked to its political goals. *Marx's Concept of Man* presented a romanticized account of Marx's personal life and stressed his humanistic values. These counteract the anti-Marxist propaganda promoted by American political leaders who were determined to win the Cold War against the Russians. But *Marx's Concept of Man* also presented a detailed and careful textual reading of the major writings that Marx penned in his twenties before he was involved in radical political activity. Fromm stresses how central human freedom, autonomy, and the dignity of work were to Marx's early vision for a new society.

Fromm offers a cultural explanation for the misreading of Marx that stresses not the differences between communist dictatorships and Western democracies but their similarities. Modern alienation and spiritual decline created by the industrial search for material comfort and economic well-being created a philosophical framework that distorts how we read Marx. Even capitalism's critics on the left in the socialist and communist movements read Marx as a proponent of increasing the material well-being of workers to the exclusion of the broader set of humanistic values Fromm asserted were at the core of his vision.

Fromm compellingly made the case that the economic spirit of our age leads readers to believe that Marx viewed the striving for economic self-interest as a universal element of human nature. Marx argued that the particular economic and cultural arrangements of a historical epoch set unlimited greed and capitalist values in motion, not the other way around. With detailed textual support, Fromm convincingly shows that Marx did not believe that 'the strongest psychological motive in man is to gain money to have more material comfort' (Fromm, 1961a p 11). As Fromm puts it:

> The fundamental misunderstanding on which this interpretation rests in the assumption that historical materialism is psychological theory which deals with man's drives and passions. But, in fact, historical materialism is not all a psychological theory; it claims that the way man produces determines his thinking and his deserves, and not that his main deserves are those for maximal material gains. Economy in this context refers not to a psychic drive, but to the mode of production; not to a subjective, psychological, but to an objective economic-sociological factor. (1961a p 12)

Marx's Concept of Man has often been misread by academic Marxist scholars who don't see that the book is largely a work of public sociology, not an academic history of Marxism or a formal work of social theory. Fromm's introduction is scholarly in its tone and content when it defines and explains Marx's concept of historical materialism, the theory of alienation, his view on the nature of man, and his vision of socialism in relation to the Hegelian tradition. Fromm's target audience, however, was not sociological theorists or Marxist scholars but students, mass publics, and public intellectuals.

Never a best-seller like *Escape from Freedom* and *The Art of Loving*, it still sold over a million copies and was assigned widely in university classes. Fromm asked questions that public sociologists can answer. How does Marx's view of human nature conform to what the American public thinks about Marxism? Are Marx's ideas consistent with the communism practised in the Soviet Union and the People's Republic of China? In answering these questions, Fromm was centrally engaged with other public scholars, particularly the sociologist Daniel Bell, who he argued misunderstood and misrepresented Marx's humanist vision. Bell was a former Marxist who took the same position, ironically, as the Soviet Marxists on the break between the young and old Marx, arguing that the 'real' Marx was the later economic-oriented revolutionary, not the early philosophical thinker. Bell, one of sociology's great public intellectuals, and Robert Nisbet, a more traditional conservative thinker who opposed American militarism and the Vietnam War (Baehr, 2014), were both deeply sceptical of Fromm's political use of Marx's ideas in the 1960s. They both played an important role in undermining Fromm's reputation in sociology for political more than purely intellectual reasons.

As American socialist Michael Harrington has outlined the issues, Bell rejected Fromm's reading of the humanist Marx, implicitly taking the orthodox Marxist Althusser's side in the broader debate because Bell 'rejects a Marxist critique of capitalism based on Marx's economic work' (Harrington, 1976 p 159). Bell had been a Marxist in his youth, but by the late 1960s, he was a centralist who rejected New Left politics and Marxism. There is debate about whether to call Daniel Bell a neo-conservative, a term coined by Harrington to describe New York intellectual factional fights even though it was a label Bell rejected. Harrington, as well as sociologist Philip Selznick, both made the case that Fromm's reading of the issues was fundamentally right (Harrington, 1976; Selznick, 1992; Selznick 2008).

Bell's perspective on the humanist Marx ironically converged with the neo-Stalinist French Marxist Althusser. The core argument of *Marx's Concept of Man* is Fromm's powerful case against Russian and pro-Soviet intellectuals like Althusser who tried to distinguish the young 'immature' philosophical Marx represented in these 'Economic and Philosophical Manuscripts' from the 'mature' scientific Marxism practised under communism in the Soviet Union. The Russian position that split the 'young Marx' from the 'old Marx' was dishonest, flowing from the ideological necessity of defending their own form of managerialism and anti-democratic state run industrial system. As Fromm put it,

> They could hardly do anything else, since their thinking, as well as their social and political system, is in every way a contradiction of Marx's humanism. In their system, man is the servant of the state and of production, rather than being the supreme aim of all social arrangements. Marx's aim, the development of the individuality of the human personality,

is negated in the Soviet system to an even greater extent than in contemporary capitalism. (1961a p 70)

Fromm also wished to stimulate interest in the humanist tradition among reformist social democrats, democratic socialists, and the emerging youth movement in the early 1960s. The reformist socialist and non-Stalinist Marxist traditions of the early part of the twentieth century did not have access to Marx's humanist tradition because key texts such as Marx and Engels' *The German Ideology* were not available until the 1930s. The *Grundrisse*, a key unpublished text related to the connections between the early Marx and *Das Kapital* was also not available until the 1950s (Avineri, 1968; McLellan, 1973). In *Marx's Concept of Man*, Fromm advocated for a humanistic socialism, aligning himself with dissident Marxists in Poland, East Germany, Hungary, France, and Yugoslavia.

Fromm outlined a sophisticated analysis of the changes in Marx's social theory in his lifetime, arguing compellingly that despite a change in focus and language, there was a basic continuity in the humanist foundation of his thought from his early Hegelian philosophical writings to the political economy of *Das Kapital*. Marx scholars would complicate and refine his basic point (Blauner, 1964; Avineri, 1968; Ollman, 1971; McLellan, 1973; Selznick, 1992; Braune, 2014; Durkin, 2014; Anderson, 2015, 2016). Scholarly quibbles aside, the book played an important role in the emergence of a radical socialist humanist politics in the 1960s in the United States and around the world. This was a truly global public sociology in action.

Fromm's socialist activism in the 1960s

Marx's Concept of Man and Fromm's influence on Marxist academic sociology was connected to both his socialist activism during the 1950s and early 1960s and his global human rights and humanistic efforts in the middle of the decade. Fromm had joined the Socialist Party in 1958 (Freidman, 2013 p 227), and was impressed by Norman Thomas, the leader of the party at the time. Friedman puts it this way, 'Prompted by Thomas's quest for organizational revitalization, Fromm was assigned to prepare a position paper in pamphlet form so that party members and socialists generally could gain a clearer sense of their goals' (Friedman, 2013 p 227). Fromm held a formal leadership position in the Socialist Party of America while he was writing *Marx's Concept of Man*.

To make sense of his place in the party, however, it is important to realize that it was a marginal organization. Like the Democratic Socialists of America (DSA) in the 1980s and 1990s before its contemporary revival (Sunkara, 2019), it was common for socialist organizations in America without any electoral prospects to appoint widely respected figures as ceremonial on their leadership bodies in order to gain legitimacy and recruits. In reality, Fromm knew very little about grassroots organizing. His connections were mostly with elite networks, particularly through the aging but well-respected Norman Thomas. Fromm and Thomas shared an ethical-religious sensibility as Thomas was a Presbyterian minister. They were both strong critics of the militaristic elements of the Zionist movement and Israel, an issue on which Thomas became more vocal about after the Suez Crisis in 1956–1957.

By the time Fromm became involved in the American socialist movement, Thomas had largely lost control of the party as it was slowly being taken over by the followers of an obscure but brilliant and sectarian American ex-Trotskyist named Max Shachtman (1904–1972) (Ross, 2015). Increasingly critical of the independent presidential campaigns that Norman Thomas engaged in, they were moving towards a realignment strategy for moving the Democratic Party to the left by working with the labour and civil rights movements. Fromm understandably had only a vague and general sense of the politics on the ground since he lived in Mexico and was generally distant from organizational activism.

Fromm's pamphlet entitled 'Let Man Prevail' was effective at recruiting new socialists drawn to the movement no matter how out of step with the party's electoral strategy it was. It was popular on campuses where he spoke, for example, to over 1,200 students at Yale and over 2,000 at the University of Chicago during this period (Friedman, 2013 p 227). Fromm's manifesto promoted a 'third solution' that not only rejected the 'managerial free enterprise system' of the United States and the West, but also the 'managerial communist system' of the Soviets and allies (Friedman, 2013 p 227).

The core problem facing the modern world was that both capitalism and communism were excessively focused on material gain, not human growth and potential. This view was a continuation of the argument he had made in *The Sane Society* and Fromm's Socialist Party pamphlet shared the earlier book's assumption that both American capitalism and Russian communism had solved the problems of production. Pivotal to the manifesto was a call for the Socialist Party to respond aggressively to the threat of nuclear war. Fromm appealed to both camps in the Cold War to accept the existing political arrangements in Europe as they moved towards disarmament. Fromm also outlined a domestic reform agenda that included racial and gender equality, socialized medicine, and economic assistance for the poor, unemployed, the elderly, and the infirm.

A well-written and popular pamphlet is not the same thing as a party platform. Shachtman's obscure theoretical pamphlet on what he called the 'bureaucratic collectivism of the Soviet State' was hardly selling at all, while Fromm's pamphlet was wildly popular among members and new recruits (Ross, 2015). Shachtman's piece was sectarian and excessively theoretical but Fromm's ethical appeals, while more clearly written, said very little about the strategic issues facing the civil rights and union movements of the time. Fromm could help bring young people into the movement, but his manifesto was ineffective in the factional battles that were wresting control of the party away from Thomas. Fromm consistently underestimated the economic instability that modern capitalism created as he had done in *The Sane Society*. While he was far more aware of the depth of racism in America than most of the other Frankfurt School intellectuals and most sociologists of the time (McLaughlin and Steinberg, 2016), he did not understand the strategic centrality of the civil rights movement in America. Fromm was disappointed that the party did not adopt his ideas as their programme but that was an unrealistic hope that would have, in any case, led to political disaster. Fromm's ethical socialism would have simply speeded up the inevitable decline of the Socialist Party of America.

There is a happy as well as a tragic ending to this. In the wake of the Bernie Sanders campaign, the current upsurge in the DSA represents a vindication of the 'realignment' strategy. Harrington (1976) was sympathetic to Fromm's humanistic Marxism although he found Fromm's specific political proposals lacking strategic insight. One of the great political assets in the Socialist Party of the time was Bayard Rustin, a key African-American organizer in Martin Luther King's movement. Fromm's ideas had an influence on King himself.[1]. As skilled as Fromm was in bringing people into the Socialist Party with his best-selling books and inspiring rhetoric, it was Harrington and Rustin who had a much better sense of what they should do to build the party and the movement. They were central to making realignment a viable politics beyond Shachtman's sectarianism.

The tragedy is that the right-wing Shachtmanites in the Socialist Party of America were gathering power and influence in this period, a different group of people whom Harrington knew well but opposed. Eventually the Shachtmanites would be neutral in the election contest between George McGovern and Richard Nixon in 1972. Legitimate political critiques of communist tyranny led some progressive activists to support fanatical anti-communism which in turn led them to right-wing, albeit pro-labour, politics. By that time, Fromm was living in Switzerland and disillusioned with socialism, something that was all but inevitable given his own naïvety about practical left politics. Fromm's temperament and overcommitment to too many responsibilities diminished his effectiveness.

Harrington would take his followers and allies out of the old Socialist Party in the early 1970s leaving it the empty shell of the Social Democrats USA. His efforts eventually resulted in the DSA which, thirty years after his death, is undergoing remarkable growth as part of the upsurge of left-wing politics represented by two Bernie Sanders campaigns and the movement against Donald Trump (Sunkara, 2019). Fromm's ideas have shaped the current DSA in indirect ways over the years by influencing many activists from the New Left era. Fromm would also later influence the Green movement in Germany in the 1970s, but Fromm's humanistic socialist vision could never be the basis for a practical electorally oriented party, something he never fully understood. Harrington was a political person, while Fromm was a writer and an intellectual.

Fromm was disappointed that he did not have as much influence on the Socialist Party of America as he wished, but this experience, alongside his human rights efforts on behalf of his imprisoned cousin, generally spurred him forward into global socialist politics. This trajectory would lead to the publication of an international edited collection, *Socialist Humanism*.

In 1960, Fromm was moved to action by a proposal for a coalition of humanistic socialist intellectuals conceived by the great Hungarian economist and historian Karl Polanyi (Friedman, 2013 p 238). Polanyi's book *The Great Transformation* (1944) is a classic work of social science at the level of *Escape from Freedom*. It emphasized a powerful historical sociological critique of the mythology by mainstream neo-classical economists that markets can be understood and should be valorized as efficient mechanisms for creating wealth and well-being. Attention to the role of the state and to social relations of care and reciprocity was unnecessary. Polanyi wanted to develop a global network of influential thinkers who were anti-fascist, anti-Stalinist, and opposed to marketplace capitalism. Fromm volunteered to take the lead on this; Polanyi agreed since Fromm and he shared similar politics and a twenty-year friendship (Friedman, 2013 p 238). Fromm's organizing efforts connected some of the most important global scientific and intellectual figures of the twentieth century in an intellectual movement for humanistic socialism. This work was part of Fromm's contribution to global human rights work, but it also led to Fromm's edited book *Socialist Humanism: An International Symposium*.

The social movements of the mid-1960s saw global protests and a revival of humanism sparked by victories of the civil rights movement in the United States despite the brutal war in Vietnam. Fromm's introduction to *Social Humanism* made the case for the building of intellectual and political bridges between East and West based on common ground between religious and secular humanists across the political divide of liberalism versus Marxism. The book included an essay by Bertrand Russell, the great English philosopher, Norman Thomas who represented American socialism, and Herbert Marcuse from the Frankfurt School. Among the important philosophers represented were Ernest Bloch, Eugene Kamenka, and Maximilien Rubel. The volume was heavily weighted towards Eastern and Central European philosophers as well several from the intellectuals around the Praxis group of reform Marxists in the former Yugoslavia. The book also included an essay by Léopold Senghor who was then the sitting President of the Republic of Senegal and the most influential African intellectual of the twentieth century. Senghor was a non-Marxist African socialist and poet and a central figure in the emergence of the Negritude intellectual movement. Many of these figures played important political roles in the twentieth century in addition to their work as creative and accomplished intellectuals.

Fromm's contribution to the book 'The Application of Humanistic Psychoanalysis to Marx's Theory', argued that Marxism requires a psychological theoretical foundation in order to understand and change the world. Dennis Wrong and George Homans had argued that sociology needed an orthodox Freudian and Skinnerian behaviourist foundation respectively in order to avoid over-socialized sociology absent of human beings (Wrong, 1961; Homans, 1964). Fromm rejected both libido theory and an excessive focus on operant conditioning to make the case that a revised psychoanalysis be synthesized with humanistic Marxism. Although Marx did not have access to Freudian theory in the mid-nineteenth century, he got close to developing a psychological view of human needs in his philosophical writings of 1844. Fromm makes the case for the connection between the early humanist Marx and the economics of *Das Kapital*. To do so, he had earlier developed a comprehensive critique of Althusser's purely scientific Marxism in *Marx's Concept of Man*.[2] In Fromm's essay in *Social Humanism*, he summarizes his own theory of human needs and presents the case for eliminating simplistic libido theory from the Freudian tradition. The theory of social character is then offered to help Marxists explain how capitalism reproduces itself, valuable insights in the struggle for a radical global humanist alternative.

Fromm's book on socialist humanism is similar to the manifesto he wrote for the Socialist Party of America early in the decade except this time it concludes with a practical set of proposals sent by a group of American leftists to the White House in 1964. The proposal's purpose was to advise political leaders on how to deal with the 'Triple Revolution' of cybernetics, nuclear weapons, and human rights. The book was Fromm at his most practical and political. Impelled by his global public sociological vision, it brought his Marxist ideas to bear upon mass politics and policy. Around the same time, Fromm also published an essay entitled 'The Psychological Aspects of the Guaranteed Income' in an edited book on an issue that was becoming widely debated in the United States at the time (Fromm, 1966b) as it is being discussed at the time of writing in the midst of the COVID-19 pandemic. Fromm was now moving in the direction of domestic American politics as the protests against the war in Vietnam dominated world attention in the middle of the 1960s. After the war escalated in 1965, Fromm threw himself into anti-Vietnam War activism. In 1966, he suffered a heart attack just after giving an anti-war talk in New York's Madison Square Garden (Friedman, 2013). Taking 1967 off to recover, he returned to politics and writing in 1968. This period of Fromm's life was when he did intense political work in the American presidential primaries and wrote *The Revolution of Hope*.

A book for a political campaign: *The Revolution of Hope*

Published in 1968, *The Revolution of Hope* was a political contribution to public sociology in which Fromm was attempting to mobilize Americans for anti-Vietnam War protest, New Left activism, and electoral politics. It was written just after Fromm's campaign work for Eugene McCarthy's presidential primary run that year (Friedman, 2013). The primary contest was framed by protests against the Vietnam War in the United States. Sitting American President Lyndon Johnson had withdrawn from a re-election bid because of the pressure from the anti-Vietnam War movement and the resulting primary to replace him as the candidate for the Democratic Party led to the riots at the Chicago Democratic Convention in the summer of 1968. Fromm was living in Mexico at the time but remained involved in American politics by giving speeches and donating money to political causes. Fromm was passionately attempting to create a democratic socialist/radical humanist current in American intellectual life, fighting conservatives, liberals, and Stalinists. He engaged the Democratic Party when needed.

Fromm's recovery from his health issues allowed him to get back involved in politics just as Eugene McCarthy, the junior Senator from Minnesota, was emerging as a mainstream critic of the Vietnam War (Friedman, 2013 p 268). Fromm identified with McCarthy partly because of the Senator's Catholic-influenced criticism of capitalism. McCarthy was an intellectual among politicians and had worked as something of a public sociologist himself teaching sociology at a small Catholic college in St. Paul before becoming an elected politician in the late 1950s. Fromm supported intellectually oriented politicians. Indeed, it was McCarthy's nomination of the original American 'egghead' politician Adlai Stevenson (Brown, 2020) at the 1960 Democratic Party convention that brought him to Fromm's attention (Friedman, 2013 p 269). Fromm's relationship with Governor Stevenson, a Democratic Party candidate nominated to run for president in 1952, was central to how Fromm became an activist (Friedman, 2013). Fromm donated to the Stevenson campaign, sent him a signed copy of *Escape from Freedom*, and offered help and more money for a second campaign after he lost (Friedman, 2013 pp 200–205).

Friedman emphasizes how Fromm's political naïvety is reflected in the letters between Fromm and Stevenson. Fromm seemed to have no understanding of either politicians' busy schedules or the practical constraints that they work under (Friedman, 2013). Nonetheless, Fromm did develop a relationship with the governor who then became the US Ambassador to the United Nations during the Kennedy Administration, giving Fromm modest access to policy circles particularly around questions related to German politics where he had real expertise. Fromm was an activist on the outside of the mainstream while also having access to policy makers. This kind of activism initially was more of a personal campaign as Fromm leveraged his fame as the author of *Escape from Freedom* to put together public statements on issues and to connect with politicians. Not centrally engaged in politics at a collective level, his knowledge of German politics was still sophisticated and current enough to maintain policy makers' attention (Friedman, 2013).

The McCarthy campaign changed Fromm's approach to his political engagement. By the middle of the 1960s, McCarthy was following Pope John XXIII's encyclical *Pacem in Terris*, a strong anti-war perspective that had also impressed Fromm. Fromm and McCarthy argued for a spiritual foundation for the fight against nuclear weapons and modern warfare (Friedman, 2013 p 269). In 1968, when McCarthy sought the Democratic nomination for president to replace wartime President Lyndon Johnson, he ran on a platform to end the bombings of Vietnam, start serious negotiations, and then withdraw American troops from Indochina. Fromm was one of the earliest large donors to the campaign (Friedman, 2013 p 269); by this time, the sales of *The Art of Loving* provided him with significant extra funds to spend on politics.

From the perspective of socialist politics in the 1960s, Eugene McCarthy was an important but flawed candidate. Progressive politics was impossible in America while the Vietnam War was raging, having been escalated first by Democrat John Kennedy and then by Lyndon Johnson, the Democratic President who replaced Kennedy after his assassination in 1963. Long-haired students influenced by the counterculture were willing to 'go clean for Gene' in order to deliver an effective anti-war message and force Lyndon Johnson out of the White House. McCarthy was the first mainstream Democrat willing to take on a sitting president on the issue of the war and he gained Fromm's support on that basis.

McCarthy was, however, a complicated political figure. He opposed Johnson and the war, but as sociologist and activist Todd Gitlin puts it, McCarthy 'damned the war but held back'. A product of his time, and representing largely white Minnesota, he took good positions on race in America but 'was squeamish about campaigning in the ghettoes' and was vague about addressing racial inequality (Gitlin, 1993 p 297). McCarthy had appeal among students and suburban reformers but was not an exciting candidate among African-Americans or trade unions, the reason why socialist Michael Harrington switched from supporting McCarthy to Robert Kennedy in the Democratic primaries in 1968 once 'Bobby' entered the race. Harrington believed that Kennedy could unite a broader and more progressive coalition against Richard Nixon. Harrington returned to support McCarthy when Robert Kennedy was assassinated, but Fromm's more unconditional support for McCarthy illustrates his limitations as a political actor and analyst. McCarthy's anti-war movement was dominated by middle-class reformers and thus was no match for the Democratic establishment. Militant radical protests at the Democratic Convention in Chicago in 1968 turned off many unions and moderate voters, all but sealing Nixon's election as president in November of that year.[3]

More of a public sociologist and a prophetic radical socialist than an experienced political campaigner, Fromm entered the political fray as public intellectuals often do, by writing a memo that would lead to a new book. His 'Memo on Political Alternatives' would be the outline for his many talks on college campuses as the anti-war movement and the McCarthy campaign heated up (Friedman, 2013 p 270). Fromm argued for socialist humanism and for participatory democracy along the lines of the SDS's 'Port Huron' statement that was influenced by Fromm and C. Wright Mills (Miller and Miller, 1994). In the 'Memo', Fromm made the case for an end to the Vietnam War and the nuclear arms race. Fromm was in private contact with McCarthy during the primary campaign, paying for his own expenses and donating about $150,000 in today's money to the primary challenge (Friedman, 2013). Fromm paid for the expenses of Michael Maccoby who represented Fromm on the McCarthy campaign, travelling around the country and attending the Chicago Convention. The 'California Citizen for McCarthy', organization paid to place Fromm's essay 'Why I Am for McCarthy' in the *Los Angeles Times*, a glowing case for the nominee's character and vision (Friedman, 2013 p 272). Despite these efforts, McCarthy lost and Richard Nixon was elected in 1968.

Fromm was not temperamentally oriented to this kind of practical party politics despite his willingness to put in time and money, a limitation he himself acknowledged (Fromm, 1962). By 1968, Fromm was in his late sixties, exhausted, and his declining health would soon force his withdrawal from all political activities and see his eventual retirement to Switzerland in his seventies (Friedman, 2013). The political options for a democratic socialist in America in 1968 were grim with Martin Luther King dead and the student movement in militant opposition to the Democratic Party and their war in Vietnam. Richard Nixon was in the wings speaking for the 'silent majority' and their backlash to the civil rights, student, anti-war, and feminist movements. Fromm was about to enter a period of political despair; the practical ideas he outlined in *The Revolution of Hope* were simply not politically compelling, especially for young radicals who had seen the American state repress the Black Panther Party and the anti-war movement. The Democratic Party was politically bankrupt, and Nixon and then California Governor Ronald Reagan were ascending (Gitlin, 1987).

After the election campaign was over, Fromm wrote and quickly published *The Revolution of Hope* as his response to both the rising radicalism that he viewed as extremist, and the reactionary and divisive politics of Richard Nixon. The book was a repetition of some of his old ideas as he searched for a new vision that would later lead to the best-selling radical humanist manifesto, *To Have or to Be* in the 1970s. In *The Sane Society*, Fromm had argued that the localism syndicalist and communitarian socialist tradition should be drawn upon to create local discussion groups that would encourage people to move away from the propaganda promoted by the corporate dominated media and the self-interest of professional politicians and political parties. In *The Revolution of Hope,* Fromm developed these earlier ideas, suggesting the creation of local clubs for the debate of social issues.

The intellectual framework for *The Revolution of Hope* started with the claim that American and modern societies were at a crossroads leading to either revolutionary despair and violence or a totally administered technocratic dystopia. Most of the book was essentially a re-framing of his existential psychoanalytic theory of human needs, a discussion of how modern technology was creating alienation and despair among people who were becoming more like passive consumers than active citizens, and suggestions for regulating corporate advertising, planning for the humanization of technology and creating a psycho-spiritual revival. Fromm sought to create a movement for the face-to-face democracy he had written about in *The Sane Society* and radical American students were calling participatory democracy (Gitlin, 1987; Miller and Miller, 1994).

The most engaging section of the book is a chapter entitled 'Hope', in which Fromm uses his psychoanalytic insights and political experience to provide a theoretical commentary on the paradox of hope that young radicals and older progressives were facing in 1968. It was a time of national polarization between Richard Nixon and segregationist populist third-party candidate George Wallace together on the right, and the growing anger of student anti-war activists and the Black Panther Party in the left. Fromm argued against naïve optimism because the prospects for peace, real democracy and a global humanistic movement for a better society were becoming grimmer. Still, he insisted on the value of faith, fortitude and what he described as a 'messianic hope' (Braune, 2014) to anchor movements for change building on the positive aspects of the McCarthy movement and the upsurge of radicalism among students and religious humanistic activists around the world. Fromm believed that the way forward was 'neither tired reformism nor pseudo-radical adventurism' (1968 p 9).

The Revolution of Hope sold over 2.5 million copies. The book struck emotional chords with readers who felt trapped between the reactionary right-wing movements of the time, unrealistic calls for revolution, and a corporate-media-university establishment that did not inspire trust. Young people and people new to politics, especially, were left feeling disillusioned. More politized activists would not have found the book as compelling as *The Sane Society* and *Marx's Concept of Man,* but there was a large general audience who found the book persuasive.

Money was key to both the strength and the limitations of Fromm's political activism. Fromm was wealthy from his best-selling books, as well as his speaking engagements, therapeutic practice, and the significant pay-off he had received from the Frankfurt School in the 1930s (Burston, 1991; McLaughlin, 1999; Friedman, 2013; Funk, 2019). Friedman's archival research shows how Fromm exaggerated the influence of the money he donated and the fame he brought to McCarthy's campaign. Fromm believed he had significant intellectual and policy influence on McCarthy when it seems far more likely that the candidate admired Fromm's books but was more interested in his campaign donations and the publicity an endorsement from a famous leftist could bring. Freidman offers compelling evidence that McCarthy's interest in the long letters he received from Fromm was less than central to his political activities in this period than Fromm imagined (Friedman, 2013).

Even with its sales and the hundreds of supportive letters that Fromm received, *The Revolution of Hope* was one of his intellectually weakest books. Originally conceived as a pamphlet, it showed once again how little Fromm understood of how to win votes. Based on his campaign speeches, the book stressed the pathological logic of technology in modern society, the raging nuclear arms race, and the bombing and violence of the Vietnam War, the latter likely being the only potentially winning argument in 1968. Fromm stressed a need for a politics of hope to replace the despairing politics of rage that Americans had seen after the assassinations of Malcolm X, Martin Luther King, Robert Kennedy and the Democratic Party convention riots. Fromm was on his way out of electoral politics, a decision sped up by the lacklustre response from readers to the mail-in form enclosed with the book. This intervention is further evidence of how unrealistic was Fromm's understanding of how one builds political organizations and movements.[4] It was particularly frustrating for Fromm that after the campaign was over and a follow-up meeting had been set up to build a movement, McCarthy did not show up as he had promised. Fromm's limitations as a political operative were on display.

After *The Revolution of Hope*, Fromm dramatically cut back his involvement in politics and soon moved to Switzerland. The radical humanism advanced in the book gradually replaced Fromm's earlier focus on democratic socialism. Fromm's health prevented further intense political campaigning, and he would soon turn his attention to more theoretical and empirical questions in *Social Character in a Mexican Village* and *The Anatomy of Human Destructiveness*. Before discussing these books, we will evaluate Fromm's intellectual and political work from the late 1950s to 1968 with attention to how activism, social criticism, and scholarship interact.

The double-edged sword of political engagement

Fromm's political writing during the early 1960s represents important examples of public sociology. What was the quality of Fromm's public sociology in this decade by the standards of professional sociology? Did Fromm's activism damage the quality of his academic scholarship or improve it? How did his political activism shape the quality of his public sociological work? How good an activist was he? What can all of this tell us about the general issues facing public sociologists, activist-academics and social critics? We will address these questions by looking at *May Man Prevail?* and *Marx's Concept of Man*.

The literature needs to move further towards evaluating public sociology on its own terms. While Fromm's *May Man Prevail?* may not meet the standards of the best political sociology or political science today, it needs to be compared to other works of public sociology like C. Wright Mills' *The Causes of World War III* (1958) and *Listen Yankee* (1960) or the public intellectual work represented by Noam Chomsky's *Necessary Illusions* (1995) and *Manufacturing Consent* (with Edward Herman, 2010). Mills' *Causes of World War III* was published in 1958 and is both less insightful and political engaged than *May Man Prevail?*. Selling around 100,000 copies after it came out (Treviño, 2012), the book was a polemical pamphlet that castigates what Mills calls the 'military metaphysics' and crackpot realism of both American and Soviet leaders who were leading the world to potential annihilation. The book was effective in inspiring revolt among young American students and anti-nuclear weapons activism. But Fromm reached far more readers and offered a more detailed, sophisticated, and balanced analysis of the sociological forces that were operating during the Cold War. Fromm backed up his analysis with money given to peace organizations and more public speaking for the cause.

Later in the 1960s, Chomsky, like Fromm, dedicated personal funds to anti-Vietnam War activism but even more significantly, he risked his career by advocating tax resistance and militant opposition to the war (Barsky, 2007). Chomsky's many books on American foreign policy in Vietnam, Central and Latin America, and the Middle East are comparable to Fromm's book also mostly pulled together from newspaper accounts (Chomsky 1972, 1995; Chomsky and Herman 1979a, 1979b). Chomsky engaged with foreign policy issues for decades at a level of detail that Fromm simply did not match, perhaps preoccupied as he was by therapy, writing about Freudian theory and various research projects. Fromm's dual insider/outsider status also probably limited his ability to write critically about American militarism and Israel in the ways that Chomsky did. Fromm's contributions to critical public sociology on questions of Soviet, Chinese, and Western militarism, however, are an important part of the history of public sociology. Fromm, like Chomsky, believed that the general citizen could form opinions about foreign policy in a democratic society freed from the dominance of state and corporate propaganda.

Fromm's distance from professional sociology and academic social science hurt the quality of his work in this period. In his disarmament writings on the Soviet Union, as well as his work on socialist-humanism, Fromm generally gave too much credit to the Soviet regime for running an economy that, over the long term, he suggested was sustainable. Fromm's critique of Soviet Marxism was moral and political but Fromm would have benefited from scholarly engagement with mainstream economists and political scientists. The Soviet Union after Stalin was deeply undemocratic and destructive of human dignity, but Fromm overestimated its economic success. Professional sociologists like Randall Collins would later predict the fall of the Soviet Union based on structural factors (Collins, 1995). Fromm did not think this way. Fromm's critique of mass consumerism and the industrial model itself led him to over-estimate the stability of the Soviet state, and by the 1950s he was not reading enough mainstream sociologists to facilitate a more robust analysis.

Fromm's promotion of Marx's early writings contributed a great deal to American sociology even though the book had its limitations as professional sociology and philosophy. The past sixty years has seen the institutionalization of studies of alienation starting with Robert Blauner (Blauner, 1964) and Melvin Kohn (Kohn, 1989; 2015, 1989; Kohn and Schooler, 1969; Kohn et al, 1997), and continuing with Arlie Hochschild's sociology of work and emotions (Hochschild, 1979; 1982, 2016). Fromm never followed up his theoretical writings on alienation with the careful empirical research done by later sociologists, but within academic Marxism and professional sociology he is part of the history of this tradition. Blauner laid out an important macro agenda with a critical edge (Blauner, 1964), and Kohn was a master in quantifying Fromm's work on the family as the socializing agent of class societies. Kohn was instrumental in creating a critical and comparative social psychology of work, something Fromm was simply not capable of doing. Hochschild attended to situational logics and rules of emotion combining Goffman, feminist insights, Fromm's popularization of Marx's theory of alienation and his earlier focus on the commercialization of feelings developing Fromm's notion of social character further. Fromm was not a major professional sociological Marxist but he helped make later research possible.

Philosophers and historians would also improve on Fromm's analysis. There is a massive literature on the theory of alienation that develops the details of Marx's philosophical perspective in far more scholarly ways as we see with Raya Dunayevskaya and Herbert Marcuse as well as the Praxis scholars to whom Fromm was close (Anderson, 1993, 2015). Philosophical work by Bertell Ollman (1971), Marshall Berman (1982), Agnes Heller (2018), and sociologist Philip Selznick in *The Moral Commonwealth: Social Theory and the Promise of Community* (Selznick, 1992) gave us a more scholarly analysis of Marx's early writing although he draws on Fromm's basic insights and inspiration.

There is a now a massive literature on Marx's life and character and his relationship to Engels in addition to historical scholarship contextualizing Marxism. Lawrence Friedman shows a lack of generosity and care in reading *The Sane Society* and *Beyond the Chains of Illusions*, when he suggests that Fromm was unaware of Marx's flaws and limitations. It is clear that Fromm decided in *Marx's Concept of Man* to highlight the humanist elements of Marx's ideas and life as a counterweight to the massive anti-Marxist propaganda that dominated American intellectual life at the time. What better example do we have of a public sociologist who created a humanist Marxist tradition in Cold War and 1960s era America? This was a major accomplishment for Fromm's public sociology even though his book is polemical more than scholarly. *The Sane Society* is actually quite critical of Marx.

Fromm's distance from scholarly and political elites later in his life was also an advantage. Fromm's position on the margins of both political scientists working within the foreign policy establishment and Marxist scholars led to real insights unavailable to professional sociologists. In retrospect, it is clear that Fromm was generally correct that after the death of Stalin, the Soviet Union was largely a conservative authoritarian regime focused on dominating the nations at its borders. Marxism in Soviet Russia was a stale ideology and American fears of world revolution led by Moscow were grossly exaggerated. Fromm was talking about the break between the Russians and Chinese versions of communism that we now call the Sino-Soviet split in real time something that should have raised questions about the American strategy in Indochina that led to the Vietnam War.

Fromm's reading of Marx and his activism among dissident Marxists in Poland, Hungary, and the former Yugoslavia made him sceptical of the claim that there was an expansionist and unified Marxist threat to the democratic world. Academics should have listened more carefully to Fromm given the important role played by scholars and scholar-activists in the United States government who helped imagine, plan, and execute the Vietnam War. Exaggerated assumptions of the Marxist motivations of America's enemies in this period were often promoted by academics who knew little about Marx or communism. Such assumptions contributed to the devastation and killing of the Vietnam War, undermining America's standing in the world and leading to massive domestic turmoil until the resignation of Richard Nixon.

How activism sharpened Fromm's intellectual vision

One of the missing pieces in the literature on public sociology is the specific intellectual insights that scholars gain from movement activism. Activism can distort objectivity even though there are good normative arguments for contributing to social change. There are trade-offs involved in public sociological engagement. Fromm's professional sociological work both gained from and was diminished by his activism.

There are issues where his judgement seems off, in retrospect. Owing to his understandable fears of the militarism of his homeland, Fromm may have overestimated the dangers of German reunification. It would be fair for democrats in Lithuania, Estonia, and Latvia to be critical of Fromm's willingness to accept the borders established after the Second World War as the price for peace.

He also got things right. Unlike the great public sociologist W. E. B. Du Bois who justified and supported the occupation of the Baltics and even wrote a glowing obituary for Stalin upon his death in 1953 (Du Bois, 1953), Fromm never wavered from his moral critique of Soviet expansion and brutality. Fromm did not equate Khrushchev and Stalin, nor did he believe either of them were motivated by a messianic Marxist vision for world revolution. Fromm was more critical of the fanaticism of Chinese communism than he was of the essentially conservative Soviet state Marxism of the time. He also appreciated the anti-colonial imperative of the Chinese revolution, something mainstream American political scientists had trouble recognizing.

Some of Fromm's insights about communism flowed as much from his activism on human rights in the Soviet sphere as from his readings of Marx, but it was the combination of the two that made him unique. Today's hawks might aver that the Soviet Union collapsed in the early 1990s due to the economic pressure created by the arms race. This view dismisses what the world would have looked like if the United States had bypassed the Vietnam War, opposed the South Africa apartheid regime instead of propping it up, and worked to ensure a more just resolution to the Israeli–Palestinian conflict. Fromm would be far less surprised than are most analysts today at the emergence of the Chinese Communist Party, whose authoritarian leaders adopted one-party state-led capitalism. Fromm doubted the influence of Marxist ideas on the actions of modern communist leaders, seeing instead the power of nationalism and self-interest especially evident in the Soviet Union. Wallerstein's world systems theory and more orthodox Marxists would emphasize the imperialist inevitability of colonial wars but Fromm never accepted that kind of determinism. Fromm was attempting to do something about the coming violence, not simply understand the Vietnam War as an inevitable reaction to the decline of imperial nations.

A public sociology that is purely left-wing or Marxist leads to a lack of political balance. Left-wing political orthodoxy is an inadequate lens through which to conceptualize the world as clearly as it must in order to change it, something Fromm not only believed in strongly but practised. Just as Marx had learned from Prussian state philosopher Hegel, Fromm drew on nineteenth-century aristocratic and reactionary thinker Bachofen's ideas on mother right and pre-modern systems of matriarchal rule to critiquing Freud's patriarchal thinking (Burston, 1991; Funk, 2019). To develop his analysis of twentieth-century communism, moreover, he consulted the work of centrist and conservative scholars (Fromm, 1961b). Today, the left tends to ignore the corrections that can come from debates among a politically diverse set of scholars (Gross, 2013; Lukiannoff and Haidt, 2018). In Fromm's time, it was easier for him to engage liberals and centrists who were critical of the authoritarian right than it is for leftists to do so today when the middle is not holding up under contemporary polarization (Wolfe, 1996). But Fromm did especially well by this political openness metric, often doing better than the liberal centre.

Beyond unusual figures like liberal David Riesman it is important to not exaggerate the openness of liberal elites in this period. On some of the major issues in Cold War and early 1960s America, it was often public intellectuals and public sociologists on the right and the liberal centre who were most vocal and effective in limiting the debate on American foreign policy, taking money from questionable sources and red-baiting dissidents (Bloom, 1986; Jumonville, 1991; Wald, 2017). One of the reasons why we don't remember Fromm's public sociology on the Soviet Union and China from this period is that he was subjected to a bitter set of criticisms by public intellectuals associated with the political view we now call 'neo-conservativism'.

Fromm's views on disarmament, the Vietnam War, and the role of Marxism in the contemporary world challenged what Noam Chomsky would later call 'the Washington Consensus' (Chomsky and Herman, 1979a, 1979b). While contemporary political liberals celebrate experts, we should not forget that the Harvard intellectual elite were central to providing legitimation for the immoral and disastrous Indochina wars. The intellectuals who objected to Fromm most intensely and who damaged his intellectual reputation most severely in the 1960s and 1970s were not, in fact, the China and Russia area experts in elite academic departments. Fromm's major enemies were former Marxists in the process of becoming conservative public sociologists and elite liberal public intellectuals.

Fromm was viciously attacked in the 1960s by intellectuals, some of them sociologists, who had shifted from Marxism to militant anti-communism often in an alliance with American state actors. Philosopher Sidney Hook attacked Fromm on many occasions. His two pieces published in 1961, 'Escape from Reality' and 'Marx and Alienation' in *The New Leader* (cited in Anderson, 2015) the house organ of what we would now call neo-conservativism, illustrates the extent of the threat that Fromm posed to the intellectual consensus of the time. Hook had been a student of pragmatist philosopher John Dewey and was America's great expert on Marx and Marxism. He taught at New York University before he moved far to the right as his socialist commitments transformed into a militant anti-communism. Hook accused Fromm of appeasement in ways that would lead to the victory of world communism. Martin Perez, later the editor of the influential Cold War liberal outlet *The New Republic*, also attacked Fromm's 'logic of surrender' in *The New Leader* (also cited in Anderson, 2015). This conservative and Cold War liberal critique of Fromm's writings echoed inside sociology, damaging his intellectual reputation. Edward Shils (Shils, 1980), Daniel Bell, and Seymour Martin Lipset (Lipset, 1996) were not sympathetic to Fromm's Marxism and critique of the American empire. Shils played a role in undermining Fromm's reputation in sociology given his opinions about Fromm, Marxism, and his influence in the field during the Cold War (Shils, 1980).[5]

Fromm's political involvement with dissident Marxists in the Soviet sphere, as well as his efforts working behind the scenes and with Amnesty International to gain freedom for his cousin imprisoned in East Germany, sharpened his intellectual work. It helped him avoid both Cold War liberalism and popular apologetics for communist tyranny. The Marxist academics of Fromm's generation came out of the Marxist movement when it was located outside the university.

The 1960s and 1970s Marxist sociologists like Burawoy and Erik Olin Wright (Wright, 2010) were a transitional generation formed by the movements of the New Left era. Having lived through the crushing of the Prague Spring in 1968, they were not naïve about authoritarian communism. By the 1980s and 1990s and the early years of the twenty-first century, Marxist sociologists were often more academic than Marxist.

It is extraordinary that the impressive revival of interest in the work of W. E. B. Du Bois, for example, almost completely ignores the problematic relationship he had with Stalinism later in his life (Du Bois, 1953; Fleck and Hess, 2011; Morris, 2015). Fromm's analysis of Stalin's sadistic behaviour in *The Anatomy of Human Destructiveness*, in contrast, flowed from knowledge of Stalinism gained from his human rights activism. For many Marxist sociologists today, the tradition is about texts, dialectics, and abstractions. Scholars can read Althusser and deliberate about socialism and communism without any knowledge of the reality of life and death under Stalinism or Maoism. Fromm was not a successful socialist activist, but he brought many thousands into the movement with his powerful writing. Fromm also helped infuse the discipline of sociology with critical perspectives on left-wing authoritarianism, something needed in the post-pandemic and post-Trump era of economic crisis, right-wing populism, amnesia about Stalinism, and the rise to global power of authoritarian Chinese Communist Party-led capitalism.

Evaluating Fromm's activism and policy sociology, both inside and outside the system

On anti-war and nuclear weapons issues, Fromm was reasonably effective as an activist, donating funds to help sustain SANE and working with Riesman on the Committee for Correspondence newsletter, a hub for nuclear disarmament issues that he also financially supported. Fromm was an effective anti-war and disarmament speaker on American campuses and at community events, and his name recognition and writing skills brought large numbers of people into the movement. Willing to stand up at elite events of American policy makers and scientists and in Moscow at the important Soviet-sponsored global peace conference, Fromm made his arguments with passion and balance. Few others would challenge nuclear extremists like the American strategist Herman Kahn who proclaimed his view that a nuclear war would be survivable while also challenging Khrushchev's lackeys in Moscow itself (Friedman, 2013).

Fromm's work with Riesman on peace and anti-nuclear issues is another good example of what can be accomplished if our public and policy sociology is done with collaboration across political camps. Fromm and Riesman were personally close, but their political views were different. SANE was on the moderate to centrist side of the peace movement in the United States in the 1960s responding to McCarthyism by banning communists from their organization and by stressing respectability, expertise, and middle-class American values as the basis of their organizing. Riesman was far more comfortable with this general approach than was Fromm, although they shared anti-Stalinist viewpoints.

Yet their differences were real. Riesman always rejected Fromm's socialism and what Riesman saw as his unrealistic utopian streak. As a long-time friend and collaborator of both men and influential scholar and writer in his own right (Maccoby, 1972, 1980, 2003), Michael Maccoby stresses that Fromm was ambivalent about Riesman both intellectually and politically. Seeing him as too willing to accept all sides of a matter, Fromm judged Riesman as having no clear political commitments (Maccoby, 2015 p 188). As Maccoby puts it, 'Riesman was an empathetic liberal democrat and Fromm was a radical socialist humanist. While Riesman valued civility and was skeptical of radicals, Fromm admired revolutionary fervor' (Maccoby, 2015 p 188).

Along with their ability to work together and trust each other, this combination was creative and helped them channel their shared opposition to American militarism in effective ways. Fromm contributed to the creation of arms reductions and nuclear weapons treaties through his work in SANE. The fact that he was willing to do so in collaboration with liberal forces avoided some of the extremes seen later in the 1960s as the peace movement erupted into Marxist-Leninist 'days of rage' (Gitlin, 1987). Many activists and social movement scholars would argue that there was a need for more militant action in the 1960s than SANE could provide (Piven, 2006, 2008). Fromm played a valuable role in creating democratic socialist opposition to the system speaking at radical protests and raising larger structural issues that Riesman would not do. Intellectual life requires both what Goldfarb called 'civility and subversion' (Goldfarb, 1998) and the Fromm–Riesman collaboration represents an attempt at a synthesis. The issue is not that these differences can be easily resolved or evaded. Fearing a right-wing backlash, Riesman was critical of Fromm for supporting the Columbia student protests in the late 1960s, while Fromm viewed Riesman as being too cautious and insufficiently visionary. Riesman and Fromm argued these strategic differences out, agreed to disagree and moved on, a productive lesson in these days of cancel culture.

Some of the work Fromm did in this period should be evaluated as policy sociology. There exists no right answer for how one should best do policy sociology since we cannot possibly know policy outcomes in advance. The conservative insistence on unintended consequences brought into the discipline by Max Weber and Robert Merton is a concept worth remembering (Merton, 1998). While Fromm's prophetic voice sometimes overwhelmed his analytic good sense (Maccoby, 1995) with what Burawoy called the pathologies of 'critical sociology', Riesman made compromises with the American political system that Fromm's visionary critique usefully challenges. Fromm's analysis and politics often becoming excessively utopian. The Fromm–Riesman dyad suggests lessons for policy sociology.

Noam Chomsky represents a different model for militant intellectual opposition to American foreign policy. Chomsky's uncompromising opposition to the foreign policy establishment, as well as his critique of the role of the mainstream media in providing ideological cover of the misuse of power, provides inspiration for contemporary media sociologists (Herman and Chomsky, 2010). At the same time, most academic media critics view Chomsky's account of the media as lacking nuance, even for those on the left such as Todd Gitlin who is no defender of mainstream media elites (Todd Gitlin, personal communication, June 2020). Fromm was very similar politically to Chomsky although he did not share Chomsky's unwillingness to collaborate with liberals and with the mainstream media (Chomsky, 1967, 1972, 1995; Brown, 2020). While Fromm become a forgotten intellectual partly due to his critiques of the liberal establishment, Chomsky was harder to cancel because of his less-challenged status inside his own specialized field. There is research to be done by professional sociologists looking at the 'space of opinion', (Jacobs and Townsley, 2011), in order to think sociologically about figures like Chomsky and Fromm.

One of the most intense political conflicts among American elite intellectuals in the twentieth century was the feud historian Michael Brown documented between Chomsky and Arthur Schlesinger Jr. (Brown, 2020). Chomsky called out Schlesinger's lies on behalf of the United States Government, particularly connected to the Bay of Pigs invasion of Cuba. Schlesinger was playing a dual role of policy advisor to President John Kennedy and historian at Harvard, the second position coming with a greater obligation to articulate the truth (Chomsky, 1967; Brown, 2020). For Chomsky, he was the perfect example of the New Mandarins of compromised intellectuals while Schlesinger viewed Chomsky as a dogmatic ideologue (Brown, 2020), a view that is common in elite media circles in the United States even today (Lannigan and McLaughlin, 2017).

Fromm, on the other hand, critiqued American foreign policy while maintaining channels to elites as observed in the 'The Berlin Crisis' memo and his personal relationship to top American politicians. Fromm and Riesman addressed the memo to Schlesinger while he was Special Assistant to President Kennedy in the summer of 1961 when the threat of US–Soviet nuclear war loomed over access to the divided German capital (Fromm and Riesman, 2015).[6] It is very possible that Friedman (2013) exaggerates the influence Fromm and Riesman would have had on Schlesinger, a hard-nosed power player (Todd Gitlin, personal communication, June 2020). The Fromm–Riesman collaboration raises interesting questions about how public and critical sociologists might avoid echo chambers by conversing and working with scholars with different political views both inside and outside elite circles.

Fromm also got things done. Lawrence Friedman's biography makes the case that Fromm had significant influence on the Kennedy Administration's foreign policy on nuclear weapons. Kennedy had read both *Escape from Freedom* and Fromm's arms race proposal in the elite policy journal *Daedalus*. In his article, 'The Case for Unilateral Disarmament', Fromm recommended reasoned and reversible de-escalation of the nuclear arms race (Fromm, 1960b).[7] In Kennedy's famous address six months before he was assassinated, he 'advocated détente with the Soviets, open discussions on arms control measures, a ban on nuclear testing, and ultimately the elimination of all nuclear weapons' (Friedman, 2013 p 211). It is possible that Fromm had indirect influence on Kennedy through Norman Cousins (Todd Gitlin, personal communication. June 2020), another topic for specialized historians on Kennedy's foreign policy.

Chomsky and critical sociologists and intellectuals today would argue – and not without merit – that Friedman's claims on behalf of Fromm's behind-the-scenes policy work is too kind to the Kennedy Administration. In part, this reflects Friedman's own political insider status and sympathies to the Riesman–Erikson style of negotiation that Fromm flirted with (Friedman, 2013). The practice of radical and prophetic sociologist as outside critic with few connections to communities and political constituents is vulnerable to critiques of dogmatism expressed by scholars (Maccoby, 1995; Walzer, 1988; Burawoy, 2005). These are larger issues for public and policy sociologists to debate, with the Fromm–Riesman collaboration as a case study.

Freidman's (2013) account of these issues is flawed by his own preference for the insider Harvard-based politics and Democratic Party channels (Friedman, 2013). But he is right that Fromm's political activism linked to *The Revolution of Hope* was damaged by his political inexperience and reliance on his money and fame for access to political influence. Friedman shows that Fromm's involvement in American electoral politics started not with his grassroots involvement in campaigns or parties but with his direct access to politicians. Starting with the presidential campaign of Adlai Stevenson in 1952, moving through Fromm's relationship to Senator J. William Fulbright (an anti-war Republican from the South who somewhat reluctantly opposed major civil right reforms), and with his efforts on behalf on the anti-war Democratic Party primary challenge of Eugene McCarthy in 1968, Fromm's politics was mediated through personal relations created by his fame. Fromm connected with these different but powerful political figures because they had read his writings, particularly *Escape from Freedom*. He developed political relationships by donating money to their campaigns, sending them things to read and, in Fulbright's case, becoming friends. Fromm's fame as an intellectual, however, damaged his ability to engage in electoral politics as a citizen as effectively as his values would have predicted. Fromm's geographic and cultural distance from America left him unconcerned about Fulbright's mixed democratic credentials as a liberal on foreign policy with a poor record on civil rights.

The verdict on Fromm's political activism between the late 1950s and 1968 is mixed. Fromm had an undeniable influence on the emergence of the anti-nuclear weapons and anti-Vietnam movements of the 1950s and 1960s. He played a significant role in promoting Amnesty International and human rights. Fromm's policy work with David Riesman on the Berlin Crisis and arms control electoral policy had some influence although how much is hard to say. It is certainly possible that elites in the government liked to talk to Riesman and Fromm to create an appearance of openness, more than being actually being influenced by their ideas. Furthermore, one could certainly argue, as Noam Chomsky and many public sociologists and social movement scholars such as Frances Fox Piven would, that he would have been better off exposing government lies and building alternative movements outside establishment circles in the turmoil of the 1960s. Like today, those were polarized times; finding a middle ground was not easy.

Yet Fromm helped socialize thousands of young readers of his books into the socialist tradition in America. He legitimated democratic Marxist ideas in the United States more than anyone until Michael

Harrington in the 1970s and 1980s and Bernie Sanders from 2016 to 2020. Like Harrington and Sanders, Fromm supported feminism and civil rights. Also like them, his political framework was forged well before these movements and as a result, much of his language and instincts are outdated in today's terms. But Fromm's basic framework is progressive and open enough to be revised and reformulated for the twenty-first century.

Fromm was an important part of the rise of global Marxist humanism, reaching out to, supporting, and engaging with intellectuals and activists in Poland, Hungary, Latin America, and to a lesser extent, Africa, Asia, and the Middle East. His humanist Marxism was, in political terms, far more important than the excessively abstract and narrow professional critical theory common on university campuses today. Academic Marxists are more concerned with dialectics and close textual readings than making the powerful ethical appeals of Marx's original vision, what Michael Harrington called (drawing on Fromm's analysis), Marx's 'spiritual materialism' (1976). Cornel West's book about the 'ethical dimensions of Marxist thought' (West, 1991b) is generally consistent with Fromm's humanism. But even West, in many ways an admirable and more politically engaged replacement for Fromm in America in the twenty-first century as a celebrity public intellectual socialist, has a tendency to revert to academic jargon and Adorno-influenced pessimism.

Fromm's commitments to radical engagement, especially in the period from the late 1950s to 1968, was impressive. Like C. Wright Mills, who died after a heart attack in 1962, Fromm was pushing himself to the limits in his political activism in the late 1950s and 1960s. After Richard Nixon was elected president in 1968 and proceeded to escalate the brutal bombings and counterinsurgency in Vietnam and to invade Cambodia in an illegal and secretive strategy to end the conflict with terms favourable to the United States, Fromm became despairing of traditional political electoral politics and democratic socialism.

Lawrence Friedman understands this despair as reflecting the ills of old age as Fromm knew his time was limited, given his declining health. I would argue, however, that Fromm's disillusionment with political movements was created partly by the fact that he was only half engaged with political activism and did not fully understand how it operated. As a consequence, Fromm was more disappointed than the seasoned activists who accepted inevitable defeats and moved on to the next battle.

The case of Erich Fromm as a public sociologist is also a case study in the damage that celebrity status can do to the intellectual and political work of scholars. Fromm's fame distorted his perception of how politics works on the ground. Fromm's distance from the Socialist Party of America establishment and the American Democratic Party, however, did allow him to raise larger and tougher critiques of American society and foreign policy than many others did. Fromm often spoke from what I have called an 'optimally marginal' position (McLaughlin, 2001a) that was close enough to the centre of cultural capital and networks to be able to be heard, but independent enough not to be compromised. Fromm's fame and money compromised his influence as a radical but was effective in other ways.

With *May Man Prevail?* and *Marx's Concept of Man*, Fromm took advantage of 'what a book can do' (Murphy, 2005) by helping create a socialist and New Left upsurge and socialist humanist conversation in the United States and globally. All this would be exhausting and his health was declining. Fromm would spend the early 1970s returning to academic work with two major scholarly books, *Social Character in a Mexican Village* and *The Anatomy of Human Destructiveness*, both attempts to refine and develop his theoretical and methodological approach to critical, professional, policy, and public sociology.

6

Studying Social Character and Theorizing Violence

Fromm's declining health in the later part of the 1960s called him home to Europe. Living out the last decade of his life on a lake at Locarno, Switzerland, Fromm finished his academic career with two major scholarly books: *Social Character in a Mexican Village* (written with Michael Maccoby, 1970) and *The Anatomy of Human Destructiveness* (1973). These two books represent Fromm's final framing of his intellectual and public sociological legacy and a response to the criticisms of social character theory and his revision of psychoanalysis respectively. Contrary to the myth that Fromm had become a purely popular writer who produced little of academic value (Coser, 1984; Friedman, 2013), these two books were his most scholarly despite being published by commercial presses. *Social Character* and *Anatomy* represent Fromm's analytic voice and a return to the scholarly writing he did in the 1930s and 1940s.

Reminiscent of the working class in Weimar and authoritarian family studies conducted while part of the Frankfurt School, Fromm had a number of goals for *Social Character in a Mexican Village*. First, he wanted to provide evidence for his theory of social character by revisiting and refining the interpretive questionnaire method from the Weimar study in the late 1920s and early 1930s using Mexico as a case study. Second, he wanted to provide policy advice on local village development to different levels of government. In addition, he raised normative questions about existing theories of capitalist growth for what was then referred to as the Third World (Fromm and Maccoby, 1970; Maccoby and McLaughlin, 2020). The book was thus professional, policy and critical sociology.

The Anatomy of Human Destructiveness was a continuation of Fromm's earlier revisions of psychoanalytic theory in order to develop a theory of violence. Drawing from the mechanism of 'destructiveness' in *Escape from Freedom*, and account of 'necrophilia' in *The Heart of Man: Its Genius for Good and Evil* (1964), Fromm responded to the charge that he was a simplistic and naïve proponent of feel-good thinking. Fromm articulated a psychoanalytically influenced interdisciplinary theoretical account of human violence that avoided both liberal optimism and sociobiological pessimism. The book was to be both part of his psychoanalytic legacy and a public sociology intervention in public debates about violence and human nature.

A sociology of knowledge perspective

Fromm's sociological positioning in various academic fields would have important consequences for the content and quality of both books. His creation of the Mexican Psychoanalytic Institute in Mexico City had helped isolate him from attacks from orthodox Freudians in the United States. Based in Mexico, Fromm could focus on his own therapeutic practice and his writing without the distractions of New York City. Fromm continued to obtain major research funding and publish in major commercial presses well into his seventies, but he was outside of the core networks where academic capital circulates (Bourdieu, 1988; Collins, 1998).

Fromm's increasing marginality within mainstream sociology shaped how *Social Character in a Mexican Village* came to be written and received. A more important book in the history of professional sociology than has often been acknowledged, *Social Character* elaborates a theory of social character that is a more psychologically insightful version of Bourdieu's concept of habitus. Remarkable for its empirical contribution to the study of development, it is also the single most important example of Fromm's policy sociology. The book is less successful, however, than it could have been within sociology due to Fromm's distance from the professional core.

A similar dynamic was at play with *The Anatomy of Human Destructiveness*, a book completed in relative isolation in Switzerland in Fromm's twilight years. A return to key theoretical questions about the human passions for violence and hatred that animated his career, *Anatomy* was among his more scholarly, even technical, books. The book also represented a public intellectual intervention in debates about the roots of human evil and the power of evolutionary sociobiological factors in shaping human societies. *Anatomy* showcases Fromm's psychoanalytic as well as interdisciplinary commitments. Attempting to develop an integrated theory of human destructiveness grounded in his own revision of Freudian theory, the book engages the best work in archaeology, anthropology, history, psychology, and even the neurosciences.

Fromm's fame and status, alongside the financial independence he had carved out for himself, boosted the theoretical power of the book. Few scholars operating in the highly professionalized and specialized fields of psychology, anthropology, or historical sociology would have attempted such a comprehensive and broad interdisciplinary analysis. The professional logics of specialization in each field had gained significant conformist and limiting power over scholars by the 1970s.

Even fewer scholars would engage public debates about the roots of destructiveness. Fromm had the stature and the confidence gained by his scholarly and popular writing to publish an interdisciplinary treatise on violence with a commercial press. This is a form of public intellectual work that was innovative at the time but is common today (Pinker, 2011; Bregman, 2019; Christakis, 2019). Reading widely in archaeology, anthropology, and history, Fromm also consulted with experts in neurosciences. He integrated his revised psychoanalytic theory with empirical social and biological sciences.

The power of his analysis, however, is weakened by the multiple audiences for which the book was written. Half popular polemic against the public intellectual work of sociobiologist Konrad Lorenz and militant behaviourist B. F. Skinner, and half scholarly theoretical treatise on the origins of human violence, *Anatomy* only partly succeeds. Fromm's marginality among both academics and elite intellectuals enabled him see things that others could not. Despite the value of his studies of Stalin and Hitler, Fromm's marginality to mainstream social science had negative consequences both for the quality of his ideas and his reputation as a global public sociologist.

This chapter reviews each of these two major books, provides the historical and biographical context to their production, and evaluates them in light of recent research. We compare and contrast Fromm's theory of social character in *Social Character* with Pierre Bourdieu's concept of habitus and his sociological account of Algeria conducted around the same time that Fromm studied Mexico. Our analysis of *Anatomy* allows us to address the proper relationship of sociology to evolutionary psychology and the neurosciences. I also discuss how Fromm's analysis of various pathological historical figures combines a sociological analysis of what Bourdieu called habitus with Fromm's insights into the logics of character and emotions.

It is worth reflecting on why Fromm's work in the early 1970s found such a small audience in sociology. Each of these books were part of Fromm's career-long efforts to combine professional, critical, public, and policy forms of sociological and broader public intellectual content. *Social Character* represents his professional and policy work with an element of critical sociology; *Anatomy* is professional interdisciplinary work, public psychoanalysis and sociology, and critical social science. I also consider how the celebrity status that he had attained by the 1970s shaped his reputation and the quality of this work. These works were ignored in sociology partly because his broader reputation had been damaged in the 1960s and early 1970s, especially in English-language social science.

A neglected community study: *Social Character in a Mexican Village*

Fromm had two main goals for this study. Unhappy with criticism that suggested his work was unscientific, Fromm wanted to establish scholarly support for his concept of social character by developing and testing the theory with empirical data. The second purpose was to do research that would be useful for predicting and planning positive social change in peasant societies, a set of policy sociology goals that Fromm especially wanted to pursue in Mexico as an act of reciprocity. The book was thus concerned both with the theoretical and methodological puzzles of professional sociology (and anthropology) and the practical goals of policy sociology.

Although Fromm was often attacked unfairly for being a mystical thinker and popular writer, it would be a mistake to ignore his roots in nineteenth-century utopian radicalism as well as the sociological traditions concerned with scientifically designing a better society. Fromm, like Bourdieu, was a critic of this 'positivism', but they both shared with Comte and Saint-Simon a commitment to gathering social science data, using theory to interpret empirical reality, and using science to create social change.

Before writing *Social Character in a Mexican Village*, Fromm had argued for the creation of a committee of respected scientific and humanistic intellectuals who could be consulted on social and political issues. His commitment to helping design a better Mexico was rooted in a long-standing vision of democratic social engineering common in sociology even on the left. In this way, Fromm was similar to the great French sociologist Pierre Bourdieu who, in the 1990s, would also call for the establishment of a committee of intellectuals to shape social change in the French social engineering tradition of what Marx once called utopian socialism (Swartz, 2013). Fromm's utopian vision was oriented around helping Mexico avoid what he saw as the inhumanely destructive path of capitalist development that the nation was ready to embark upon in the 1950s and early 1960s. It was also an opportunity to develop his theory of social character and his method of the interpretive questionnaire both first outlined in his workers study in Germany in the 1920s and 1930s (Brunner, 1994).

The conventional wisdom that Fromm left serious social science after he broke with the Frankfurt School in the 1930s ignores the empirical research he did in Mexico. Based on the template that Fromm created with his interpretive questionnaire in the late 1920s and early 1930s when he was associated with the Horkheimer school of critical theory, the book was concerned with explaining how social character shaped support for Hitler (Brunner, 1994). The study looked at the role social character played in explaining economic development under conditions of poverty in a formerly colonized and then underdeveloped society. While the working class in Weimar study was based on larger but a non-random sample from different locations, the Mexican study focused on depth not breadth, intensely studying one small village.

When the Weimar study was conducted, Fromm was a pioneer in this method, but by the time *Social Character in a Mexican Village* was completed in the 1960s, anthropologists had developed psychological methods of analysis (Redfield, 1956; Foster, 1967). Pierre Bourdieu had begun his own version of a social character study in Algeria around the same time, later absorbed within his broader theory of habitus, field, and capital (Bourdieu, 1984, 1990b, 2013a, 2013b; Swartz, 1997). Fromm had more resources at his disposal than did Bourdieu in the early years of his career (Swartz, 1997; Maccoby and McLaughlin, 2020). Fromm had the cooperation of the national and regional Mexican Government, the local elites in the village, Father William Wasson, the founder of a large orphanage in the surrounding area, and American Friends Service volunteers. He was also able to recruit volunteers from his Mexican Psychoanalytic Institute and he received significant funding from the American Foundations Fund for Research in Psychiatry.

Fromm selected Chiconcauc, a small village of 280 families, formerly landless *campesinos*, who had been given small plots of land after the revolution of 1910–1920. Interviews were conducted with every villager over the age of sixteen along with half of the children. Supplementing this with economic surveys, statistical analysis, psychological tests, and participant observation, Fromm sought to demonstrate that his socio-psychoanalytic concept of social character could explain relationships between economic, social, and psychological factors. With a team of researchers, Fromm worked at the project for years while he was engaged in a range of other professional and political activities in the late 1950s and early 1960s. A local internist was hired to interview adult villagers using a questionnaire eliciting responses that could be interpreted according to Fromm's theory of character types. Mexican psychologists administered Rorschach tests and Thematic Apperception Tests (TAT), a common research tool that involved asking the research participants to interpret images of people involved in various scenes.

From 1958 to 1960, Theodore and Lola Schwartz, two American anthropologists linked to Fromm's old friend Margaret Mead, carried out participant observation and an economic survey of village families. There were conflicts between the Schwartzes and Fromm (Friedman, 2013). One was a theoretical difference; Fromm felt they were uncommitted to the psychoanalytic theoretical frame for the study. Another involved ethics; Lola Schwartz wanted to use the data for her dissertation in ways that Fromm felt would compromise his promise of anonymity to the village. Fromm further alleged they were helping villagers get to the United States, an ethical problem in his view (Friedman, 2013).

Fromm was reasonably well connected to American anthropologists in the 1950s, having taught at Yale, and he kept up with some of his colleagues from the culture and personality school of anthropology (Burston, 1991). He also remained very close to American anthropologist Ashley Montagu, a major critic of scientific racism (Burston, 1991). As a result of these connections, Fromm was more up to date with anthropology than sociology.

In 1960, Michael Maccoby, then a young Harvard-trained scholar and social psychologist connected to David Riesman, joined the project as an eventual replacement for the Schwartz couple who left in 1961 (Maccoby and McLaughlin, 2020). Maccoby – who was funded by a research and training fellowship from the US National Institute for Mental Health – interpreted all of the questionnaire responses and projective text material in relation to social character types and, at regular project meetings, discussed many of the interpretations and results with Fromm. Together with an anthropologist and psychologist, Maccoby studied the village children (Maccoby, 1964, 1966) and led an agricultural club for adolescent boys with help from the American Friends Service Committee. Maccoby produced the statistical analysis, wrote up all the results, and was responsible for the history chapter that contextualized the study in relation to the colonial destruction of traditional culture and the oppressive nature of Spanish economic rule. For comparison, he also interviewed *campesinos* in another village (Maccoby and Foster, 1970).

Fromm recognized that the study would be strengthened with illustrative descriptions of individuals and families, but he had promised the villagers that they would remain anonymous. In a small village in which some of the inhabitants suffered from alcoholism and domestic violence was not uncommon, Fromm believed that it would be ethically unacceptable to identify the village or individuals. There was no reasonable way to present ethnographic evidence without breaching obvious ethical obligations for social research. Fromm cared about these issues (Friedman, 2013).

The conflict between Fromm and Theodore and Lola Schwartz extended for some years, despite the unsuccessful attempts of David Riesman at mediation (Friedman, 2013). If the young scholars had been more involved, the final publication might well have been more ethnographic and in more dialogue with mainstream anthropologists. The incident may well have been unavoidable, however, given the ethical and theoretical issues at stake. Some observers feel that Fromm's behaviour exhibited a certain authoritarianism (Friedman, 2013). Before getting to these larger issues, it is necessary to review the theoretical goals and the empirical results of the study.

Social character theory: habitus with depth psychology

The concept of social character was Fromm's most original and important contribution to social theory; it can be understood as an earlier and more psychoanalytic version of Bourdieu's theory of habitus. While Fromm was a psychoanalytic theorist and Bourdieu was a sociologist generally hostile to the Freudian tradition, the concept of social character refers neither to a unique character structure nor a psychological personality as it exists in an individual. The theory cannot be dismissed as psychologically reductionist. Social character relates to what Fromm called a character matrix – a syndrome of character traits that developed as an adaptation to the economic, social, and cultural conditions common to that group. Fromm's theory emerged and developed in the 1930s, 1940s, and 1950s, around the same time as the development of other national character theories, and his work during this period was loosely associated with culture and personality research that is now unfashionable. Fromm was not a national character theorist, however, as he believed that nations were shaped by historical and sociological logics connected to a social character that is both psychological and sociological.

Social Character in a Mexican Village was also explicitly framed as a critique of modernization theories that highlighted culture in uncritical ways. Modernization theories explained poverty in Latin America as partly caused by Catholic or Mexican traits. Fromm rejected all of this, very explicitly. Distinct from national character theories, Fromm's social character theory alternative to the modernization perspective has more affinity to Bourdieu's theory of habitus, albeit with more psychoanalytic and less cognitive psychology. Fromm integrated what he viewed as core insights from both Karl Marx and Sigmund Freud while rejecting orthodox dogma from the theoretical systems of Marxism and psychoanalysis respectively. In 1962, Fromm described the basis of his theory:

> Marx postulated the interdependence between the economic basis of society and the political and legal institutions, its philosophy, art, religion, etc. The former, according to Marxist theory, determined the latter, the 'Ideological superstructure'. But Marx and Engels did not show, as Engels admitted quite explicitly, *how* the economic basis is translated into the ideological superstructure. I believe that by using the tools of psychoanalysis, this gap in Marxian theory can be filled, and the economic basis structure and the superstructure are connected. One of these connections lies in what I have called the *social character*. (Fromm, 1962 p 17)

The core of the theory was expressed in 'The social and individual roots of neurosis', in the *American Sociological Review*:

> The particular ways in which a society functions are determined by a number of objective economic and political factors, which are given at any point of historical development. Societies have to operate within the possibilities and limitations of their particular historical situation. In order that any society may function well, its members must acquire the kind of character which makes them want to act in the way they have to act as members of the society or of a special class within it. They have to desire what objectively is necessary for them to do. Outer force is to be replaced by inner compulsion, and by the particular kind of human energy which is channeled into character trait. (Fromm, 1944 p 381)

Drawing on Marx, Fromm also rejected the inattention to emotions, morality and human nature in orthodox Marxism. Fromm used Freud's dynamic character types to describe the nucleus of social character in ways that Marxists never could with their focus on economic and class relations. Fromm also rejected Freud's theory of character development based on libidinal ties as well as what he viewed as Freud's commitment to patriarchal and nineteenth-century bourgeois values. Fromm proposed instead a synthesis: a psychological theory of character formation connected to a Marxist-influenced analysis of the social relationships rooted in the form of economic development and class relations of a particular historical period. Fromm's broader purpose was the creation of a healthier, more productive social character.

Results of the study

Social Character in a Mexican Village contributes to our knowledge on the relationship between social character and behaviour and the interaction between economic, social, cultural, and psychological factors. At its outset, Fromm raised the following question: What happened to the *campesinos* after the Mexican revolution? Despite the fact that they were given land, many *campesinos* failed to take advantage of these new opportunities. Alcoholism appeared to increase, and there was a high incidence of violence. Why did this happen? Fromm concluded that those villagers who were raised before the revolution in the culture of the semi-feudal hacienda lacked the self-confidence and the self-directed, hard-working character associated with successful peasants throughout the world. Their submissive, receptive, unproductive character, which was adapted to life in the hacienda, made them vulnerable to alcoholism and exploitation after the revolution. The children of these villagers were likely to share some of these character traits. In contrast, the villagers who had been landowners demonstrated adaptive productive hoarding traits. They farmed their land effectively, and they attempted to maintain conservative patriarchal values and traditions. Those few villagers with a modern outlook and an entrepreneurial character, the productive exploitative types, proved best able to take advantage of the new opportunities. They also took advantage of the unproductive villagers by renting land from them, and then opening small businesses. They took the lead in transforming the culture, abolishing costly fiestas, and building roads and schools. The study demonstrated that although the revolution left the villagers in a state of relative equality, a new class system would inevitably emerge building on differences in social character unless there was comprehensive structural and emotional change.

One of the most significant findings of the study concerns the relationship between character and the actual farming behaviour of the *campesinos*. Those who were psychologically more 'productive', based on the questionnaires, were also economically more productive. What Fromm and Maccoby called 'productive peasants' planted the major part of their land in cash crops such as rice and vegetables which demanded a great deal of care and hard work. While some of the psychologically receptive unproductive landholders rented out their land, the others farmed it with sugar cane which produced a much lower profit but greater security. Cane required fewer days of work and less upkeep. The difficult, dirty job of harvesting the cane was done by migrant workers who occupied the lowest class in Mexican rural society and were hired by the sugar refinery, the 'cooperative' which took on the paternalistic role of the old hacienda. Some landholders who tried to escape the control of the cooperative found their crops ploughed under.

The most economically astute villagers planted a small percentage of their land with just enough sugar cane to satisfy the cooperative, gain its benefits in the form of scholarships for their children, health care, and low-cost loans, and avoid political conflict while optimizing their income. Given the new rules of the game after the revolution, some peasants were able to improve their class position relative to others by perceiving the new rules of the game quickly and developing new strategies for advancement. Fromm never assumed this was only about personal choice. He was concerned precisely with the reproduction of inequality in the everyday life of dominated classes and social strata, something French sociologist Bourdieu later theorized (Bourdieu 1977, 2013b; Swartz, 2013). We turn now to a brief comparison of Fromm and Bourdieu.

Bourdieu's theory of habitus

Bourdieu's sociological analysis of field, capital, and habitus is his most important contribution to the study of culture, education, and work within sociology. Fromm would have viewed Bourdieu's use of the categories of cultural, economic, social, and symbolic capital as reifying existing power relations. Their theoretical frameworks, however, overlap with the concepts of social character and habitus. Habitus is:

> a system of durable, transposable dispositions, structured structures predisposed to function as structuring structures,

that is, as principles which generate and organize practices and representations that can be objectively adapted to their outcomes without presupposing a conscious aiming at ends or an express mastery of the operations necessary to attain them. (Bourdieu, 1990a p 53)

In various other places in his considerable scholarly output, Bourdieu, as David Swartz has documented, used the terms 'cultural unconscious', 'habit-forming force', 'set of basic, deeply interiorized master-patterns', 'mental habit', 'mental and corporeal schemata of perceptions, appreciations, and actions', and 'generative principle of regulated improvisations' to designate his key concept (Swartz, 2013 p 101). Bourdieu relies on sociological and cognitive frames, downplaying an explicit psychoanalytic analysis of emotions, which is the strength of Fromm's social character theory.

Bourdieu's intellectual commitments underplay psychoanalytic insights. George Steinmetz has argued that Bourdieu's concept of habitus could be further developed through the use of Lacanian theory (Steinmetz, 2006). Others have compellingly argued that Fromm's revision of analysis could highlight the emotional elements of habitus that go deeper than the purely structural and cognitive orientation anchoring Bourdieu's framework (Cheliotis, 2011a, 2011b; Grillo, 2018). Despite the obvious insights that Fromm's theory of social character offer Bourdieu's field theory and the sociology of development more generally, *Social Character in a Mexican Village* was largely ignored.

A neglected community study

The reception of the book was actually a little more complicated. Reasonably positive academic reviews of the book appeared in the top American sociology outlets and a major general social science journal (Foster, 1971; Padgett, 1971; McMahon, 1972). Social scientists largely ignored the book and it did not sell widely among general readers at just over 100,000 copies worldwide, unusually low for Fromm. Initially published by the commercial press Prentice-Hall, the book went out of print until republished in 1996 by Transaction Press, an academic press that often publishes social science classics.[1] *Social Character* had almost no influence in either elite public intellectual or sociology debates in the United States, although it did have modest influence in Latin America.

To explain this, it is necessary to look both at the reputational and content-fit dynamics within sociology (Camic, 1992) and the broader political and cultural environment. It was unlucky timing that *Social Character* was published just when William Ryan's concept of 'blaming the victim' became an influential trope. Linked to an earlier debate about Oscar Lewis' concept of 'culture of poverty' and debates among historians about the black family during slavery, scholars were increasingly hesitant to make cultural arguments regarding the reproduction of inequality. These narrowly academic debates led to a widespread public controversy in the United States in response to American Senator and public intellectual Patrick Moynihan's infamous 1965 report on the breakdown of the black family in America (Zinn, 1989; Bobo and Charles, 2009; Wilson, 2009; Patterson, 2010; Geary, 2015). Because of this and the rise of black nationalism in the late 1960s, left-liberal intellectuals, especially white scholars, lost interest in studying the psychology of the marginalized as a factor reproducing inequality. This was generally a positive development. The broader intellectual debate tended to put the blame for poverty and underdevelopment on the shoulders of the marginalized in ways that erased processes of colonialization, racialization, and exploitation. There is a better balance that needs to be struck, however, so that we can think about history, society, and psyche.

Fromm and Maccoby understood the poverty that existed in the Mexican village they studied was caused by the historical legacy of earlier generations of exploitation and authoritarian elite rule in Latin America. They did not blame peasants for the enormous hardships they endured in their lives. For Fromm and Maccoby, hunger, poverty, domestic violence, alcoholism, and despair were not caused by the character traits of individuals. They were careful to tell the history of the village and set the stage for a structural analysis before they examined social psychological variables and questions of choice.

It was inevitable that the book's emphasis on peasant social character would be dismissed as blaming the victim. In the 1970s, Fromm was beginning to be ignored by radical thinkers for a variety of reasons and they had legitimate criticisms. Marxists in Latin America saw the book as lacking a sufficiently trenchant critique of the capitalist world system, American dominance of the region, and exploitative local political and economic elites (as one sees in Frank, 1967; Wallerstein, 1979). Maccoby later went on to become a social character leadership consultant who worked with corporations, unions and the Swedish Government, while writing quality research and maintaining loose ties to elite scholars and universities (Maccoby, 1976, 1980, 2003, 2007).

This likely diminished the status of the Fromm–Maccoby research for radical scholars of development.

Changes in the world have undermined the book's contemporary relevance. Fromm and Maccoby were deeply concerned about alcoholism but understandably less cognizant about drugs and drug cartels – social problems that emerged in the 1980s after Fromm's death – in ways that would make many of their proposals politically unrealistic. Fromm and Maccoby were concerned about domestic violence and macho attitudes among men, but from a contemporary perspective, the book underestimates what scholars describe as 'femicide' (Wright, 2001, 2011). Current research would pay far more attention to Indigenous communities and perspectives, although in actual fact, there were no Indigenous identified peasants in this particular village where the category of mestizo was used. The famous Subcomandante Marcos (Rafael Sebastián Guillén Vicente) who led a rebellion in the Chiapas region of Mexico, was influenced by Fromm in his youth, but scholars today tend to be more interested in grassroots movements than in studies like the Fromm and Maccoby community (Khasnabish, 2008, 2013). Perhaps most importantly, Fromm's tendency to make overly confident judgements about what is humanistic development and productive character became increasingly out of touch in modern anthropology, for good reasons.

The changing political and policy debates about Mexico and broader development issues explains, however, only some of the erasure of *Social Character* in sociology and academic social science. The book was caught between the competing intellectual logics and research methods of economics, psychology, anthropology, and sociology as well as Fromm's broader reputational decline in the English-speaking intellectual and academic world in the late 1960s. Fromm's decline was also created by attacks on him by orthodox Marxists, Freudians, neo-conservatives, and anti-humanist thinkers of various ideological stripes exacerbated by his bitter feud with the Frankfurt School (McLaughlin, 1998a).

Academic reputations are formed by relatively closed scholarly networks, but they travel and often shape perceptions outside peer-reviewed networks. This is especially true in the age of the 'celebrity intellectual' and social media. Anthropologists had moved from the culture and personality research that Fromm was doing from the 1940s to the 1960s. Margaret Mead had also suffered reputational decline for similar reasons (Lutkehaus, 2008). Sociologists studying development in the later part of the twentieth century were world systems theorists (Wallerstein, 1979), radical political economists (Attewell, 1984), the neo-institutionalists, feminists (Chancer, 1992), and post-colonial theorists (Fanon, 1967; Connell, 2007; Coulthard, 2014; Denis, 2020). Fromm was not connected to the cutting edges of where theory and methods was going.

Fromm's declining influence is related to the career directions that his intellectual followers took after working with him. A comparison to Bourdieu is helpful here. Fromm's most successful students did not become professors as Bourdieu's graduate students did. Fromm's strongest following was in Mexico and Germany, not among American academics (Funk, 2019). There is a network of Mexican scholars and psychoanalysts (Millán and Millán, 2015) who do important participatory action research using Fromm's methods. In Germany, an international Erich Fromm Society led by Fromm's former assistant Rainer Funk do both applied and theoretical work on social character (Funk, 2009, 2019). *Social Character*'s co-author, Michael Maccoby, never stayed in the academic profession, despite various appointments at major universities but instead went on to develop social character theory outside the academy in a series of best-selling works of applied social science for business leaders and executives (Maccoby, 1976, 2003, 2007, 2015). Many of the major promoters of social character theory built their careers as therapists rather than professors (Cortina, 2015).

In comparison, while Bourdieu started out very much on the margins of French intellectual life in the 1960s (Kauppi, 1996), he was anything but marginal in academic institutions by the time of Fromm's death in 1980 (Swartz, 2003, 2013). Bourdieu moved from the periphery of French society as a lower-middle-class provincial youth to a faculty position at the prestigious Collège de France in Paris. Many of Bourdieu's students went on to take leadership roles in the social sciences; the Bourdieu school within the sociology of culture was created by intense teacher–student relationships forged at the elite research universities in France and later the United States.

Bourdieu's theory is now at the centre of sociology and Fromm is all but forgotten. Bourdieu's concept of habitus is more important than Fromm's social character theory precisely because he developed it with methodological rigour and well-resourced research teams Fromm could not compete with. Social character theory, however, can add insights to Bourdieu's field theory and habitus research agenda. Apart from Bourdieu's thoughts about Freud (Steinmetz, 2006), and his own explicit argument for reflexivity (Bourdieu and Wacquant, 1992), his autobiographical reflections are almost totally free of psychological insight. Bourdieu's research agenda is largely structural and cognitive rather than psychoanalytic, and he has very little to say about passions, violence, or the sociology of emotions (Cheliotis, 2011b).

Social Character is worth re-examination and building on. The most important contribution Fromm made to sociology, however, does not come from the details of this book but from the socio-psychoanalytic theory he developed in it as well as his broader insights into violence and destructiveness outlined in *The Anatomy of Human Destructiveness*.

Theorizing violence: beyond instincts and behaviours

As Fromm's reputation declined in the 1960s and 1970s, he was painted by his critics as a naïve and excessively optimistic thinker who wrote sentimental pop psychology about love. This charge is unpersuasive; the central argument of *Escape of Freedom* was about the human potential for fascism that Fromm warned could happen in the United States as it took over Germany. In fact, one of the core insights that Fromm's work offers for professional sociology is his revision of psychoanalytic theory, providing what scholars today might call a 'micro-foundation' for theorizing political passions, malignant individual and social narcissism, and the sociology of emotions (McLaughlin, 1996). It was precisely these insights that were buried and forgotten in scholarly debates about Fromm's work, especially in the United States in the 1960s and 1970s.

Fromm published *The Anatomy of Human Destructiveness* in 1973 in no small part to address these theoretical issues. The book was, however, also a major public intellectual and scholarly intervention. Fromm started the book in Mexico and completed it while living in Switzerland. An impressive work of social theorizing, scholarly synthesis, and political engagement, it addresses the human roots of violence and destructiveness informed by an original and powerful social-psychoanalytic perspective. *Anatomy* is not professional or public sociology since by this time in his career Fromm was distant from the 'intellectual self-concept' of a sociologist (Gross, 2008). In the book, Fromm clearly defined his expertise as a psychoanalytic theorist, clinician, and an unorthodox Freudian (Burston, 1991).

Fromm first developed his theoretical approach to Freud's ideas in his early analytic social psychology published in the 1930s when he was part of the Frankfurt School (Fromm, 1992 [1963]). After leaving the critical theory network and becoming famous with *Escape from Freedom* and *Man for Himself*, Fromm wrote extensively as a public intellectual critic of psychoanalytic orthodoxy (Philipson, 2017). His numerous books on Freudian ideas sold millions of copies. Fromm was, with the exception of Erik Erikson, the most visible and important popularizer of the psychoanalytic tradition in America (Erikson, 1950, 1958, 1968,

1969, 1975; Friedman, 1999; Philipson, 2017). The preface to *The Anatomy of Human Destructiveness* describes it as the 'first volume of a comprehensive work on psychoanalytic theory' (Fromm, 1973 p xi).[2] Fromm published *Anatomy*, a scholarly book over 500 pages long, in order to deal with destructiveness as 'one of the fundamental problems in psychoanalysis' as well as making a 'practically relevant' contribution given 'the wave of destructiveness engulfing the world' in the early 1970s (Fromm, 1973 p xi).

For a contemporary professional sociology that does not integrate historical sociological analysis with insights from both neurosciences and psychoanalysis, *Anatomy* is provocative and ambitious.[3] Furthermore, in a moment of world history where the political consequences of Donald Trump's narcissism has been felt around the world during his four-year presidency, Fromm's powerful theoretical account of the importance of character for political leaders warrants more attention. Fromm's theory of malignant aggression and necrophilia is illustrated with detailed case studies on pathological leaders like Stalin, Himmler, and Hitler that are sociological and psychoanalytic.

Anatomy also offers an implicit critical sociology when he rejects the behaviourist assumptions in psychology. Fromm was opposed to the extreme behaviourist assumptions that view violence as created purely by environmental conditions and reward and punishment structures since this framework places too little emphasis on human passions. The book also criticizes the various instinctual theories influential within the fields of psychoanalysis and certain branches of social science; it offers a powerful repudiation of theories that overestimate the importance of instincts and evolutionary biological dynamics for explaining violence as intrinsic to human nature.

Anatomy of Human Destructiveness also offers highly sophisticated theorizing on the human roots of violence and organized killing. Published by a commercial press, its prose is clear and relatively easy to understand. *Anatomy* is an early example of books such as psychologist Steven Pinker's *The Better Angels of Our Nature: Why Violence Has Declined* (2011) and sociologist Nicholas Christakis' *Blueprint: The Evolutionary Origins of a Good Society* (2019).[4] As an example of a certain genre of public intellectual work, *Anatomy of Human Destructiveness* merits more attention in sociology. Many sociologists are influenced by philosopher Judith Butler and social constructionist traditions within our discipline. Many have legitimate fears of supporting eugenics or sexism. An unfortunate result of this, however, is few sociologists today consult with experts in the neurosciences.[5] Fromm pushes us to address neurosciences seriously, something that most certainly does not require accepting discredited race science, patriarchal thinking, or hetronormativity.

The Anatomy of Human Destructiveness is organized into three major sections and ends with a political epilogue on hope and a theoretical appendix on Freud. The first section 'Instinctivism, Behaviourism, and Psychoanalysis', is a detailed critique of the instinct-based theory of aggression in the work of zoologist and ethologist Konrad Lorenz, Freud's libido and death instinct theories and the neo-behaviourism of psychologist B. F. Skinner. Fromm then documents the evidence for his rejection of instinct theories of violence with a discussion of the literature in neurophysiology, animal behaviour, paleontology, and anthropology.

The final section of the book distinguishes between what Fromm calls benign aggression rooted in our animal nature and malignant aggression. The worship of destructiveness, sadism, and the logic of what Fromm calls necrophilia is uniquely human. The concluding chapters make the case for Fromm's psychoanalytically informed alternative theory of human violence with detailed clinical case studies of malignant aggression: Soviet dictator Joseph Stalin, German Nazi SS leader Heinrich Himmler, and a detailed psychohistory of Adolf Hitler. The epilogue at the end of the book muses on how to sustain hope for human survival and flourishing despite the brutality and cruelty we see in the world. Fromm also provides a theoretical summary of his revision of the Freudian theory of violence.

Why Freud, Lorenz, Skinner, and popular social psychology are wrong

The Anatomy of Human Destructiveness begins with a spirited critique of popular post-Second World War books and research about the roots of human destructiveness. As Fromm argued in his earlier book *The Heart of Man: Its Genius for Good and Evil*, human beings are neither wolves driven wholly by predatory instincts nor sheep simply following social norms. Fromm makes the case against both the popular 'death instinct' theory of Sigmund Freud and the purely environmental perspective popularized by psychologist B. F. Skinner. Fromm begins and ends the book with a critique and revision of Freud, but the first chapter features a scathing critique of the logical flaws and empirical inadequacies of Konrad Lorenz's best-selling *On Aggression* (1966).

Lorenz was an Austrian-born paleontologist and physician widely regarded as a founder of the field of ethnology (the systematic study of animal behaviour) and best known for popularizing the concept of 'imprinting'. Fromm was understandably appalled by Lorenz's history – he had served in the German Army during the Second World War and embraced the concept of Germany's 'racial strength' (Friedman, 2013). We now know more about Lorenz's complicity with the Nazi regime (Klopfer, 1994). Before the war, Lorenz mostly published academic articles based on his descriptive and detailed study of geese and other animals. Lorenz joined the Nazi Party for which he later expressed regret. He survived capture by the Soviets. In the post-war period, Lorenz combined a successful academic career as an Austrian professor who shared a Nobel Prize in 1973. He was well regarded in his specialized field and published extensively in German. Lorenz also wrote popular books in English starting with *King Solomon's Ring* (1955b), *Man Meets Dog* (1955a), and *On Aggression* (1966).

The popular appeal of Lorenz's books helped inspired Fromm's decision to write of *The Anatomy of Human Destructiveness*. He was triggered when American Senator William Fulbright expressed admiration for the book; this made Fromm conclude that it was having more influence even among people he respected (Friedman, 2013). Only three years younger than Fromm, Lorenz was also a German speaker with an ability to write well in English. Fromm viewed Lorenz as an intellectual and political competitor. He was not concerned primarily about academic status considerations (Collins, 1998) but about the political implications of Lorenz's thought. Fromm understood full well that other books, particularly Robert Ardrey's *The Territorial Imperative* (1966) and Desmond Morris' *The Naked Ape* (1967), were popularizing a simplistic and reactionary evolutionary psychological form of thinking (Friedman, 2013 p 300). Fromm was fighting a political as well as intellectual battle in this respect.

Given Lorenz's political history, national origins, and stature as an academic, the conflict was personal. Fromm was concerned that Lorenz's work would appeal to people because it connected to the pre-existing mood of those who 'believe our drift towards violence and nuclear war is due to biological factors beyond our control', rather than being rooted in 'social, political, and economic circumstances of our own making' (Fromm, 1973 p 16).

Fromm asserted that Lorenz presents a 'Hobbesian cliché of war as the natural state of man' (Fromm, 1973 p 18) arising from the hunter-food gathering societies that emerged around 50,000 years ago. Lorenz relied mostly on evidence from his own expertise on animals, 'proof by analogy' (Fromm, 1973 p 21), using examples from his observation of fish and mammals, mostly in captivity, to explain human aggression. As Fromm puts it, Lorenz's method was to discover 'similarities between human behaviour and the behaviour of the animals' in order to conclude 'that both kinds of behaviour have the same cause' (Fromm, 1973 p 21).

Fromm claims that Lorenz's perspective shares the same flawed 'hydraulic' model of aggression that Freud articulated, one in which 'human aggressiveness is an instinct fed by an ever-flowing foundation of energy' and is thus not 'necessarily the result of a reaction to outer stimuli' (Fromm, 1973 p 17). To Fromm, Lorenz's ideas are naïve, even dangerous. Sublimating human violence through sport is, for Fromm, just as likely to increase nationalist conflict as to replace it. And Lorenz's claim that we can save humanity from destruction in the nuclear era by understanding the laws of evolution is, for Fromm, a form of chauvinistic paganism that represents a quasi-religious attitude towards Darwin.

As an alternative to the Lorenz–Freud instinct hydraulic model of violence that Fromm critiqued so thoroughly, the dominant approach in the post-Second World War social sciences was behaviourism. Fromm viewed this alternative as equally dangerous and thus offers an extended scholarly and polemical critique of the work of psychologist B. F. Skinner and the famous Milgram and Zimbardo social psychological experiments. Fromm believed that they ignored psychological perspectives, substituting a naïve environmentalism for Lorenz's pessimistic evolutionary psychology. Long critical of behaviourist approaches to violence, Fromm argued against theories that attempted to explain human destructiveness simply as response to incentives and a creation of social context, what Dennis Wrong called an over-socialized view of human nature (Wrong, 1961, 1994). But the major proponent in twentieth-century psychology of what Steven Pinker would later call the blank slate view was Harvard professor and behaviourist theorist B. F. Skinner, whom Fromm considered a naïve rationalist and denier of the importance of passions. As far back as *Escape from Freedom*, Fromm had always been critical of social science work that was tinged with behaviourism and would often make critical remarks about Skinner's work. In *Anatomy*, however, he abandons propriety and directly attacks the theory of violence outlined in Skinner's work.

Fromm's critique of Skinner is similar to that made by radical linguist Noam Chomsky in the late 1950s and early 1970s (Chomsky, 1959, 1971). Chomsky and Fromm had similar politics although their theoretical frameworks regarding psychology were quite different. They shared the view that Skinner's experimental results on 'operant conditioning' on animals was not useful in understanding human behaviour. Both were critical of the anti-democratic stance of social engineering outlined in Skinner's popular writings including the book *Beyond Freedom and Dignity* (1973) and shared a similar critical perspective on the politics of mainstream social science. Chomsky would have agreed with Fromm's view that 'Skinnerism is the psychology of opportunism dressed up as a new scientific humanism' (Fromm, 1973 p 41). The disrespect was mutual, as Skinner mocked Fromm openly in the second volume of his memoir, joking that he had operationally conditioned the great humanist proponent of human freedom when he gave a guest lecture at Harvard (Skinner, 1981).

Sophisticated historians of psychology have painted a more nuanced picture of Skinner's intellectual influence than Fromm allows for (Rutherford, 2009). Sociologist George Homans developed social exchange theory out of the key insights of behaviourism modified by later developments in sociology and cognitive psychology (Homans, 1964). It is worth recounting Fromm's critique of the behaviourist assumptions about violence that he outlined in *The Anatomy of Human Destructiveness*. It is important because, as Fromm puts it, 'most investigators of aggression in the United States have written with a behaviourist orientation' (Fromm, 1973 p 42).

The problem with Skinner's approach is that it assumes that the 'deed, not the doer' is the object for scientific observations and analysis (Fromm, 1973 p 43). Skinner, like so many other social scientists, misses what Freud understood. While instincts and environment shape behaviour, weight must be given to the unconscious and powerful forces that shape human action. Character plays a key role in determining the meaning and motivation for action. Fromm argued that a person who is shouting and red in the face is engaging in a different action depending on whether they are motivated by a deep sense of impotence, a more straightforward fear of something in the environment, or a justified sense of indignity and rage at injustice (Fromm, 1973 p 44). Skinner's exclusive focus on behaviour and his rejection of deeper analysis of emotions set the stage, from Fromm's perspective, for later work in behaviourism-tinged social psychology that led further away from, rather than closer to, a sophisticated analysis of human violence.

Fromm moves from a critique of Skinner's behaviourist assumptions to the most important empirical works on destructiveness in twentieth-century North American experimental social science: Stanley Milgram's 'Behavioural Study of Obedience' in the early 1960s, and Zimbardo's Stanford prison study of the early 1970s. Fromm was interested in both of these classic experiments partly because, like the work of Lorenz and Skinner, they misled the public about the human roots of violence. Both studies are familiar to millions of university and high school students. The massive scholarly debate and documentary films about the ethics of these experiments have permeated popular culture. Fromm was generally sceptical of this kind of experimental research design, preferring his own interpretive questionnaire, historical analysis, and insights gained from clinical work. What Fromm found most important in both studies was not that they documented human beings' natural viciousness, but that people had to be coerced and coaxed into shocking subjects with electricity in the Milgram experiment, and to humiliate and degrade people in the Stanford prison study.

For Fromm, both studies raised questions about the instinct and behaviourist theories of violence. Contrary to standard textbooks, Fromm noted evidence in both studies that people who were tricked into behaving in cruel ways tended to suffer symptoms of anxiety. This suggested that violence does not come naturally to people as Lorenz assumed. Fromm was sceptical of the behaviouralist assumptions embedded in both studies that suggested that it was the environmental conditions that determined behaviour.

Fromm's theoretical frame, in contrast, emphasized the character structure of groups and individuals. Drawing on Bettelheim's famous studies of concentration camp survivors (Fleck and Muller, 1998), Fromm argued that people's character, political ideology, and worldview had a major influence on how they react to traumatizing situations. Recent research on these studies, especially the now discredited Stanford prison study, reinforces Fromm's point with more evidence (Bregman, 2019).

For Fromm, instinct theory, behaviourism, and frustration-aggression theory (which he was familiar with through the work of major figures in the field like John Dollard) were inadequate for understanding human passions and violence. Fromm returns to Freud using his ideas to critique the existing social science literature and lay out the contours of a psychoanalytic theory of aggression. But all this was largely an entrée for the conclusion of the book where Fromm offers his own psychoanalytic theory of violence and destructiveness. Before doing so, however, Fromm would go deeper into the vast interdisciplinary literature on violence in order to fully move beyond the instinct theories that were distorting both popular political debates and scholarly research on human destructiveness.

Is human destructiveness hard-wired?

The middle section of *The Anatomy of Human Destructiveness* is a dense literature review of research in neurophysiology, animal psychology, paleontology, and anthropology. In it, Fromm attempts to refute the hypothesis that human beings are 'innately endowed with a spontaneous and self-propelling aggressive drive' (Fromm, 1973 p 89). He critiques the hydraulic model of Lorenz and his followers and the simplistic version of the 'death instinct' defended by Herbert Marcuse and orthodox Freudians. Fromm was interested in creating a space for discussion of the human roots of destructiveness by signaling his commitment to look at biological and evolutionary aspects of human passions. He wished to do so in ways that avoided what we would call today the 'blank slate' approach (Pinker, 2002). Contrary to the myth that Fromm's later work descended into popular platitudes, large sections of *Anatomy* are technical and framed around a set of major scholarly questions.

Fromm posits that neurophysiology helps us distinguish between instincts designed to lead to defensive reactions of either fight or flight versus the predatory behaviour of land animals such as wolves and bears. These sciences help us understand 'life-preserving, biologically adaptive, defensive aggression' (Fromm 1973 p 100), but do not offer evidence for Lorenz's instinctivistic-hydraulic theory (Fromm, 1973 p 101). By the 1970s, these fields had not taken up the question of human destructive passions in the ways that psychoanalytic theories did, except in research on brain damage (Fromm, 1973 p 101). Unlike some sociologists today, especially public sociologists, who tend to openly reject neurosciences, Fromm demonstrates his commitment to develop a psychoanalytic theory of destructiveness that extends beyond neurophysiology but is consistent with its findings.

While Fromm emphatically rejects scholars like Lorenz and Skinner who simplistically analogize human behaviour from ethnological research, he draws from scholarship that distinguishes between predatory aggression, intraspecific aggression against members of the same species, and interspecific aggression against different species. The literature suggests that we treat the predatory instinct as a distinct phenomenon and most aggression as largely a 'threatening post, which serves as a warning'. Further, if we talk about aggression in captivity as opposed to life in the wild, there is little evidence for Lorenz's position. For Fromm, 'man is the only mammal who is a large-scale killer and sadist' (Fromm, 1973 p 103). While the large volume of research done since 1973 modifies and refines Fromm's views (Cortina,

2015), his basic critique of instinct theories holds. Fromm is right that with the exception of pathological killers and psychopaths, human beings have an innate inhibition against killing that has to be overcome organizationally and sociologically to induce mass violence and war (Collins, 2009).[6]

In the 1930s, 1940s, and 1950s, Fromm worked more closely with anthropologists than sociologists (Burston, 1991). Against the hydraulic model that suggests that early human beings were driven by deep-seated biological urges for violence, Fromm drew from anthropologists who argued that early hunter-gatherer societies were generally less warlike than those that emerged with the neolithic revolution and early agriculture, cities, and trade. Building on on Lewis Mumford's work on the fourth and fifth millennia BC, Fromm stresses the patriarchal and exploitative nature of new urban societies (Fromm, 1973 pp 161–167).

For Fromm, the levels of aggressiveness in cultures is a variable, not a given. He offers a secondary analysis of thirty 'primitive tribes' (Fromm, 1973 pp 167–177) that is flawed both by his language and evolutionary assumptions but does help illustrate his general theory of social character. Fromm argued that hunter-gatherer societies are either: (1) life-affirmative societies, (2) non-destructive-aggressive societies, or (3) destructive societies. For Fromm, 'the instinctivist interpretation of human destructiveness is not tenable' (Fromm, 1973 p 177) precisely because human cultures vary so greatly. Violence in humans is largely oriented for survival and varies with the cultural system linked to historical conditions. Yet this does not mean that pathological violence is not part of human nature because human beings are the 'only primate who can feel intense pleasure in killing and torturing' (Fromm, 1973 p 181).

Varieties of aggression: theory and case studies on sadism and necrophilia

The concluding section of *The Anatomy of Human Destructiveness* opens with a discussion of what Fromm calls benign aggression, essentially the animal nature of human beings concerned with survival, safety, play, and assertion. Fromm then reviews his theory of human existential needs, making the case that they are sources of the malignant aggression and the destructive passions that lead to what Fromm calls the necrophilous character, a distinctively human form of violence and pathology. He ends with historical case studies of individual destructive characters, the most important and original element of the book for sociologists. Fromm discusses the early twentieth-century German political extremist Ernst von Salomon's destructive idolatry, the political sadism of Soviet communist leader Joseph Stalin, the Nazi Heinrich Himmler, and finally the malignant necrophilia of Adolf Hitler.

Benign aggression, for Fromm, consists of forms of pseudo-aggression that includes accidental aggression, playful aggression, and self-assertive behaviour that is appropriate and necessary in social life. Defensive aggression in humans, like the similar set of mechanisms in animals, is functional for social life even though the range of human forms of defensive reactions is greater than in our closest primate relatives. Fromm outlines a number of examples. Aggression in humans often flows from the mechanism of resistance: people react with anger to being told unpleasant truths about themselves. Conformist aggression leads people to obey orders to kill. Instrumental aggression is violence done to accomplish a specific personal or political goal. Human beings are different from animals because of their ability to envision future threats, their weakness to brainwashing and fearmongering by nefarious leaders, and the ways they respond to symbolic threats and challenges to meaning systems apart from their vital and immediate interests. This means that people can be mobilized to defend abstract notions of freedom and the nation, creating individual and social forms of narcissism that greatly increase the likelihood of war.

Fromm's political and moral vision demands that we oppose unjust wars, the violence underpinning slavery, the patriarchal oppression of women, and modern neo-colonial conflicts like the Vietnam War which he resisted so vocally. It is not the scale of destruction that distinguishes different forms of destruction, especially in modern times when hundreds of thousands, even millions, of people can be killed with the pressing of a nuclear weapons button. For Fromm, 'the soldier who kills and maims, the bomber pilot who destroys thousands of lives in one moment, are not necessarily driven by a destructive or cruel impulse, but by the principle of unquestioning obedience' (Fromm, 1973 p 207). Fromm distinguishes between benign aggression and a psychoanalytic malignancy, but the former is also shaped by a sociological analysis of instrumental rationality and the social organization of human societies.

Fromm's analysis is superior to that of both Lorenz and Skinner but also to most psychoanalysts who write about politics. His historical sociological background and training is illustrated clearly here when he states that, 'the thesis that war is caused by innate human destructiveness is plainly absurd for anyone who has even the slightest knowledge of history' (Fromm, 1973 pp 210–211). Building on the sociological analysis he developed in *Escape from Freedom* and refined in *May Man*

Prevail? and *The Heart of Man*, Fromm points out that 'The Babylonians, the Greeks, up to the statesmen of our time, have planned war for what they thought were very realistic reasons and weighed the pros and cons very thoroughly' (Fromm, 1973 p 211). Revenge, irrationality and passion for destruction can play roles in certain circumstances, but Fromm would agree with historical sociology's great students of war from Max Weber to Michael Mann that the motives for war are 'land for cultivation, riches, slaves, raw materials, markets, expansion—and defense' (Fromm, 1973 p 211). For Fromm, modern Europeans and North Americans, along with the leaders of some powerful non-Western states, project their own motives for conquest and power onto the history of the hunter-gatherer societies they colonize and exploit.

Fromm's two major contributions to the study of political aggression in sociology are the concepts of social narcissism and his analysis of the political consequences of the narcissism of leaders. Donald Trump's obvious narcissism during his four-year presidency has stimulated a revival of interest in Fromm's work on the political importance of character. In *Anatomy*, Fromm describes individual narcissism in vivid ways that are relevant to contemporary politics. Fromm argued that 'Narcissism can be described as a stage of experience in which only the personal himself, *his* body, *his* needs, *his* feelings, *his* thoughts, *his* property, everything and everybody pertaining to *him* are experienced as fully real' while at the same time everything else is 'not interesting, is not fully real, is perceived only by intellectual recognition, while affectively without weight and colour' (Fromm, 1973 p 201). It is precisely because of the distorting lens of narcissism that people with this character show 'severe defects in judgement' and lack 'the capacity for objectivity' (Fromm, 1973 p 201).

Extreme narcissism is common among political leaders; it is often effective for convincing 'large audiences who are attracted by men who appear to be so absolutely certain' (Fromm, 1973 p 202). This poses real dangers for society because 'extremely narcissistic persons are often almost forced to become famous' in order to maintain their sanity (Fromm, 1973 p 203). Narcissistic political leaders get angry when they are challenged or insulted, bullying and threatening to get their way. This promotes social narcissism among their followers. The story is all too familiar to contemporary students of recent American politics; we can usefully understand Trump as a 'marketing character' with no core convictions as well as a narcissist and authoritarian (Maccoby, 2020).

Fromm developed the concept of 'social narcissism' at length in *The Heart of Man* (1964). There is an extensive scholarly literature on clinical and individual narcissism to which Fromm contributes. The perceptions and emotions of whole societies, social classes, ethnic-racial groups, and religions can be distorted by collective narcissism whereby one's own group is seen as exceptional, even perfect. A set of emotional filters functions to degrade, attack, and dismiss outsiders.

Contemporary sociologists can utilize Bobo's 'group position theory' to address these issues (Denis, 2020) but the theory of social narcissism adds an important analysis of distorted emotions and powerful passions. In *The Heart of Man*, Fromm described 'national hysteria in all the belligerent countries of the First World War, Hitler's racialism, Stalin's party idolization, Muslim and Hindi religious fanaticism, [and] Western anti-communist fanaticism' (Fromm, 1964 p 83) as examples of the destructive logic of social narcissism.

The central concern of *Anatomy* is not social narcissistic aggression, however, but the malignant aggression he calls necrophilia. Fromm believed this was one of his most important theoretical contributions, a debatable proposition among clinicians and scholars of serial killers. My own view is that the most valuable contribution of *The Anatomy of Human Destructiveness* for sociologists is his detailed case studies on political leaders motivated by malignant aggression.

Fromm is often seen by elite intellectuals and sociologists today as a simplistic and naïve thinker who believed human beings were naturally good. This is not true because Fromm always highlighted the radical evil human beings were capable of. Fromm rejected instinct theories and evolutionary psychology that exaggerated the violence of early humans and suggested that a hydraulic model for human destructiveness was misguided. His view was that human beings were more potentially violent than other animals, arguing that humans were unique in being 'driven by impulses to kill and to torture' and a 'destroyer of his own species without any rational gain, either biological or economic' (Fromm, 1973 p 218). The ways humans transcended their animal nature through language, consciousness and culture set the stage for Fromm's concept of malignant destructiveness.

The mechanism represented by malignant narcissism provoked a level of cruelty in humans that is more destructive than animal predatory violence precisely because of its human qualities rooted in human existential needs as Fromm defined them. For Fromm, Darwin's work was flawed because he did not mention 'passions and emotions like tenderness, love, hate, cruelty, narcissism, sadism and masochism' in his lists of psychic traits in humans (Fromm, 1973 p 221). Maslow, an influential twentieth-century psychologist who was guilty of underestimating human destructiveness as Fromm was accused of doing, offers his famous hierarchy of needs without, as Fromm puts it, offering an analysis of 'the common origins of such needs in the nature of man' (Fromm, 1973 p 222).

Fromm again repeats his existentialist influenced analysis of the uniqueness of human destructiveness that flows from the gift and the curse of human consciousness, the awareness of death created by reason, and the imagination of a creature who is a 'freak of nature' (Fromm, 1973 p 225). Human beings have a nature that flows not just from evolutionary selection but also from the set of existential dilemmas that human consciousness creates. Humans have a need for a 'system of orientation and devotion'. They require 'rootedness' and a sense of 'unity' with the natural world and other humans. They are driven to have a sense of 'effectiveness' in a world out of their control, they are passionately driven to seek 'excitation and stimulation', and they can suffer extreme chronic depression and boredom in ways not common among animals. Philosophers and psychologists have long debated various models for human 'needs'; his offers only one such framework (Cortina, 2015). Where Fromm's ideas differ from most frameworks is his revised Freudian theory of character that explains how these existential needs are met and mediated by the formation of distinct character structures that simplify and structure experience. There are parallels here to Bourdieu's sociological perspective on habitus (Maccoby and McLaughlin, 2020).

Fromm's theory of social character differs from Bourdieu's in that he emphasizes emotions far more centrally, leaves more room for neurophysiological conditions, and offers a specific typology for non-instrumental violence. Human destructive passions are rooted in character. In addition to spontaneous bursts of violence rooted in situations (Collins, 2009), Fromm stresses vengeful destructiveness, ecstatic destructiveness, and a worshipping of violence alongside masochistic, sadistic passions, and what he calls necrophilia. Fromm's four case studies are worth examining in detail.

Human beings can be more destructive than other species partly because we have the capacity to worship destructiveness, something Fromm illustrates with a short case study based on the autobiographical novel by Ernst von Salomon (1930). Von Salomon was one of the conspirators to the murder of liberal German foreign minister Walther Rathenau in 1920 by the fanatical far-right-wing ex-military officer Erwin Kern. Representing the protype for the Nazis in the early years after the German defeat in the First World War, von Salomon was burning with hatred towards German leftist revolutionaries. He desired the 'total destruction of the existing social and political structure and its replacement by a nationalistic, militaristic order' but he had no concrete plan for what that would look like or how to get there (Fromm, 1973 p 278). Kern and von Salomon were motivated by anger at the attacks on 'their values of nationalism', and their 'feudal concepts of honour and obedience' (Fromm, 1973 p 279). Class resentments provides fuel, and prisons served as socializing agents for their radicalism. Yet Fromm goes further than Bourdieu or Mann would in his analysis of the psychic reality of both men as 'destroyers and not revolutionaries' (Fromm, 1973 p 279) who 'hated life itself' and felt 'utterly unrelated and unresponsive to anybody alive' (Fromm, 1973 p 279). Drawing on the analysis of fascist ideology, Fromm observed that von Salomon and Kern (who eventually killed himself) represented people who were drawn to a 1930s Spanish fascist motto, 'Long live death!' (Fromm, 1964 p 37). They worshipped destruction.

Fromm then moves to a theoretical discussion of Joseph Stalin's non-sexual sadism. Fromm's analysis of authoritarianism and destructiveness was more politically sophisticated than Adorno's because unlike the other members of the Frankfurt School, Fromm believed in the existence of left-wing as well as right-wing authoritarianism. Even sociologists who were not compromised by Stalinist political viewpoints can recognize the instrumental elements of the rapid industrialization that lifted millions in the Soviet Union and billions in the People's Republic of China out of poverty (Mann, 2005). Abstract and ideological denouncing of communist atrocities in the twentieth century is common without careful historical sociological analysis of the murderous cleansing organized by Stalin, Mao, and Pol Pot (Mann, 2005). This type of analysis must be combined with theoretical and historical accounts of genocide in the Americas and Africa by settler-colonial and colonial states. Fromm is an important thinker about these issues because he was consistently opposed all forms of human destructiveness and used a historical-comparative lens while adding a much-needed psychological analysis to the sociology.

The Anatomy of Human Destructiveness documents the non-instrumental sadistic nature of Stalin's behaviour. Political scientists, historians, sociologists, and economists have written extensively on the strategic elements of Stalin's will – his murder of opponents, conquering of neighbours, political repression, and his forced collectivization of agriculture and the famines that resulted (Gouldner, 1977; Medvedev and Shriver, 1989; Tucker, 2017). Deeply and consistently anti-Stalinist well before his crimes were widely known in the West, Fromm's discussion of Stalin makes another point. The literature on Stalin is full of examples of his cruelty, viciousness, and sadism that Fromm theorizes as the 'transformation of impotence into the experience of omnipotence' (Fromm, 1973 p 290).

The details must surely give pause to any sociologist who believes it is possible to understand politics or organizational social life without a robust psychoanalytically influenced theory. Having introduced torture to the Bolshevist revolution, Stalin would give personal instruction on the methods to be used, their cruelty surpassing even the Czarist police. A master of psychological torture, he often assured people he had worked with for years that they were safe from brutal purges only to have them arrested days later. Stalin enjoyed abusing people with the unpredictability of his actions, clearly taking pleasure in humiliating high-level functionaries by securing their agreement to the arrests of their own wives and children. Stalin was also notorious for arresting and torturing former comrades in the movement, having them serve long and brutal sentences, and then later appointing them to high posts with no explanation (Fromm, 1973 p 287). Stalin's old comrade Sergei Ivanovich Kavtaradze was sentenced to death for plotting Stalin's assassination, reprieved at the last minute after a long stay in an execution cell, and then released. Following this, Stalin would invite Kavtaradze to the occasional dinner. After a night of joking and reminiscing, he again accused Kavtaradze of plotting his murder. None of this behaviour is purely instrumental or rational. It was clearly rooted, Fromm argued, in a sadistic pathology unique to humans.

Stalin represents a broader social type that is a uniquely human form of destructiveness with traits and behaviours that 'can never be understood if one isolates them from the whole character structure' (Fromm, 1973 p 291). For people with sadistic characters, 'living beings become things' and are 'transformed into living, quivering, pulsating objects of control' (Fromm, 1973 p 291). Fromm ends his discussion of Stalin by theorizing the highly stratified social conditions and personal trajectories of trauma that tend to lead to his form of destructiveness.

Building on this analysis of sadism, Fromm then moves on to discuss SS leader Heinrich Himmler, a vicious sadist who also illustrates what Fromm calls the 'bureaucratic, authoritarian character' (Fromm, 1973 p 299). Known as the 'bloodhound of Europe', Himmler worked closely with Hitler and was 'responsible for the slaughter of between fifteen and twenty million unarmed and powerless Russians, Poles and Jews' (Fromm, 1973 p 299). Fromm's analysis here is similar to the more famous account of the 'banality of evil' by Hannah Arendt in *Eichmann in Jerusalem* (1964).

Fromm knew Arendt as a fellow German refugee intellectual based in New York where they overlapped in the 1940s. They shared an interest in theorizing Nazis who followed orders and ran the bureaucracies of death in Nazi Germany. Both Fromm and Arendt were old-style theoretically oriented Jewish European intellectuals who shared a universalistic critique of Israel's treatment of Arabs and Palestinians. Fromm also viewed Himmler as a man of 'lifelessness', 'banality', 'insignifi cance', and 'submission to Hitler', but these similarities should not distract us from how their analysis diff ers. Arendt was notoriously uninterested, even hostile, to psychoanalysis and in the end, her analysis of Eichmann grossly underestimated his hatred and anti-Semitism. Fromm's framework allows us to avoid this mistake.

Fromm's account of Himmler allows for Bourdieu's sociological category of class habitus alongside an emphasis on effi ciency and order that Arendt underlined but Fromm insists on a depth analysis of character. Exhibiting 'insecurity and gaucheness' (Fromm, 1973 p 300), Himmler was a pedant, a trait he shared with his authoritarian father, and he carried with him a sense of social inferiority that flowed from his social origins. When he was the leader of the SS, he recorded on index cards every object he gave to anyone (Fromm, 1973 p 301), a pedantic mentality that he combined with brutality. Himmler was an opportunist who moved up the Nazi bureaucracy, coined the SS motto 'Loyalty is our Honour' (Fromm, 1973 p 322), and effi ciently organized mass executions. Yet he betrayed Hitler after years of submission and obsequiousness. As Bourdieu and Arendt would stress respectively, a lower-middle-class insecurity and the banality of evil were operant. But for Fromm one cannot understand Himmler without taking serious account of his masochism and sadism.

In *Escape from Freedom*, Fromm used the concept of sadomasochism to understand the broader politics of the far right, an analysis developed in new ways elsewhere (Chancer, 1992). Fromm's analysis of Himmler's destructiveness, modifi ed as it must be by new scholarship, is important for sociological theorizing and research because it suggest that one cannot fully understand the behaviour of bureaucrats without theorizing the characterological origins of destructiveness. Himmler was submissive as well as sadistic from the beginning of his life. Himmler drifted through his early years, exhibiting both submissive and sadistic traits. Fromm illustrates the submissiveness with a detailed summary of Himmler's early years; the sadism is illustrated with an incident in Himmler's young adult life where he forces his older brother to end a relationship and then humiliate his former fiancée.

Himmler rose to the top of the Nazi Party after the violent internal purge of the anti-capitalist wing led by his old comrade Ersnt Röhm on the Night of the Long Knives in 1934 (Fromm, 1973 p 314).

Himmler readily betrayed Röhm, an action that makes sense given his early character development. He was weak, masochistic, and driven by a sense of impotence, making him a disloyal and inveterate liar and envious of those with more strength and self-respect.

When Himmler was finally captured hiding with false papers identifying him as a corporal, his narcissism could not allow himself to be treated as an unknown soldier. He poisoned himself with cyanide after telling the camp commander who he was. Himmler chose to die rather than give up his narcissistic image of his power and importance, fantasies he played out in the service of Hitler. Fromm believed that there are many thousands of people like Himmler among us, and under the right circumstances they can emerge within bureaucracies to do great evil. Unlike many sociologists and the great political theorist Hannah Arendt, however, Fromm insisted there was nothing banal about this kind of sadomasochistic character structure that could lead to a brutality that our closest primate relatives could never imagine. Unlike Arendt, Fromm never underestimated Eichmann's hatreds; he did not over-emphasise organizational banality. Neglect of the psychosocial elements of Nazism may have enabled Arendt to evade confronting the radical evil of her former lover and teacher, Martin Heidegger (Ezra, 2007).

Necrophilia and Hitler's pathologies

The Anatomy of Human Destructiveness ends with Fromm's theory of the necrophiliac character. Building on earlier research in abnormal psychology and criminology on the sexual desire for corpses and the pathological need to gaze at, be near, or dismember dead bodies, Fromm described a character-rooted passion that explains elements of the most destructive forms of war and human violence. Aware that much of his work was dismissed by scholars and psychoanalysts as simplistic popularization, Fromm's distinctive theory was an attempt to create a scholarly and theoretical legacy that would contribute theorizing to violence and war. Illustrating the theory with a detailed case study on Adolf Hitler flowing from his earlier analysis of the Nazi leader in *Escape from Freedom*, Fromm delves into Hitler's life and motivations.

Drawing on his wide reading in philosophy, psychoanalysis, and history, as well as clinical cases, and empirical research done with Michael Maccoby in the 1960s, Fromm outlined his theory of necrophilia. He describes it in the characterological sense as 'the passionate attraction to all that is dead, decayed, putrid, sickly' (Fromm, 1973 p 332). From this character structure flows a 'passion to transform that which is alive into something unalive; to destroy for the sake of destruction; the exclusive interest in all that is purely mechanical' (Fromm, 1973 p 332). Neither an instinct nor a behaviour that people learn, necrophilia is a passion 'to tear apart living structures' (Hentig cited in Fromm, 1973 p 332). The necrophiliac character appears in a very small percentage of the population and pure versions of it are rarer still.

Fromm offers diverse sources as evidence. These include dreams from psychoanalytic case material, a study of Nixon voters using Michael Maccoby's interpretive questionnaire in the late 1960s (Maccoby, 1972), Lewis Mumford's historical analysis connecting Mesopotamia and Egypt to modern society, scholarship on the Italian Futurists, the United States military campaign in Vietnam, the Nazi Holocaust, literature on the bombing of Dresden and Hiroshima, and the writings of strategists for nuclear war during the Cold War.

Fromm explains that the necrophilia involves social structural, psychoanalytic, and biological levels of analysis. The sociologist and Marxist in Fromm believed that societies based on massive levels of inequality, brutal exploitation of the less powerful, and the arrogant use of advanced technologies to transform the world in godlike ways were bound to promote a death-loving culture. It produces individuals whose childhood was absent of 'affective bonds' outside the 'shell of autistic self-sufficiency' (Fromm, 1973 p 362), a condition that Fromm calls a 'malignant incestuousness' in relation to the mother. Fromm described an early adolescence that reinforces dependency and a lack of realism alongside likely genetic factors. This character becomes reinforced and intensified through young adulthood in response to authoritarian ideologies and trauma encountered both within and outside of the family. These processes produce both the 'haters, the racists, those in favour of war, bloodshed and destruction', as well as 'executioners, terrorists and torturers' (Fromm, 1973 p 368). Less extreme versions of the syndrome are observed in the committed followers of authoritarian and violent leaders depending on broader political, sociology and historical factors. Fromm engages Freud's theory of the death instinct, attempting a preliminary synthesis with his own approach and then presents an extended case study on Hitler.

Fromm's analysis of the roots of Hitler's malignant destructiveness does not conform to Freudian clichés. Hitler's incestuous but emotionally disconnected tie to his mother was the source of a pathological lack of realism characterizing Hitler's youth, having emerged during his first five or so years of life. Fromm did not blame either parent, however, least of all the mother. He viewed Klara Hitler as a well-adjusted and sympathetic woman who as a working-class girl had worked as a maid in the home of her uncle, Alois, whom she would later marry. Hitler's father, in Fromm's account, was less sympathetic and more authoritarian. Fromm insists, however, that it is a mistake to assume that evil is produced by parents alone. Alois was no monster. Hitler never developed a warm relationship to either parent, and his mother never represented a real person for young Adolf for whom she became a 'symbol for the impersonal power of earth, fate—and death' (Fromm, 1973 p 377).

The next step in the development of his pathology was Adolf's desire for freedom between the ages of six and eleven, which meant 'irresponsibility, lack of constraints and, most importantly, freedom from reality'(Fromm, 1973 p 379). As a young adult, Adolf Hitler moved to Vienna. In his unsuccessful effort to become an artist, he became increasingly resentful, angry, and narcissistic. The details of Hitler's artist period are well known, and Fromm relies on the standard biographical sources available at the time. The key psychological point is Hitler's growing pathological narcissism. His sanity was coming to depend on his efforts to turn his 'grandiose fantasies' of greatness into reality, something that had failed in the art world in Munich. The outbreak of the First World War was a boon for Adolf Hitler turning him from an 'outcast' into 'a hero fighting for Germany, for its existence and glory and for the value of nationalism' (Fromm, 1973 p 394).

When looking at Hitler's life, Fromm observes a likely biological source of pathology, an incestuous tie to his mother that he projected onto the nation, and a series of failures that grew by stages from high school student to middle-class drop-out and art academy rejection. As a talented speaker and opportunist, Hitler would soon avenge his humiliations and wounded narcissism by becoming a demagogue who sought revenge for Germany's war defeat as a rationalization for setting the world on fire.

Restoring Fromm's academic reputation

Contemporary political scientists, historians, and historical sociologists provide more detailed analyses of the rise and fall of Nazism, but Fromm's psychological account of Hitler's pathological destructiveness remains relevant. Hitler's mania for destruction is best understood first by political science and historical sociology, not psychohistory, despite the criticism that must be raised about conventional wisdom within social science.[7] One can and should be sceptical of Fromm's specific reading of Hitler, but it is difficult to ignore his argument that Nazism and other forms of extremism cannot be understood with rational political actor models that shape the influential historical sociology of Randall Collins, Theda Skocpol, and Michael Mann.

The Anatomy of Human Destructiveness sold far more copies than *Social Character* and achieved a reasonable reception in the academic and elite intellectual world, but it was not enough to prevent the decline of Fromm's scholarly reputation. The general waning of psychoanalysis in the culture at the time did not help, nor did the fact that Fromm had little expertise in neuroscience, anthropology, and the like. While some scholars have developed the concept of necrophilia, many find some of Fromm's psychoanalytic interpretations unconvincing and his general theory regarding the love of death uncompelling.[8] Fromm was unable to restore his scholarly reputation, especially among leftists in the English-speaking world, partly because his politics of hope conflicted with the rage and anger that had become dominant in the United States as the Vietnam War dragged on. Fromm opposed the war and the American empire, but his political vision and his analytic framework avoided an excessively romantic view of left-wing opposition to injustice.[9] Fromm knew that left-wing authoritarianism was always a danger, even while the focus of his analysis remained a critique of capitalism, fascism, and right-wing extremism.

There are limitations to Fromm's social science analysis and psychoanalytic perspective that was recognized at the time but are more apparent in light of recent research. In his thoughtful review of *Anatomy*, Berkeley sociological theorist Guy Swanson suggests that Fromm's analysis of thirty societies can be recoded in ways that do not support his argument for a connection between the variables of 'narcissism and destructiveness' (Swanson, 1975 p 1244). Swanson challenges what he views as Fromm's exaggerated critique of 'cybernetic, bureaucratized', 'capitalist societies' as 'malignant aggression' and analysis of the 'lower-middle and upper working classes and their susceptibility to extremist movements in the 1930s' (Swanson, 1975 p 1244). Swanson is right that *Anatomy* would have been more successful if Fromm had grappled with the 'findings of Barrington Moore, Richard Hamilton, Melvin Kohn and Carmi Schooler' (Swanson, 1975 p 1244).

Sociologist William Amis also gave *Anatomy* a decent review in *Contemporary Sociology*, the official book review journal for the American Sociological Association. Amis gave Fromm credit for complicating popular competing models that suggest violence can be explained by either instinct or conditioning. Fromm's book provided 'an impressive review of research from many disciplines' (Amis, 1974 pp 513–514) and offered a useful study of the '*motivation* to aggression'

(Amis, 1974 p 514). Taking a sensible position on how psychoanalytic perspectives can supplement sociological research, Amis recognizes that behaviourist social science ought to be critical of some of Fromm's methodological choices but that 'triviality of conclusions can be the price paid for accuracy if our models are pared down to fit the safest methodology' (Amis, 1974 p 515).

In this spirit, sociologists should draw on Fromm's analysis of destructiveness. Neil Smelser compellingly argued that psychoanalysis can be used to understand irrationality (Smelser, 1998) without rejecting the rational choice and organizational models that employ rigorous empirical methods that are less speculative than those of depth psychology. Professional sociology need not choose one or the other.

Fromm's psychoanalytic approach and his existential theory of needs is not without limitations (Cortina, 2015). Fromm's focus on the bond to the mother was a productive intervention in the context of Freudian theory in 1930s. Building on Karen Horney and Fromm's early critique of Freud's patriarchal assumptions, scholars created object relations and relational perspectives in psychoanalysis often shaped by feminist politics and epistemologies (Greenberg and Mitchell, 1983; Chodorow, 1985, 1989; Chancer, 1992; Kurzweil, 1995; Green, 2008a, 2008b; Silver, 2017).

Fromm was writing at the same time that Bowlby was conducting his pioneering work on the infant child's ties to the mother (Bowlby, 1958, 1969, 1979) but before empirical research in the attachment theory tradition became dominant within psychoanalysis. This literature created a new consensus on the need for secure attachments now viewed as the Bowlby/Ainsworth route to autonomy (Ainsworth, 1979; Bowlby 1979). More importantly, however, is Cortina's assertion that Fromm's reading of routes to extremism travelled by the individuals in his case studies puts too little emphasis on emotional schemes that must be internalized to the point that the 'psychical presence of mother is not needed for confident exploration' (Cortina, 2015). A revised and refined version of Fromm's psychoanalytic theory modified by attachment theory would be far more useful for contemporary sociologists in theorizing violence. Such an approach should include a nuanced analysis of what is now known as 'toxic masculinity' best understood through the insights of contemporary feminist and gender theories (Theweleit, 1989; Connell, 2002; Chancer, 2017).

More fundamentally, the core of Fromm's theory, including his analysis of early human evolution and the historical development of modern individualism, is flawed by his exaggeration of the loss of our instinctual equipment (Cortina, 2015). Fromm underplayed the violence of some of our close primate relatives (Riesman, 1973), and recent research documents far more complex social and emotional dynamics among animals (Cortina, 2015; Christakis, 2019). Fromm was right to critique both the brutal pessimism of Lorenz as well as the orthodox Freudian theory that anchored so much thinking about human nature circulating in public discourse in the mid-twentieth century. This reactionary view of human nature has now reappeared in Jordan Peterson's influential reframing of Hobbesian ideas through a Jungian framework (McLaughlin, 2019; Peterson, 2018). Fromm's critique of Social Darwinian theories and reactionary thinking is generally valid but must be modified. The same may be said of his attack on excessively optimistic defences of capitalist modernity, a liberal emphasis dominant in his time and reappearing in recent years with Harvard psychologist Steven Pinker (Pinker 2011, 2018)

The problems with Fromm's existential psychoanalytic humanism and his related theory of necrophilia are both political and intellectual. Politically, Fromm's emphasis on the break from nature in *Anatomy* tends to excessively valorize modern individualism severing his work from the political and moral insights emerging from Indigenous theorists and movements around the world today (Denis, 2020; Watts, Hooks, and McLaughlin, 2020). Potentially aligned with Fromm's radical humanism, these traditions would be justifiably critical of Fromm's account of pre-modern cultures that needlessly pathologizes communal cultures, connections to nature and land and native forms of spiritualism for which, in principle, he had sympathy. Fromm, having lived through the Nazi era in Germany with its 'blood and soil' rhetoric, understandably viewed claims about ties to nature with scepticism. Fromm was opposed to colonialism and racism, but his social narcissism theory of nationalism led him to overgeneralize about tribal culture and nations and their psychologies. Fromm was unaware of later critical race theorists influenced by Foucault like Cornel West who would put greater emphasis on the racism encoded in rituals, myths, colonialism, the slave trade, and anti-Semitism shaped by scientific discourse (West, 1989). As a result, Fromm's analysis was incomplete.

Fromm's theory of violence is overly psychological and inadequately structural leading him to overemphasize his flawed theory of necrophilia. Drawing on attachment theory and clinical experience, Cortina is sympathetic to Fromm's general viewpoint but ultimately concludes that the theory of necrophilia was 'wrong in assuming that biophilia (love of life) and necrophilia are polar developmental opposites'. Fromm remained strongly committed to the Freudian tradition in *Anatomy* demonstrated in the book's extended appendix. There, he puts his theory of necrophilia into dialogue with the psychoanalytic theory of the death instinct. For Cortina, however, the opposite of the love of life is 'depression, feeling defeated and feeling shamed', not a necrophilia that exists only in extreme cases like Hitler and Himmler who are 'deeply alienated (schizoid), paranoid, grandiose and have strong sadistic traits' (Cortina, 2015 p 396). Bureaucracies are not full of little Himmlers and Hitlers, and it is a mistake to think, as Fromm and Maccoby did, that Nixon supporters in the early 1970s were motivated by necrophilia (Maccoby, 1972). Fromm's theory can lead contemporary critical theorists to formulate misleading conclusions seeing, for example, the support for Trump in America in overly abstract ways (Kellner, 2016; Thorpe, 2016; Langman and Lundskow, 2016). This approach is often tinged by academic and class elitism.

Neither this kind of abstract critical theory nor Fromm's overemphasis on the human break with nature is necessary. Cutting-edge scientific research reinforces Fromm's core intellectual points and hopeful (not naïve) radical political vision. Cortina summarizes the most recent scholarly research:

> Our human ancestors survived by becoming a highly cooperative and social species, and this development required the development of social instincts, already present to a lesser degree among our ape relatives (chimpanzees, bonobos, gorillas, and orangutans). This cooperative mode of survival among small groups of nomadic hunter-gatherers was the result of dramatic climate changes that produced severe droughts in East Africa. (Cortina, 2015 p 406)

In order to live in open African Savannah, our ancestors had to adapt to a new environment with less rainforest than had existed for millions of years. In this new climate, *homo erectus* emerged over 1.8 million years ago and these conditions 'created selective pressures on learning to cooperate to hunt and scavenge meat left behind by lions and predators and to distribute this food among other group members' (Cortina, 2015 p 406).

The contemporary relevance of all this for professional sociology is clear. Sociologists can draw on Fromm's insights into psychoanalytic emotional dynamics and his hopeful political vision. At the same time, however, they should downplay his focus on necrophilia in *Anatomy* and combine his approach with up-to-date research (Cortina, 2015). Popular interventions on human nature by sociologist Nicholas Christakis, *Blueprint: The Evolutionary Origins of a Good Society* (2019), and by Dutch journalist Rutger Bregman, *Humankind: A Hopeful History* (2019) do what Fromm was trying to accomplish. There were times when Fromm underplayed the violence in human history that Steven Pinker documents at length in *The Better Angels of Our Nature* (2011), an issue also in Rutger Bregman's *Humankind* (2019). Fromm's book would have been better if he had kept up with major scholars in related fields, although some of the most important challenges to his ideas came after his death. In the end, however, *Anatomy* remains a valuable account of human violence worth serious reconsideration.

Fromm had many goals when he first outlined the basics of a social character theory and analysis of fascist violence in *Escape from Freedom* in 1941, and he developed his approach in more scholarly detail in both *Social Character in a Mexican Village* and *The Anatomy of Human Destructiveness*. Fromm's analysis was deepened and made more sophisticated in each of these books even while they have limitations as well as offering insights. It is necessary to both draw on Fromm's ideas *and* to move beyond his framework to build a scholarly global public sociology that also contributes to professional literatures in our discipline. In the conclusion, I will address the lessons Fromm's public sociology offers for us, how this case study can help us study public sociology, and how Fromm's theories and research can be refined to apply to our current situation. But first we need to discuss the revival of Fromm's global public sociology that is evident around the world.

Conclusion: The Revival of a Global Public Sociologist

By 1975, Fromm was essentially a forgotten public sociologist in the United States and the English-speaking world. Yet Fromm's analysis of the mechanisms of escape involved in both far-right-wing movements and left-wing authoritarianism, his emphasis on the distorting power of the market as it permeates character and reshapes personalities, his contribution to theories of alienation and the development of humanistic Marxism, and his empirical work on the relationship between social character, alienated work, and economic development all brought insights and ideas into sociology.

Fromm's theoretical account of the power of emotions, passions and narcissism in human destructiveness and his insights into the psychosocial logic of social life (McLaughlin, 2019) are sociological perspectives worthy of renewed attention. The undertheorized power of emotions amplified so intensely by social media today (Gardner and Davis, 2013; Lukiannoff and Haidt, 2018) has become apparent to sociologists who prematurely dismissed psychoanalytic insights (Cavalletto and Silver, 2014). Fromm's unique account of human nature and motivations, and his pioneering critique of the patriarchal and the positivistic limitations of Freud's theories, are an indispensable intellectual resource for social theory today.

Fromm's pathbreaking role is a largely unacknowledged part of the history of public sociology. There was no Marxist sociology in America when Fromm published *Escape from Freedom* but conservative sociologist Edward Shils understood the importance of this book. In *The Calling of Sociology* (1980), Shils argued that *Escape from Freedom* offered:

> Without the dogmatism of a political party, a plausible conception of a cataclysmic event of human history, and it was, moreover, one which was harmonious with the

> enhanced and widened political sensitivity of the new generation of sociologists. (Shils, 1980 p 113)

Assisting in Americans' self-understanding, Fromm also 'offered a critique of the social order of capitalism' that applied to the 'situation of the United States as well as Germany' (Shils, 1980 p 113). Shils was famously pro-West and pro-capitalist and opposed the rise of academic Marxism that swept American sociology in the 1960s and 1970s. Shils was insightful and honest enough, however, to see how pivotal Fromm's *Escape from Freedom* was for the radicalization of sociology. As Shils puts it, that book 'brought into the center of analysis the class system, the motivations which impelled its acceptance and rejection, and the political consequences of such motivations' (Shils, 1980 p 113). Fromm did more than anyone to bring Marxism into American sociology, with the possible exception of W. E. B. Du Bois.

Fromm was also pivotal in creating the template for what twentieth-century public sociology might look like. Fromm mentored David Riesman, the major traditional public sociologist of the twentieth century. When Riesman died, Orlando Patterson called him 'sociology's last public intellectual' (Patterson, 2002) with no mention of Fromm's inspiration for *The Lonely Crowd*. Riesman conducted empirical research (Riesman and Glazer, 1952) but, like Fromm, he was largely an essay writer and book publisher (Riesman, 1954, 1964) despite his academic position at the centre of the American field (Riesman, 1990). Fromm showed Riesman the path to a career at the University of Chicago and Harvard, and they supported each other in their similarly optimally marginal positions outside the core of professional sociology.

While we think of C. Wright Mills as the model for engaged Cold War and 1960s era public sociology, it was Fromm who pioneered the genre of best-selling radical works of public sociology that Mills later successfully emulated. Fromm sold far more books than C. Wright Mills ever did and was more politically active. Contemporary public sociologists are more specialized than they were in the 1950s (Brint, 1994). But the great contemporary public sociologists such as William Julius Wilson, Arlie Hochschild, Eric Klinenberg, and Annette Lareau (Hallett, Stapleton, and Saunder, 2019) built upon the cultural capital and emotional energy (Collins, 1998) the Fromm–Riesman collaboration created. Fromm, in particular, provided the public sociology template that travelled globally in ways that neither Riesman nor even Mills managed. Fromm still gets between 4,000 and nearly 5,000 citations every year in Google Scholar, well over half of which are not in English. This is a remarkable global reach not often attained in self-referential and overly parochial American sociology.

The rediscovery and revival of Fromm's global public sociology

National sociologies have their own public sociological traditions discussed in the emerging literature on public sociology around the world.[1] Core foundational texts in the public sociology debate, however, rely excessively on provincially American writers like C. Wright Mills and David Riesman. Fromm was a more global public sociologist who wrote in two major languages and spoke three. Fromm had a massive influence in Latin America, Eastern and Central Europe, the United Kingdom, Japan, and in German-speaking countries.

For Fromm, this was never a marketing strategy. Fromm was committed to engaging scholars around the world, supporting the human rights of dissenting intellectuals in Latin America and Eastern and Central Europe, and to think about the world comparatively and globally. The remarkable revival of interest in Fromm's work (Funk and McLaughlin, 2015; Funk, 2019) is truly global and likely to restore his name to the pantheon of great public sociologists.

There were always national and regional differences in the reception of Fromm's work, and the same is true with his revival. Fromm's work was well received and appreciated in Catholic majority nations partly because of his critique of Protestant authoritarianism in *Escape from Freedom*. It helped that Fromm lived in Mexico for decades and influenced Brazilian Paulo Freire (Freire, 1970), a major radical intellectual in the region. Fromm was also praised by Pope John Paul II for his critiques of modern spiritual emptiness and regularly made the case for the positive aspects of Catholic communitarianism and the matriarchal elements of the religion.

From the Cold War period to his death, Fromm defended socialist humanists and Marxist critics of Soviet official Marxism, and he had personal relationships with important intellectuals in Poland and the former Yugoslavia. Fromm's critique of both Stalinism and the inequalities that flowed from market societies explains his sustained influence in Eastern and Central Europe (Anderson, 2015). Fromm retains more influence in Germany, the land of his birth and his mother language, than he does anywhere else (Funk, 2019).

The revival of Erich Fromm began with the publication of his last major book, *To Have or to Be*. A theoretically informed political vision for radical humanist social change, the best-selling book was published by a commercial press and had massive influence in Germany, continental Europe, and the English-speaking world. After writing *Social Character in a Mexican Village* and *The Anatomy of Human Destructiveness*, Fromm pivoted from an analytic to a prophetic voice (Maccoby, 1995) in *To Have or to Be*. Returning to his mother tongue, Fromm wrote the book from his final home in Switzerland, bringing a message of hope and radical change back to his homeland, decades after the defeat of Nazism. Fromm helped inspire the Green movement in Germany that has since spread around the world.

This concluding chapter will look at the revival of Fromm's public sociology. We then recast Fromm's public sociology through Burawoy's framework, evaluating the consequences of Fromm's sociological positioning and career choices to gauge the influence and quality of his professional sociology. We conclude with some lessons that can be learned from Erich Fromm as a public sociologist, offering both a research agenda and practical lessons for contemporary public sociologists.

In his final years, Fromm saw himself as a prophetic and political figure who wanted not only to interpret the world but to change it following Karl Marx's famous formulation. *To Have or to Be* represents his final call to action, a visionary manifesto. Written and published as a short and relatively accessible book, *To Have or to Be* was a best-seller in Germany and around the world in English and other translations. It sold over 8 million copies, second to only *The Art of Loving*.

Sociologists know that books alone do not create movements, but the case of Erich Fromm shows the role that books can play as a recruitment device and source of inspiration for social movements. Millions of young Germans were inspired by *To Have or to Be*, many of whom went on to create the worldwide Green movement starting with the original parliamentary party. Fromm's vision was anti-capitalist, anti-communist and critical of the ruling German Social Democratic Party. His politics and visionary writing played a role in helping construct new space for a countercultural environmental left. As he entered the final phase of public engagement in his life, his appearances on German and English radio and TV helped spearhead a new global environmental movement.

After Fromm's death in 1980, his legacy and interest in his ideas was kept alive by Rainer Funk and a network of scholars in and around the Erich Fromm Society, many working in the German language. Michael Maccoby and his students conducted applied organizational research in the private sector (Maccoby, 1988, 2003, 2007, 2015), and Mexican researchers engaging in important participatory action research (Millán and Millán, 2015). Fromm retained an audience in Poland, parts of

Central Europe, and Latin America, particularly in Brazil where his relationship with Paulo Freire and influence on Lula's Workers' Party and movement sustained support for his ideas (Costa, 2019). There is new interest among some key Frankfurt School scholars who had revisited the old Marcuse–Fromm–Adorno debates and decided that the critical theorists shared more than what had earlier divided them (Rickert, 1986; Kellner, 1989; Bronner, 1994). But among elite intellectuals, and inside professional sociology in America in particular, Fromm was *persona non grata*.

Following the 2016 US Presidential election of the deeply narcissistic and authoritarian Donald Trump and in the wake of his four-year term, we have seen a significant revival of Fromm's work. The rise of right-wing populism in America, Hungary, Poland, and Brazil, and the growing psychological anxiety that the contemporary capitalist and social media world has created are drawing people to Fromm's insights. There were more dissertations written on Fromm in the last decade in China than in the rest of the world combined (Funk and McLaughlin, 2015). Fromm's Marxist analysis of the alienation that comes with industrialization and his radical humanist political critique of Stalinist and Maoist authoritarianism of one-party states is finding an audience in Asia just as his dissenting Marxist humanism was once influential in communist Poland, Hungary, and the former Yugoslavia.

Recent books have facilitated the revival (Braune, 2014; Durkin, 2014; Funk, 2019; Durkin and Braune, 2020). Lawrence Friedman's comprehensive biography (Friedman, 2013) is one element of this momentum but perhaps the most important factor is the growing dissatisfaction with professional and policy sociology in the neo-liberal university. Sociology is becoming increasingly technical and specialized, dominated by the most elite American universities (Markovits, 2019). Knowledge about inequality and injustices has increased as has despair in taking action against it, although protests in 2020 and the defeat of Donald Trump suggest room for hope. American research universities that create knowledge about inequality, however, have become expensive elitist institutions that reinforce inequality as much as challenge it.

The perception of an institutional crisis in research universities is felt acutely inside the professional core of major disciplines; out of it came the newly invented concepts of 'public intellectual' and 'public sociology' (Jacoby, 1987; Burawoy, 2005; McLaughlin, 2018; McLaughlin and Townsley, 2011; McLaughlin and Turcotte, 2007). These debates give us a language to reinterpret Fromm's work. Fromm is not an outdated professional sociologist or psychologist but a major global public intellectual and public sociologist ahead of his time. There are limitations in his work, however, that must be addressed.

Reframing and reformulating Fromm's insights

Fromm's ideas and example cannot be brought back into the professional literature and public sociology practice without significant revision and reformation. Updating Fromm's gender analysis must be first on the list. Janet Afary and Roger Friedland (Afary and Friedland, 2018) drew on Fromm's interpretive questionnaire methodology to show how attitudes about the place of women in society in Iran are linked to the contemporary versions of authoritarian political movements represented by Islamism. As Lynn Chancer has perceptively argued, any revival of Fromm's work must draw on his critique of patriarchy while avoiding the elements of essentialism and outdated language that permeated some of his writings (Chancer, 2017). The literature on sexualities would benefit from drawing on the object relations-oriented forms of psychoanalysis that Fromm helped create (Chodorow, 1985, 1989; Green 2008a).[2]

A revival of Fromm's social character theory would have to occur in dialogue with more contemporary theorists of race, emotion, and post-colonial theories in sociology. Foucault has tended to dominate recent race scholarship despite some scepticism of his political judgement (Afary and Anderson, 2010). But compared to Fromm, the discourse analysis traditions that flow from Foucault's work places a stronger emphasis on the structures and logics of various ideas that shape racism and white supremacy. Fromm came too late to fully appreciate the critiques of Orientalist logics developed by Edward Said (Said, 2012a). Fromm's analysis of Nazism would have benefited from more attention to anti-Semitism, anti-Roma bigotry, and anti-black racism. Good Marxist and Freudian that he was, Fromm tended to assume it was the material conditions of a society along with the psychological logic of character that shaped social narcissisms and bigotry. His powerful analysis of emotions must be integrated into larger contemporary literatures on race and emotions (hooks, 2002; Srivastava, 2005; Bonilla-Silva, 2019) that puts more stress on ideas (West, 1989) such as scientific racism (Williams, 2016), and racism against Asians (Glenn, 2011), Muslims (Bail, 2014), Roma (Levine-Rasky, 2016), and Jews (Smith, 1996).

One important way into productive contemporary debates is to retheorize Fromm's concepts of social narcissism and clinical insights along with more recent group-position theories that pay more attention to post-colonial and Indigenous thought (Denis, 2020). More theoretical work comparing and building on Fromm and Fanon would help us get beyond Bourdieu's dismissal of psychological levels of analysis. This approach would avoid abstract philosophy and would instead help produce an empirical sociology of people's lives in dealing with bigotry and discrimination (Lamont et al, 2016).

Various contemporary critical sociologists and critical theorists have returned to Fromm, especially since Trumpism (Smith and Hanley, 2018). Despite the insights in this work, there is a need to combine Fromm's analysis with mainstream professional sociology. Understanding Trumpism as a contemporary version of necrophilia (Thorpe, 2016, 2020), or as representing a lower-middle-class rebellion and the expression of American reactionary character rooted in guns and religion (Langman and Lundskow, 2016), or reflecting Trump's own profound narcissism (Kellner, 2016) and the hatreds of his base (Smith 2019, 2020) capture part of the truth but require more sociological sophistication. Further ethnographic research is required to interpret the complexities and nuances of the Trump vote in the United States (Hochschild, 2016) and in the reactionary movements in Brazil, Hungary, and Poland. In an analytic political sociology, Fromm's tendency to label political pathologies should be avoided.

The assertions still made by critical scholars of the alleged lower-middle-class roots of far-right movements is particularly problematic. Any attempt to use Fromm's social character theory today must engage the work of the best historical sociologists such as Michael Mann, Theda Skocpol, and Randall Collins in order to be ruthlessly empirical about the actual social class basis of far-right-wing movements. Clearly, strategists like Steve Bannon are making the case for a working-class and nationalist far right. It will no longer be enough to simply to point to billionaires and the capitalist class as the source of reactionary politics, an outdated Marxism that is even less compelling now than in the 1930s. The working-class support for Trumpism could be seen at the rallies and on 6 January 2021 storming of the Congress. This cannot be explained away by simply critiquing the propaganda of Fox News and the reactionary influence of the Koch brothers' dark money.

But working-class and lower-middle-class authoritarianism cannot be assumed, as social scientists and historians in mid-century America too often did (Lipset, 1959). As David Riesman stated in his review of *The Anatomy of Human Destructiveness*, Fromm's critique of modern technological societies is 'overdrawn' and his work is often 'pervaded by distaste for the bourgeois and especially the lowermiddle class' (Riesman, 1973 p 26).[3] As were many other German critical theorists,

Fromm was simply too judgemental to render an objective analysis of America (McLaughlin, 2001b). A critical distance from one's own political views is an essential element of good sociology, something that can aid in the political project of understanding and defeating reactionary global Trumpism (Hochschild, 2016).

Riesman, as well as many of the New York intellectuals of the period (Wolfe, 2018), were too complacent and uncritical of America. Fromm's work is essential for contemporary public and critical sociology. Yet work that builds on his insights needs to express far less of both class prejudice and European anti-Americanism (Markovits, 2009). Clearly there was working-class and lower-middle-class support for Trumpism that was seen in his rallies and the voting patterns but the vote for the Republican Party overall went up with family income in the 2020 election. Fromm's psychosocial analysis underplays the authoritarianism of what Barbara Ehrenreich called the professional managerial class (Ehrenreich, 2009). Without a willingness to look at the liberal authoritarianism of the centre and to be critical of the elitism of academics, left psychosocial analysis is a recipe for a remarkably unreflexive sociology.

Fromm insisted on the theoretical centrality of left-wing authoritarianism (Fromm, 1984), a position being taken up in an unsophisticated and reactionary way by Jordan Peterson today. Any tenable critical theory must confront the political and psychological pathologies embedded in Stalinism and its outgrowths whether they be in the People's Republic of China or the Republic of North Korea (David-West, 2014). The more diffuse left authoritarianism we see on Western university campuses risks closing down a range of speakers and ideas beyond through de-platforming instead of debating, critiquing, or ignoring offensive views (Lukiannoff and Haidt, 2018). Political lies are not exclusively a right-wing phenomenon. A Fromm-influenced public sociology would engage with principled conservative and moderate political voices while avoiding dogmatism through a commitment to universalistic humanism.

Research based on Fromm's social character could make important contributions today, particularly in dialogue with the Bourdieu school of cultural sociology. Fromm's theory of social character is similar to Bourdieu's more influential concept of habitus (Maccoby and McLaughlin, 2020). While Bourdieu's disciplined focus on producing a professional research programme within the sociology of culture and education was more successful, it has conceptual gaps that social character theory can help fill. Embedded in a larger theoretical apparatus that includes the concepts of capital and field, habitus theory was designed to overcome the polarity between structure and agency but does so in ways that are overly cognitive and lack psychological depth (Cheliotis, 2011a; Grillo, 2018; Maccoby and McLaughlin, 2020).

Attempts to bring Freudian-influenced psychoanalysis to fill in gaps in Bourdieu's theory is an obvious theoretical move, something George Steinmetz has argued can be accomplished by Lacan's psychoanalytic theorizing (Steinmetz, 2006). Fromm's framework, however, came out of sociology itself and is far more compatible with doing empirical research, particularly in a critical realist form (Grillo, 2018).

Indeed, Fromm did important professional sociology (Fromm and Maccoby, 1970). It is not likely that empirical studies like *Social Character in a Mexican Village* could and should be done today. The amount of resources required and the complexities in studying marginalized communities as an outsider like Fromm ultimately require new post-colonial methods and approaches (Denis, 2020). Yet Fromm's work had affinity with Fanon's analysis of internalized racism (Fanon, 1967), something that Bourdieu patently dismissed. A new synthesis is required both beyond Bourdieu and Fromm.

Synthesizing critical race theories and Fromm's social character theory would benefit both schools of thought. Social character research on issues of dependency and anti-fragility in higher education, studies on sadism among police officers and the military, questions of projection and narcissism on social media, research on sex work, commercialization of intimacy and the Nordic model, debates about domestic violence, and research on the politics of professors under particular institutional arrangements are examples of existing literature where Fromm's ideas could be useful if inserted carefully. Fromm scholars cannot stay isolated in insular sects as we see among Freudians (Kurzweil, 1989, 1995; Noll, 1997) and intellectual movements more generally (Coser, 1965; Frickel and Gross, 2005; McLaughlin, 2017b). Social character theory must traverse Bourdieu's field analysis framework and Fanon's post-colonial theory without getting trapped inside narrow theoretical camps.

Towards a psychosocial social science

Renewal of Fromm's professional sociology depends on the broader intellectual movement of the psychosocial perspective (McLaughlin, 2019). Originally emerging from the Freudian clinical tradition, psychosocial work now is done in social work, psychology, sociology, criminology, and psychosocial departments where attempts are being made to integrate depth psychological insights into social analysis, both theoretical and applied. Fromm's ideas initially grew in influence in the 1930s during the crises of economic depression and fascism. At the time of writing there is a need for social science perspectives that go beyond the rational choices theories that dominate much economics and political science (Smelser, 1998), and the generic behaviourist and one-sided structural sociology that dominates disciplinary paradigms. Cognitive sociology moves us forward but does not address the power of feelings adequately (Chodorow, 1999).

It is difficult to institutionalize psychosocial perspectives in modern research universities where neurosciences and experimental research designs increasingly dominate. Like earlier psychohistory, psychosocial thinkers often over-reach, trying to explain social and political events with too much psychology and not enough history, structural context, and careful empirical research. Sectarian battles between the followers of Lacan, Jung, Klein, Winnicott, and other Freudian offshoots make the field inaccessible to sociologists and broader publics. Fromm was a psychosocial thinker who had a sociological framework and knew how to take his insights beyond the warring camps of Freudians (McLaughlin, 2019).

As sociologists George Cavalletto and Catherine Silver (2014) have documented, psychoanalytic ideas were once important in the discipline. There is now a growing intellectual movement (Frickel and Gross, 2005) arguing that we should return to the insights in the Freudian tradition, reframing them in broader interdisciplinary psychosocial ways now shaped by feminist and critical race theory insights (Silver, 2014, 2017; Chancer, 2017; Bonilla-Silva, 2019). They build on the earlier insights of Neil Smelser (1998) on the 'rational and irrational', the pathbreaking psychoanalytic feminist sociology of Jessica Benjamin (1988), and Nancy Chodorow (1985, 1989, 1999). It is in this context that Fromm's psychosocial ideas and public sociology merit renewed attention. Lynn Chancer's (1992, 2017) research agenda on sadomasochism and everyday life and Janet Afary's account (Afary and Friedland, 2018) of authoritarian gender politics show how this could be done with a feminist lens.

Lessons for public sociologists: Fromm and beyond

Fromm's insights and influence throughout his career come from the fact that he was an optimally marginal public sociologist (McLaughlin, 2001a). Fromm had insights into the power of the authoritarian character, the pathologies of narcissistic personalities and cultures, the alienation of consumer societies, and the irrationalities of nationalism.

Blind spots in professional sociology and the political consensus enforced by political and economic elites hide these issues in plain sight.

Fromm was deeply embedded in the interactional ritual changes, emotional energies and cultural capital (Collins, 1999) of the Marxist tradition, the sociology of Weber, Simmel, and Durkheim and the Freudian tradition. Connections to the Frankfurt School (McLaughlin, 2008), the world of clinical practice (Rogow, 1970), and the mass-market book publishing industry (Coser, Kadushin, and Powell, 1982) gave him access to resources that allowed him to avoid a career in professional sociology. This independence also reinforced his marginality inside mainstream sociology. What lessons can be learned from thinking about Fromm's public sociology from a sociological perspective?

The quality of Fromm's work would have benefited from more engagement with cutting-edge empirical sociology, especially after 1956 when the celebrity status created by publication of *The Art of Loving* further isolated him from peer-reviewed scholarship. Fromm's activism was both facilitated by and made less effective by the fame and wealth that removed him from the networks of activists within the civil rights, socialist, and feminist movements. Relationships there could have helped Fromm update and refine his ideas.

A more politically engaged Fromm who acted as an equal in the socialist movement would have learned about new theories of race and racism. He would have been more connected to practical economic proposals promoted by progressive economists and political economy-oriented sociologists, as well as labour and feminist activists. Michael Harrington and Fromm shared a socialist humanist politics and a reading of the democratic elements of Marx's thought. While Fromm was ultimately a more original thinker, Harrington was a far better activist intellectual. His more direct engagement with mass politics furnished him with better insights into the economics of capitalist societies and the cultural politics of the 1960s (Harrington, 1962, 1976, 1989; Isserman 2000). Fromm's stubborn use of male humanist language might have been overcome by stronger engagement with social movements, particularly feminism and gay liberation (Chancer, 2017). The broader point is that rather than only damaging objectivity as much of the debate on public sociology in the United States tends to assert (van den Berg, 1980; Nielson, 2004; Tittle, 2004), activism and critical sociology can also help refine scholarship.

Fromm tended to over-reach with psychoanalytic judgements, bringing them into political debates, contributing to the hollowing-out of public life just as Hannah Arendt warned (Baehr, 2019).

A synthesis of their approaches is needed. Arendt could have thought more psychoanalytically about her relationship to Heidegger. Her analysis of the banality of evil needed a theoretical framework that highlighted human passions and hatreds. But Arendt also had things to teach Fromm. Intellectuals often engage in what Arendt scholar and sociologist Peter Baehr has called the 'unmasking' style of political debate in which they dismiss their political opponents by claiming to reveal their true underlying motives as xenophobia, Islamophobia, or more recently, transphobia, undermining the democratic public sphere (Baehr, 2019).

Bigotry, hatred, and discrimination are real and must be opposed morally and politically. An analysis that relies on the language of phobia, however, risks substituting the psychoanalysing of one's political opponents with the political engagement of ideas in the public sphere. Fromm was guilty of some of this when he dismissed supporters of Richard Nixon as 'necrophiliac' characters (Maccoby 1972) and when he claimed that Herbert Marcuse was a nihilist who did not love life (Fromm, 1992 [1963]). More broadly, *Escape from Freedom* was central to creating a social science framework for thinking about populism as xenophobia. This is a classic double-edged sword. There *are* emotional logics operating in the current polarized political climate and ultimately Fromm's insights into social psychology of authoritarianism of both the left and the right are valuable. But he also contributed to what Philip Rieff famously called the 'triumph of the therapeutic' (Rieff, 1987) that helped both depoliticize and polarize societies.

Research on public sociologies

There are many broader research questions that *Erich Fromm and Global Public Sociology* can open up. Fromm's best-selling books shaped the political movements of the 1960s by bringing young people into the anti-war and socialist movements. We need to develop a research agenda for how books shape politicization and recruitment in ways that do not fall into the 'big book' myth or downplay the influence of YouTube and social media for this generation.

We also need new research on the role of friends in intellectual collaboration. Fromm's relationship to Riesman is not the only example of a collaboration that involves 'instrumental intimacy' that crossed political divisions (Farrell, 2001). Studying other close friendships between public sociologists may reveal more about how public sociologists are created. Peter Baehr has studied the collaboration between Marxist sociologist Tom Bottomore and conservative Robert

Nisbet (Baehr, unpublished). Jonathan Haidt has theorized the social psychology of conversations across political divides (Haidt, 2012). There is an important research tradition on friendships and collaborative work that should be developed in studying the making of public sociologists (Farrell, 2001). In the period after Trump, sociologists need to study opportunities for political dialogue and intellectual common ground alongside of public sociological work to defend democracy and create change.

This study on a forgotten public sociologist involved a different kind of analysis than work on canonized public sociologists like C. Wright Mills (Geary, 2009; Aronowitz, 2012) or newly rediscovered thinkers such as W. E. B. Du Bois (Morris and Ghaziani, 2005; Morris, 2015). *Erich Fromm and Global Public Sociology* opens up possibilities for new research about the relationship between professional sociological work, activism, and public writing. Mills, for example, is often presented as a heroic and controversial figure in the field (Sterne, 2005), but in comparison to Fromm he was never fully marginalized and was far less political. Mills continued to be cited in core sociology journals after his death. Part of the public sociology canon, his writing continues to be discussed in introductory sociology classes (Burawoy, 2005). Ironically, however, while Mills is often praised for his radical principles (Aronowitz, 2012), he was relatively uninvolved in concrete activism. Mills was a professional and policy researcher who became a symbolic generational figure of inspiration in ways that downplayed the material base of his success (Sterne, 2005). Fromm was far more politically engaged and influential.

What explains the processes by which some public sociologists are chosen as heroes and others ignored? What role do these inspirational figures play in bringing young scholars into the profession? And how should we understand the differences between public sociologists who build careers without involving themselves in movements? There are those who, like Frances Fox Piven, succeed in both movement building and scholarship (Piven, 2006). Yet there are others who make sacrifices for politics in ways that damage their scholarly reputation. There is research to be done to reveal how activism, advocacy, and research are related and interact, for better or worse.

Additional related questions emerge from our case study on Fromm that could be expanded to other cases. How effective was Bourdieu as a political activist? How did Foucault's anti-prison activism and mental health advocacy and Du Bois' early liberal and later communist political commitments shape their intellectual work? How do the political commitments of feminist sociologists on both sides of the contentious debates on the Nordic Model or the legalization of sex work shape the quality of their research and public interventions? Public sociology would do well to move away from normative debates about whether it is beneficial or whether it is ruining the discipline, instead emphasizing empirical case studies.

In this age of celebrity academics, a research agenda on public sociology needs to be more attentive to how both fame and controversy shape intellectual and political work as observed by Daniel Bell, William Julius Wilson, and more recently Tressie McMillan Cottom and Eric Klinenberg. Fromm acquired fame comparable to that of Margaret Mead in the 1930s (Lutkehaus, 2008), Noam Chomsky after 9/11 (Lannigan and McLaughlin, 2017), and, on the political right, Jordan Peterson today. As the academic field becomes permeated by celebrity cultures, the number of famous public sociologists or public social psychologists worth study is likely to increase.

Fromm was a public sociologist with a truly global reach, something that even the most famous American sociologists did not have. Riesman is largely unknown outside the United States and most American public sociologists are known only to academics in other countries. Mills is an exception and Du Bois' Pan-Africanism and militant radicalism also brought him global fame (Morris, 2015). Raewyn Connell's work, *Southern Theory* (2007), focused our attention on public intellectuals, activists, and theorists outside the United States. What explains the differences in disciplinary cultures and broader political cultures in Latin America and Eastern and Central Europe, places where Fromm's public sociology retained more influence for longer? Research on Foucault, for example, reveals how he moved between public and academic work (Kauppi, 1996; Afary and Anderson, 2010). These are issues that should be explored with case studies on sociologists who speak to global audiences in languages other than English, as Fromm did.

Fromm was successful in avoiding the hyper-professionalism of contemporary sociology, managing to write persuasively outside of closed scholarly networks. We need more research into the conditions that make this kind of work possible. We are immersed today in social media along with a decline in tenured jobs, issues that raise important questions for research on the reproduction of public sociological careers.

Fromm avoided the battle for a tenure-track job by working with the Frankfurt School and doing therapy before bursting onto the scene with *Escape from Freedom*. The academic, publishing, and therapy fields are structured differently today. Many young scholars today planning for professional success in sociology, politics, and public intellectual life must make disciplined choices in a risky and competitive environment.

Ambitiously aiming beyond narrow professionalism paid off for Fromm and will do so for younger scholars today even in a very different historical context. But a sociology of public sociology can illuminate the constraints as well as help theorize and create possibilities.

Fromm's global sociological legacy

The intellectual value and the reputational costs associated with Fromm's willingness to challenge all orthodoxies is worth serious attention. Fromm's public sociology was clearly and unambiguously left-wing but avoided simplistic political orthodoxies. His intellectual vision and courage (Roazen, 1996) can be seen in his early work with the Horkheimer circle theory when he insisted on the existence of left-wing authoritarianism, a controversial position among critical theorists (McLaughlin, 1999). The authoritarian personality research tradition led by Adorno and later reinforced by Canadian social psychologist Robert Altemeyer's 'right-wing authoritarianism' research (Altemeyer, 1981) emphasized the right-wing roots of political pathology but exhibited both political and methodological biases (Shils, 1954; Jay, 1973).

As important a thinker and public sociologist as W. E. B. Du Bois was, his inability to see the brutality of Stalinism is an example of how the credibility of public sociology can be damaged if we do not abide by Fromm's insights on the dangers of authoritarianism on the left. Sociologist must be clearer on the authoritarianism of the Communist Party of the People's Republic of China today (Fleck and Hess, 2011). Fromm understood full well the role that Chinese communists played in decolonization and addressing the poverty of billions. The story of Du Bois and twentieth-century communism cannot be told without an account of the deep and pervasive racism and state repression that he faced (Morris, 2015). It is crucial to avoid simplistic ahistorical moralism. Yet if left-wing public sociologists do not stand against one-party states and the brutality of the Chinese regime today and fail to raise questions about the far softer, but still serious problem of excessive authoritarianism on campus (Lukiannoff and Haidt, 2018), space is opened for conservative reaction.

No other public sociologist wrote as clearly and as passionately about the range of political and social issues as Fromm did. Young people all around the world, especially outside the United States, were inspired by him for decades precisely because he rejected the narrow professionalism and expert tone so deadly to real dialogue between intellectuals and the public. The issues and political nuances are different today, and certainly Twitter, YouTube, social media, and the changing nature of both commercial publishing and the academy affect how this work will be done. If sociologists wish to compete with the likes of conservative Canadian psychologist Jordan Peterson for popular influence, following Fromm's example is vitally important.

C. Wright Mills, W. E. B. Du Bois, David Riesman, Arlie Hochschild, and the scores of public scholars who bring the sociological imagination to policy and public audiences today are better public sociologists, in the end, than Fromm. Fromm was as much a public psychoanalyst (Philipson, 2017), a spiritual prophetic thinker, and a therapist as he was a scholar (Funk, 2019). These additional roles sit uneasily with sociology's core mission, especially for professional sociology at elite American universities. Fromm belongs in the pantheon of great public sociologists but not at its centre with Du Bois, Mills, and the newly emerging scholars today who will define public sociology in the twenty-first century. This new public sociology will be more feminist, more post-colonial, and more diverse than it was in the twentieth century.

Fromm had a global vision, however, that most American sociologists in the twentieth century did not have. Ultimately a German Jewish intellectual of his generation, Fromm drew on Buddhist insights (1960a) and Muslim poets, and identified with the centuries-long struggles for liberation from colonial and then American domination in Latin America. His truly cosmopolitan European vision for democratic socialism, rooted in a particular conception of the historical emergence of individualism, requires rewriting and reformulating from a global angle. Yet Fromm's understanding of the great opportunities and profound dangers that modernity holds on this troubled and violence-ridden planet is shaped by a sociological framework.

The forgetting of Fromm's public sociology is not simply a story of injustice as was the history of Du Bois' racist exclusion from the sociological canon. Fromm's relationship to the discipline was more conflicted than was the case for Du Bois, Mills, or even Riesman. Du Bois chose a difficult but admirable role as an activist challenging white supremacy in the twentieth century, partly because he was excluded by racism within our discipline but also because he had a radical vision (McLaughlin and Steinberg, 2016). Du Bois' work is being rediscovered partly because of political organizing and high-quality scholarship (Morris, 2015) but also because his basic theoretical framework, like Mills and Bourdieu in their time, was unambiguously sociological. Fromm, on the other hand, combined a sociological vision with a psychoanalytic perspective that calls into question some of the usefulness and validity of our sociological paradigms.

African American philosopher Cornel West (1991b) identified the core of this issue in a influential 1991 *Dissent* magazine article entitled, 'Nihilism in Black America'. In it, he questioned the false choice between 'conservative behaviourism' and 'liberal structuralism' in thinking about inequality and injustice. Fromm would have agreed with West that poverty and oppression cannot be explained by the behaviour of the marginalized without a serious account of capitalist exploitation, colonial dispossession, and various processes of exclusion that spread across generations. Most sociologists would agree. But West raises difficult questions about the social psychology of the oppressed as Fanon did more than half a century before (Fanon, 1967; West, 1991b). Fromm contributes to this conversation.

There is a deeper question at play developed by the great American critical sociologist Alvin Gouldner (Gouldner, 1980). For Gouldner, all theoretical systems have an emotional and symbolic life of their own and a need to defend the boundaries between what is acceptable discourse within schools of thought, expelling ideas that pose a challenge to the theoretical system itself. Ideas that challenge an intellectual system can never be fully expelled from discussion. The most serious challenges tend to emerge within the theoretical system as an unconscious 'nightmare' that keeps theorists up at night and on guard in the interests of protecting the purity and consistency of their system. The repressed nightmares never go away, however, because the problem is with the theoretical system itself.

Fromm drew from and challenged both Marxist and Freudian orthodoxies. It was Marxism's nightmare that eliminating private property alone is not the route to a better and more just society and the working class is not the universal class (Fromm, 1955a; Gouldner, 1980). The psychoanalytic nightmare is that social structures trump psychological logics so that social change, not therapy, is required for people to heal emotionally damaged lives. Fromm's great contribution as a theorist and public sociologist is that he challenged all these false assumptions. Structures, histories, and inner emotional lives must all be addressed.

The ultimate reason Fromm was ignored in public sociology is that he challenges our orthodoxies on social structure. The sociological imagination is powerful but it will not be enough alone to allow us to understand and change the world. If we don't systematically draw on the insights of other disciplines while also getting outside of the very academic system itself, then the sociological promise that C. Wright Mills wrote so eloquently about will come to naught.

Nihilism, self-destructive behaviour, the potential irrationality that can flow from oppression, and the role that people can play in constructing their own living hells of alcoholism, drug addiction, and violence, for example, can best be theorized with a sociological perspective that also draws on psychoanalytic lens. Fromm, more than any other twentieth-century thinker, conceptualized society in both structural and psychological ways. Fromm engaged in global public sociological debate, analysis and dialogue using this lens. Going beyond both Freudian and sociological orthodoxies cost him in terms of his reputation but improved the quality of his ideas.

In the end, that is what our best critical and public sociologists must be called upon to do. This raises questions that risk putting them on the margins of the field. Revising and developing a new version of psychoanalytic theory that is more feminist, more post-colonial, and less distorted by Fromm's personal lens is an important, even essential, task for public sociologists today. The power of emotions in social life is far too salient to ignore. It cannot be understood through a traditional sociological imagination that represses sociology's nightmares about emotions and human nature in ways our discipline ignores.

We are living in traumatic, frightening, but exciting, almost revolutionary, times. Global Trumpism, climate change, economic insecurities, and the threat of wars raise real questions about the sustainability of human life while rebellions and counter-movements are on the offensive. This is a final reason for re-reading Fromm and integrating him into the history of public sociology.

Contrary to the distortions promoted by his critics, Fromm was not a naïve thinker. He understood fully the dangers of totalitarianism in both its communist and fascist forms. He was not particularly optimistic that human beings would survive the changes wrought by industrialization, the threat of nuclear war, and uncontrolled technology. Optimism and pessimism are false choices in human life, Fromm always argued. We must penetrate deeply underneath the surface of elite ideology and draw on human hope and the humanist spirit to do whatever is necessary to bring about radical change. Fromm's global public sociology is a major resource for the humanist intellectual movement today, a counterweight to the despair and nihilism so many are experiencing. No single intellectual has a better theoretical response to the despair and anger that is feeding reactionary views than Fromm.

The best recent research on human nature in the fields of evolutionary ethnology and psychology rejects race science and simplistic analogies based on lobsters (Peterson, 2018) while arguing that humans have profound social instincts and deep roots in an evolutionary past that transmit hope for the future (Cortina, 2015; Bregman, 2019; Christakis, 2019). Far from being a naïve liberal or a dangerous radical, Fromm was grappling in good faith with universal questions of good versus evil. He sought pathways to right living and political opportunities for a better society despite risks of destruction, war, and death. Fromm did not live to see this new scholarship but it is very likely, as Mauricio Cortina (2015) has suggested, that he would have been delighted with its implications.

Fromm was no naïve leftist. If anything, he overemphasized the destructive dangers of necrophilia and underplayed the possibilities for gaining control of modern technology in order to create a better society, understandable errors given his experiences in Nazi Germany. But like so many young public sociologists today, Fromm held on to hope for a better society. He attempted to do sociological and intellectual work in clear language so that it could find an audience among mass publics outside narrow academic networks.

Fromm would not be shocked or surprised by the irrationality and hatreds that we face in the increasingly authoritarian world in which we live. The rise of Trumpism would not have surprised him. Far too many liberal and left sociologists were caught off guard by events that Fromm's framework helps make understandable. Fromm's framework does not lead to despair or political apathy because he rejects the view that destruction, violence, and inequality are inevitable. Fromm had his limitations as all political actors and theorists do given our common and flawed humanity. Nonetheless, Fromm's commitment to hope, humanism, and political engagement, along with his powerful theoretical ideas and the research tradition he created provides an invaluable set of intellectual resources for a global public sociology for the twenty-first century.

Notes

Introduction

1. We see this among intellectual historians (Friedman, 2013), political theorists and scientists (Wilde, 2004; David-West, 2014), philosophers (Braune, 2014; Kellner, 2016), psychoanalysts and psychologists (Cortina, 2015; Silver, 2017; Funk, 2019; Maccoby, 2020), feminists (Afary and Friedland, 2018), critical theorists (Dirken and Braune, 2020) and most of all, sociologists (Cheliotis, 2011a, 2011b; Durkin, 2014; Anderson, 2015; Langman and Lundskow, 2016; Thorpe, 2016; Chancer, 2017; Grillo, 2018; McLaughlin, 2019).
2. Following the lead of the literature on the sociology of ideas on Richard Rorty (Gross, 2008); W. E. B. Du Bois (Morris, 2015) and George Herbert Mead (Huebner, 2014) and the historical literature on individual sociologists such as C. Wright Mills (Geary, 2009), Jane Addams (Deegan, 1988), Gunnar Mydral (Jackson, 1994), the life and work of Erich Fromm makes for a valuable case study in global public sociology.
3. In the years after Burawoy's statement, we have witnessed a spirited debate by international scholars and national associations on the relationship between local forms of sociology and the juggernaut of American professional sociology (Burawoy, 2005; Connell, 2007; Holmwood, 2007; Baviskar, 2008; Helmes-Hayes and McLaughlin, 2009; Perlatto, 2013; Rafael, 2014; Lazano, 2018).
4. *The Art of Loving* sold five times as many copies and *To Have or To Be* sold more than 8 million copies.

Chapter 1

1. Fromm's account of individuation begins with a discussion of 'primary ties' – the ties that exist before the complete emergence of the self. Fromm, influenced by the 'birth trauma' theories of the Freudian Otto Rank, wrote of the 'comparatively sudden change from fetal into human existence and the cutting off of the umbilical cord that mark the independence of the infant from the mother's body' ([1941] 1969 p 41). Along with the growing strength of individuation comes 'growing aloneness' ([1941] 1969 p 41).
2. Fromm's analysis here, of course, is outdated regarding both empirical studies of the formation of the self in children as well as historical accounts of individualism. For some discussion of recent work in the empirical study of the self within psychoanalysis, see Greenberg and Mitchell (1983). Fromm's notion of the modern self as opposed to the pre-modern self was flawed, like the German sociological

concepts of Gemeinschaft and Gesellschaft that he drew upon and, one could argue, was overly influenced by.

3   Fromm's criticism of the Durkheimian approach has also been made by sociologists influenced by George Herbert Mead. For all the insights of such symbolic interactionist thinkers as Mead and Erving Goffman, however, few contributors to this tradition (with the notable exception of C. Wright Mills and Randall Collins) placed the formation of the self in an adequately historical and comparative context as W. E. B. Du Bois had done a generation before (Du Bois, 1903).

4   Adorno and Horkheimer both underplayed Fromm's contribution to this research tradition, although the history of Fromm's involvement was quite widely known in the 1940s and 1950s. By the late 1960s, however, Fromm had largely been written out of the history of the Frankfurt School (McLaughlin, 1999).

5   Randall Collins gives too much credit to Max Weber for developing an analysis of the 'means of emotional production' (1981 p 41). For Collins, Weber 'made a discovery analogous to those of Durkheim and Freud (and above all, Nietzsche, on whom he drew), when he recognized that people have emotional desires and susceptibilities, and that these are crucial for their social lives' (Collins 1981 p 41). *Escape from Freedom* can be read as an attempt to fill in the psychological gaps in Weber's political sociology.

6   Reich deserves a place in intellectual history for bringing an analysis of sexuality, character, and the body into social theory. Fromm drew on Reich's work extensively, and contemporary theorists have developed Reichian themes (Chancer, 1992). Fromm's work, however, is more useful for sociologists. The issue here is not primarily the paranoid and bizarre writings of Reich's later years. Even Reich's work *The Mass Psychology of Fascism* ([1933]) lacked historical depth and sociological detail relative to *Escape from Freedom*, and Reich overemphasized the role of German sexual repression in explaining the appeal of Nazism. For a useful discussion of both Reich and Fromm's relationship to the circle around Otto Fenichel see Harris and Brock (1991). Fromm reflects at length on Reich in a relatively balanced way in a book published after his death (Fromm, 1992).

7   In 1941, Mead called *Escape from Freedom* 'an important and challenging book' in the *New York Herald Tribune*. Montagu claimed that it was 'one of the most important books published in our time' (1942 p 122), and Macdonald agreed, calling it 'a book of the greatest importance' (1942 p 19). Eleanor Kittredge called *Escape from Freedom* an 'eloquent warning to America' in *The New York Times Book Review* (1942). The reviewer in the *Saturday Review* called it the 'best diagnosis of the psychological aberrations of Nazism' (Mattingly, 1941 p 6). .

8   According to Frank Knight (one of the founders of the Chicago School of Economics), Fromm's analysis of Western cultural history 'shows real penetration and knowledge of history' (1942 p 299).

9   Goodman also took Fromm to task for defending representative instead of direct democracy and for being a 'pale imitation' of Comte (1945 p 198). C. Wright Mills and Patricia J. Salter defended Fromm and Horney against Goodman's 'misunderstanding', arguing that 'Fromm and Horney are part of a general drift in current research and theory which moves towards a historical and a sociological psychology. We agree wholly with that drift and with its positive political relevance' (Mills and Salter, 1945 p 313).

10   In Fromm's treatment of the rise of the Nazi Party, 'the economic and political power of finance capital, the influence of social democratic ideas, leadership and organization, the arming of fascist bands, and the employment of force and terror

under the Weimar 'democracy' – all these recede into the background' (Bartlett, 1942 pp 189).

11. Bartlett left room for a return to the Marxist faith. Fromm had the 'equipment to produce something of great value' and 'some of his errors seem to stem in part from his bias against the Soviet Union.' Fromm's anticommunism, according to Bartlett, did not yet seem to be an 'all-consuming passion', so it was hoped that 'events and his own part in the anti-fascist struggle will change his mind' (Bartlett, 1942 p 190). Bartlett would have been disappointed, of course, for Fromm died in 1980 as an anti-Stalinist democratic radical humanist (Durkin, 2014; Funk, 2019).

12. *Escape from Freedom* (1941) remains Fromm's most cited book with nearly 9,000 citations according to Google Scholar in the spring of 2019.

13. For a somewhat different view see Kuechler (1992). Thomas Childers also modified the conventional wisdom, arguing 'the nucleus of the NSDAP's following was formed by the small farmers, shopkeepers, and independent artisans of the old middle class' (1983 p 264). The most important account of the multi-class nature of Nazism as well as the ways that the class basis of fascism differed according to national context is found in Mann (Mann, 2004).

14. This overly harsh view may have been coloured by Fromm's reaction to the anti-Semitism of Luther's later years, an understandable reaction to the Nazism Fromm was living through. Specialists in this history provide more nuance.

15. Thomas Scheff's *Bloody Revenge: Emotions, Nationalism and War* (1994), makes a similar compelling case that collective shame and humiliated fury were central causes in the rise of the Nazi Party. Germans often referred to the Versailles agreement as the 'treaty of shame', and Hitler called the Weimar Republic 'fourteen years of shame and disgrace' (Scheff, 1994 p 108).

16. Hamilton is more sociologically rigorous in rooting the anger about the Versailles Treaty in the Nazi cadre of demobilized soldiers and officers. In addition, Hamilton stresses the fear of communism among the German middle class as an important source of the appeal of the Nazi Party. Mann's comparative analysis, however, shows that fear of communism was not always central to the rise of fascism (Mann, 2004).

17. The great strength of Anderson's *Imagined Communities* is his detailed knowledge of the history and culture of Cambodia, China, Indonesia, and Vietnam, case studies that allow him to develop convincing reflections on the origins and spread of nationalism. Fromm, in contrast, was not a historian and never wrote the kind of detailed works that have secured Anderson's reputation.

18. David Riesman has pointed out that for all of his theoretical interest in American culture and Protestantism, Fromm did not show any interest in studying either Mormons or Southern Baptists (personal interview, Boston, summer 1992). In addition, Fromm's account of the Middle Ages in *Escape from Freedom* is excessively romantic. And any attempt to revise Fromm's social theory must surely address Indigenous theorizing that calls for a reworking of the very modernist categories that shaped his training and ideas (Watts, Hooks, and McLaughlin, 2020).

Chapter 2

1. There are rich literatures on both the sociology of intellectuals (Coser, 1965; Gouldner, 1979; Kauppi, 1996; Townsley, 2006; Collins, 2009; Jacobs and Townsley, 2011; McLaughlin and Townsley, 2011) and creativity (Joas, 1992; Farrell, 2001; Leschziner and Brett, 2019) as well as an emerging scholarship on public academic

2   As Martin Jay points out, when the institute was founded in 1923, it was 'to have a single director with 'dictatorial' control' (Jay, 1973 p 11). Max Horkheimer took over the directorship from Carl Grünberg in 1930. As Jay points out, 'in subsequent years, the dominance of Max Horkheimer in the affairs of the Institute was unquestioned. Although in large measure attributable to the force of his personality and the range of his intellect, his power was also rooted in the structure of the Institute as it was originally conceived' (Jay, 1973 p 11).

3   A key element of Fromm's argument was that some workers who had voted for left parties had authoritarian characters, a position that Edward Shils and Seymour Martin Lipset would later articulate as a conservative critique of left-wing authoritarianism (Shils, 1954; Lipset, 1959). Fromm, in contrast, was motivated by a left-wing concern with understanding the factors that draw workers to fascism. Unlike Jordan Peterson today, however, Fromm does not make anti-communism an obsession even thought Fromm was a principled critic of Stalinism and Chinese Communism, something Peterson falls to note in his almost paranoid attacks on cultural Marxism, post-modern Marxism, critical theory and sociology.

4   Although Fromm was tenured and deeply involved in the early work of the Frankfurt School, he did not spend that much time around the Institute (partly because of illness, but also because of the time constraints of his psychoanalytic work).

5   This was published as 'Die gesellschaftliche Bedeutung der psychoanalytischen Therapie', *Zeitschrift für Sozialforschung*, 4:3 (1935) 365–97.

6   One need not be in therapy to engage in debates about psychoanalytic theory but it is interesting that Adorno, Marcuse, and Pollock had not been in any kind of psychoanalysis nor did they have formal training, while Löwenthal had been analysed.

7   Ultimately, too impressionistic to meet the standards of professional social science, and often promoting ideas that looked like stereotypes in the context of postwar culture, 'culture and personality' theories became unfashionable and partly took the work of Horney and the neo-Freudians down with them. For a discussion of the 'rise and fall' of 'culture and personality' within anthropology, see *The Making of Psychological Anthropology* (Spindler, 1978).

8   Daniel Burston's *The Legacy of Erich Fromm* is right to highlight the important role played by the network around Sullivan, but his analysis is insufficiently sociological. Burston (1991 p 24) describes the Zodiac Club as an informal discussion group and then suggests that Fromm was not officially a member. The dynamics that Burston is trying to describe could be illuminated by the sociological idea of social circles first developed by Simmel (Znaniecki, 1965; Kadushin, 1974; and Coser, Kadushin, and Powell, 1982).

9   Some have argued that Horney's difficulties establishing relationships with men and Fromm's tendency to get involved with older women to take care of him were at the root of their problems. Paris' book contains an interesting discussion of Horney's published case studies, suggesting that the relationship between Horney and Fromm was described in Horney's own books.

10 One can understand Fromm's attitude towards American psychoanalysts by reading the extensive correspondence between Fromm and Lewis Mumford in the Erich Fromm Archives run by German psychoanalyst, Rainer Funk. Fromm cared more about how radical intellectuals like Mumford reacted to his writings than he worried about the opinions of thinkers in the broad Freudian camp. The

arrogance that many American neo-Freudians complained about was rooted not simply in Fromm's personality, but had much to do with the fact that his major reference group was international radical humanist social critics, not American clinicians. Fromm had the same attitude about American sociologists, who he viewed as parochial and conformist.

Chapter 3

1. In 1944 Fromm published an article entitled 'Individual and Social Origins of Neurosis' in the *American Sociological Review*. He outlined a sociological and historical critique of Freud's theory of the Oedipus Complex, making the case for his concepts of the 'culturally patterned defect' and the 'pathology of normalcy'. Taking his critique of Freudian libido theory and the analysis of neurosis in increasingly sociological directions, Fromm argued that social science should be making moral and ethical judgements about the nature of societies.

2. A couple of years later, in 1946, sociologist Arnold Green published a critique of the ideas of Fromm and Karen Horney in a paper entitled, 'Sociological Analysis of Horney and Fromm', in the *American Journal of Sociology* (*AJS*), the journal that came out of the University of Chicago sociology department, then the dominant intellectual force in the field (Abbott, 1999). The 'cultural orientation' of the Neo-Freudian psychoanalysts was criticized as lacking 'systematization' and was flawed by its allegedly 'easy assumptions regarding the universality of total-cultural influences within a given culture'. What emerged 'is a confused mélange of historical developments, family influences, group activities, conflicts of values—all descriptively unsorted and unweighted' and lacking 'sociological relevance and adequacy' (Green 1946). Since positioning himself within professional sociology was not the direction he was heading, Fromm turned down the opportunity to respond to this critique in the *AJS*. Fromm's personal and professional relationship with Horney was not positive at that time (McLaughlin, 1998a). Further, he did not see mainstream American sociology as a worthy intellectual opponent for his emerging theoretical perspective.

3. Friedrich was a cultivated European scholar and later theorist of totalitarianism and foreign policy.

4. There is no way of knowing, of course, what went on in Riesman's therapy with Fromm. It is certainly a private matter, although Riesman has been quite candid. There is a strange way that Fromm's renegade career and radical political views were perfectly suited to helping Riesman carve out his own unusual career. Riesman himself suggests that he lacked confidence in his intellectual abilities partly due to the demanding standards of his parents, particularly his highly cultured mother. Riesman's insecurities must have been reinforced by the fact that in 1946 he went on to a sociologically complicated career as a social science professor without a PhD at the University of Chicago and then at Harvard. Fromm was a European intellectual who was disdainful of the mainstream sociologists who often rejected Riesman. Fromm was thus positioned to strengthen Riesman's resolve to ignore many sociologists' low opinion of his work. The combination of Riesman's own inclinations and elite background and Fromm's excessively harsh criticisms of mainstream work probably played an important role in creating the David Riesman who creatively wrote from the margins of American mainstream sociology while being based at elite institutions such as Chicago and Harvard. The history of twentieth-century American sociology would have been very different if Riesman

had had a therapist who told him to grow up, keep his job in law, or adjust to mainstream sociology, seeing Riesman's rebellion as resistance to growing up and fitting into the professional world. As a therapist, Fromm tended to take the side of the artist, the intellectual, and the political radical against the mainstream society and the demands of business, professions, and middle-class culture and politics. Whether Fromm's approach was always good for his clients is a question worth exploring in another context (Maccoby 1995). Maccoby felt that Fromm never really confronted his own narcissism or learned to address counter-transference. There is little doubt, in my mind at least, that all of this was extremely good for American sociology.

5   Riesman had done a book jacket blurb for Fromm's *Marx's Concept of Man* (1961) but would not do one for Fromm's *The Anatomy of Human Destructiveness* (1973) even though he reviewed it favourably for *The New Republic* (Riesman, 1973). The correspondence between Fromm and Riesman is extensive and deals with numerous intellectual, personal, professional, and political issues. A very significant proportion of their letters deals with their mutual interest in American foreign policy, world peace, and the nuclear arms race. Riesman and Fromm shared similar values, but Riesman was consistently more sympathetic to the American foreign policy establishment. This makes sense given Charles Kadushin's finding that Riesman was the intellectual with the most credibility among the political elite in the United States in the late 1960s and early 1970s (Kadushin, 1974).

6   Bloom underestimates Riesman's originality, suggesting he simply popularized Fromm's ideas. Fromm, in turn, is said to have simply absorbed these destructive ideas 'from a really serious thinker, Nietzsche's heir, Martin Heidegger' (Bloom, 1987 p 144). Fromm's *Escape from Freedom* was an important book in the development of Riesman's ideas, but for Bloom it is,

> Just Dale Carnegie with a little bit of middle-European cultural whipped cream on top. Get rid of capitalist alienation and Puritan repression, and all will be well as each man chooses for himself. But Woody Allen really has nothing to tell us about inner directedness. Nor does Riesman nor, going further back, does Fromm. One has to get to Heidegger to learn something of all the grim facts of what inner-directedness might really mean. (Bloom, 1987 p 146)

The political philosopher John Schaar takes Fromm more seriously in his book-length critique, *Escape from Authority: The Perspectives of Erich Fromm* (1961), but he also dismisses Riesman and decries a culture that could mistake Riesman's 'masked and pedantic complacencies' for 'serious moral discourse' (Schaar, 1961 p 9). Alan Wolfe takes Riesman very seriously indeed in *Marginalized in the Middle* (1996) while repeating the cliché that Fromm was simplistic.

7   While I am arguing that Fromm's *Man for Himself* provides the most direct template for *The Lonely Crowd*, at a deeper level much of Riesman's work is a dialogue with *Escape from Freedom*. Wilfred McClay's excellent essay on *The Lonely Crowd* makes the case that the book is more centrally concerned with the moral philosophy of freedom in modern America than it is a piece of empirical social science (McClay, 1998). Fromm's *Escape from Freedom* was also really about the freedom in the modern world as much as it was about Nazism, a point Fromm made clear in a private letter he wrote to Robert Lynd (a major sociologist whom Fromm had also psychoanalysed) as the book was being written. Reading both Riesman and

8   Neither Fromn nor Riesman read well in relationship to questions of Indigenous culture and philosophy coming as they did decades before the explosion of original and powerful challenges to Western colonial dismissals of what Vanessa Watts (2013) calls Indigenous 'social being'. Both Fromm and Riesman draw far too sharp a distinction between the 'modern' and 'pre-modern'; their thinking about Indigenous cultures and psychologists must be reformulated and rethought in light of recent scholarship (Tuck and Yang, 2012; Watts 2013; Coulthard, 2014; Simpson, 2014; Denis, 2020; Watt, Hooks, and McLaughlin, 2020). For Riesman, 'tradition-directed' is the past, all lumped into one pre-modern category, while contemporary theorists must surely revisit tradition and pre-colonial forms of culture alongside reframed contemporary attempts to imagine a new synthesis quite different from Riesman's vision of liberal autonomy and subjectivity. Fromm's later interest in Zen Buddhism offered some insights and ways forward in this project, but in the end Fromm's own modernist assumptions must also be reformulated. For an appreciation and reformulation of Fromm's humanism see Durkin (2014).

9   For analysis that suggests Fromm goes too far in stressing a break between humans and other species, especially considering recent advances in the scientific study of evolutionary psychology, animal behaviour, and contemporary developmental psychology, see Cortina (2015).

Chapter 4

1   Two of my first three publications as a graduate student were in *Dissent* magazine and I owe Howe an enormous debt for helping teach me to write clearly and well, to the extent I manage that. I will never forget him telling me to stop trying to impress my sociology professors and make an argument! I once heard Irving speak on Hannah Arendt's theory of totalitarianism at the New School for Social Research and got up the courage to ask him how he thought Fromm's *Escape from Freedom* compared to Arendt's analysis. Howe made it very clear that he did not take Fromm seriously, so I never brought it up again. I take Howe's critique of Fromm's politics very seriously but ultimately it shows some of Howe's limitations as a theoretical thinker, as brilliant and principled as he was.

2   At least until Ansari was derailed by a widely circulated story of his own dating misbehaviours.

3   For a thoughtful and careful archive based analysis of this, see the as yet unpublished work of Brazilian scholar Matheus Romanetto who holds an Erich Fromm research fellowship in German administered by Rainer Funk.

Chapter 5

1   This can as be clearly heard in an audio recording of a speech King delivered in London on 6 December 1964 on his way to receive the Nobel Prize in Oslo. The speech was discovered in the archives of Pacifica Radio and aired on Democracy Now in 2015.

2   Fromm's counterattack on the orthodox Marxist view was also editorial; he rejected an article from Althusser for *The Socialist Humanism*, seeing it as a Stalinist reading of Marx (Anderson, 2015).

3   In truth, it would be more accurate to refer to this conflict as police riots but that is not how it was understood at the time.
4   Russell Jacoby would mock this gesture in *Social Amnesia: Conformist Psychology from Adler to Laing* (1975). I have discussed the influence of Jacoby's critique of Fromm's psychoanalytic ideas elsewhere (McLaughlin, 2018) along with the irony that a scholar who was part of the Frankfurt School was so unfairly critical of Fromm's revision of Freudian theory, obscuring the fact that was just the kind of public intellectual argued for in his important book *The Last Intellectuals* (Jacoby, 1987). But on the political naïvety of Fromm's practical proposals in *The Revolution of Hope*, Jacoby was not wrong.
5   We know from Michael Burawoy's autobiographical essay (2005) that while he was a graduate student, Shils had tried to ruin the career of the creator of public sociology by submitting a noxious letter of recommendation.
6   Fromm and Riesman actually sent Michael Maccoby, Riesman's former student and Fromm's collaborator on the Mexico study to Washington to lobby McGeorge Bundy on the Berlin crisis. Working with Mark Raskin, later a founder of the left-wing think tank the Institute for Policy Studies, Maccoby managed to get support from thirteen elected officials for a document based on the Riesman/Fromm memo read into the Congressional Record.
7   Friedman's claim that Kennedy himself may have phoned Fromm in Mexico during resolution of the Cuban Missile Crisis and before his 1963 American University commencement speech is almost certainly not true, given Michael Maccoby's much closer connections in the White House and memory of receiving calls from Bundy at the time.

Chapter 6

1   I was involved, as a graduate student over twenty-five years ago, encouraging the republication of the book, framed as it was by a new Maccoby introduction where some of the larger issues addressed here were discussed.
2   Fromm never managed to write major works on his techniques for clinical practice despite the fact that he played a major role in teaching in psychoanalytic institutes in the United States and Mexico. Fromm's technique and role in the political life of psychoanalytic institutes in Germany, United States and Mexico is something discussed in an edited book by Rainer Funk (Fromm 2009). Catherine Silver is particularly insightful for thinking about how to adapt Fromm's clinical insights for today (Silver, 2017).
3   Some of the most important works of historical comparative works in the discipline, such as Barrington Moore's *The Social Origins of Dictatorship and Democracy* (1966), Theda Skocpol's *States and Social Revolutions* (1979), and Michael Mann's *Fascists* (2004), are more methodologically sophisticated than Fromm's historical sociology, but they also tend to underestimate the human psychological dynamics that *Anatomy* stresses.
4   It is also relevant to the work of generalist academics such as Russell Jacoby's *Bloodlust: On the Roots of Violence from Cain and Abel to the Present* (2011) and journalist-public intellectuals such as Barbara Ehrenreich's *Blood Rites: Origins and the History of the Passions of Wars* (1998).
5   There are important political issues at stake. While *Anatomy* is clearly rooted in Fromm's Marxist influenced radical humanism, Fromm directly engages perspectives across a range of political views relatively untouched by the narrowing of the

political viewpoints that we see among academics in North America after the 1980s (Burawoy, 2005; Haidt 2012; Gross, 2013). Fromm's growing isolation from North American academic networks from the late 1960s had both positive and negative consequences for the political content and tone of his work. Fromm had always drawn insights from traditional European conservative thinkers, particular the Swiss aristocratic theorist Johann Jakob Bachofen. Engaged with ideas that he found compelling, Fromm was not interested in a thinker's status within elite academic circles as a measure of their scholarship. By the time he was writing *Anatomy*, for example, he had become close to American historian-writer Lewis Mumford (Mumford, 1967) and Ivan Illich, the Croatian-Austrian philosopher, neither of whom were part of the academic establishment. This both helped and damaged the quality of Fromm's later work.

6   The Paleontology section is the shortest and thinnest, likely requiring the most updating with recent research. It is primarily oriented to making the case that human beings are not a species who evolved into a predatory animal. Instead we are carnivorous and created by cultural evolution just as much as biology.

7   Fromm's theory of passions and emotions and perhaps elements of his theory of necrophilia can help explain dynamics of this nature: Adolf Hitler's pathological sex life and relationship with women; his familiar evil smirk; the pleasure he exhibited upon France's surrender; his hatred for Jews; and his willingness to destroy Germany and its people. Too cowardly to kill his victims with own hands, near the end of his life, he demanded to be shown the 'film taken of the torture and execution' of his own generals and the images of the 'corpses in their prison garb hanging from meat hooks' (Fromm, 1973 p 405).

8   There is a moralism in that basic framework that takes away from the many other insights. It is hard not to be critical of some of Fromm's confidence that he can see the real motivations behind small facial gestures and tics, like the example he offers of Churchill lining up dead flies at a dinner table. There are good reasons to be critical of Churchill's retrograde views on race, the Irish and the British working class, but one can also appreciate the role he played in leading the fight against Nazism in Britain and offer a powerful critique of his political views and actions in South Africa and Bengal. This can be done without resorting to an implausible psychoanalytic diagnosis as Fromm does here. At the same time, however, there is insight in the book. Fromm see the destructiveness in both colonial leaders and empires, far-right-wing populist reaction, and communist dictators and he leaves theoretical room for theorizing the opponents of injustice as also being capable of pathological violence.

9   Fromm was actually asked to testify on behalf of the Baader-Meinhof terrorists in Germany in the 1970s by lawyers seeking to leverage Fromm's combined political critique of the Vietnam War and capitalism and psychoanalytic knowledge. He demurred. For Fromm, urban terrorism in Germany or the United States in the 1970s was destructive, not radical (Friedman, 2013). Fromm was too radical for the mainstream political establishment, with his critiques of America, Israel, and capitalism but never at the centre of militant action in the 1960s as Marcuse was.

Conclusion

1   Connell, Wood, and Crawford, 2005; Kalleberg, 2005; Connell, 2007; Baviskar, 2008; Braga, Garcia, and Silva, 2008; Lee and Shen, 2009; Warren, 2009; Kolasa-Nowak, 2015).

2   Some new synthesis is not yet on the horizon in feminist debates that can go far further in theorizing and valourizing woman's sex-based rights, the human and dignity rights of trans and non-binary people and gay and lesbian rights beyond the brutal cultural wars going on today. In that context, Fromm's ideas about gender and sex were too traditional to be helpful except to the extent that he helps us see how a society permeated by market values and celebrity culture and now, constant peer pressure created by online 'likes' and comparisons alongside the collapsing of boundaries between intimacy and economic exchange are damaging to mental health.

3   The American historian Christopher Lasch, in contrast, clung to orthodox Freudian theory (Lasch, 1985) and reactionary views about gender and sexuality (Lasch, 1977) but his analysis of the modern 'culture of narcissism' did a far better job than Fromm was capable of in creating space for sympathetic but critical view of blue-collar, white-collar, and non-college-educated Americans.

References

Abbott, A. (1999) *Department and Discipline: Chicago Sociology at One Hundred*, Chicago: The University of Chicago Press.
Abrams, P. (1968) *The Origins of British Sociology 1834–1914*, Chicago: The University of Chicago Press.
Acker, J. (2005) 'Comments on Burawoy on public sociology', *Critical Sociology*, 31(3): 321–31.
Adler, J. (2014) 'Sociology as an art form: one facet of the conservative sociology of Robert Nisbet', *The American Sociologist*, 45(1): 8–21.
Adorno, T. (1967) 'Sociology and psychology', *New Left Review*, 46 (November/December): 67–80.
Adorno, T. (1968) 'Sociology and psychology II', *New Left Review*, 47 (January/February): 79–97.
Adorno, T. (2002) *Adorno: The Stars Down to Earth and other Essays on the Irrational Culture*, London: Routledge.
Adorno, T. W. (2005) *Minima Moralia: Reflections on a Damaged Life*, London: Verso.
Adorno, T. W. (2013) *The Jargon of Authenticity*, London: Routledge.
Adorno, T. W., Frenkel-Brunswik, E., Levinson, D. J., and Sanford, R. N. (1950) *The Authoritarian Personality*, New York: Harper.
Afary, J. (1996) *The Iranian Constitutional Revolution, 1906–1911: Grassroots Democracy, Social Democracy, & the Origins of Feminism*, New York: Columbia University Press.
Afary, J. and Anderson, K. B. (2010) *Foucault and the Iranian Revolution: Gender and the Seductions of Islamism*, Chicago: The University of Chicago Press.
Afary, J. and Friedland, R. (2018) 'Critical theory, authoritarianism and the politics of lipstick from the Weimar Republic to the contemporary Middle East', *Critical Research on Religion*: 6(3): 243–68.
Ainsworth, M. S. (1979) 'Infant–mother attachment', *American Psychologist*, 34(10): 932–7.
Alford, R. (1998) *The Craft of Inquiry: Methods, Theories and Evidence*, Oxford: Oxford University Press.

Altemeyer, R. A. (1981) *Right-Wing Authoritarianism*, Winnipeg: University of Manitoba Press.

Amis, W. (1974) 'Review of *The Anatomy of Human Destructiveness* by Erich Fromm', *Contemporary Sociology*, 3 (November): 513–15.

Anderson, B. (1983) *Imagined Communities*, New York: Verso.

Anderson, K. (1993) 'On Hegel and the rise of social theory: a critical appreciation of Herbert Marcuse's *Reason and Revolution*, fifty years later', *Sociological Theory*, 11(3): 243–67.

Anderson, K. (2015) 'Fromm, Marx and humanism', in R. Funk and N. McLaughlin (eds) *Towards a Human Science: The Relevance of Erich Fromm for Today*, Gessen: Psychosozial-Verlag, pp 209–18.

Anderson, K. (2016) *Marx at the Margins: On Nationalism, Ethnicity, and Non-Western Societies*, Chicago: The University of Chicago Press.

Ansari, A. (with Klinenberg, E.) (2015) *Modern Romance*, New York: Penguin Books.

Ardrey, R. (1966) *The Territorial Imperative*, New York: Atheneum.

Arendt, H. (1964) *Eichmann in Jerusalem*, New York: Viking Press.

Aronowitz, S. (2012) *Taking It Big: C. Wright Mills and the Making of Political Intellectuals*, New York: Columbia University Press.

Aronson, R. (1995) *After Marxism*, New York: Guilford Press.

Attewell, P. A. (1984) *Radical Political Economy since the 1960s: A Sociology of Knowledge Analysis*, New Brunswick, NJ: Rutgers University Press.

Avineri, S. (1968) *The Social and Political Thought of Karl Marx*, Cambridge: Cambridge University Press.

Baehr, P. (2002) 'Identifying the unprecedented: Hannah Arendt, totalitarianism, and the critique of sociology', *American Sociological Review*, 67(6): 804–31.

Baehr, P. (2014) 'Totalitarianism in America? Robert Nisbet on the "Wilson War State" and beyond', *The American Sociologist*, 45(1): 84–102.

Baehr, P. (2016) *Founders, Classics and Canons*, New Brunswick, NJ: Transaction.

Baehr, P. (2019) *The Unmasking Style in Social Theory*, London: Routlege.

Baert, P. (2015) *The Existentialist Moment: The Rise of Sartre as a Public Intellectual*, Cambridge: Polity.

Bail, C. A. (2014) *Terrified: How Anti-Muslim Fringe Organizations Became Mainstream*, Princeton, NJ: Princeton University Press.

Barsky, R. (2007) *The Chomsky Effect: A Radical Works Beyond the Ivory Tower*, Cambridge, MA: MIT Press.

Bartlett, F. (1942) 'Review of *Escape from Freedom*', *Science and Society*, 6(1): 187–90.

Bauman, Z. (1999) *Liquid Modernity*, London: Polity Press.

Baviskar, A. (2008) 'Pedagogy, public sociology and politics in India: what is to be done?', *Current Sociology*, 56(3): 425–33.
Becker E. (1973) *The Denial of Death*, New York: The Free Press.
Beiner, R. (2018) *Dangerous Minds: Nietzsche, Heidegger, and the Return of the Far Right*, Philadelphia: The University of Pennsyvania Press.
Bell, D. (1977) 'The once and future Marx', *American Journal of Sociology*, 83(1): 187–97.
Bell, D. (1991) *The Winding Passage: Sociological Essays and Journeys*, New Brunswick, NJ: Transaction.
Bellah, R., Madsen, R., Sullivan, W., Swidler, A., and Tipton, S. (1985) *Habits of the Heart: Individualism and Commitment in American Life*, Berkeley: University of California Press.
Bellah, R., Madsen, R., Sullivan, W., Swidler, A., and Tipton, S. (1992) *The Good Society*, New York: Vintage.
Bello, W. 'Inconvenient truths: a public intellectual's pursuit of truth, justice and power', *Current Sociology*, 62(2): 271–8.
Benedict, R. (1942) 'Review of *Escape from Freedom*', *Psychiatry*, 5(1): 111–13.
Benjamin, J. (1977) 'The end of internalization: Adorno's social psychology', *Telos* 32: 42–64.
Benjamin, J. (1988) *The Bonds of Love: Psychoanalysis, Feminism, & the Problem of Domination*, New York: Pantheon.
Benton, T. (1984) *The Rise and Fall of Structural Marxism: Althusser and His Influence*, New York: St. Martin's Press.
Berger, B. (ed) (1990) *Authors of Their Own Lives*, Berkeley: University of California Press.
Berlin, I. (1969) 'Two concepts of liberty', in *Four Essays on Liberty*, Oxford: Clarendon, pp 121–54.
Berman, M. (1982) *All That Is Solid Melts into Air*, New York: Penguin.
Blauner, R. (1964) *Alienation and Freedom: The Factory Worker and His Industry*, Chicago: The University of Chicago Press.
Bloom, A. (1986) *Prodigal Sons: The New York Intellectuals and Their World*, Oxford: Oxford University Press.
Bloom, A. (1987) *The Closing of the American Mind*, New York: Simon & Schuster.
Blyth, M. (2016) 'Global Trumpism: why Trump's victory was 30 years in the making and why it won't stop here', *Foreign Affairs*, November: 1–12.
Bobo, L. D. and Charles, C. Z. (2009) 'Race in the American mind: from the Moynihan report to the Obama candidacy', *The Annals of the American Academy of Political and Social Science*, 621(1): 243–59.

Bonikowski, B. (2017) 'Ethno-nationalist populism and the mobilization of collective resentment', *The British Journal of Sociology*, 68(S1): 181–213.

Bonilla-Silva, E. (2019) 'Feeling race: theorizing the racial economy of emotions', *American Sociological Review*, 84(1): 1–25.

Bonss, W. (1984) 'Introduction', in E. Fromm, *The Working Class in Weimar Germany*, Cambridge, MA: Harvard University Press, pp 1–38.

Bottomore, T. and Nisbet, R. (eds) (1978) *A History of Sociological Analysis*, New York: Basic Books.

Bourdieu, P. (1977) *Outline of a Theory of Practice* (vol. 16), Cambridge: Cambridge University Press.

Bourdieu, P. (1986) 'The forms of capital', in J. Richardson (ed) *Handbook of Theory and Research for the Sociology of Education*, Westport, CT: Greenwood, pp 241–58.

Bourdieu, P. (1988) *Homo Academicus*, Stanford, CA: Stanford University Press.

Bourdieu, P. (1990a) *In Other Words: Essays Towards Reflexive Sociology*, Stanford, CA: Stanford University Press.

Bourdieu, P. (1990b) *The Logic of Practice*, Stanford, CA: Stanford University Press.

Bourdieu, P. (2007) *Sketch for a Self-Analysis*, Cambridge: Cambridge University Press.

Bourdieu, P. (2013a) *Algerian Sketches*, London: Polity.

Bourdieu, P. (2013b) *Distinction: A Social Critique of the Judgement of Taste*, London: Routledge.

Bourdieu, P. and Wacquant, L. J. (1992) *An Invitation to Reflexive Sociology*, Chicago: The University of Chicago Press.

Bowlby, J. (1958) 'The nature of the child's tie to his mother', *International Journal of Psycho-Analysis*, 39: 350–73.

Bowlby, J. (1969) *Attachment* (Vol 1), New York: Basic Books.

Bowlby, J. (1979) 'The Bowlby-Ainsworth attachment theory', *Behavioral and Brain Sciences*, 2(4): 637–38.

Boyer, P. (1985) *By the Bomb's Early Light: American Thought and Culture at the Dawn of the Atomic Age*, New York: Pantheon.

Brady, D. (2004) 'Why public sociologies may fail', *Social Forces*, 82(4): 1629–38.

Braga, R., Garcia, S. G., and Mello e Silva, L. (2008) 'Public sociology and social engagement: considerations on Brazil', *Current Sociology*, 56(3): 415–24.

Braune, J. (2014) *Erich Fromm's Revolutionary Hope: Prophetic Messianism as a Critical Theory of the Future*, Amsterdam: Sense.

REFERENCES

Bregman, R. (2019) *Humankind: A Hopeful History*, New York: Little, Brown and Company.

Brint, S. (1994) *In an Age of Experts*, Princeton, NJ: Princeton University Press.

Brint, S. (1998) *Schools and Societes*, New York: Sage.

Bronner, S. (1994) *Of Critical Theory and Its Theorists*, Oxford: Blackwell.

Brown, M. (2020) *Hope and Scorn: Eggheads, Experts, and Elites in American Politics*, Chicago: The University of Chicago Press.

Brunner, J. (1994) 'Looking into the hearts of the workers, or: How Erich Fromm turned critical theory into empirical research', *Political Psychology*, 15(4): 631–54.

Burawoy, M. (2005) 'For public sociology', the *American Sociological Review*, 70(1): 4–28.

Burston, D. (1991) *The Legacy of Erich Fromm*, Cambridge, MA: Harvard University Press.

Calhoun, C. (2005) 'The promise of public sociology', *British Journal of Sociology*, 56(3): 355–63.

Camic, C. (1992) 'Reputation and predecessor selection: Parsons and the institutionalists', *American Sociological Review*, 57(4): 421–45.

Campbell, B. and Manning, J. (2014) 'Microaggression and moral cultures', *Comparative Sociology*, 13(6): 692–726.

Carnegie, A. (1938) *How to Make Friends and Influence People*, New York: Simon & Schuster.

Carson, R. (1962) *The Silent Spring*, New York: Houghton Mifflin.

Cavalletto, G. and Silver, C. (2014) 'Opening/closing the sociological mind to psychoanalysis', in L. Chancer and J. Andrews (eds) *The Unhappy Divorce of Sociology and Psychoanalysis*, Basingstoke: Palgrave Macmillan, pp 17–52.

Chancer, L. (1992) *Sadomasochism in Everyday Life: The Dynamics of Power and Powerlessness*, New Brunswick, NJ: Rutgers University Press.

Chancer, L. S. (2017) 'Sadomasochism or the art of loving: Fromm and feminist theory', *The Psychoanalytic Review*, 104(4): 469–84.

Cheliotis, L. K. (2011a) 'For a Freudo-Marxist critique of social domination: rediscovering Erich Fromm through the mirror of Pierre Bourdieu', *Journal of Classical Sociology*, 11(4): 438–61.

Cheliotis, L. K. (2011b) 'Violence and narcissism: a Frommian perspective on destructiveness under authoritarianism', *Canadian Journal of Sociology*, 36(4): 337–60.

Childers, T. (1983) *The Nazi Voter*, Chapel Hill, NC: University of North Carolina Press.

Chodorow, N. (1978) *The Reproduction of Mothering: Psychoanalysis and the Sociology of Gender*, Berkeley: The University of California Press.

Chodorow, N. J (1985) 'Beyond drive theory', *Theory and Society*, 14(3): 271–319.

Chodorow, N. J. (1989) *Feminism and Psychoanalytic Theory*, New Haven, CT: Yale University Press.

Chodorow, N. (1999) *The Power of Feelings: Personal Meaning in Psychoanalysis, Gender, and Culture*, New Haven, CT: Yale University Press.

Chomsky, N. (1959) 'A review of BF Skinner's verbal behaviour', *Language*, 35(1): 26–58.

Chomsky, N. (1967) 'The responsibility of intellectuals', *New York Review of Books*, 8(3): 23.

Chomsky, N. (1972) *Problems of Knowledge and Freedom: The Russell Lectures*, New York: Vintage.

Chomsky, N. (1995) *Necessary Illusions: Thought Control in Democratic Societies*, Toronto: House of Anansi.

Chomsky, N and Herman, E. (1979a) *The Washington Connection and Third World Fascism*, Boston: South End Press.

Chomsky, N and Herman, E. (1979b) *After the Cataclyism: Postwar Indochina and the Reconstruction of Imperial Ideology*, Boston: South End Press.

Christakis, N. (2019) *Blueprint: The Evolutionary Origins of a Good Society*, New York: Little, Brown Spark.

Christie, R. and Jahoda, M. (1954) *Studies in the Scope and Method of the Authoritarian Personality*, Glencoe, IL: Free Press.

Clawson, D., Zussman, M. J., Gerstel, N., and Stokes, R. (eds) (2007) *Public Sociology: Fifteen Eminent Sociologists Debate Politics and the Profession in the Twenty-First Century*, Berkeley: University of California Press.

Collini, S. (2006) *Absent Minds: Intellectuals in Britain*, Oxford: Oxford University Press.

Collins, R. (1981) *Sociology since Midcentury*, New York: Academic Press.

Collins, R. (1992) 'The rise and fall of modernism in politics and religion', *Acta Sociologica*, 35(3): 171–86.

Collins, R. (1995) 'Prediction in macrosociology: the case of the Soviet collapse', *American Journal of Sociology*, 100(6): 1552–93.

Collins, R. (1998) *The Sociology of Philosophies*, Cambridge, MA: Harvard University Press.

Collins, R. (2009) *Violence: A Micro-Sociological Theory*, Princeton, NJ: Princeton University Press.

Collins, R. (2014) *Interaction Ritual Chains*, Princeton, NJ: Princeton University Press.

Connell, R. W. (2002) *Gender*, Cambridge: Polity.

Connell, R. W. (2007) *Southern Theory*, London: Polity.

Connell, R. W., Wood, J., and Crawford, J. (2005) 'The global connections of intellectual workers: an Australian study', *International Sociology*, 20(1): 5–26.

Cortina, M. (2015) 'The greatness and limitations of Erich Fromm's humanism', *Contemporary Psychoanalysis*, 51(3): 388–422.

Coser, L. (1965) *Men of Ideas: A Sociologist's View*, New York: Free Press.

Coser, L. (1984) *Refugee Scholars in America: Their Impact and Their Experiences*, New Haven, CT: Yale University Press.

Coser, L. and Howe, I. (1957) *The American Communist Party*, Boston, MA: Beacon Press.

Coser, L., Kadushin, C., and Powell, W. (1982) *Books: The Culture and Commerce of Publishing*, New York: Basic Books.

Costa, P (dir). (2019) *The Edge of Democracy*, documentary.

Coulthard, G. (2014) *Red Skin, White Masks: Rejecting the Colonial Politics of Recognition*, Minneapolis, MN: University of Minnesota Press.

Crane, D. (1972) *The Invisible Colleges: Diffusion of Knowledge in Scientific Communities*, Chicago: The University of Chicago Press.

Crenshaw, K. (1989) 'Demarginalizing the intersections of race and sex', *University of Chicago Legal Forum*, 1989(8): 139–67.

David-West, A. (2014) 'Erich Fromm and North Korea: social psychology and the political regime', *Critical Sociology*, 40: 575–600.

Davies, S. (1995) 'Leaps of faith: shifting currents in critical sociology of education', *American Journal of Sociology*, 100: 1448–78.

DeBenedetti, C. (1990) *An American Ordeal: The Antiwar Movement of the Vietnam Era,* Syracuse, NY: Syracuse University Press.

Deegan, M. J. (1988) *Jane Addams and the Men of the Chicago School, 1982–1918*, New Brunswick, NJ: Transaction.

Denis, J. (2020) *Canada at a Crossroads: Boundaries, Bridges, and Laissez-Faire Racism in Indigenous-Settler Relations*, Toronto: The University of Toronto Press.

Deshazor, B. (2015) 'The lost Dr. Martin Luther King speech: how the Pacifica Radio Archives unearthed a piece of history', *Democracy Now*, 19 January, Available from: https://www.democracynow.org/2015/1/19/the_lost_dr_martin_luther_king [Accessed 21 June 2020].

De Tocqueville, A. (1969) *Democracy in America*, New York: Harper and Row.

Dinnerstein, D. (1976) *The Mermaid and the Minotaur: Sexual Arrangements and Human Malaise*, New York: Harper and Row.

Dobrenkov, V. I. (1976) *Neo-Freudians in Search of Truth*, Moscow: Progress Publishers.

Du Bois, W. E. B. (1903) *The Souls of Black Folk*. Chicago: A.C. McClung and Co.

Du Bois, W. E. B. (1953) 'On Stalin', *National Guardian*, March 16.

Duneier, M. (2002) 'What kind of combat sport is sociology?', *American Journal of Sociology*, 107(6): 1551–76.

Durkheim, E. (1897) *Suicide*, New York: The Free Press.

Durkin, K. (2014) *The Radical Humanism of Erich Fromm*, New York: Palgrave.

Durkin, K. (2019) 'Erich Fromm and Theodor W. Adorno reconsidered: a case study in intellectual history', *New German Critique*, 48(1/136): 103–26.

Durkin K. and Braune, J. (2020) *Erich Fromm's Critical Theory: Hope, Humanism and the Future*, London: Bloomsbury Academic.

Epstein, C. F. (1987) *Deceptive Distinctions*, New Haven, CT: Yale University Press.

Ericson, R. (2005) 'Publicizing sociology', *The British Journal of Sociology*, 56(3): 365–72.

Erikson, E. (1950) *Childhood and Society*, New York: Norton.

Erikson, E. (1958) *Young Man Luther*, New York: Norton.

Erikson, E. (1964) *Insight and Responsibility*, New York: Norton.

Erikson, E. (1968) *Identity: Youth and Crisis*, New York: Norton.

Erikson, E. (1969) *Gandhi Truth*, New York: Norton.

Erikson, E. (1975) *Life History and the Historical Moment*, New York: Norton.

Ehrenreich, B. (2009) *Bright-Sided: How the Relentless Promotion of Positive Thinking has Undermined America*. New York: Henry, Holt and Company.

Ehrenreich, B. (2011) *Blood Rites*, New York: Granta.

Etzioni, A. (2005) 'Bookmarks for public sociologists', *The British Journal of Sociology*, 56(3): 373–8.

Eyal, G. and Buchholz, L. (2010) 'From the sociology of intellectuals to the sociology of interventions', *Annual Review of Sociology*, 36: 117–37.

Ezra, M. (2007) 'The Eichmann polemics: Hannah Arendt and her critics', *Democratiya*, 9(3): 141–69.

Fanon, F. (1967) *Black Skin, White Masks: The Experiences of a Black Man in the White World*, New York: Grove Press.

Farrell, M. (2001) *Collaborative Circles: Friendship Dynamics and Creative Work*, Chicago: The University of Chicago Press.

Fenichel, O. (1944) 'Psychoanalytic remarks on Fromm's book *Escape from Freedom*', *Psychoanalytic Review*, 31(2): 133–52.

Fetner, T. (2019) 'The religious right in the United States and Canada: evangelical communities, critical junctures, and institutional infrastructures', *Mobilization: An International Quarterly*, 24(1): 95–113.

Fine, G. A., (2001) *Difficult Reputations: Collective Memories of the Evil, Inept, and Controversial*. Chicago: The University of Chicago Press.

Fleck, C and Hess, A. (2011) 'Sociology and communism: Coming to terms with a discipline's past', *Comparative Sociology*, 10: 670–90.

Fleck, C. and Muller, A. (1998) 'Bruno Bettelheim and the concentration camps', *Journal of the History of the Behavioral Sciences*, 33(1): 1–37.

Foster, G. (1967) *Tzinzunzan: Mexican Peasants in a Changing World*, New York: Little Brown.

Foster, G. (1971) 'Review of *Social Character in a Mexican Village*', *American Journal of Sociology*, 77(2): 336–8.

Frank, A. G. (1967) *Capitalism and Underdevelopment in Latin America* (vol. 93), New York: New York University Press.

Frickel, S. and Gross, N. (2005) 'A general theory of scientific/intellectual movements', *American Sociological Review*, 70(2): 204–32.

Frie, R. (2003) 'Erich Fromm and contemporary psychoanalysis: from modernism to postmodernism', *The Psychoanalytic Review*, 90(6): 855–68.

Friedan, B. (1963) *The Feminine Mystique*, New York: Norton.

Friedenberg, E. (1962) 'Neo-Freudianism and Erich Fromm', *Commentary*, 34: 305–13.

Friedman, L. J. (1990) *Menninger: The Family and the Clinic*, Lawrence, KS: University of Kansas Press.

Friedman, L. (1999) *Identity's Architect: A Biography of Erik H. Erikson*, New York: Scribner.

Friedman, L. J. with Schreiber, A. M. (2013) *The Lives of Erich Fromm – Love's Prophet*, New York: Columbia University Press.

Freire, P. (1970) *Pedagogy of the Oppressed*, New York: Continuum.

Fromm, E. [1941] (1969) *Escape from Freedom*, New York: Holt, Rinehart, & Winston.

Fromm, E. (1944) 'Individual and social origins of neurosis', *American Sociological Review*, 9(4): 380–4.

Fromm, E. (1947) *Man for Himself, an Inquiry into the Psychology of Ethics*, New York: Rinehart.

Fromm, E. (1950) *Psychoanalysis and Religion*, New Haven, CT: Yale University Press.

Fromm, E. (1951) *The Forgotten Language*, New York: Rinehart.

Fromm, E. (1955a) *The Sane Society*, New York: Holt, Rinehart, & Winston.

Fromm, E. (1955b) 'The human implications of "instinctivistic" radicalism: a reply to Herbert Marcuse', *Dissent*, 2(4): 342–9.

Fromm, E. (1956a) *The Art of Loving*, New York: Harper & Row.

Fromm, E. (1956b) 'A counter-rebuttal', *Dissent*, 3(1): 81–3.

Fromm, E. (1958) 'Psychoanalysis: scientism or fanaticism?', *The Saturday Review*, 14 June: 11–13.

Fromm, E. (1959) *Sigmund Freud's Mission: An Analysis of His Personality and Influence*, New York: Harper and Brothers.

Fromm, E. [1960a] *Psychoanalysis and Zen Buddhism*, New York: Open Road Media.

Fromm, E. (1960b) 'The case for unilateral disarmament', *Daedalus*, 89(4): 1015–28.

Fromm, E. (1961a) *Marx's Concept of Man*, New York: Ungar.

Fromm, E. (1961b) *May Man Prevail?: An Inquiry into the Facts and Fictions of Foreign Policy*, New York: Doubleday.

Fromm, E. (1962) *Beyond the Chains of Illusion. My Encounter with Marx and Freud*, New York: Simon & Schuster.

Fromm, E. (1964) *The Heart of Man*, New York: Harper & Row.

Fromm, E. (1966a) *You Shall be as Gods: A Radical Interpretation of the Old Testament and its Tradition*, New York: Holt, Rinehart and Winston.

Fromm, E. (1966b) 'The psychological aspect of the Guaranteed Income', in R. Theobald (ed) *The Guaranteed Income*, New York: Doubleday, pp 5–10.

Fromm, E. (1968) *The Revolution of Hope: Toward a Humanized Technology*, New York: Harper Collins.

Fromm, E. (1970) *The Crisis of Psychoanalysis*, New York: Holt, Rinehart, & Winston.

Fromm, E. (1973) *The Anatomy of Human Destructiveness*, New York: Holt, Rinehart, & Winston.

Fromm, E. (1976) *To Have or to Be?*, New York: Harper & Row.

Fromm, E. (1984) *The Working Class in Weimar Germany: A Psychological and Sociological Study*, Cambridge, MA: Harvard University Press and Berg Press.

Fromm, E. (1989) *The Art of Being*, London: Open Road Media.

Fromm, E. (1992 [1963]) *The Dogma of Christ and Other Essays on Religion, Psychology and Culture*, New York: Henry Holt.

Fromm, E. (1997) *Love, Sexuality and Matriarchy*, Berlin: Fromm International.

Fromm, E. and Maccoby, M. (1970) *Social Character in a Mexican Village: A Socio-Psychoanalytic Study*, Englewood Cliffs, NJ: Prentice Hall.

Fromm, E and Riesman, D. (2015) 'The Berlin crisis', in K. Kerr, B. Harden, and M. Aldredge (eds) *David Riesman's Unpublished Writings and Continuing Legacy*, Farnham: Ashgate, pp 57–65.

Fuller, S. (2000) 'A very qualified success, indeed: the case of Anthony Giddens and British sociology', *The Canadian Journal of Sociology*, 25(4): 507–16.

Funk, R. (1982) *Erich Fromm: The Courage to Be Human*, New York: Continuum.

Funk, R. (ed) (2009) *The Clinical Erich Fromm: Personal Accounts and Papers on Therapeutic Technique* (vol. 9), Amsterdam: Rodopi.

Funk, R. (2019): *Life Itself Is an Art: The Life and Work of Erich Fromm*, New York: Continuum.

Funk, R. and McLaughlin, N. (eds) (2015) *Towards a Human Science: The Relevance of Erich Fromm for Today*, Gessen: Psychosozial-Verlag.

Galbo, J. (2004) 'From *The Lonely Crowd* to *The Cultural Contradictions of Capitalism* and beyond: the shifting ground of liberal narratives', *Journal of the History of the Behavorial Sciences*, 40(1): 47–76.

Gans, H. (1988) *Middle American Individualism*, New York: Free Press.

Gans, H. (1997) 'Best-sellers by sociologists: an exploratory study', *Contemporary Sociology*, 26(2): 131–5.

Gardner, H. and Davis, K. (2013) *The App Generation: How Today's Youth Navigate Identity, and Imagination in a Digital World*, New Haven, CT: Yale University Press.

Geary, D. (2009) *Radical Ambition: C. Wright Mills, the Left, and the American Social Thought*, Berkeley: University of California Press.

Geary, D. (2015) *Beyond Civil Rights: The Moynihan Report and Its Legacy*, Philadelphia, PA: University of Pennsylvania Press.

Gerhardt, U. (1993) *Talcott Parsons on National Socialism*, New York: Aldine de Gruyter.

Gerth, H. and Mills, C. W. (1953) *Character and Social Structure: The Psychology of Social Institutions*, New York: Harcourt, Brace and World.

Gessen, M. (2017) *The Future is History: How Totalitarianism Reclaimed Russia*, New York: Granta Books.

Ghamari-Tabrizi, B. (2005) 'Can Burawoy make everybody happy', *Critical Sociology*, 31(3): 361–9.

Giddens, A. (1990) *The Consequences of Modernity*, Stanford, CA: Stanford University Press.

Giddens, A. (1992) *The Transformation of Intimacy*, London: Polity.

Gitlin, T. [1987] (1993) *The Sixties: Years of Hope, Days of Rage*, New York Bantam.

Glazer, N. (1990) 'From socialism to sociology', in B. Berger (ed) *Authors of Their Own Lives*, Berkeley: University of California Press, pp 190–209.

Glenn, E. N. (2011) 'Constructing citizenship: exclusion, subordination, and resistance', *American Sociological Review*, 76(1): 1–24.

Go, J. (2013) 'Decolonizing Bourdieu: colonial and postcolonial theory in Pierre Bourdieu's early work', *Sociological Theory*, 31(1): 49–74.

Goffman, E. (1961) *Asylums: Essays on the Social Situation of Mental Patients and Other Inmates*, New York: Doubleday.

Goldberg, M. (2017) 'Fifty shades of orange', *The New York Times*, 22 December.

Goldfarb, J. C. (1998) *Civility and Subversion: The Intellectual in Democratic Society*, Cambridge: Cambridge University Press.

Goodman, P. (1945) 'The political meaning of some recent revisions of Freud', *Politics*, 2 (July): 197–203.

Gorski, P. (2017) 'Why evangelicals voted for Trump: a critical cultural sociology', *American Journal of Cultural Sociology*, 5(3): 338–54.

Gouldner, A. W. (1977) 'Stalinism: a study of internal colonialism', *Telos*, 34 (Winter): 5–48.

Gouldner, A. (1979) *The Future of Intellectuals and the Rise of the New Class*. London: Palgrave.

Gouldner, A. W. (1980) *The Two Marxisms: Contradiction and Anomalies in the Development of Theory*, London: Macmillan Education.

Grant, G. and Riesman, D. (1978) *The Perpetual Dream: Reform and Experiment in the American College*, Chicago: The University of Chicago Press.

Green, A. I. (2008a) 'Erotic habitus: toward a sociology of desire', *Theory and Society*, 37(6): 597–626.

Green, A. I. (2008b) 'The social organization of desire: the sexual fields approach', *Sociological Theory*, 26(1): 25–50.

Green, A. W. (1946) 'Sociological analysis of Horney and Fromm', *American Journal of Sociology*, 51(6): 533–54.

Greenberg, J. and Mitchell, S. (1983) *Object Relations in Psychanalytic Theory*. Cambridge, MA: Harvard University Press.

Greenfeld, L. (1992) *Nationalism: Five Roads to Modernity*, Cambridge, MA: Harvard University Press.

Greenfeld, L. (2009) *The Spirit of Capitalism*, Cambridge, MA: Harvard University Press.

Greenfeld, L. (2013) *Mind, Modernity, Madness*, Cambridge, MA: Harvard University Press.

Grillo, C. M. (2018) 'Revisiting Fromm and Bourdieu: contributions to habitus and realism', *Journal of Theory for Social Behaviour*, 48(4): 416–32.

Gross, N. (2008) *Richard Rorty: The Making of an American Philosopher*, Chicago: The University of Chicago Press.

Gross. N. (2013) *Why Are Professors Liberal and Why Do Conservatives Care?* Cambridge, MA: Harvard University Press.

Gross, N. and Fosse, E. (2012) 'Why are professors liberal', *Theory and Society*, 41(2): 127–68.

Habermas, J. (1971) *Knowledge and Human Interests*, Boston, MA: Beacon Press.

Haidt, J. (2012) *The Righteous Mind: Why Good People Are Divided by Politics and Religion*, New York: Vintage.

Hale, N. (1995) *The Rise and Crisis of Psychoanalysis in the United States*, New York: Oxford University Press.

Hallett, T., Stapleton, O., and Sauder, M. (2019) 'Public ideas: their varieties and careers', *American Sociological Review*, 84(3): 545–76.

Hamilton, R. F. (1982) *Who Voted for Hitler?* Princeton, NJ: Princeton University Press.

Hamilton, R. F. (1986) 'Review of Erich Fromm *The Working Class in Weimar Germany*', *Society*, March/April: 82–3.

Hamilton, R. F. (1996) *The Social Misconstruction of Reality: Validity and Verification in the Scholarly Community*, New Haven, CT: Yale University Press.

Hamilton, R. F. and Wright, J. D. (1986) *The State of the Masses*, New York: Aldine.

Hanafi, S. (2014) 'Complex entanglements: moving from policy to public sociology in the Arab world', *Current Sociology*, 62(2): 197–208.

Hanemaayer, A. and Schneider, C. (eds) (2014) *The Public Sociology Debate: Ethics and Engagement*, Vancouver: University of British Columbia Press.

Haney, D. (2008) *The Americanization of Social science: Intellectuals and Public Responsibility in the Postwar United States*, Philadelphia, PA: Temple University Press.

Harrington, M. (1962) *The Other America*, New York: Macmillan.

Harrington, M. (1976) *The Twilight of Capitalism*, New York: Simon & Schuster.

Harrington, M. (1989) *Socialism: Past and Future*, New York: Skyhorse Publishing.

Harris, B. and Brock, A. (1991) 'Otto Fenichel and the left opposition in psychoanalysis', *Journal of the History of the Behavioral Sciences*, 27(2): 157–65.

Hartman, F. H. (1962) 'Review to *May Man Prevail?*', *The Journal of Politics*, 24(3): 594–5.

Hausdorf, D. (1972) *Erich Fromm*, New York: Twayne.

Hedges, C. (2018) *American, The Farewell Tour*, Toronto: Alfred Knopf.

Heller, A. (2018) *The Theory of Need in Marx*, London: Verso.

Helmes-Hayes, R. and McLaughlin, N. (2009) 'Public sociology in Canada: debates, research and historical context', *Canadian Journal of Sociology*, 34(3): 573–600.

Herman, E. (1995) *The Romance of an American Psychology*, Berkeley: University of California Press.

Herman, E. S. and Chomsky, N. (2010) *Manufacturing Consent: The Political Economy of the Mass Media*, New York: Random House.

Hess, A. (2014) *The Political Theory of Judith N. Shklar: Exile from Exile*, New York: Palgrave Macmillan.

Hetherington, M. J. and Weiler, J. D. (2009) *Authoritarianism and Polarization in American Politics*, Cambridge: Cambridge University Press.

Hill, L. B. (1942) 'Review of *Escape from Freedom*', *Psychiatry*, 5(1): 117–18.

Hochschild, A. R. (1979) 'Emotion work, feeling rules, and social structure', *American Journal of Sociology*, 85(3): 551–75.

Hochschild, A. (1982) *The Managed Heart: The Commercialization of Feeling* Berkeley: University of California Press.

Hochschild, A. (2016) *Strangers in Their Own Land: Anger and Mourning on the American Right*, New York: The New Press.

Holmwood, J. (2007) 'Sociology as public discourse and professional practice: a critique of Michael Burawoy', *Sociological Theory*, 25(1): 46–66.

Homans, G. C. (1964) 'Bringing men back in', *American Sociological Review*, 29(5): 809–18.

hooks, b. (2002) *Communion: The Female Search for Love*, New York: William Morrow.

Horkheimer, M. (1936) 'Studien über Autorität und Familie', *Schriften des Instituts für Sozialforschung*, 5: 947.

Horkheimer, M. (1974) *Eclipse of Reason*, New York: Continuum.

Horkheimer, M. and Adorno, T. W. (1944) *Dialectic of Enlightenment*, New York: Seabury Press.

Horney, K. (1937) *The Neurotic Personality of Our Time*, New York: Norton.

Horney, K. (1946) *Our Inner Conflicts*, New York: Norton.

Horney, K. (1950) *Neurosis and Human Growth*, New York: Norton.

Hornstein, G. (2000) *To Redeem One Person Is to Redeem the World: The Life of Frieda Fromm-Reichmann*, New York: The Free Press.

Horowitz, D. (1994) *Vance Packard and American Social Criticism*, Chapel Hill, NC: University of North Carolina Press.

Horowitz, D. (2019). *Dark Agenda: The War to Destroy Christian America*, New York: Humanix Books.

Horowitz, I. L. (1983) *C. Wright Mills: An American Utopian*, New York: The Free Press.

Howe, I. (1954) 'This age of conformity', *Partisan Review*, 21(1): 1–33.

Howe, I. (1976) *World of our Fathers: The Journey of the East European Jews to America and the Life they Found and Made*, New York: Open Road Media.

Howe, I. (1984) *A Margin of Hope: An Intellectual Autobiography*, New York: Harcourt.

Huebner, D. (2014) *Becoming Mead: The Social Process of Academic Knowledge*, Chicago: The University of Chicago Press.

Huxley, A. L. (1932) *Brave New World*, London: Chatto and Windus.

Illich, I. (1971) *Deschooling Society*, New York: Harpers and Row.

Illouz, E. (1997) *Consuming the Romantic Utopia*, Berkeley: University of California Press.

Inglehart, R. (1977) *The Silent Revolution: Changing Values and Political Styles among Western Publics*, Princeton, NJ: Princeton University Press.

Inglis, F. (2010) *A Short History of Celebrity*, Princeton, NJ: Princeton University Press.

Inkeles, A. (1963) 'Sociology and psychology', in Sigmund Koch (ed) *Psychology: A Study of a Science* (vol. 6), New York: McGraw-Hill, pp 317–87.

Israel, J. (1979) *Alienation: From Marx to Modern Sociology*, Atlantic Highlands, NJ: Humanities Press.

Isserman, M. (2000) *The Other American: The Life of Michael Harrington*, New York: Public Affairs.

Jackson, W. A. (1994) *Gunnar Myrdal and America's Conscience: Social Engineering and Racial Liberalism, 1938–1987*, Chapel Hill, NC: University of North Carolina Press.

Jacobs, J. (2001) *In Defence of Disciplines: Interdisciplinarity and Specialization in the Research University*, Chicago: The University of Chicago Press.

Jacobs, J. (2014). *The Frankfurt School, Jewish Lives, and Antisemitism*, Cambridge: Cambridge University Press.

Jacobs, R. N. and Townsley, E. (2011) *The Space of Opinion: Media Intellectuals and the Public Sphere*, New York: Oxford University Press.

Jacobsen, K. (2009) *Freud's Foes: Psychoanalysis, Science, and Resistance*, Lanham, MD: Rowman & Littlefield.

Jacoby, R. (1975) *Social Amnesia: A Critique of Conformist Psychology from Adler to Laing*, Boston, MA: Beacon.

Jacoby, R. (1986) *The Repression of Psychoanalysis: Otto Fenichel and the Freudians*, Chicago: The University of Chicago Press.

Jacoby, R. (1987) *The Last Intellectuals*, New York: Basic Books.

Jacoby, R. (2011) *Bloodlust*, New York: Simon & Schuster.

Jahoda, M., Lazarsfeld, P. F., and Zeisel, H. (1933) *Marienthal: The Sociography of an Unemployed Community*, London: Taylor and Francis.

Jamison, A. and Eyerman, R. (1994) *Seeds of the Sixties*, Berkeley: University of California Press.

Jasper, J. (1997) *The Art of Moral Protest*, Chicago: The University of Chicago Press.

Jay, M. (1973) *The Dialectical Imagination: A History of the Frankfurt School and the Institute of Social Research*, Boston, MA: Little, Brown.

Jeffries, S. (2016) *Grand Hotel Abyss: The Lives of the Frankfurt School*, London: Verso.

Jencks, C. and Riesman, D. (1968) *The Academic Revolution*, New York: Doubleday.

Jennes, K. (2017) 'The unassailable self: Freud's image among postwar American intellectuals', *Psychoanalysis and History*, 19(1): 55–75.

Joas, H. (1992) *The Creativity of Action*. Chicago: The University of Chicago Press.

Jumonville, N. (1991) *Critical Crossings: The New York Intellectuals in Postwar America*, Berkeley: University of California Press.

Kadushin, C. (1974) *The American Intellectual Elite*, Boston, MA: Little, Brown and Company.

Kahn, H. (1960) *On Thermonuclear War*, Princeton, NJ: Princeton University Press.

Kalleberg, R. (2005) 'What is "public sociology"? Why and how should it be made stronger?', *The British Journal of Sociology*, 56(3): 387–93.

Kardiner, A. (1961) *They Studied Men*, Cleveland, OH: World Publishing Company.

Kater, M. (1983) *The Nazi Party: A Social Profile of Members and Leaders, 1919–1945*, Cambridge, MA: Harvard University Press.

Kauppi, N. (1996) *French Intellectual Nobility: Institutional and Symbolic Transformations in the Post-Sartrian Era*, Albany, NY: State University of New York.

Kellner, D. (1984) *Herbert Marcuse and the Crisis of Marxism*, Berkeley: University of California Press.

Kellner, D. (1989) *Critical Theory, Marxism and Modernity*, Baltimore, MD: Johns Hopkins University Press.

Kellner, D. (2016) 'Donald Trump as authoritarian populist: a Frommian analysis', *Logos*, 15, pp 2–3, Available from: http://logosjournal.com/2016/kellner-2/ [Accessed 19 January 2021].

Kerr, K., Harden, B. K., and Aldredge, M. (2015) *David Riesman's Unpublished Writings and Continued Legacy*, London: Ashgate.

Khasnabish, D. A. (2008) *Zapatismo beyond Borders: New Imaginations of Political Possibility*, Toronto: University of Toronto Press.

Khasnabish, D. A. (2013) *Zapatistas: Rebellion from the Grassroots to the Global*, London: Zed Books.

Kittredge, E. (1942) 'Review of *Escape from Freedom*', *New York Times Book Review*, 4 January: 12.

Klopfer, P. (1994) 'Konrad Lorenz and the national sociologists: on the politics of ethology', *International Journal of Comparative Psychology*, 7(4): 202–8.

Klopfer, W. G. (1949). *Suggestions for the Systematic Analysis of Rorschach Records*. Berkeley: University of California.

Knapp, G. (1989) *The Art of Living: Erich Fromm's Life and Works*, New York: Peter Lang.

Knight, F. (1942) 'Review of *Escape from Freedom*', *American Journal of Sociology*, 48(2): 299.

Kohn, M. L. (1989) 'Social structure and personality: a quintessentially sociological approach to social psychology', *Social Forces*, 68(1): 26–33.

Kohn, M. L. (2015) *Change and Stability: A Cross-National Analysis of Social Structure and Personality*, London: Routledge.

Kohn, M. L. and Schooler, C. (1969) 'Class, occupation, and orientation', *American Sociological Review*, 34(5): 659–78.

Kohn, M. L., Slomczynski, K. M., Janicka, K., Khmelko, V., Mach, B. W., Paniotto, V., Zaborowski, W., Gutierrez, R., and Heyman, C. (1997) 'Social structure and personality under conditions of radical social change: a comparative analysis of Poland and Ukraine', *American Sociological Review*, 62(4): 614–38.

Kolasa-Nowak, A. (2015) 'Critical sociology in Poland and its public function', *Polish Sociological Review*, 3(191): 381–99.

Koonz, C. (1987) *Mothers in the Fatherland: Women, the Family and Nazi Politics*, New York: St. Martin's Press.

Kornhauser, W. (1959) *Politics of Mass Society*, New York: The Free Press.

Kuechler, M. (1992) 'The NSDAP vote in the Weimar Republic: an assessment of the state-of-the-art in view of modern electoral research', *Historical Social Research*, 61(17): 22–52.

Kurzweil, E. (1989) *The Freudians: A Comparative Perspective*, New Haven, CT: Yale University Press.

Kurzweil, E. (1995) *Freudians and Feminists*, Boulder, CO: Westview.

Lamont, M. and Fournier, M. (eds) (1992) *Cultivating Differences: Symbolic Boundaries and the Making of Inequality*, Chicago: The University of Chicago Press.

Lamont, M., Silva, G. M., Welburn, J., Guetzkow, J., Mizrachi, N., Herzog, H., and Reis, E. (2016) *Getting Respect: Responding to Stigma and Discrimination in the United States, Brazil, and Israel*, Princeton, NJ: Princeton University Press.

Lang, G. E. and Lang, K. (1988) 'Recognition and renown: the survival of artistic reputation', *American Journal of Sociology*, 94(1): 79–109.

Langman, L. and Lundskow, G. (2016) *God, Guns, Gold and Glory: American Character and Its Discontents*, London: Brill.

Lannigan, J. and McLaughlin, N. (2017) 'Professors and politics: Noam Chomsky's contested reputation in the United States and Canada', *Theory and Society*, 46(3): 177–99.

Lasch, C. (1977) *Haven in a Heartless World: The Family Besieged*, New York: W. W. Norton & Company.

Lasch, C. (1979) *The Culture of Narcissism: American Life in an Age of Diminishing Expectations*, New York: W. W. Norton & Company.

Lasch, C. (1985) *The Minimal Self: Psychic Survival in Troubled Times*, New York: W. W. Norton & Company.

Lasch, C. (1991) *The True and Only Heaven: Progress and Its Critics*, New York: W. W. Norton & Company.

Lasch, C. (1995) *The Revolt of the Elites and the Betrayal of Democracy*, New York: W. W. Norton & Company.

Lee, C. K. and Shen Y. (2009) 'China: the paradox and possibility of a public sociology of labor', *Work and Occupations*, 36(2): 110–25.

Lemert, C. (1995) *Sociology after the Crisis*, New York: Westview.

Lenkerd, B. (1994) 'Theoretical approach: Erich Fromm's theory of social character as adapted by Michael Maccoby', in 'Meanings and motivations at work', unpublished PhD thesis, Department of Anthropology, Catholic University of America, Washington, DC.

Leschziner, V. and Brett, G. (2019) 'Beyond two minds: cognitive, embodied, and evaluative processes in creativity', *Social Psychology Quarterly*, December, 1–27.

Levine-Rasky, C. (2016) *Writing the Roma: Histories, Policies, and Communities in Canada*, Halifax: Fernwood Publishing.

Lifton, R. J. (1961) *Thought Reform and the Psychology of Totalism: A Study of 'Brainwashing' in China.* New York: Norton.

Lipset S. M. (1959) 'Working class authoritarianism', *American Sociological Review*, 24(4): 482–502.

Lipset, S. M. (1960) *Political Man: The Social Bases of Politics*, New York: Doubleday & Company.

Lipset, S. M. (1986) 'Historical traditions and national characteristics: a comparative analysis of Canada and the United States', *The Canadian Journal of Sociology*, 11: 113–55.

Lipset, S. M. (1996) 'Steady work: an academic memoir', *Annual Review of Sociology*, 22: 1–27.

Lipset, S. M. and Löwenthal, L. (eds) (1961) *Culture and Social Character: The Work of David Riesman Reviewed*, Glencoe, IL: The Free Press.

Loewenberg, P. (1971) 'The psychohistorical origins of the Nazi youth cohort', *American Historical Review*, 76: 1457–1502.

Lorenz, K. (1955a) *Man meets Dog*, London: Methuen.

Lorenz, K. (1955b) *King Solomon's Ring*, London: Methuen.

Lorenz, K. (1966) *On Aggression*, London: Methuen.

Löwenthal, L, (1987) *An Unmastered Past*, Berkeley: University of California Press.

Lozano, A. (2018) 'Reframing the public sociology debate: towards collaborative and declonial praxis', *Current Sociology*, 66(1): 92–109.

Lukiannoff, G. and Haidt, J. (2018) *The Coddling of the American Mind: How Good Intentions and Bad Ideas Are Setting Up a Generation for Failure*, New York: Penguin.

Lutkehaus, N. (2008) *Margaret Mead: The Making of an American Icon*, Princeton, NJ: Princeton University Press.

Lynd, R. (1939) *Knowledge for What? The Place of Social Science in American Culture*, Princeton, NJ: Princeton University Press.

Lynd, R. and Lynd, H. M. (1929) *Middletown: A Study in Contemporary American Culture*. New York: Harcourt, Brace.

Maccoby, M. (1972) 'Emotional attitudes and political choices', *Politics & Society*, 2(2): 209–34.

Maccoby, M. (1976) *The Gamesman*, New York: Simon & Schuster.

Maccoby, M. (1980) *The Leader*, New York: Simon & Schuster.

Maccoby, M. (1988) *Why Work?*, New York: Simon & Schuster.

Maccoby, M. (1995) 'The two voices of Erich Fromm: prophet and analyst', *Society*, 32(5): 72–82.

Maccoby, M. (2003) *The Productive Narcissist: The Promise and Peril of Visionary Leadership*, New York: Broadway Books.

Maccoby, M. (2007) *The Leaders We Need, and What Makes Us Follow*, Boston, MA: Harvard Business School.

Maccoby, M. (2015) *Strategic Intelligence*, Oxford: Oxford University Press.

Maccoby, M. (2020). 'Trump's marketing narcisstic leadership in an age of anxiety' in Maccoby, M. and Fuchsman, K. (eds) *Psychoanalytic and Historical Perspectives on the Leadership of Donald Trump: Narcissism and Marketing in an Age of Anxiety and Distrust*, New York: Routledge, pp 11–23.

Maccoby, M. and Foster, G. M. (1970) 'Methods of studying Mexican peasant personality: Rorschach, TAT, and dreams', *Anthropological Quarterly*, 43: 225–43.

Maccoby, M and McLaughlin, N. (2020) 'Sociopsychoanalysis and radical humanism: A Fromm–Bourdieu synthesis', in Durkin and Braune, *Erich Fromm's Critical Theory: Hope, Humanism and the Future*, London: Bloomsbury, pp 108–27.

Maccoby, M. and Modiano, N. (1966) 'On culture and equivalence', in J. S. Bruner, R. Olver, and P. Greenfield (eds) *Studies in Cognitive Growth*. New York: Wiley, pp 257–69.

Maccoby, M., Modiano, N., and Lander, P. (1964) 'Games and *Social Character in a Mexican Village*', *Psychiatry*, 27: 150–62.

MacDonald, D. (1942) 'A new dimension', *Common Sense*, 11(1): 29.

Mann, M. (2004) *Fascists*, Cambridge: Cambridge University Press.

Mann, M. (2005) *The Dark Side of Democracy: Explaining Ethnic Cleansing*, Cambridge: Cambridge University Press.

Manning, P. (2005) *Freud and American Sociology*, London: Polity Press.

Marcuse, H. ([1941] 1956) *Reason and Revolution: Hegel and the Rise of Social Theory*, Boston, MA: Beacon Press.

Marcuse, H. (1954) *Reason and Revolution: Hegel and the Rise of Social Theory*, New York: Humanities Press.

Marcuse, H. (1955a) *Eros and Civilization: A Philosophical Inquiry into Freud*, Boston, MA: Beacon Press.

Marcuse, H. (1955b) 'The social implications of Freudian revisionism', *Dissent*, 2: 221–40.

Marcuse, H. (1956) 'A reply to Erich Fromm', *Dissent*, 3: 79–81.

Marcuse, H. (1964) *One-Dimensional Man: Studies in the Ideology of Advanced Industrial Society*, London: Routledge.

Marcuse, H. (1969) *An Essay on Liberation*, Boston, MA: Beacon Press.

Marcuse, H. (1972) *Counterrevolution and Revolt*, Boston: Beacon Press.

Markovits, A. S. (2009) *Uncouth Nation: Why Europe Dislikes America* (Vol. 5), Princeton, NJ: Princeton University Press.

Markovits, D. (2019) *The Meritocracy Trap*. London: Penguin Random House.

Martin, J. L. (2001) 'The authoritarian personality, 50 years later: What questions are there for political psychology?', *Political Psychology*, 22(1), 1–26.

Marx, K. and Engels, F. (1967) *The Communist Manifesto*, trans. Samuel Moore. London: Penguin Random House.

Mattingly, G. (1941) 'Review of *Escape from Freedom*', *The Saturday Review of Literature*, 24 (30 August): 6.

McClay, W. M. (1998) 'Fifty years of the lonely crowd', *The Wilson Quarterly*, 22(3): 34–42.

McGee, M. (2005) *Self-Help, Inc.: Makeover Culture in American Life*, Oxford: Oxford University Press.

McLaughlin, J. B. and Riesman, D. (1990) *Choosing a College President: Opportunities and Constraints*, Princeton, NJ: Princeton University Press.

McLaughlin, N. (1996) 'Nazism, nationalism and the sociology of emotions: *Escape from Freedom* revisited', *Sociological Theory*, 14(3): 241–61.

McLaughlin, N. (1998a) 'How to become a forgotten intellectual: intellectual movements and the rise and fall of Erich Fromm', *Sociological Forum*, 13(2): 215–46.

McLaughlin, N. (1998b) 'Why do schools of thought fail? Neo-Freudianism as a case study in the sociology of knowledge', *Journal of the History of the Behavioral Sciences*, 34(2): 113–34.

McLaughlin, N. (1999) 'Origin myths in the social sciences: Fromm, the Frankfurt School, and the emergence of critical theory', *Canadian Journal of Sociology*, 24(1): 109–39.

McLaughlin, N. (2001a) 'Optimal marginality: innovation and orthodoxy in Fromm's revision of psychoanalysis', *The Sociological Quarterly*, 42(2): 271–88.

McLaughlin, N. (2001b) 'Critical theory meets America: Riesman, Fromm, and the lonely crowd', *The American Sociologist*, 26(2): 5–26.

McLaughlin, N. (2008) 'Collaborative circles and their discontents. Revisiting conflict and creativity in Frankfurt School critical theory', *Sociologica*, 2(2): 1–35.

McLaughlin, N. (2017a) 'When worlds collide: sociology, disciplinary nightmares, and Fromm's revision of Freud', *Psychoanalytic Review*, 4(10): 415–35.

McLaughlin, N. (2017b) 'Movements, sects and letting go of symbolic interactionism', *Canadian Journal of Sociology/Cahiers canadiens de sociologie*, 42(2): 203–9.

McLaughlin, N. (2018) 'The two Jacobys: contradictions, ironies and challenges in new left critical social psychology', *Free Associations*, 72(1): 21–46.

McLaughlin, N. (2019) 'The coming triumpth of the psychosocial perspective: lessons from the rise, fall and revival of Erich Fromm', *Journal of Psychosocial Studies*, 12(1/2): 9–22.

McLaughlin, N. and Townsley, E. (2011) 'Contexts of cultural diffusion: a case study of "public intellectual" debates in English Canada', *Canadian Review of Sociology/Revue canadienne de sociologie*, 48(4): 341–68.

McLaughlin, N. and Trilupaityte, S. (2013) 'The international circulation of attacks and the reputational consequences of local context: George Soros's difficult reputation in Russia, post-Soviet Lithuania and the United States', *Cultural Sociology*, 7(4): 431–46.

McLaughlin, N. and Turcotte, K. (2007) 'The trouble with Burawoy', *Sociology*, 41(5): 813–28.

McLaughlin, N. and Steinberg, S. (2016) 'Evereet Hughes on race: wedded to an antiquated paradigm', in R. Helmes-Hayes and M. Santoro (eds) *The Anthem Companion to Evereet Hughes*, London: Anthem Press, pp 211–34.

McLaughlin, N., Kowalchuk, L., and Turcotte, K. (2005) 'Why sociology does not need to be saved: analytic reflections on public sociologies', *The American Sociologist*, 36(3/4): 133–51.

McLellan, D. (1973) *Karl Marx: His Life and Thought*, New York: Springer.

McMahon, D. F. (1972) 'Review of *Social Character in a Mexican Village*', *Contemporary Sociology*, 1(3): 229–30.

McMillan Cottom, T. (2017) *Lower Ed: The Troubling Rise of For-Profit Colleges in the New Economy*, New York: The New Press.

McMillan Cottom, T. (2019) *Thick*, New York: The New Press.

Mead, G. H. (1934) *Mind, Self and Society*, Chicago: The University of Chicago Press.

Mead, M. (1928) *Coming of Age in Samoa*, New York: William Morrow.

Mead, M. (1935) *Sex and Temperament in Three Primitive Societies*, New York: William Morrow.

Mead, M. (1941) 'Review of *Escape from Freedom*', *The New York Herald Tribune Book Review*, 21 September: 18.

Medvedev, R. A. and Shriver, G. (1989) *Let History Judge: The Origins and Consequences of Stalinism*, New York: Columbia University Press.

Menninger, K. (1942) 'Loneliness in the modern world', *The Nation*, 154 (14 March): 317.

Merton, R. K. (1968) 'The Matthew effect in science', *Science*, 159(3810): 53–63.

Merton, R. K. (1998) 'Unanticipated consequences and kindred sociological ideas: a personal gloss', in C. Mongardini and S. Tabboni (eds) *Robert K. Merton and Contemporary Sociology*, New Brunswick, NJ: Transaction, pp 295–318.

Merton, R. and Wolfe, A. (1995) 'The cultural and social incorporation of sociological', *The American American Sociologist*, 26: 15–39.

Meštrović, S. G. (1997) *Postemotional Society*, New York: Sage.

Meyer, D. S. and Rohlinger, D. A. (2012) 'Big books and social movements: a myth of ideas and social change', *Social Problems*, 59(1): 136–53.

Millán, G. and Millán, S. (2015) 'Understanding social motivation for encouraging children's development. social character studies in Mexico', in R. Funk and N. McLaughlin (eds) *Towards a Human Science: The Relevance of Erich Fromm for Today*, Gessen: Psychosozial-Verlag, pp 149–58.

Miller, J. and Miller, J. (1994) *Democracy Is in the Streets: From Port Huron to the Siege of Chicago*, Cambridge, MA: Harvard University Press.

Mills, C. W. (1951) *White Collar: The American Middle Classes*, New York: Oxford University Press.

Mills, C. W. (1956) *The Power Elite*, Cambridge: Cambridge University Press.

Mills, C. W. (1958) 'The structure of power in American Society', *The British Journal of Sociology*, 9(1): 29–41.

Mills, C. W. (1958) *The Cause of World War Three*, New York: Simon & Schuster.

Mills, C. W. (1959) *The Sociological Imagination*, New York: Oxford University Press.

Mills, C. W. (1960) *Listen Yankee; The Revolution in Cuba*, New York: McGraw-Hill.

Mills, C. W. and Salter, P. (1945) 'The barricade and the bedroom', *Politics*, 2(10): 313–15.

Mitchell, J. (1974) *Psychoanalysis and Feminism*, New York: Vintage.

Mitchell, S. (1993) *Hope and Dread in Psychoanalysis*, New York: Basic Books.

Mitchell, S. and Black, M. (1995) *Freud and Beyond: A History of Modern Psychoanalytic Thought*, New York: Basic Books.

Mitscherlich, A. (1969) *Society without the Father*, New York: Harcourt, Brace and World.

Montagu, A. (1942) 'Review of *Escape from Freedom*', *Psychiatry*, 5(1): 122–9.

Moore, B. (1966) *The Social Origins of Dictatorship and Democracy*, Boston, MA: Beacon.

Morris, A. (2015) *The Scholar Denied: W. E. B. Du Bois and the Birth of Modern Sociology*, Berkeley: University of California Press.

Morris, A. and Ghaziani, A. (2005) 'Duboisian sociology: watershed of professional and public sociology', *Souls*, 7(3–4): 47–54.

Morris, D. (1967) *The Naked Ape*, New York: Random House.

Mullahy, P. (1973) *The Beginnings of Modern American Psychiatry; the Ideas of Harry Stack Sullivan*, Boston, MA: Houghton Mifflin.

Mullins, N. (1973) *Theory and Theory Groups in Contemporary Sociology*, New York: Harper and Row.

Mumford, L. (1967) *The Myth of the Machine: Technics and Human Development* (vol. 1), New York: Harcourt Brace Jovanovich.

Murphy, P. C. (2005) *What a Book Can Do: The Publication of Reception of Silent Spring*, Boston, MA: University of Massachusetts Press.

Nader, R. (1965) *Unsafe at any Speed*, New York: Grossman.

Nakhaie, R. and Brym, R. (1999) 'The political attitudes of Canadian professors', *The Canadian Journal of Sociology*, 24(3): 329–53.

Neier, A. (2012) *The International Human Rights Movement: A History*, Princeton, NJ: Princeton University Press.

Neill, A. S. (1960) Summerhill: A Radical Approach to Child Rearing, New York: Hart.

Nettler, G. (1956) 'Review of *The Sane Society*', *American Journal of Sociology*, 61(6): 644–6.

Nielson, F. (2004) 'The vacant "we": remarks on public sociology', *Social Forces*, 82(4): 1619–27.

Nisbet, R. (1952) 'Conservatism and sociology', *American Journal of Sociology*, 58(2): 167–75.

Nisbet, R. (1988) *The Present Age: Progress and Anarchy in Modern America*, New York: Harper and Row.

Noll, R. (1997) *The Jung Cult: The Origins of a Charismatic Movement*. New York: Simon & Schuster.

Oakes, G. and Vidich, A. J. (1999) *Collaboration, Reputations and Ethics in American Academic Life: Hans H. Gerth and C. Wright Mills*, Chicago: University of Illinois Press.

Ollman, B. (1971) *Alienation: Marx's Conception of Man in Capitalist Society*, Cambridge: Cambridge University Press.

Pachter, H. M. (1963) 'Amateur diplomats and the peace literature', *Social Research*, 30(1): 95–107.

Padgett, V. (1971) 'Review of *Social Character in a Mexican Village*', *The Annals of the American Academy of Political and Social Science*, 397: 170–1.

Paris, B. (1995) *Karen Horney: A Psychoanalyst's Search for Self-Understanding*, New Haven, CT: Yale University Press.

Park, D. W. (2004) 'The couch and the clinic: the cultural authority of popular psychiatry and psychoanalysis', *Cultural Studies*, 18(1): 109–33.

Patterson, J. T. (2010) *Freedom Is Not Enough: The Moynihan Report and America's Struggle over Black Family Life – from LBJ to Obama*, New York: Basic Books.

Patterson, O. (2002) 'The last sociologist', *The New York Times*, 19 May.

Peale, N. V. (1952) *The Power of Positive Thinking*, New York: Fawcett Crest.

Perlatto, F. (2013) 'Public sociology: the Brazilian sociological imagination and public problems', PhD thesis, Instituto de Estudos Sociais e Políticos, Rio de Janeiro, Brazil.

Perry, H. (1982) *The Psychiatrist of America: The Life of Harry Stack Sullivan*, Cambridge, MA: Belknap.

Peterson, J. (2018) *Twelve Rules for Life*, Toronto: Random House, Canada.

Philipson, I. (2017) 'The last public psychoanalyst?: why Fromm matters in the 21st century', *Psychoanalytic Perspectives*, 14(1): 52–74.

Pinker, S. (2002) *The Blank Slate: The Denial of Human Nature in Modern Intellectual Life*, New York: Viking.

Pinker, S. (2011) *The Better Angles of Our Nature: Why Violence Has Declined*, New York: Penguin.

Pinker, S. (2018) *Enlightenment Now: The Case for Reason, Science, Humanism and Progress*, New York: Penguin.

Piven, F. F. (2006) *Challenging Authority: How Ordinary People Change America*, Lanham, MD: Rowman & Littlefield.

Piven, F. F. (2008) 'Can power from below change the world?', *American Sociological Review*, 73(1): 1–14.

Platt, J. (2007) 'Some issues in comparative, marco and international work in the history of sociology', *The American Sociologist*, 38(4): 352–63.

Plenta, P. (2020) 'Conspiracy theories as a political instrument: utilization of anti-Soros narratives in Central Europe', *Contemporary Politics*, 26(5), 512–30.

Polanyi, K. (1944) *The Great Transformation*. Boston, MA: Beacon Press.

Posner, R.A. (2001) *Public Intellectuals: A Study of Decline*, Cambridge, MA: Harvard University Press.

Quinn, S. (1987) *A Mind of Her Own: The Life of Karen Horney*, New York: Summit.

Rafael, E. (2014) 'Is sociology in the Philippines a professionalized discipline', *Philippine Sociological Review*, 1 January: 213–36.

Redfield, R. (1956) *Peasant Society and Culture: An Anthropological approach to Civilization*, Chicago: The University of Chicago Press.

Reich, W. [1933] *The Mass Psychology of Fascism*, New York: Pocket.

Rickert, J. (1986) 'The Fromm–Marcuse debate revisited', *Theory and Society*, 15(3): 181–214.

Rieff, P. (1987) *The Triumph of the Therapeutic: Uses of Faith after Freud*, Chicago: University of Chicago Press.

Riesman, D. (1950) *The Lonely Crowd: A Study of the Changing American Character*, New Haven, CT: Yale University Press.

Riesman, D. (1954) *Individualism Reconsidered and Other Essays*, Glencoe, IL: Free Press.

Riesman, D. (1956) *Constraint and Variety in American Education*. Lincoln, Nebraska: University of Nebraska Press.

Riesman, D. (1964) *Abundance for What?*, New Brunswick, NJ: Transaction Press.

Riesman, D. (1973) 'Review of *The Anatomy of Human Destructiveness*', *The New Republic*, 169(23): 24–6.

Riesman, D. (1990a) 'Becoming an academic man', in B. Berger (ed) *Authors of Their Own Lives*, Berkeley: University of California Press, pp 22–74.

Riesman, D. (1990b) 'The Innocence of *The Lonely Crowd*', *Society*, January/February: 339–42.

Riesman, D. with Glazer, N. (1952) *Faces in the Crowd*, New Haven, CT: Yale University Press.

Roazen, P. (1974) *Freud and His Followers*, New York: Knopf.

Roazen, P. (1976) *Erik H. Erikson: The Power and Limits of a Vision*, New York: The Free Press.

Roazen, P. (1977) 'A stranger to narrow fashion', *The Nation*, 5(2): 151–4.

Roazen, P. (1996) 'Fromm's courage', in M. Cortina and M. Maccoby (eds) *A Prophetic Analyst: Erich Fromm's Contributions to Psychoanalysis*, Northvale, NJ: Jason Aronson, pp 415–25.

Roazen, P. (2001) 'The exclusion of Erich Fromm from the IPA', *Contemporary Psychoanalysis*, 37(1): 5–42.

Robinson, P. (1969) *The Freudian Left*, New York: Harper & Row.

Rodden, J. (1989) *The Politics of Literary Reputation: The Making and Claiming of 'St. George' Orwell*, New York: Oxford University Press.

Rogow, A. (1970) *The Psychiatrists*, New York: G. P. Putnam's Sons.

Rosen, B. C. (1956) 'Review of *The Sane Society*', *American Sociological Review*, 21(5): 641–2.

Ross, J. (2015) *The Socialist Party of America*. Lincoln, NE: University of Nebraska Press.

Rubin, L. (1976) *Worlds of Pain: Life in the Working Class Family*, New York: Basic Books.

Rubin, L. B. (1983) *Intimate Strangers: Men and Women Together*, New York: Perennial Library.

Rubin, L. B. (1985) *Just Friends: The Role of Friendship in our Lives*, New York: Harper & Row.

Rutherford, A. (2009) *Beyond the Box: B.F. Skinner's Technology of Behavior from Laboratory to Life, 1950s–1970s*, Toronto: University of Toronto Press.

Ryan, W. (1976) *Blaming the Victim*, New York: Vintage.
Sagall, S. (2013) *Final Solutions: Human Nature, Capitalism and Genocide*, London: Verso.
Said, E. W. (2012a) *Representations of the Intellectual*, London: Vintage.
Said, E. W. (2012b) *Out of Place: A Memoir*, London: Vintage.
Salomon, von E. (1930) *Die Geächteten*, Berlin: Rowohlt.
Samelson, F. (1974) 'History, origin myth and ideology: "discovery" of social psychology', *Journal for the Theory of Social Behaviour*, 4 (Fall): 467–88.
Sayers, J. (1991) *Mothers of Psychoanalysis*, New York: Norton.
Schaar, J. (1961) *Escape from Authority: The Perspectives of Erich Fromm*, New York: Basic Books.
Scheff, T. (1994) *Bloody Revenge: Emotions, Nationalism and War*, Boulder, CO: Westview.
Schneider, L. (1956) 'Review of *The Sane Society*', *Social Problems*, 4(2): 181–2.
Schoefeld, C. G. (1965) 'Erich Fromm's attack upon the Oedipus Complex: a brief critique', *The Journal of Nervous and Mental Disease*, 141(5): 580–5.
Schroyer, T. (1973) *The Critique of Domination: The Origins and Development of Critical Theory*, New York: G. Braziller.
Seeman, M. (1959) 'On the meaning of alienation', *American Sociological Review*, 24(6): 783–91.
Seidman, S. (1994) *Contested Knowledge: Social Theory in the Postmodern Era*, Cambridge, MA: Blackwell.
Selznick, P. (1992) *The Moral Commonwealth: Social Theory and the Promise of Community*, Berkeley: University of California Press.
Selznick, P. (2008) *A Humanist Science: Values and Ideals in Social Inquiry*, Stanford, CA: Stanford University Press.
Sennett, R. (1993) *Authority*, New York: W. W. Norton & Company.
Sennett, R. (1998) *The Corrosion of Character: The Personal Consequences of Work in the New Capitalism*, New York: Norton.
Shils, E. (1954) 'Authoritarianism: "Left" and "Right"', in R. Christie and M. Jahoda (eds) *Studies in the Scope and Method of the Authoritarian Personality*, Glencoe, IL: Free Press, pp 24–49.
Shils, E. (1980) *The Selected Papers of Edward Shils, Volume 3: The Calling of Sociology and Other Essays on the Pursuit of Learning* (Vol. 3), Chicago: University of Chicago Press.
Shlomo, A. (1968) *The Social and Political Thought of Karl Marx*, Cambridge: Cambridge University Press.

Sica, A. and Turner, S. (2005) *Michael Burawoy, 'Antinomian Marxist', The Disobedient Generation: Social Theorists and the 1960s*, Chicago: The University of Chicago Press.

Silver, C. B. (2014) 'Paranoid and institutional responses to psychoanalysis among early sociologists: a socio-psychoanalytic interpretation', in L. Chancer and J. Andrews (eds) *The Unhappy Divorce of Sociology and Psychoanalysis*, Basingstoke: Palgrave Macmillan, pp 53–76.

Silver, C. B. (2017) 'Views of social change in Freud, Fromm, and the culture of psychoanalysis', *Psychoanalytic Review*, 104(4): 389–414.

Simpson, A. (2014) Mohawk Interruptus, Durham, NC: Duke University Press.

Skinner, B. F. (1973) *Beyond Freedom and Dignity*, New York: Bantam/Vintage Books.

Skinner, B. F. (1981) *The Shaping of a Behaviorist: Part Two of an Autobiography*, New York: Alfred A. Knopf.

Skocpol, T. (1979) *States and Social Revolutions*, New York: Cambridge University Press.

Skocpol, T. and Hertzel-Fernandez, A. (2016) 'The Koch network and Republican party extremism', *Perspectives on Politics*, 14(3): 681–99.

Smelser, N. (1998) 'The rational and the ambivalent in the social sciences', *American Sociological Review*, 63(1): 1–16.

Smith, D. N. (1996) 'The social construction of enemies: Jews and the representation of evil', *Sociological Theory*, 14(3): 203–40.

Smith, D. N. (2019) 'Authoritarianism reimagined: the riddle of Trump's base', *The Sociological Quarterly*, 60(2): 210–23.

Smith, D. N. (2020) 'Whiter than white: patterns of race, class and prejudice in the divided Midwest', in Barney Warf (ed) *Political Landscapes in the Age of Donald Trump*, London and New York: Routledge, pp 1–27.

Smith, D. N. and Hanley, E. (2018) 'The anger games: who voted for Donald Trump in the 2016 election, and why?', *Critical Sociology*, 44(2): 195–212.

Smith, R. (1997) 'The bearing of Erich Fromm's *The Working Class in Weimar Germany* on current studies of Nazism', paper presented to the annual meeting of the American Sociological Association, Toronto, Ontario, August.

Spindler, L. (1978) 'Researching the psychology of culture change and urbanization' in L. Spindler (ed) *The Making of Psychological Anthropology*, Berkeley: The University of California Press, pp 187–95.

Srivastava, S. (2005) '"You're calling me a racist?" The moral and emotional regulation of antiracism and feminism', *Signs: Journal of Women in Culture and Society*, 31(1): 29–62.

Stacey, J. (2004) 'Marital suitors court social sciences spinsters: the unwittingly conservative effects of public sociology', *Social Problems*, 51(1): 131–45.

Stein, A. and Daniels, J. (2017) *Going Public: A Guide for Social Scientists*, Chicago: The University of Chicago Press.

Steinberg, S. (1996) *Turning Back*, Boston, MA: Beacon Press.

Steinmetz, G. (2006) 'Bourdieu's disavowal of Lacan: psychoanalytic theory and the concepts of "habitus" and "symbolic capital"', *Constellations*, 13(4): 445–64.

Steinmetz, G. (ed) (2013) *Sociology and Empire: The Imperial Entanglements of a Discipline*, Durham, NC: Duke University Press.

Steinmetz, G. (2017) 'Sociology and colonialism in the British and French empires, 1945–1965', *The Journal of Modern History*, 89(3): 601–48.

Stepansky, P. (2009) *Psychoanalysis at the Margins*, New York: Other Press.

Sterne, J. (2005) 'C. Wright Mills, the Bureau for Applied Social Research, and the meaning of critical scholarship', *Cultural Studies: Critical Methodologies*, 5(1): 65–94.

Strozier, C. (2001) *Heinz Kohut: The Making of a Psychoanalyst*, New York: Farrar, Straus and Giroux.

Sullivan, H. S. (1953) *The Interpersonal Theory of Psychiatry*, New York: Norton.

Sunkara, B. (2019) *The Socialist Manifesto*, New York: Basic Books.

Swanson, G. (1975) 'Review of *The Anatomy of Human Destructiveness* by Erich Fromm', *American Journal of Sociology*, 80(5/March): 1243–5.

Swartz, D. L (1997) *Culture and Power: The Sociology of Pierre Bourdieu*, Chicago: The University of Chicago Press.

Swartz, D. L. (2003) 'From critical Sociology to public intellectuals: Pierre Bourdieu and politics', *Theory and Society*, 32(51–6): 791–823.

Swartz, D. L. (2013) *Symbolic Power, Politics, and Intellectuals: The Political Sociology of Pierre Bourdieu*, Chicago: The University of Chicago Press.

Schwartz, P. (1995) *Love Between Equals: How Peer Marriage Really Works*, New York: Simon & Schuster.

Schwartz, P. (2005). 'Sociology as public practice: toward a better utilization of research and theory: 2005 presidential address to the Pacific Sociological Association', *Sociological Perspectives*, 48(4), 423–31.

Schwartz, P. (2006). *Finding your Perfect Match*, New York: Penguin Random House.

Tar, Z. (1985) *The Frankfurt School: The Critical Theories of Max Horkheimer and Theodor W. Adorno*, New York: Schocken Books.

Tawney, R. W. (1921) *The Acquisitive Society*, London: Collins.

Taylor, V. (1989) 'Social movement continuity: the woman's movement in abeyance', *American Sociological Review*, 54(5): 761–75.

Teitelbaum, B. (2020) *War for Eternity: Inside Bannon's Far-Right Circle of Global Power Brokers*, New York: Harper Collins.

Theobald, R. (1966) *The Guaranteed Income: Next Step in Economic Evolution*, New York: Doubleday.

Therborn, G. (1970) 'Frankfurt Marxism: a critique', *New Left Review*, 63 (September/October): 65–96.

Theweleit, K. (1989) *Male Fantasies*, 2 vols, Minneapolis, MN: University of Minnesota Press.

Thorpe, C. (2016) *Neculture*, New York: Palgrave Macmillan.

Thorpe, C. (2020) 'Escape from reflexivity: Fromm and Giddens on individualism, anxiety, and authoritarianism', in K. Durkin and J. Braune (eds) *Erich Fromm's Critical Theory: Hope, Humanism, and the Future*, London: Bloomsbury Academic, pp 166–93.

Tittle, C. (2004) 'The arrogance of public sociology', *Social Forces*, 82(4): 1639–43.

Townsley, E. (2006) 'The public intellectual trope in the United States', *The American Sociologist*, 37(3): 39–66.

Treviño, A. J. (2011) *The Social Thought of C. Wright Mills*. New York: Sage Publications.

Tuchman, G. with Fortin, N. (1986) *Edging Women Out: Victorian Novelists, Publishers and Social Change*, New Haven, CT: Yale University Press.

Tuck, E. and Yang, K. W. (2012) 'Decolonization is not metaphor', *Decolonation: Indigeneity, Education and Society*, 1(1): 1–40.

Tucker, R. C. (ed) (2017) *Stalinism: Essays in Historical Interpretation*, London: Routledge.

Turkle, S. (1992) *Psychoanalytic Politics: Freud's French Revolution*, New York: Guilford Press.

Turner, B. S. (2014) 'Robert Nisbet and the problem of community', *The American Sociologist*, 45(1): 68–83.

Turner, J. (2000) *On the Origins of Human Emotions: A Sociological Inquiry into the Evolution of Human Affect*, Stanford, CA: Stanford University Press.

Turner, J. (2005) 'British sociology and public sociology', *British Journal of Sociology*, 57(3): 169–88.

Turner, S. and Turner, S. (1990) *The Impossible Science: An Institutional Analysis of American Sociology*, London: Sage.

van den Berg, A. (1980) 'Critical theory: is there still hope', *American Journal of Sociology*, 86(3): 449–78.

Vaughan, D. (1986) *Uncoupling: Turning Points in Intimate Relationships*, New York: Oxford University Press.

Vaughan, D. (2006) 'NASA revisited: theory, analogy, and public sociology', *American Journal of Sociology*, 112(2): 353–93.

Wald, A. M. (2017) *The New York Intellectuals: The Rise and Decline of the Anti-Stalinist Left from the 1930s to the 1980s*, Chapel Hill, NC: University of North Carolina Press.

Wallerstein, I. (1979) *The Capitalist World-Economy*, Cambridge: Cambridge University Press.

Walzer, M. (1988) *The Company of Critics*, New York: Basic Books.

Waskow, A. (1962) 'Review of *May Man Prevail?*', *The Annals of the American Academic of Political and Social Sciences*, 343 (September): 144–5.

Watts, J. (1994) *Heroism and the Black Intellectual: Ralph Ellison, Politics, and the Afro-American Intellectual*, Chapel Hill: University of North Carolina.

Watts, V. (2013) 'Indigenous place-thought and agency amongst humans and non humans (first woman and sky woman go on a European world tour!)', *Decolonization: Indigeneity, Education & Society*, 2(1): 20–34.

Watts, V., Hooks, G., and McLaughlin, N. (2020) 'A troubling presence: indigeneity in English-language Canadian sociology', *Canadian Review of Sociology*, 57(1): 7–33.

Weber, M. (1905) *The Protestant Ethic and the Spirit of Capitalism*, New York: Charles Scribner's Sons.

West, C. (1989) *Toward a Socialist Theory of Racism*, New York: Institute for Democratic Socialism.

West, C. (1991a) *The Ethical Dimensions of Marxist Thought*, New York: Monthly Review Press.

West, C. (1991b) 'Nihilism in black America: a danger that corrodes from within', *Dissent*, 38(2): 221–6.

Westkott, M. (1986) *The Feminist Legacy of Karen Horney*, New Haven, CT: Yale University Press.

Wheatland, T. (2009) *Frankfurt School in Exile*, Minneapolis, MN: University of Minnesota Press.

White, R. and Parsons, T. (1961) 'The link between character and society', in S. M. Lipset and L. Löwenthal (eds) *Culture and Social Chararacter*. New York: Free Press, pp 89–135.

Whitebook, J. (1995) *Perversion and Utopia: A Study in Psychoanalysis and Critical Theory*, Cambridge, MA: MIT Press.

Whitley, R. (1984) *The Intellectual and Social Organization of the Sciences*, Oxford: Clarendon Press.

Wiggershaus, R. (1995) *The Frankfurt School: Its History, Theories, and Political Significance*, Cambridge, MA: MIT Press.

Wilde, L. (2004) *Erich Fromm and the Quest for Solidarity*, New York: Palgrave.

Wilkinson, R. (1988) *The Pursuit of American Character*, New York: Harper and Row.

Williams, J. E. (2016) *Decoding Racial Ideology in Genomics*, Lanham, MD: Lexington Books.

Wilson, E. O. (1978) *On Human Nature*, Cambridge, MA: Harvard University Press.

Wilson, J. Q. (1993) *The Moral Sense*, New York: The Free Press.

Wilson, W. J. (2009) 'The Moynihan report and research on the black community', *The Annals of the American Academy of Political and Social Science*, 621(1): 34–46.

Wirth, L. (1942) 'Review of *Escape From Freedom*', *Psychiatry*, 5(2): 129–31.

Wolfe, A. (1989) *Whose Keeper? Social Science and Moral Obligation*, Berkeley: University of California Press.

Wolfe, A. (1993) *The Human Difference: Animals, Computers and the Necessity of Social Science*, Berkeley: University of California.

Wolfe, A. (1996) *Marginalized in the Middle*, Chicago: The University of Chicago Press.

Wolfe, A. (1998) *One Nation, After All*, New York: Viking.

Wolfe, A. (2011) *Political Evil: What It Is and How to Combat It*, New York: Knopf.

Wolfe, A. (2018) *The Politics of Petulance: America in an Age of Immaturity*, Chicago: The University of Chicago Press.

Wolfesenstein, E. V. (1993) *Psychoanalytic Marxism: Groundwork*, New York: Guilford.

Wolin, R. (1992) *The Terms of Cultural Criticism: The Frankfurt School, Existentialism, Poststructuralism*, New York: Columbia University Press.

Wright, E. O. (2010) *Envisioning Real Utopias* (vol. 98), London: Verso.

Wright, M. W. (2001) 'A manifesto against femicide', *Antipode*, 33(3): 550–66.

Wright, M. W. (2011) 'Necropolitics and femicide: gendered violence on the Mexico–US border', *Signs: Journal of Women in Culture and Society*, 36(3): 707–31.

Wrong, D. (1961) 'The oversocialized conception of man', *American Sociological Review*, 26(2): 183–93.

Wrong, D. (1990) 'Imagining the real', in Bennett Berger (ed) *Authors of Their Own Lives*, Berkeley: University of California Press, pp 3–21.

REFERENCES

Wrong, D. (1992) 'The lonely crowd revisited', *Sociological Forum*, 7(2): 381–9.

Wrong, D. (1994) *The Problem of Order: What Unites and Divides Society*, Glencoe, IL: Free Press.

Zaretsky, E. (2015) *Political Freud: A History*, New York: Columbia University Press.

Zaroulis, N. and Sullivan, G. (1984) *Who Spoke Up? American Protest against the War in Vietnam, 1963–1975*, New York: Doubleday.

Zinn, M. B. (1989) 'Family, race, and poverty in the eighties', *Signs: Journal of Women in Culture and Society*, 14(4): 856–74.

Znaniecki, F. (1965) *The Social Role of the Man of Knowledge*, New York: Octagon Books.

Index

A
Abbott, Andrew 97
The Acquisitive Society (Tawney) 103
activism 135–6, 139, 143–82, 231
Addams, Jane 79
Adorno, Theodor 8, 24–5, 68, 70–1, 114, 116, 235
  and critical theory 141
  and Freudian orthodoxy 140
  and the F-scale 10, 69
  and Jacoby 138
Afary, Janet 226, 230
Africa 14, 79, 101, 151, 181, 210, 219
African-American intellectuals 59, 60, 120, 130
aggression 199, 201, 203, 204–15
On Aggression (Lorenz) 199, 200
alcoholism 99, 191, 195
Alcove 1 115
Alexander, Franz 73–4
alienation 2, 3, 82, 83, 109, 171, 225
  and Fromm's sense of from his family 56
  and Marcuse 119
  and *Marx's Concept of Man* 155, 156, 157
  and *The Revolution of Hope* 168
  and *The Sane Society* 13, 103, 104
  and social character 172
'The Alleged Radicalism of Herbert Marcuse' (Fromm) 139
Altemeyer, Robert 235
Althusser, Louis 158, 163
American Communist Party 116
American culture 82, 83, 89, 90, 91, 114
American foreign policy 14, 82–3, 84, 144, 146
  and The Berlin Crisis memo 179
  and Chomsky 170–1
  and Cuba 178
  and *Marx's Concept of Man* 156
  and *May Man Prevail?* 2, 11

  and negotiating nuclear disarmament deals 151
  and Russia 148
American Foundations Fund for Research in Psychiatry 187
American Friends Service Committee (AFSC) 152, 187, 188
American Journal of Sociology 11, 27, 133
American militarism 2, 158, 171, 177
American Sociological Association 5
American Sociological Review 4, 11, 133, 190
Amis, William 216–17
Amnesty International 154, 175, 180
The Anatomy of Human Destructiveness (Fromm) 11, 182, 183, 184–5, 186, 197, 204–15
  and necrophilia 218–19
  and psychoanalytic theory 198–9
  and Riesman 227
  and Stalin 176
  and Swanson and Amis 216–17
  and violence 202, 220
Anderson, Benedict 44
Ansari, Aziz 132
anthropologists 66, 74, 76, 188
anthropology 22–3, 72, 90, 99, 185, 188
  and *The Anatomy of Human Destructiveness* 199, 204
  and *Social Character in a Mexican Village* 195
anti-nuclear activism 2, 144, 151, 152, 170, 177, 180
anti-Semitism 6, 41–2, 47, 59–60
anti-Stalinist left 115
anti-war movement 131, 144, 166, 167, 168, 232
  and SANE 152, 153
anxiety 24, 90, 92, 99, 103, 203, 225
  and *The Art of Loving* 123
  and death 124, 125

'The Application of Humanistic
    Psychoanalysis to Marx's Theory'
    (Fromm) 163
Arab Spring 44
archetypes 126
Ardrey, Robert 200
Arendt, Hannah 114, 211–12,
    213, 231–2
arms control 179, 180
The Art of Loving (Fromm) 12, 13, 81,
    111, 112, 113–14, 122–32
    and celebrity status 231
    and Fromm–Marcuse debate 137, 138
    sales 2, 136, 166
Asylums (Goffman) 32
attachment theory 217
authoritarian belief systems 108
authoritarian character 9, 10, 24, 26, 43
authoritarianism 2, 129, 210, 216, 228,
    232, 235
    in Poland 3, 43
    and sadomasochistic character 25
    in the United States 46
    working class 45
The Authoritarian Personality (Adorno et
    al) 10, 24, 25, 69, 114
authority, rational 103, 107, 129
automation conformity 42, 78, 98

B
Baader-Meinhof group 153
Bachofen, Johann Jakob 64, 174
Baehr, Peter 31, 232–3
banality of evil 211, 212, 232
Bannon, Steve 46
Bartlett, Francis 27
Bear Mountain meeting 152
'Behavioural Study of Obedience'
    (Milgram) 202–3
behaviourism 199, 201, 202, 203
Bell, Daniel 157–8, 175, 234
Bellah, Robert 82, 85, 96
Benedict, Ruth 74, 76
Benenson, Peter 154
benign aggression 199, 205, 206
Benjamin, Jessica 230
Benjamin, Walter 68
Berlin, Isaiah 29–30
Berlin Crisis 179, 180
Berlin Institute for Psychoanalysis 73
Berman, Marshall 172
*The Better Angels of Our Nature:
    Why Violence Has Declined*
    (Pinker) 198, 220
Beyond Freedom and Dignity (Skinner) 202
'big books' 12, 13
Black Panther Party 168

black self-love 130
blaming the victim 194
Blauner, Robert 171
Bloch, Ernest 163
Bloom, Allan 84–5, 96, 141
*Blueprint: The Evolutionary Origins of a
    Good Society* (Christakis) 198, 219–20
Bolsonaro, Jair 5, 47
Bonilla-Silva, Eduardo 6
Bonss, Wolfgang 9, 24, 69
Bottomore, Tom 232–3
Bourdieu, Pierre 3, 6, 131, 186–7, 209,
    212, 228–9
    and habitus 189, 192–3, 196
bourgeoisie 27–8
Bowlby, J. 217
Brandt, Heinz 153, 154
Brave New World (Huxley) 128
Brazil 47, 225
Bregman, Rutger 220
Brint, Steven 93
brotherly love 126
The Brothers Karamazov (Dostoevsky) 22
Brown, Michael 178
Brunner, José 9
Buber, Martin 58
Burawoy, Michael 6, 14, 32, 82, 143, 176
    and critical sociology 94, 113, 122,
        141–2, 178
    'For Public Sociology' 1, 3–5
bureaucrats 102, 104, 155, 161, 211,
    212, 216
Butler, Judith 198

C
'California Citizen for McCarthy' 167
The Calling of Sociology (Shils) 221–2
Calvinism 25
capitalism 25, 26, 56, 91, 119, 174, 222
    and *Escape from Freedom* 86–7
    and 'Let Man Prevail' 160
    and *Man for Himself* 88
    and *The Sane Society* 101, 103, 104
    and social character theory 164
care 125, 126
Carnegie, Dale 129
Carson, Rachel 12
'The Case for Unilateral Disarmament'
    (Fromm) 179
Catholic Church 35, 37
The Causes of World War III
    (Mills) 152, 170
Cavalletto, George 133, 230
celebrity culture 94, 234
celebrity intellectuals 14, 15, 52, 120,
    136, 137, 181–2
    and *The Art of Loving* 2, 13, 122, 231

INDEX

Central Europe 1, 223, 225
centrality 54
Chancer, Lynn 123, 226, 230
charismatic leaders 39, 45
Chicago Institute for Psychoanalysis 73
Chiconcauc 187–8
children, rights of 10
China 147, 148, 149, 155, 156, 172, 173, 235
Chinese Communist Party 174, 235
Chodorow, Nancy 109, 134, 230
Chomsky, Noam 151, 170–1, 175, 178–9, 201–2, 234
Christakis, Nicholas 198, 219–20
City College of New York (CCNY) 115
civil rights 161, 163, 181
class 25, 28, 38, 109, 227
    German Workers study 10, 24, 69
    lower middle 26, 34, 36–7, 45–6
The Closing of the American Mind: How Higher Education Has Failed Democracy and Impoverished the Souls of Today's Students (Bloom) 84–5, 141
Cohen, Hermann 58
Cold War 112, 115, 145–6, 148, 170, 175, 214
    Fromm's reputation at height of 109
    and 'Let Man Prevail' 160
    and Marcuse 114
    and *Marx's Concept of Man* 155
    and Mills 222
    and threat of Soviet communism 149
Collins, Randall 35, 37, 38, 171
colonial wars 151, 174
Columbia University 9, 10, 66, 69, 74
Coming of Age in Samoa (Mead) 77, 137
commercialization of feelings 2, 3, 172
Committee for Non-Violent Action (CNVA) 152
Committee of Correspondence newsletter 152, 176
communism 104, 147, 155, 156, 158–9, 160, 173, 174
    Soviet and Chinese alliance 149
Communist Manifesto (Marx and Engels) 45–6
conflict theory 116
conformist aggression 206
conformist psychology 134
conformity, automation 42, 78, 98
Connell, Raewyn 3, 6, 234
Contemporary Sociology 11, 216
Cornell University 85
Cortina, Mauricio 217, 218, 219, 239
Coser, Lewis 14, 115–16
Counterrevolution and Revolt (Marcuse) 139
Cousins, Norman 179

The Crisis magazine 79
The Crisis of Psychoanalysis (Fromm) 139
critical pedagogy 107
critical public sociology 82, 97, 171
critical sociology 94, 113, 122, 141–2, 178
critical theory 10, 65, 66, 67–70, 71, 121, 141
Cuba 151, 178
cultural anthropology 72
cultural capital 15, 53, 54, 64, 67, 182, 231
    and *Escape from Freedom* 66
    and Fromm–Riesman collaboration 222
culture and personality movement 66, 76, 77–8, 90
'Culture and Personality' seminar 76
The Culture of Narcissism: American Life in an Age of Diminishing Expectations (Lasch) 86
cybernetics 164

D

Daedalus 151, 179
The Dark Agenda: The War to Destroy Christian America (Horowitz) 47
Darwinian theories 201, 208, 218
Davis, Angela 120, 139
death 39, 40–1, 124, 125, 216
death instinct theory 23, 116, 117, 199, 204, 214, 219
defensive aggression 204, 206
Democratic Convention, Chicago 1968 164, 166
Democratic Party 164, 165, 167, 182
democratic socialism 115, 116, 151, 236
Democratic Socialists of America (DSA) 161, 162
Department and Discipline: Chicago Sociology at One Hundred (Abbott) 97
depression 99, 209, 219
depth psychology 33, 73, 133, 229
deschooling society 107
destructiveness 23, 185, 201, 202–3, 217
    and *The Anatomy of Human Destructiveness* 184, 198, 199, 204–5
Dewey, John 29, 175
The Dialectical Imagination (Jay) 68
dialectical materialism 155
Dialectic of Enlightenment (Horkheimer and Adorno) 99
disarmament 43, 151, 160, 175, 176
Dissent 110, 111, 115, 116, 121, 137, 138
    and 'The Implications of Institutional Radicalism' 118
    and 'Nihilism in Black America' 237
Distinguished George W. Gay Lecture 98

287

'The Dogma of Christ' (Fromm) 108
Dollard, John 76
domestic violence 189, 194, 195, 229
domination 125, 126, 130
Dostoevsky, Fyodor 22
drive theory 64, 118
drug addiction 99, 124, 195, 238
Du Bois, W. E. B. 6, 14–15, 135, 173, 176
  and fame 234
  and racism 53, 79, 235, 236
Dunayevskaya, Raya 172
Durkheim, Émile 24, 32, 59, 104

E

Eastern Europe 11, 223
'Economic and Philosophical Manuscripts of 1844' (Marx) 154
education, and *The Sane Society* 107–8
Egypt 44, 151
Ehrenreich, Barbara 135, 228
Eichmann, Adolf 212, 213
Eichmann in Jerusalem (Arendt) 211
Einstein, Albert 104
emotional energy 23, 66, 67, 222
emotions 22, 31, 209, 221, 226, 238
  sociology of 37–9, 41, 90, 109, 131, 197
Epstein, Cynthia 135
Erich Fromm Society 196, 224
Erikson, Erik 60
Eros and Civilization: A Philosophical Inquiry into Freud (Marcuse) 99, 111, 114, 120
erotic love 126, 127
Escape from Freedom (Fromm) 11, 13, 15, 19–49, 56, 112, 149
  and capitalism 86–7
  core ideas 59
  and critical theory 67
  and culture and personality movement 76
  empirical research for 65–6
  and Freudian theory 72
  and human potential for fascism 1–2, 197
  and neo-Freudian school of psychoanalysis 72
  and origins of Nazism 78
  and populism as xenophobia 232
  read by President Kennedy 179
  and sadomasochism 212
  shaped by experience of First World War 57
  and Shils 221–2
  sold over 5 million copies 12, 136
'Escape from Reality' (Hook) 175

An Essay on Liberation (Marcuse) 139
ethnomethodology 23
European social democracy 41, 104, 224
evangelical religion 47
evil, banality of 211, 212, 232
evolutionary psychology 23, 98, 200, 201, 208
existential dread 23
existentialist philosophy 11, 20, 23, 123
existentialists 22–3
existential psychoanalysis 33, 38, 39, 41, 168, 218
extremism 38, 39
Eyerman, R. 13

F

face-to-face democracy 107
fame 80, 98, 114, 136–7, 234
  and politics 165, 169, 180, 182
fanatical thinking 148
Fanon, F. 229
Farrell, Michael 77, 84, 145
far-right-wing movements 227
fascism 2, 21, 26, 33–4, 36, 78, 197
  and lower middle class 45, 46
feelings, commercialization of 2, 3, 172
femicide 195
feminism 73, 132, 181, 230
The Feminist Mystique (Friedan) 12
feminists 109, 130, 131, 135
Fenichel, Otto 27, 64, 73, 140–1
field theory 131, 196
First World War 8, 57
foreign policy, American *see* American foreign policy
Foucault, Michel 226
Founders, Canons and Classics (Baehr) 31
Frankfurt Psychoanalytic Institute 65
Frankfurt School 8–10, 65, 66, 67–70, 114, 115, 225
  and critical sociology 141–2
  and Fromm–Marcuse debate 121
  and Jacoby 138
Frankfurt School for Social Research 74
freedom 20, 22, 24, 26, 28, 29–30
Free Jewish Teaching Institute 58
Freire, Paulo 107, 223, 225
Freud, Sigmund 21, 33, 57, 59, 72, 74, 133
  and Adorno 114
  and libido and death instinct theories 199
  and Marcuse 116, 118–19, 120
  and social character theory 191
Freudian orthodoxy 12, 22, 59, 63, 66, 133, 218
  and Karen Horney 64, 72, 74

INDEX

and Marcuse 140
and Parsons 134
and 'Psychoanalysis: Scientism or Fanaticism' 121
Freudian theory, revision of 70–1, 116, 117, 119, 126, 185, 217
Frickel, S. 76
Friedan, Betty 12
Friedland, Roger 226
Friedman, Lawrence 58, 60, 61, 62, 128, 146, 154
   facilitated the revival of Fromm 225
   on Fromm's political activism 159, 160, 180, 181
   and Fromm's sense of alienation 56
   on the Kennedy Administration 179
   on Marx 172
   on McCarthy 169
Friedrich, Carl Joachim 84
friends in intellectual collaboration 232–3
Fromm, Erich
   birth 1
   death 1, 84
   university studies 1, 58, 60–1
   youth 55–8
Fromm–Marcuse debate 110, 111, 114–15, 116–19, 120–1, 137–42
frustration-aggression theory 203
F-scale 10, 69, 114
Fulbright, William 200
functionalism 99, 116, 180
Funk, Rainer 61, 196, 224
The Future is History: How Totalitarianism Reclaimed Russia (Gessen) 43

G

Gans, Herbert 93
Gemeinschaft 90
gender analysis, need to update 226
gendered language 102, 123, 132, 135, 226, 231
gender inequality 10
German reunification 173
German Workers 1929 – A Survey, Its Methods and Results 9, 10, 11, 24, 69–70, 187
Germany 20, 24, 150, 162, 196, 223, 224
Gessellshaft 90
Gessen, Masha 43
Giddens, Anthony 2
Gitlin, Todd 152, 166, 178
global Marxist humanism 181
global protests 163
Goffman, Erving 32
Goldberg, Michelle 47
Goldfarb, Jeffrey 94, 177
Goodman, Paul 27

The Good Society (Bellah et al) 96
Google Scholar 222–3
Gouldner, Alvin 237
The Greatness and Limitations of Freud's Thought (Fromm) 22
Great Refusal 119, 139
The Great Transformation (Polanyi) 162
Green, Adam 131
Greenberg, Jay 21–2
Green movement 162, 224
Groddeck, Georg 63–4
Gross, N. 76
Grossman, Henryk 68
Grünberg, Carl 68
Grundrisse 159
The Guaranteed Income (Theobald) 106
Gurland, Henny 131

H

Habermas, Jürgen 8, 68
Habits of the Heart (Bellah et al) 82, 86, 96
habitus 189, 192–3, 196, 228–9
Haidt, Jonathan 233
Hamilton, Richard 34, 37, 38, 41, 93
Harper, Stephen 5
Harrington, Michael 12, 104, 158, 161, 162, 231
   and Robert Kennedy 166
   on spiritual materialism 180–1
Harvard 98
Hausdorf, Dan 29
To Have or to Be (Fromm) 12, 167, 223–4
Hayden, Tom 104
The Heart of Man: Its Genius for Good and Evil (Fromm) 199, 207–8
Heidegger, Martin 114, 213, 232
Heidelberg University 60
Heller, Agnes 172
higher education 107–8
Hill, Lewis B. 27
Himmler, Heinrich 199, 206, 211, 212
historical materialism 21, 36, 59, 73, 105, 157
historical sociology 35, 36, 44, 162, 206, 216
   and Nazism 215
   and war 207
Hitler, Adolf 20, 21, 26, 30, 199
   mass appeal of 39
   necrophiliac character 206, 213–15
   and the working class 69
Hitler, Alois 215
Hitler, Klara 214–15
Hochschild, Arlie 3, 83, 109, 131, 135, 171

and *Strangers in Their Own Land: Anger and Mourning on the American Right* 47, 48
Holocaust 214
Homans, George 163, 202
homophobia 141
homosexuality 123, 132
Homo Sovieticus 43
Hook, Sidney 175
hooks, bell 13, 130
Horkheimer, Max 8, 9–10, 65, 68–9, 70, 71, 114
Horney, Karen 55, 63, 66, 71–2, 73–5, 76, 217
  and Freud 64
  and Marcuse 116, 117
  and *The Neurotic Personality of Our Time* 77
Horney, Marianne 75
Horowitz, David 44, 47
Howe, Irving 99, 115, 138
How to Win Friends and Influence People (Carnegie) 129
Hughes, H. Stuart 152
'The Human Implications of Institutional Radicalism' (Fromm) 118
human irrationality 21, 23
humanism 59, 62, 108, 163, 181, 218, 225
humanistic socialism 104, 159, 162, 167
humanistic spirituality 108
human nature 201, 218, 219–20
  and *The Anatomy of Human Destructiveness* 184, 198, 205
  and Marx 105, 155, 156, 157, 191
  and *The Sane Society* 98
human needs 98–9, 163–4, 168
human rights 153–4, 159, 162–3, 164, 173, 180
hunter-gatherer societies 205, 207, 219
Huxley, Aldous 104, 128

I

ideal types 126
identity crisis 60
Illich, Ivan 107
Imagined Communities (Anderson) 44
Imago 63
'The Implications of Institutional Radicalism' (Fromm) 118
income, national guaranteed 106
individualism 37, 40, 82, 91, 96, 217, 236
  and *The Anatomy of Human Destructiveness* (Fromm) 218
  and Marx 155
  and modernity 23, 236
individuation 23
industrialists 21, 37, 150

inequality 10, 194, 225
Inkeles, Alex 29
'inner-directed' characters 90, 91, 92
instinctivistic-hydraulic theory 204
instinct theory 72, 116, 117, 124, 205, 208
  and violence 199, 201, 203, 205
Institute for Social Research 65, 67, 69, 71
instrumental aggression 206
instrumental intimacy 77, 84, 145
intersectionalist theorists 54
Intimate Strangers (Rubin) 131
irrationality 21, 22, 23, 99, 217, 238
Islamism 43–4
Islamofascism 44
isolation 22, 23, 39
Israel 138, 146, 159

J

Jacobs, J. 146
Jacoby, Russell 122, 134, 138, 139, 140, 141
Jahoda, Marie 9
Jamison, A. 13
Japan 223
Jay, Martin 68, 70
'Jewish Law: A Contribution to the Study of Diaspora Judaism' (Fromm) 60–1
Jewish socialism 60
John Paul II, Pope 223
Johnson, Lyndon 164, 166
John XXIII, Pope 165
Judaism 54, 55–6, 58, 59, 61
Jung, Carl 23
Junkers 21
Just Friends (Rubin) 131

K

Kadushin, Charles 146
Kahn, Herman 150–1, 176
Kamenka, Eugene 163
Kardiner, Abram 76–7
Kavtaradze, Sergei Ivanovich 211
Kennedy, President 179
Kennedy, Robert 166
Kern, Erwin 209, 210
Khrushchev, Nikita 148, 176
Kierkegaard, Søren 22
King, Martin Luther 13, 130, 161
King Solomon's Ring (Lorenz) 200
Kirchheimer, Otto 68
Klinenberg, Eric 132, 234
knowledge, and love 126
Kohn, Melvin 109, 171
Kraepelin, Emil 63
Krause, Ludwig 58
Kulturkampf 41

INDEX

L
Landauer, Karl 65
Lasch, Christopher 86, 121–2, 134, 141
The Last Intellectuals (Jacoby) 138
Latin America 47, 151, 194, 223, 225
lay analysis 74
Lazarsfeld, Paul 9, 10
leaders, charismatic 39, 45
left-wing authoritarianism 216, 228, 235
Lemert, C. 94
'Let Man Prevail' (Fromm) 160
Lewis, Oscar 194
liberal traditional public sociology 49, 84
liberation capital 53, 67
libido theory 22, 27, 72, 116, 117, 121
  and *The Anatomy of Human Destructiveness* 199
  and Jacoby 138
  and Marcuse 120, 140
  and self-love 126–7
  in *Socialist Humanism: An International Symposium* 163
Lifton, Robert Jay 149
Linton, Ralph 74
Lipset, Seymour Martin 45, 46, 92, 152, 175
local discussion groups 167–8
The Lonely Crowd: A Study of the Changing American Character (Riesman) 2, 13, 84, 85–6, 87, 89–96, 145
Lorenz, Konrad 185, 199–201, 203, 204, 218
Los Angeles Times 167
love 113–14, 117, 122–32
Löwenthal, Leo 8, 58, 68
lower-middle-class authoritarianism 227
Luther, Martin 25
Luxemburg, Rosa 10, 104
Lynd, Helen 9
Lynd, Robert 1, 9, 19–20, 69

M
Maccoby, Michael 11, 152, 177, 188–9, 194, 195, 196
  and applied organizational research 224
  and Fromm's 'prophetic voice' 108
  and McCarthy campaign 167
  and study of Nixon voters 214
malignant aggression 197, 198, 199, 205, 208
malignant destructiveness 208, 214
The Managed Heart (Hochschild) 131
Man for Himself: An Inquiry into the Psychology of Ethics (Fromm) 13, 15, 81, 87–9, 99, 112
Man Meets Dog (Lorenz) 200
Mann, Michael 34, 35, 36, 37–8, 39

Man's Concept of Man (Fromm) 13–14
Maoism 149, 225
Marcuse, Herbert 68, 70, 111, 114–15, 116–20, 121, 135
  and alienation 172
  and critical theory 141
  and death instinct 204
  and the Great Refusal 137–40
  as nihilist 232
  and *One-Dimensional Man* 8, 102
  in *Socialist Humanism: An International Symposium* 163
marginality 54, 56, 185, 231
marginality facilitators 54, 59, 60, 64, 66, 72, 76
marginalization 53–4, 55, 194
market fundamentalism 82
marketing character 88–9, 98, 109
market society, and love 127–8
Marx, Karl 13–14, 22, 67, 104–5, 125, 154, 172
  and human nature 157
  and human needs 163
  and social character theory 190, 191
'Marx and Alienation' (Hook) 175
Marxism 8, 45, 55, 60, 83, 175–6, 180–1, 223
  and 'The Application of Humanistic Psychoanalysis to Marx's Theory' 163
  believed threat from 172–3
  and *Escape from Freedom* 33, 36
  and the Frankfurt School 9, 67–8
  and *German Workers 1929 – A Survey, Its Methods and Results* 70
  and Judaism 57–8
  and *The Sane Society* 102–3, 104
  under Khrushchev 148
Marxist Freudians 64, 140
Marxist humanism 104, 181, 225
Marxists 59, 117–18, 155–6, 164, 174, 175–6, 181
  and *Escape from Freedom* 27
  and Frankfurt School 9
  in Latin America 194
Marx's Concept of Man (Fromm) 2, 11, 144, 154–9, 163, 172, 182
masculinity, toxic 217
Maslow, Abraham 208–9
masochism 24, 125, 126, 212
mass media 93, 106
mass society 42, 87, 99, 139
materialism
  dialectical 155
  historical 21, 36, 59, 73, 105, 157
  spiritual 181
mature love 125, 126, 128

May Man Prevail?: An Inquiry into the Facts and Fictions of Foreign Policy (Fromm) 2, 11, 13, 14, 144, 147–51, 182
Mayo, Elton 104
McCarthy, Eugene 164, 165–6, 167, 169, 180
McCarthyism 115
McMillan Cottom, Tressie 234
Mead, George Herbert 30, 72
Mead, Margaret 55, 66, 74, 76, 77, 78, 188
  and fame 137, 234
  suffered from reputational decline 195
media, and Chomsky 178
media propaganda 106–7
'Memo on Political Alternatives' (Fromm) 166–7
Menninger, Karl 27
mental health crisis 100
Merton, Robert 31, 98, 112, 115, 132, 178
  and *Escape from Freedom* 1, 30
Meštrović, S. G. 94
Mexican Psychoanalytic Institute 143, 184, 187
Mexican Psychoanalytic Society 143
Mexico 131, 135, 184, 186, 187–9, 191–2, 195, 223
  and participatory action research 196, 224
Meyer, D. S. 12
middle class 25, 26, 34, 36–7, 45–6
middle-class authoritarianism 227
Middle East 43–4, 151
Middletown (Lynd and Lynd) 9
Milgram, Stanley 202–3
militarism 2, 21, 153, 171, 173, 177
Mills, C. Wright 6, 14, 53, 79, 83, 92–3, 135
  The Causes of World War III 152, 170
  and the Cold War 222
  heroic and controversial figure 233
  influenced by Fromm 82
  and Port Huron Statement 167
  and *The Sane Society* 98, 132
  and SDS 104, 107
  and social character theory 30–1
  White Collar 102
modernity 24, 28, 40, 56, 78, 99, 145
  and individualism 23, 236
  and *The Sane Society* and *Man for Himself* 15
modernization theory 35, 190
Modern Romance: An Investigation (Ansari) 132
Montagu, Ashley 29, 188

Moore, Barrington 34
moral aloneness 22, 23
The Moral Commonwealth: Social Theory and the Promise of Community (Selznick) 172
Morris, Aldon 3, 6, 53
Morris, Desmond 200
motivation 23, 40–1, 42, 202, 216
Moynihan, Patrick 194
Mumford, Lewis 205, 214
Muste, A. J. 152

N
Nader, Ralph 12
The Naked Ape (Morris) 200
narcissism 2, 45, 197, 198, 207–8, 213, 226–7
  and Hitler 206, 215
The Nation 27
National Association for the Advancement of Colored People (NAACP) 79
National Autonomous University of Mexico 131, 143
national character 29, 65, 78
national guaranteed income 106
nationalism 39, 41, 62, 150, 174, 215, 218
  and *The Sane Society* 126
Nazi Holocaust 214
Nazi Party 20, 26, 37–8, 69
Nazism 20, 25, 26, 28, 37–8, 41–2, 215–16
  and *Escape from Freedom* 13, 21, 33–6, 149
  and Gessen 43
  origins of 78
  and Scheff 39
necrophilia 198, 199, 205, 208, 216, 232, 239
  and Cortina 218–19
  and Hitler 206, 213–15
  and Trump 227
needs, human 98–9, 163–4, 168, 208–9
Neill, A. S. 107
neo-behaviourism 199
neo-conservativism 174, 175
neo-Freudianism 74, 75–6, 138
neo-Freudian psychoanalysts 65, 66, 71–2
neo-Freudians 64, 116, 117
Neumann, Franz 68
neurophysiology 204
neurosciences 198–9
neurosis 57, 72, 117
The Neurotic Personality of Our Time (Horney) 77
The New Leader 175
New Left 68, 83, 99, 104, 132, 182

and DSA 162
and Marcuse 115, 120, 139
and *The Revolution of Hope* 164
and *The Sane Society* 13, 107
New York Psychoanalytic Institute 74
The New York Times 109, 146
Nietzsche, Friedrich 22
Nietzschean philosophy 117–18
Night of the Long Knives 212
'Nihilism in Black America' (West) 237
Nisbet, Robert 158, 232–3
Nixon, Richard 166, 167, 168, 214, 232
Nobel, Rabbi Nehemiah 58
non-instrumental violence 209
nuclear arms race 145, 150, 152, 167, 169
nuclear disarmament 43, 151, 160, 175, 176
nuclear war 145–6, 147, 148, 150–1, 153, 160
and Berlin 179
and necrophiliac character 214
nuclear weapons 164, 165, 179, 180

O

Oedipus Complex 72
Office of Strategic Services (OSS) 114
Ollman, Bertell 172
One-Dimensional Man: Studies in the Ideology of Advanced Industrial Society (Marcuse) 8, 102, 120, 138–9
One Nation, After All: What Americans Really Think about God, Country, Family, Racism, Welfare, Immigration, Homosexuality, Work, the Right, the Left and Each Other (Wolfe) 95
ontological insecurity 2
optimal marginality 15, 16, 54, 182
Orbán, President Viktor 5
orthodox Freudians 27, 67, 72, 121, 131, 184, 204
orthodox Freudian theory 64, 116, 117, 118, 138
orthodox Marxism 68, 104, 191
The Other America (Harrington) 12
'other-directed' characters 90, 91–2, 94

P

Pacem in Terris 165
Palestine 146
paranoid thinking 148
parental love 126
Parsons, Talcott 30, 35, 41, 92, 100, 134
participatory action research 196, 224
participatory democracy 107, 167, 168
patriarchy 10, 59, 226
Patterson, Orlando 222

Peale, Norman Vincent 112, 117, 129, 138
peasants 191, 192, 194, 195
The Pedagogy of the Oppressed (Freire) 107
penis envy 72
Perez, Martin 175
Peterson, Jordan 6, 141, 218, 228, 234
philanthropy 144, 154
Pinker, Steven 98, 100, 198, 201, 218, 220
Piven Fox, Frances 6, 233
Platt, Jennifer 7, 11
Poland 4, 48, 159, 181, 223, 224
and dissident Marxists 172–3, 181
far-right authoritarian regime 3, 43
and right-wing populism 37, 225
Polanyi, Karl 162
policy sociology 106, 147, 150, 177, 178, 184, 186
political activism 135, 143–82
political movements 98, 130, 155, 226, 232
political radicalism 117, 118, 141
The Politics of Petulance: America in an Age of Immaturity (Wolfe) 49, 94–5
Pollock, Friedrich 68, 71
popular culture 45, 85, 203
populism 37, 225, 232
Port Huron Statement 104, 167
Posner, Richard 15
poverty 30, 67, 155, 190, 210, 235
in Latin America 190
in Mexico 187, 194
and West 237
The Power of Positive Thinking (Peale) 129
Praxis group 163, 172
primal horde 116
primitive cultures 123
The Problem of Order: What Unites and Divides Society (Wrong) 23
projection 48, 49, 129, 148, 229
The Protestant Ethic and the Spirit of Capitalism (Weber) 25, 32
Protestantism 34, 35, 36
Protestants 26, 37, 41, 47
protests 163, 164, 166
pseudo-aggression 206
pseudo-love 128–9
Psychiatry 27, 72
psychoanalysis 21–5, 27, 41, 55, 59, 60, 66
and attachment theory 217
and Berlin Institute for Psychoanalysis 73
and the Frankfurt School 68, 69
and Horkheimer and Adorno 71
and Marcuse 116
and Reichmann 63

on Riesman 83
and sociology 133–4
within critical theory 70
Psychoanalysis and Religion (Fromm) 81, 108, 127
'Psychoanalysis and Sociology' (Fromm) 65
'Psychoanalysis: Scientism or Fanaticism' (Fromm) 121
psychoanalytic feminists 109, 230
psychoanalytic libido theory 22
see also libido theory
psychoanalytic sociologists 109
psychoanalytic sociology 61, 134
psychoanalytic theory 36, 197–8, 238
'The Psychological Aspects of the Guaranteed Income' (Fromm) 106, 164
psychology, depth 33, 73, 133, 229
psychosocial analysis 33, 228, 229–30
public sociologists, reasons for becoming 51–4
'For Public Sociology' (Burawoy) 1, 4
pure relationship 2
Putinism 43

R
Rabinkow, Salman 59, 60, 62
race theory 218, 226, 229, 230, 231
racism 161, 218, 226, 229, 236
and Du Bois 53, 79, 235, 236
radical humanism 62, 169, 218
radical political activity 75, 135, 156
radical public sociology 30, 49, 82, 83, 97
Rathenau, Walther 209
rational authority 103, 107, 129
rational choice theory 23, 24
Reagan, Ronald 120, 139, 167
realism, sociological 95
Red Army Faction 153
Reformation 25–6, 36, 87
Reich, Wilhelm 26, 64, 73, 138, 140–1
Reichmann, Frieda 58, 59, 60, 61, 62–3, 64
Reik, Theodor 64
religion 35, 54, 55–6, 58, 59, 61, 108
and *The Art of Loving* 124
evangelical 47
and love 127
Renaissance 87
The Repression of Psychoanalysis: Otto Fenichel and the Political Freudians (Jacoby) 140
Republicans 46, 53
respect 117, 126, 127
responsibility 117, 125–6
revisionism 70, 77, 114, 116–18

The Revision of Psychoanalysis (Fromm and Funk) 139
The Revolution of Hope (Fromm) 144, 145, 164, 167, 168, 169
Rieff, Philip 232
Riesman, David 6, 14, 15, 83–4, 85–7, 132, 135
on *The Anatomy of Human Destructiveness* 227
and anti-nuclear activism 144
and the Berlin Crisis 180
and collaboration with Fromm 177–8
and Committee of Correspondence 152, 176
and education 107
Fromm as mentor 2, 82
and *The Lonely Crowd* 13, 89–97
and *Man for Himself* 87
and Patterson 222
and politics 145–7
and Theodore and Lola Schwartz 189
rights of children 10
right-wing authoritarianism 235
right-wing populism 37, 225
Rohlinger, D. A. 12
Röhm, Ernst 212, 213
romantic love 127, 128
Rorschach tests 188
Rubel, Maximilien 163
Rubin, Lillian 131
rural Protestants 41
Russell, Bertrand 154, 163
Russia 147, 148, 149, 151, 155, 158–9
and authoritarian character 43
and Germany 150
Rustin, Bayard 161
Ryan, William 194

S
Sachs, Hans 63, 64
sadism 125, 126, 199, 210–11, 212
sadomasochism 24, 25, 212–13, 230
Said, Edward 56
Salomon, Ernst von 206, 209–10
Sanders, Bernie 181
SANE (Committee for a Sane Nuclear Policy) 151, 152–3, 176, 177
The Sane Society (Fromm) 11, 81, 97–108, 109, 112, 124, 132
and alienation 2, 13
and capitalist modernity 15
and local discussion groups 167–8
and Marcuse 119
on Marx 172
and nationalism 126
sold over 3 million 12, 136
Sapir, Edward 76

Saturday Review 121
Schaar, John 29
Scheff, Thomas 39
schizophrenia 62, 72
Schlesinger, Arthur, Jr. 178–9
The Scholar Denied (Morris) 6
Scholem, Gershom 58
Schwartz, Lola 188, 189
Schwartz, Pepper 131
Schwartz, Theodore 188, 189
Science and Society 27
Seidman, S. 94
self, theory of 28, 72
self-love 126–7, 130
Selznick, Philip 158, 172
Senghor, Léopold 163
sentimental love 128–9
separation 23
Sex and Temperament in Three Primitive Societies (Mead) 77, 137
sexuality 41, 47, 116, 119, 127
Shachtman, Max 160, 161
shame 39, 40, 92, 123, 219
Shils, Edward 175, 221–2
Sigmund Freud's Mission: An Analysis of His Personality and Influence (Fromm) 121
The Silent Spring (Carson) 12
Silver, Catherine 133, 230
Simmel, Georg 8, 10, 59, 72, 116
Sino-Soviet split 151, 172
Skinner, B. F. 185, 199, 201–2
Smelser, Neil 217, 230
Smith, Dorothy 6
Social Amnesia: Conformist Psychology from Adler to Laing (Jacoby) 122, 138, 141
Social Character and Social Structure (Gerth and Mills) 83
Social Character in a Mexican Village (Fromm and Maccoby) 11, 182, 183, 184, 186–95, 197, 216, 220
social character theory 99, 109, 131, 172, 189–92, 220, 226
  and 'The Application of Humanistic Psychoanalysis to Marx's Theory' 163–4
  and Bourdieu 209, 228–9
  and Erich Fromm Society 196
  and *The Lonely Crowd* 90
  and marketing character 88–9
  and Mills 30–1
  and psychoanalytic analysis of emotions 193
  and *The Sane Society* 100, 101
  and *Social Character in a Mexican Village* 183, 184, 186, 187–8
social class *see* class
social democracy 41, 104, 121, 156, 224

'The Social Determination of Psychoanalytic Therapy' (Fromm) 70
social exchange theory 202
The Social Implication of Freudian Revisionism' (Marcuse) 116–19
socialism 59, 60, 104, 159
socialist humanism 104, 159, 162, 167
Socialist Humanism: An International Symposium 162, 163–4
Socialist Party of America 104, 159–60, 162, 182
socialization 93–4
social media 48–9, 93–4, 106
social movements 12, 13, 163
social narcissism 207–8, 226–7
The Social Origins of Dictatorship and Democracy (Moore) 34
Social Problems 11
social psychology 8, 9, 26, 30
social structure and personality school 109
sociobiology 23
sociological realism 95
sociology, historical *see* historical sociology
sociology of emotions 37–9, 41, 90, 109, 131, 197
Southern Theory (Connell) 6, 234
Southwest German Psychoanalytic Study Group 63–4, 65
Soviet communism 104, 105, 108, 149
Soviet Union 148, 155–6, 158–9, 171, 172, 173, 174
  and China 149
  and *May Man Prevail?* 147
spirituality 108, 127
spiritual materialism 181
Stalin, Joseph 148, 199, 206, 210–11
Stalinism 108, 176, 223, 225
Stanford prison study 202–3
Steinmetz, George 193, 229
Stevenson, Adlai 165, 180
Strangers in Their Own Land: Anger and Mourning on the American Right (Hochshild) 47, 48
student radicalism 120
  see also radical political activity
Students for a Democratic Society (SDS) 104, 107
'Studien über Autorität und Familie' (Horkheimer) 24, 69
sugar cane 192
suicide 57, 99
Suicide (Durkheim) 32
Sullivan, Harry Stack 66, 71–2, 73, 74, 75, 76, 116
  and Marcuse 117, 118, 119

Summerhill: A Radical Approach to Child Rearing (Neill) 107
Swanson, Guy 216
Swartz, David 193
Switzerland 169, 183
symbiosis 39–40
symbolic interactionism 23, 29

T
Tawney, R. W. 103
Taylor, Verta 12
technology 91, 101, 145, 168, 169, 239
Telos 138
The Territorial Imperative (Ardrey) 200
Thematic Apperception Tests (TAT) 188
theoretical systems 134, 190, 237
On Thermonuclear War (Kahn) 150–1
Third World 150, 151, 183
Thomas, Norman 159, 161, 163
Thought Reform and the Psychology of Totalism (Lifton) 149
toxic masculinity 217
'traditional' public sociology 82
'tradition-directed' characters 90–1, 92
tribes 124, 205, 218
Trotskyism 115
Trump, Donald 45, 46, 47, 48, 207, 225
Trumpism 227, 228, 239
Turner, S. 97

U
the unconscious 9, 57
The Unemployed of Marienthal (Jahoda, Lazarsfeld and Zeisel) 9
unemployment 26, 101, 106
United Kingdom 223
universal subsistence guarantee 106
Unsafe at any Speed (Nader) 12

V
Veblen, Thorstein 108
Versailles Treaty 26
Vietnam War 151, 153, 169, 173, 175, 180, 216
  and Committee of Correspondence 152
  'Memo on Political Alternatives' 167
  and necrophiliac character 214
  protests against 164
violence 38, 185, 195, 201, 203
  and *The Anatomy of Human Destructiveness* 184, 198, 199, 202, 205, 206, 220
  and attachment theory 217
  and necrophilia 218
  non-instrumental 209

W
Wallace, George 168
Wallerstein, Immanuel 174
war, motives for 206–7
Washington Consensus 175
Wasson, Father William 187
Watts, Jerry 54, 59
Weber, Alfred 8, 11, 58, 59, 60, 61
Weber, Max 8, 25, 32, 35, 36, 59, 178
Weimar study 9, 10, 11, 24, 69–70, 187
West, Cornel 181, 237
Wheatland, Thomas 69
White Collar (Mills) 102
'Why I Am for McCarthy' (Fromm) 167
Wiggershaus, R. 71
Wilkinson, Rupert 86
William Alanson White Institute 72–3
Wilson, William Julius 234
Wirth, Louis 28, 29
Wittenberg, Wilhelm 63
Wittfogel, Karl 68
Wolfe, Alan 49, 82, 93, 94–5
Woodstock 85
work conditions, research on 105–6
Workers' Party (Brazil) 225
working class 24, 28, 69
working-class authoritarianism 45, 227
The Working Class in Weimar Germany: A Psychological and Sociological Study (Fromm) 9, 10, 11, 24, 69–70, 187
World Council of Peace Meeting 153
World of our Fathers (Howe) 115
Worlds of Pain (Rubin) 131
world systems theory 174
Wright, Erik Olin 176
Wright, James 93
Wrong, Dennis 23, 93, 163, 201

X
xenophobia 232

Y
Yale University 76
Yang, Andrew 106
youth peer culture 93

Z
Zeisel, Hanz 9
Zimbardo, Philip 202–3
Zionism 62, 146, 159
Zodiac Club 74, 76

www.ingramcontent.com/pod-product-compliance
Lightning Source LLC
Chambersburg PA
CBHW070911030426
42336CB00014BA/2363